# Robert Frost and Feminine Literary Tradition

# Robert Frost and Feminine Literary Tradition

Karen L. Kilcup

*Ann Arbor*

## THE UNIVERSITY OF MICHIGAN PRESS

Copyright © by the University of Michigan 1998
All rights reserved
Published in the United States of America by
The University of Michigan Press
Manufactured in the United States of America
⊛ Printed on acid-free paper

2001   2000   1999   1998     4   3   2   1

*A CIP catalog record for this book is available from the British Library.*

Library of Congress Cataloging-in-Publication Data

Kilcup, Karen L.
    Robert Frost and feminine literary tradition / Karen L. Kilcup.
    p.   cm.
    Includes bibliographical references (p.   ) and index.
    ISBN 0-472-10967-7 (acid-free paper)
    1. Frost, Robert, 1874–1963—Knowledge—Literature. 2. Women and
literature—United States—History—20th century. 3. American
poetry—Women authors—History and criticism. 4. Frost, Robert,
1874–1963—Characters—Women. 5. Influence (Literary, artistic,
etc.) 6. Frost, Robert, 1874–1963—Influence. 7. Sentimentalism in
literature. 8. Authorship—Sex differences. 9. Sex role in
literature. I. Title.
PS3511.R94   Z7618   1998
811'.52—dc21                                           98-25386
                                          CIP

*In memory of Lauris Manning Gove (1904–86) ("Bump")*
*and Mary Ilsley Gove (1906–90)*
*my grandparents and great New Englanders*

# Acknowledgments

The exhaustion that sets in when one finishes a project that has been gestating as long as this one is only counterbalanced by the euphoria of seeing it finally to print. It is impossible to remember all the people who traveled with me at least partway down the road taken.

Allen Grossman was a very early motivating force behind my work on Frost, and I continue to be grateful not only for his help but his example. Several others were supportive and helpful in the early stages: Joyce Antler, John Burt, Billy Flesch, Michael Gilmore, Karen Klein, and Susan Staves. The members of the Nineteenth-Century American Women Writers Study Group in the United States and the International Nineteenth-Century American Women Writers Research Group in the United Kingdom provided an intellectual community in which work such as this can flourish. Paula Bennett read an early draft and pushed me to go at least a dozen better. Merryn Rutledge, Kelley Griffith, and Gail McDonald read parts of the manuscript and made helpful suggestions to which I hope I have done justice. My research assistants, Greg Tredore and Drew Perry, cheerfully tracked down fugitive references. Lesley Lee Francis provided me with copies of her important work on Susan Hayes Ward and Amy Lowell. Jay Parini and Lisa Seale offered sensitive readings of the manuscript, and I am deeply indebted to their assistance.

There are many fine readers of Frost whose work undergirds my own; especially important to me were the studies by Randall Jarrell, Katherine Kearns, Frank Lentricchia, Judith Oster, George Monteiro, Richard Poirier, and William Pritchard. All Frost scholars must be deeply indebted to Richard Poirier and Mark Richardson for their superb new edition of Robert Frost's poems and prose. Through a Research Award the University of Hull, England, provided welcome financial assistance and release time, and the University of North Carolina at Greensboro offered important research support. I want to give special thanks to Westbrook College in Portland, Maine, for honoring me with their generous research professorship in 1996; the Dorothy M. Healy Visiting Professorship in American Studies and Women's Studies provided much support for the advancement of this project. The libraries at Yale University, Dartmouth and Westbrook Colleges, and Phillips Exeter Academy provided special assistance in the project's completion. My editor at the University of Michigan Press, LeAnn Fields, was encouraging and steadfast in her support for the project, and the editorial staff at the Press offered prompt and professional assistance. As always, my husband, Chris, read, criticized, encouraged, prodded, and was quiet when he needed to be, along with making certain that I had enough to eat and that I worked my muscles as well as my mind. At home in New Hampshire, my parents, Mary and Richard Kilcup, have always provided the intellectual encouragement that enabled me to persevere; I am sad that my father died shortly after this book went to press, for its appearance would have delighted him. Finally, this book is indebted to my beloved Gove grandparents who, "north of Boston," taught me to understand and love New England in all its expressions.

*Grateful acknowledgment is made to the following authors, publishers, and journals for permission to reprint previously published materials.*

Excerpts from the notebooks and unpublished papers of Robert Frost, quoted with the permission of the Estate of Robert Lee Frost and Dartmouth College Library.

Selections from *In the Clearing* and *Complete Poems of Robert Frost,* © 1936, 1942, 1944, 1945, 1947, 1948, 1950, 1951, 1952, 1953, 1954, © 1955, 1956, 1958, 1959, 1960, 1961, 1962 by Robert Frost, and © 1964, 1967, 1968, 1970, 1973, 1975 by Lesley Frost Ballantine; © 1916, 1923, 1928, 1930, 1934, 1939, 1943, 1945, 1947, 1949, © 1967 by Henry Holt and Company, Inc. Reprinted by permission of Henry Holt and Company, Inc., and Jonathan Cape.

Excerpts from *The Selected Letters of Robert Frost,* edited by Lawrance Thompson, © 1964 by Lawrance Thompson. Reprinted by permission of Henry Holt and Company, Inc., and Jonathan Cape.

Selections from *The Letters of Robert Frost to Louis Untermeyer,* edited by Louis Untermeyer, © 1963 by Louis Untermeyer. Reprinted by permission of Henry Holt and Company, Inc., and Jonathan Cape.

Part of chapter 4 has been published as " ' "Men work together," I told him from the heart': Frost's (In)Delicate Masculinity," in *ELH* 65.3 (1998): 731–56. I am grateful for permission to reprint this material here.

Every effort has been made to trace the ownership of all copyrighted material and to obtain permission for its use.

# Contents

Abbreviations xiii

**Introduction: "Plainly the Most Deceptive Poet"** I

*Chapter 1* 17

**"The Faded Flowers Gay"**
Feminine Frost and the Sentimental Tradition

*Chapter 2* 61

**"The Feminine Way of It"**
Frost's Homely Affiliations

*Chapter 3* 103

**"Lightning or a Scribble"**
Bewitched by the Mother Tongue

*Chapter 4* 147

**"Button, Button . . ."**
Becoming a Man's Man

*Chapter 5* 191

**"No Sissy Poem"**
Reinventing the (Lyric) Poet

**Coda: "An Impregnable Harbor for the Self"** 233

Notes 245

Index 309

# Abbreviations

CP     *Frost: Collected Poems, Prose, and Plays.* Ed. Richard Poirier
and Mark Richardson. New York: Library of America, 1995.

CR    *Robert Frost: The Critical Reception.* Ed. Linda W. Wagner.
New York: B. Franklin, 1977.

LU    *The Letters of Robert Frost to Louis Untermeyer.* Ed. Louis
Untermeyer. New York: Holt, Rinehart and Winston, 1963.

SL    *The Selected Letters of Robert Frost.* Ed. Lawrance Thompson.
New York: Holt, Rinehart and Winston, 1964.

# Introduction: "Plainly the Most Deceptive Poet"

Begin both at the beginning of your subject and of yourself. I
suppose the earliest beginning of yourself is when you wake
from sleep. Picking up the subject is like picking up the thread
with the eye of a needle: it's necessary to begin further back
than with the thread itself and gather in the fiber or filament the
property beyond the thread.
—Robert Frost, notebook, 1924

A few miles east of rural Ripton, Vermont, is a park and picnic area dedi-
cated to Robert Frost, where I stopped late one summer after making the
pilgrimage to his nearby house. Tucked into the corner of a field at the end
of a long, rough driveway, the house remains inconspicuous compared to its
well-marked, busy, and relatively polished alter ego, whose attractions
include a parking area, restrooms, and, most notable, the Robert Frost
Interpretive Trail. With regular and handicapped-accessible boardwalk
paths, the trail wends through woods and fields punctuated by small plaques
inscribed with individual poems that ostensibly reflect (and were inspired
by) the landscape. As I wandered along, rereading poems like "A Young
Birch," "The Oven Bird," "Nothing Gold Can Stay," and "The Sound of
the Trees" and eating handfuls of blueberries in a pasture that the Park Ser-
vice had kept clear of trees, I reflected, with some pleasure, that there was
probably nowhere a T. S. Eliot Interpretive Trail.

Because Frost's presence in our cultural as well as literal landscape is
taken for granted by many, the first question this book may raise is prag-
matic: why should we (meaning both professional critics and "ordinary"
"lovers of poetry") have another study of someone with whom we are "so
familiar" and who remains "popular" more than thirty-five years after his
death? While understanding Frost's generic mixing and playful self-repre-
sentation may be particularly desirable at a time when the meaning and

value of the categories of "literature" and "selfhood" have been called into question, it seems to me that contemporary criticism—regularly transfigured into "theory"—is much enamored of its own brilliance and in that brilliance often indirectly or directly obscures for us the writing that has given it life, much as Frost himself so often feared.[1] Certainly, the study of poetry has diminished significantly in recent years, partly because of the advent of postmodernist approaches more amenable to work on prose fiction.[2] As with the case of poetry more generally, Frost himself is under-studied, perhaps because critics feel he is so familiar, or, conversely, because he does not fit easily or comfortably into established categories: "for all his eminence, Frost's stature as a poet among the 'moderns' is still being argued."[3] Whatever the reasons for this neglect, Frost provides an important touchstone for the poetry of his historical moment. His earlier poems in particular embody a complex set of tensions: between nineteenth- and twentieth-century verse, between poetry and prose—as well as between sentimental and realistic, old-fashioned and modern, popular and elite, and feminine and masculine.[4] Jay Parini observes that Frost's intimate familiarity "with English and American poetry is never in doubt: his work is full of quiet echoes of his predecessors." Acknowledging these border crossings while reading through his collected poems, one concludes with Louise Bogan, "It is clear that Frost served a long technical apprenticeship. Actual influences, however, even in his early work, are difficult to trace."[5]

What influences, and which predecessors, are questions that have been asked before, but until now he has been considered almost exclusively within the framework of a limited and masculine poetic history; indeed, as George Monteiro has observed in citing Frost's own desires to be read in a broad context, "Frost's poems are not . . . read against very many of 'all the other poems ever written.'"[6] Working from the end of a long tradition that has affiliated Frost with such writers as Wordsworth and Whitman, I wish to revise and extend the webs of connection to include writers whom both Frost and his critics have repressed: the popular women whose work he read and heard from childhood on and that he transformed, unconsciously or not, into a marketable masculine product. By situating him in the context of what I call "feminine literary tradition"—which includes sentimental poetry by both men and women and female-authored regionalist writing[7]— I seek not only to contribute to ongoing discussions about nineteenth-century women's writing and its significance for modernist successors (and hence to expand the scope of critics' understanding of Frost's abilities and ambitions) but also frankly and unapologetically to recuperate the poet, and by extension other male poets, as a positive model for readers who have been troubled by depictions of him as almost inevitably masculinist and misogynous. I readily grant that Frost was no feminist, that some of his statements are extremely problematic (writing to Untermeyer in 1915: "The beauty of your book is that the poems in it all get together and say something of one accord. It's a long way from you down to the ladies [they are mostly ladies in this country] who find difficulty in making the lines in one poem get together like that" [*LU* 9]). Clearly, his extraordinary investment in female voices and empathy for feminine perspectives in poems like "A Servant to Servants" and "Home Burial" do not guarantee Frost's continuing affiliations; "to assume that a male identification with the feminine is *necessarily* subversive of patriarchal privilege may be to assume too much."[8] Yet we need to be alert to ways in which male writers engage in transformations of gender, both aesthetically and personally, and to celebrate the important moments of insight that do occur. I am not interested, then, in "condemning [a writer] for not practicing or portraying an acceptable politics of gender" but, instead, in focusing on "the relationship between gender and poetic production" in a poet whose work and career are fundamentally shaped and determined by that relationship.[9]

In gathering in the filaments in his work of both explicitly female and implicitly feminine perspectives and attitudes (that is "postures" or "stances"), which contravene the notion that gender boundaries in poetic voice are circumscribed by sex, I propose to make the poet *unfamiliar*. In a related area Frost's work offers us the opportunity to say something about the work of a "great" poet that has been largely ignored, devalued, or repressed—and to ask why, to interrogate the difference *within* his opus. What makes specific instances of a "major" poet's work "less important"? Who decides and on what basis? How might cultural constructions of gender—of both the writer and the reader—enter into such appraisals and exclusions, even, or especially, for a "popular" writer like Frost? From this perspective tracking his work in the context of feminine literary tradition promises to expose some of the biases, assumptions, and values that critics bring to all poetry of the period.[10]

Popularity, as Andreas Huyssen and others have suggested, bears a negative association and, not coincidentally, a connection with femininity in American literary studies, a fact that is particularly significant in relation to Frost.[11] In spite of some suggestions that the poet's critical reputation declined after his death, his popularity over time with a general audience remains without question. We know, for example, that "between 1915 and

1980 more than three hundred articles focusing on Frost and his poetry appeared in popular journals such as *Reader's Digest* and the *Saturday Evening Post*."[12] His sales figures are even more stunning; his final volume, *In the Clearing,* sold thirty-five thousand copies in the first four days after its release, and at the time of Frost's death, according to an obituary in *Newsweek,* "more than a million copies of his books had been sold."[13] Reviewers and critics have noted, sometimes with amazement, the poet's unparalleled ability to cross boundaries between elite and popular culture. An early survey observed that "his books have been both artistic and commercially satisfactory,"[14] while in 1936 Mark Van Doren pointed out rather ambiguously that the poet "has several audiences . . . he can be appreciated on various levels. If he is not all things to all men he is something to almost anybody—to posterity, one supposes, as well as to us."[15] In tandem with providing us with an instructive instance of gender performativity, then, Frost offers a matrix for studying the tension between "highbrow" and "lowbrow" forms—and as such he becomes a representative of a larger cultural dissonance and an exemplary figure for mediating between those ostensible poles.[16] That is, in his roles as Yankee sage and paradoxical "popular modernist," Frost provides both a representative and singular cultural instance of many American poets' investment in a gendered marketplace differentially regulated by elite and ordinary readers.

Finally, we need another look at Frost because he continues to elude us. Writing in an important agent of canonization, the current *Columbia History of American Poetry,* Jay Parini calls Frost one of "the great poets of this century—or any century," and at the same time, in a wonderfully oxymoronic phrase, "plainly the most deceptive poet in the history of our literature."[17] Regarding Frost is almost like viewing a hologram: when we look straight on, we might see a Hallmark card, but when we move to one side, we see a John Singer Sargent portrait, from another angle a Frederick Church landscape, from another a Mary Cassatt mother and child pastel, and from another an "eye-dazzler" quilt. The "Hawthorne of American poetry," Frost plays hide-and-seek with his readers as he keeps his "inmost Me behind its veil."[18] To expose him wholly is impossible even if it were desirable, but I hope to offer a pleasurable likeness gathered in glimpses during some less guarded moments.

Depicting this "plainly" deceptive poet requires viewing him from many angles. Calling directly and indirectly on the resources of sociopsychological, new historicist, materialist, feminist, and reader-response perspectives, this study aims to map out Frost's transformations of his work to accord more fully with newly forming aesthetic norms marked by gender.[19] I argue that Frost's published performances represent a sensibility attuned to locations of historical, cultural, and aesthetic power inasmuch as they respond, consciously or not, to the developing standards of a modernist literary establishment and to literal, as well as imagined, readers.[20] Although Frost increasingly wanted to be a part of the canon that this increasingly masculine establishment sought to create, his work sometimes evinces a hospitality, associated with but not determined or regulated by genre, to a culturally feminine perspective; this perspective appears most vividly in his early long dramatic poems. These poems are praised by critics but often not given the sustained attention that they merit (and will receive here), in part because of this femininity.

For both male and female writers, "gender is continually in process, an identity that is performed and actualized over time within given social constructs."[21] A final aspect of this account is its desire to trace the *various* voices that the poet engenders *over time;* in most accounts of Frost's work the poems appear synchronistically and relatively ahistorically. While substantive or structural links between poems can be persuasive and significant, by dehistoricizing the work, formalist arguments flatten out certain attitudes and tones into inaudibility.[22] What is crucial to this discussion, then, is my assumption that the chronology of composition is less significant than the chronology of publication—that is, than the aesthetic self-representation and identification that Frost himself invents and reshapes over time for a public audience. In contrast to his explicit if ambiguous awareness of the *fact* of his changing self-representation, his degree of consciousness and intentionality about the gender dynamics of this transformation is a matter that I explore relatively indirectly and tentatively, choosing instead to focus more on his feminine affiliations and on the changes themselves.[23] Because his earliest work reveals his feminine voices most overtly, this account focuses on the poetry from *A Boy's Will* through that of *New Hampshire,* with the first four chapters exploring these volumes in turn (while also moving intertextually) and the last chapter tracing the echoes of these voices residual within their transformation. In turn, though with considerable overlap, these chapters trace Frost's affiliations with American sentimental poetry, regionalist fiction and nonfiction, homoerotic writing, and premodern and early modern women's writing—including children's literature—while they outline readers' responses to his changing self-representation. Frost's masculine persona was a story that he developed for high stakes: the masking of feminine (and, analogically, "effeminate"/"gay") affiliations in order to ensure his status in the evolving canon. Confirming his self-generated masculinity, Frost's sympathetic readers have increasingly reiterated the poet's own carefully constructed narrative. Not coincidentally, one border of his well-laid interpretive trail was also mapped, in broader outlines, by academic critics of American poetry.

## "The poet is a father": Poetic Identity and Gender

In his classic study *The Continuity of American Poetry* Roy Harvey Pearce affirms that the resistance of mainstream nineteenth-century culture to poetry engendered "an egocentric poetry which insisted that in its egocentrism lay its universality." Pearce makes an observation in the context of a discussion of Whitman that resonates for the poetic project more generally: "the ego asserts itself Adamically, in naming. The poem is a titanic act of adoption. The poet is a father, giving his name to all he sees and hears and feels."[24] Published at the end of Frost's career, Pearce's influential and representative story of American poetry signifies the culmination of a critical perspective that developed over the poet's lifetime; this narrative focuses on and accounts for only the "elite" poetry of Whitman and Dickinson rather than the "popular"—and, we should note, *immensely* popular—work of people like Lydia Sigourney, Alice and Phoebe Cary, Elizabeth Oakes Smith, Sarah M. B. Piatt, Celia Thaxter, and Lucy Larcom, not to mention the Fireside Poets, none of whom found their middle-class readers particularly hostile to poetry.[25] In this account of American poetic tradition, as in many others, lyric stands in for all poetry.

Recent critics have acknowledged the normative and canonizing function of such conceptions of lyric selfhood, as well as its gendered content, for if "the lyric poem . . . [speaks from] a strong and assertive 'I,' a central self that is forcefully defined, whether real or imaginary," that "I" must be fundamentally masculine.[26] This concept of the unitary self is culturally and historically situated, a romantic idea that is more particular to poetry than to prose.[27] The identification of poetry with lyric has hindered both the recognition and the creation of other kinds of poetry; Marjorie Perloff suggests that "the Romantic lyric, the poem as expression of a moment of absolute insight, of emotion crystallized into . . . timeless patterns" necessarily excludes "narrative and didacticism, the serious and the comic, verse *and* prose."[28] By implication, as my discussion of Frost will indicate, such different kinds of poetry represent (and may even require) a different kind of self-conception on the part of the poet as well as an altered relationship to her or his audience; when poetry is defined only as lyric, many other possible performances of selfhood are excluded, and poetry that represents a diffused "I" or a "representative" perspective can be disregarded as "not poetry" on the basis of its deviation from the norm. As Annie Finch has pointed out, "today, if a text lacks the central authority of an apparent ego—sometimes referred to as a 'strong voice'—many would hesitate to call it a poem at all."[29]

As well as encompassing work by women, such poetry might include, for example, poems authored by gay men and by people of color, whose historical experience, cultural values, and identity formation may diverge in significant ways from cultural norms. But it could also include poetry by canonical and "straight" male authors that we have retrospectively normalized into the tradition of Romantic lyric subjectivity. In this light *transcendence,* "the major value term for poetry in the Romantic tradition,"[30] becomes questionable in its potential application to a feminine or other "non-mainstream" writer, since the term presupposes a highly individuated self that *needs* "transcending." If one feels connected with others, then to a degree, one is *already* "outside" the "self." Indeed, the notions of "inside" and "outside" seem inapplicable to a personality possessing (in psychologist Nancy Chodorow's description of feminine selfhood) "flexible or permeable ego-boundaries."[31] What the culture sees as "weak ego boundaries" might be in fact "a negative way of describing the fact that women have tremendous powers of intuitive identification and sympathy with other people"—a kind of Keatsian "negative capability."[32]

A brief look at another very different theoretical voice confirms the complexity of this question of subjectivity and the obliquity with which mainstream critics sometimes approach poetic identity and poetic voice. Paula Gunn Allen argues that the history of Western culture (and concomitantly, of Western literature) has reflected a preoccupation with themes and modes of individuality and conflict resolution—in mainstream literary historical and psychological accounts, "masculine"—to the detriment of tribal cultures and art valuing community, collectivity, and contextuality (more "feminine"), while in traditional Indian literature "the negative effect of individuality forms a major theme in the oral literatures of all tribes."[33] This thematic concern parallels generic issues, for one of Western readers' preoccupations, she argues, is "the purity of genre": "This rigid need for impermeable classificatory boundaries is reflected in turn in the existence of numerous institutional, psychological, and social barriers designed to prevent mixtures from occurring. Western literary and social traditionalists are deeply purist."[34] Allen's work suggests, for one thing, the ethnocentric notions of selfhood embodied in Western poetic and critical traditions, at least in its relatively recent manifestations, and it invites us to consider whether a more dispersed, fluid, or multiple version of selfhood might already appear in Western male-authored poetry and we have overlooked it because of our assumptions about The Poet.[35]

As these reflections suggest, the issue of what constitutes a feminine element in poetic voice or in poetic identity is a vexed one, and, while I cannot hope to pin it down—given its complex imbrication with historical, geographical, aesthetic, biographical, and cultural situations—I would like to close the circle a bit more here. I have suggested that from a feminist psychological perspective *feminine* means possessing "flexible or permeable ego-boundaries" and that this subjectivity might eventuate in "intuitive identification or sympathy with other people." One major risk of a discussion that proceeds from this construction is that it could essentialize "femininity" to women and reinforce cultural stereotypes about women and emotion.[36] As the repeated references to Frost in this outline suggest, however, when I refer to feminine voice anywhere in this account, I mean to signify a *culturally* feminine voice, where "culture," itself a problematic term, indicates the nineteenth- and early-twentieth-century Western middle-class matrix in which Robert Frost worked and to which he responded.[37] In this account of cultural femininity, male poets can and do work out of the fluid perspective that the term invokes.

What such a perspective might entail for poetry is the poet's crossing over of boundaries (such as gender or age) to enable her or him generously to endow other perspectives with complexity and subjectivity. In Frost this movement translates into the actualization of the voices of women (and, though I will only touch upon them, poor, disabled, and working individuals) that possess emotional resonance and psychological authority vis-à-vis the reader, as we see in many of the narrative and dramatic poems. But it is not merely on the grounds of character representation that this psychological femininity comes into play; it also enables the poet to cross over hierarchical boundaries that divide the speaker and the reader. Enabling the latter's participation in the former's emotional perspective, Frost creates what I will call a poetics of empathy. One measure of a poet's femininity, then, will be her or his relative detachment from or hospitality to the reader.[38] The centrality of connection and community also translates into substantive concerns traditionally associated with women, including "domestic" matters such as home and family as well as emotion itself. Another boundary that a feminine voice enables the poet to elide is that of genre; and she or he may engage in a form of genre mixing that resists easy classification. Like Whitman, who "was commonly faulted in the 1920s and 1930s for writing prose and calling it poetry,"[39] Frost was frequently appraised in terms that questioned his participation in a poetic tradition, in spite of his commitment to traditional formal structures; as I will explore, he often wrote a kind of "not poetry" that provoked antipathetic, or at the least, confused critical response. Yet I will argue finally that with Frost it is gesture and attitude, not subject matter or genre, that most clearly intimate and illuminate his feminine voice.

In addition to this *prospective* theory of literary femininity, literary history provides a *retrospective* account. From the angle of vision elaborated by New Critics and their descendants, literary texts, and particular genres, are gendered; indeed, the strategies for the diminishment of Frost's literary achievement often paralleled the terms in which nineteenth-century American women writers were ultimately discarded by a generation of literary critics. Sentimental poetry is the most obvious example of this constructed affiliation between gender and genre. As part of the Western cultural affiliation of women with emotion, this critical construction essentializes and naturalizes gender in genre for, as the next chapter explores, male poets have written and continue to write this kind of poetry. Another form of literature that has retrospectively come to be feminized—not surprisingly, given that its most popular and distinguished practitioners were women—is late-nineteenth and early-twentieth-century New England regionalist writing, especially fiction.[40] Like sentimental poetry, this work was reinvented by a later critical tradition as overly emotional, based in part on its putative nostalgia but also, though less directly, because of its investment of the self with others and, hence, its feminine dispersal of the artist's authority. Once again essentialized with femaleness, New England regionalism was also a mode in which male writers participated. Moreover, the New Critical, modern perspective that would assign a soft femininity to both sentimental poetry and regionalist writing would not take account of either the diversity within each mode nor the ability of its practitioners to assume an ironic stance toward their materials: neither one is uniformly or inherently empathic, and both can elaborate a position of detachment from the materials (including people and events) that they describe. In critical terms, however, to participate in either tradition (or worse, as Frost did, in both, and sometimes simultaneously) is to speak in another kind of feminine voice. From this perspective Frost becomes "not the poet of New England in its great days, or in its late nineteenth-century decline (except in some of his earlier poems); he is rather a poet who celebrates the diminished but prosperous and self-respecting New England of the tourist home and the antique shop in the abandoned gristmill."[41]

As these remarks by Malcolm Cowley suggest, the role of audience in relation to these literary traditions engenders another feminine affiliation for later academic/elite critics: a mass or popular audience further feminizes the writers who work in these traditions, eliciting perspectives like the following: "Below [Longfellow and his peers] were other poets, Mrs. Sigourney and her kind, who, lacking the intelligence to assume their proper [poetic, aesthetic] responsibilities, catered to and exploited the general (or generalized) reader."[42] Mass culture has been gendered female, while elite culture is presumed to be the domain of a harder, more severe masculine artist. Any male writer who participated, as Frost did, in popular genres like sentimentalism or regionalism (or others such as children's literature and folktales) would be vulnerable to reconstruction by academics as working in a feminine voice.[43] In this authoritative and authoritarian critical history readers are also implicitly gendered, with the discriminating and detached reader who seeks "uniqueness" representing a desirable masculinity and a generous and empathic reader (who by her or his very generosity valorizes the degrading texts of mass culture) inhabiting a flaccid femininity. I hope to transvalue the modern idea of the feminine empathic reader as I explore Frost's imagination of such a reader in his earlier work, along with his resistance to an eviscerating masculine reader implicitly constructed by the detachment of his later poetry and explicitly constructed in his prose writing.[44]

Embedded in their historical moment, critical accounts are not merely descriptive but also normative inasmuch as they influence both poets' self-conceptions and readers' perceptions of them. That is, the norms that shape the lyric speaker resonate in the direction of the reader, but they are also bidirectional; a poet's readers, both "real" and "imagined," contemporary and subsequent, possess an ineluctable power to "create" his writing (as my own "story" of Frost will do): "All literary works are produced in a preexisting historical context of evaluative criteria, criteria that determine features of a text and are crucial in its initial reception," and "writers produce texts in preemptive responses to . . . standards of judgment."[45] When male writers are feminized by charges of sentimentality or merely local appeal, these strategies can be as effectual in shaping male writing (and determining canonicity) as in shaping and/or erasing women's. If Henry James's miniaturizing observation about Sarah Orne Jewett's magnificent *The Country of the Pointed Firs* ("her beautiful little quantum of achievement") represents one such strand of suppression, then comments like Amy Lowell's assertion in 1917 that "Mr. Robinson is more universal; Mr. Frost is more particular" elaborate another.[46] Male writers like Frost who sought both popularity and canonization in an elite tradition that hoarded cultural capital by basing "quality" on "complexity," "uniqueness," and "universality" would necessarily be forced into some posture of accommodation.

My outline of sources for feminine identification for poets and poetry obviously arrives from two opposing directions. The empathic and fluid feminine voice constructed from psychological accounts imagines an *interior,* self-determined, and subjective self-elaboration, while the gendering of sentimental poetry and New England regionalist fiction represents an *external* and *retrospective* projection of femininity. An enactment of cultural femininity from within is determined more by the poet's own volition and inclinations, while a projection of gender from without places the poet under constrictive aesthetic norms. Frost's understanding of the latter at some level of consciousness would come to dominate his poetic practice and self-representation, as he moved, in an admittedly irregular fashion, from a position of greater empathy (and, hence, vulnerability) to greater detachment.[47] His great joke on the critical establishment, however, was that, while he shifted toward modernist irony and distancing from his material, he retained the surface accessibility that fostered the creation of a large popular audience that could continue to appreciate his feminine investment in a New England past.

## Reading Readers

Frost once remarked, "I've often said in teaching that the best kind of criticism I know is not in abstractions . . . it's in narrative."[48] His transformation of "criticism" to narrative in this comment evokes my own concern with the relationship between genre and gender as it shapes both the poet and the critic (myself included). I am concerned, that is, not only with the privilege of lyric and its concomitant self-definition but also the purification of theory: "what constitutes theoretical [and critical] discourse, as well as . . . what constitutes poetry."[49] I want at this point to be more specific about my approach to Frost. Aimed at establishing "cognitive authority," traditional critical discourse operates according to well-established conventions that can be fundamentally at odds with a feminine, or relational, perspective: "These conventions include the use of argument as the preferred mode for discussion, the importance of the objective and impersonal, the importance of a finished product without direct reference to the process by which it was accomplished, and the necessity of being thorough in order to establish proof and reach a definitive (read 'objective') conclusion."[50] For many women, and some men, this approach feels alien, forced, and inauthentic, because it emphasizes "competition, not cooperation."[51] If we construct criticism as a form of community building, however, we are freed from the obligation to quote others as part of a construction of linguistic and epistemological authority, we take more pleasure in doing so, and we can quote them more generously (in more than one sense).

As Jane Tompkins has argued, the traditional objective approach also confirms fundamental dualisms in Western epistemology, privileging reason over emotion and hence radically compromising the "epistemic authority" of women, who are normatively affiliated with the latter.[52] Yet, in discussing a writer who draws from traditions that are themselves invested in feeling, it seems crucial to call upon emotion as a category of response, although *emotion* is itself a capacious term that will need further unpacking in the process of my discussion. Having said this, I acknowledge that at times it is very difficult to break out of the mold of "objective" argumentation for various reasons. The traditional form that I've used for some time feels a bit like an old shoe—comfortable, if not stylish, though a bit worn in the sole. The very presence of this explanatory moment is evidence of the regulatory force asserted by the conventions that these accounts critique. Though I hope that it is not disagreeable, parts of the preceding account (and parts that follow) are obviously shaped consciously around disagreement with other readers as well as by the impulse to expand on their insights and to participate in a community of ideas.[53]

Because Frost's own work frequently crosses boundaries of many kinds, I will endeavor to employ a more flexible and polyvocal approach to the writer, and my account of his gendered self-transformations will itself engage in genre mixing, including personal narrative, puns, rhetorical analysis, formalist readings of texts, and biographical and historical contextualization.[54] My responses to Frost's poetry will range from relatively detached, critical, and putatively objective to sometimes personal, emotional, appreciative, playful, and, occasionally, outrageous; I hope, too, to evoke some of Frost's sly humor. The point is not to provoke categorical confusion but, as Frost himself does over and over, to interrogate the bifurcation of such cultural categories themselves.[55] One danger of the autobiographical approach is that, while anecdotes can give to academic discourse a sense of intimacy, this intimacy threatens to dissolve into "mere" "gossip." As is intuitively obvious, and as I will explore in chapter 3, *gossip* is neither a neutral nor androgynous term.[56] Yet such a choice of interpretive diversity is appropriate not only because of my convictions but also because of Frost's own. As Sheldon W. Liebman observes, "no modern poet has spoken out so strongly and unequivocally against the whole critical enterprise." Because he especially condemned criticism that, like much of the poetry it attempted to decode, required an elite education, a "highly specialized erudition" that "reduced poetry to an esoteric puzzle,"[57] I will work toward a discussion that is accessible to "ordinary" as well as "academic" readers.

What remains to be done in this introduction is to move beyond my perspective and frame Frost's work very broadly in the discussions by his contemporaries and their successors in an effort to sketch their own gendered qualities and their (en)gendering of Frost himself. Ironically, in view of his ambivalent attitudes toward them, Frost's earlier sympathy with literal female voices was acknowledged by his contemporaries Amy Lowell and Jessie Rittenhouse. In a discussion of "Home Burial" Lowell points to the line in which the wife begs her husband not to speak of her dead child ("'Don't, don't, don't, don't,' she cried"), observing, "that cry of the woman is terrible in its stark truth. It hurts the reader, it is as unbearable as the real cry would have been, one wants to stop one's ears and shut it out. Printed words can go no farther than this." An important purveyor of verse and an arbiter of taste early in the century, Rittenhouse makes Frost's sympathies with women even more explicit, writing, "Frost has an insight into the lives of women not to be matched by any poet of our day"; "in the lyric group, 'The Hill Wife,' Frost again shows how completely he understands women."[58]

In more restrained and less laudatory terms a number of recent critics have remarked upon the poet's alertness to gender concerns. One of the poet's most perspicacious and sympathetic readers, Richard Poirier, has explored the poet's awareness of "the plight of women who have nothing but a home to keep" and the attendant "frustrations of imagination," but, although Poirier records Frost's sensitivity to female experience, he remarks upon the poet's "heterosexual 'assertiveness,' his confident masculinity." In the same vein, though from another perspective, Patricia Wallace describes Frost's women as powerful, often-frightening purveyors of the imagination, of "craft," of "disruption," occupying positions outside of culture, while Frank Lentricchia depicts Frost's women as essentially neurotic, possessing a "serious lack of drive to preserve self." In his study of the "dialogue" between the poet's men and women, Robert Swennes argues that "the joy of love is in the mutual recognition of each other's virtues—the reconciliation of the sexes, not their erasure"; similarly, in contrast to many earlier accounts, Robert Faggen observes that "Frost's women seem as capable of asserting boundaries and exercising control as his men. What makes the tree [of life] grow, flourish, develop, is always the action of *both* sexes encouraging and contradicting each other." William Pritchard touches most nearly upon Frost's femininity in terms of the present discussion, highlighting the poet's attentiveness to "the motives and hidden natures of men and women, particularly of women" and his concern for the expression of "intimacy" with a reader.[59]

The most extended account to date of Frost's engagement with women—as image, subject, and voice—is Katherine Kearns's. Like many of her predecessors underscoring the deviance or danger of Frost's female characters, Kearns argues that "Frost's world is controlled by a powerful femininity" that is associated with a "nature that is equally female and thus potentially deadly." She emphasizes his pressing need to protect his "individuality," "the structural integrity of manhood," which is threatened by the mother and, by extension, all women;[60] in this context Frost's will to individualism translates to distance from and even hostility toward the reader.[61] Like Kearns, Judith Oster explores, though not in gendered terms, the tension in Frost's work between "engagement" with others and "the need to protect, to keep whole and pure and private the inner core of the self."[62] Directly or indirectly, both Kearns and Oster posit some version of the feminine as the most pressing threat to that self, and they reiterate the narrative of the lyric poet's necessarily and continuously autonomous subjectivity.[63] To emphasize Frost's individuality and autonomy, however, is to take him too much at his word as well as to erase important differences in his work over time. In spite of occasionally recognizing Frost's sympathy for women in many early poems, none of these excellent readers articulates the *culturally* feminine perspective that appears predominantly in *A Boy's Will* and *North of Boston* and that resonates with what one of the poet's best readers, Randall Jarrell, calls "a final and identifying knowledge of the deprived and dispossessed, the insulted and injured."[64]

Through this perspective readers gain insight otherwise unavailable, for, as Frost observed: "Poetry is correspondence: Its images bring forth a response from the feelings and thoughts of the reader because the reader has similar feelings and thoughts. It goes back to the reader's performing his part in a serious engagement."[65] Much like Whitman's poetry, which would require that "the reader will always have his or her part to do, just as much as I have had mine," Frost's would "demand correspondence rather than recognition, participation rather than observation, and creation rather than criticism."[66] In a number of important moments Frost disperses a "strong intact, and invulnerable ego" to imagine powerful and powerfully authorized feminine speakers, inviting readers to share in, not merely to appraise, an intense emotional experience. Finally, the objective, masculinized, and masculinizing view that permeates not only more traditional readings of poets like Frost but also explicitly feminist ones severely curtails our ability to appreciate the originality and the conventionality of the poet himself as well as of other work by writers of either gender.[67] In spite of and because of his contemporary masculine critics, Frost negotiated a complex form of popularity on the way to becoming not only a "self-made man"[68] but also a Real Poet: one whose work would eventually engender both the Robert Frost Interpretive Trail and a conspicuous, if conspicuously problematic, place in American literary history. To understand the construction of this trail, we need to trace a new path, and, in Frost's own feminine metaphor that heads this introduction, "to begin further back than with the thread itself and gather in the fiber or filament the property beyond the thread."

*Chapter 1*

## "The Faded Flowers Gay"
Feminine Frost and the Sentimental Tradition

> But for me, I don't like grievances . . . What I like is griefs and I
> like them . . . profound. I suppose there is no use in asking, but
> I should think we might be indulged to the extent of having
> grievances restricted to prose if prose will accept the imposi-
> tions, and leaving poetry free to go its way in tears.
> —Robert Frost, "Introduction to
> E. A. Robinson's 'King Jasper'"

What constitutes "sentimentality"?[1] Most contemporary persons would
offer an example like the following: crying at a "bad" movie, where we
know from the beginning that the hero and heroine are (or aren't) going to
get together; presidential candidates' "photo-ops" with babies; Hallmark
cards; a little boy and his puppy in a TV commercial for floor wax; on other
terrain, little Eva's death and Emmeline Grangerford's poetry. I confess to
crying every time I read Stowe's novel—and to laughing (admittedly in an
irritated fashion) whenever I read Twain's, whose evocation of the lachry-
mose poetess tweaks every well-trained muscle in my modernist sensibility.[2]
These examples represent one pole of a continuing bifurcation in American
culture: between "emotional" and "rational" ways of experiencing the
world. Juxtaposed to the pleasures of the former—crying at the movies—
are the necessities of the latter, such as teaching my students how to read
"The Wasteland." These examples also represent both the commercializa-
tion and continuing cultural power, acknowledged by advertising execu-
tives and presidents, of sentimental discourse.

In spite of his pronouncements to the contrary, Frost affiliates himself,
at least earlier in his career, with the culturally feminine (often literally
female) voices and the dispersed, collective subjectivity that emerge from
the tradition of sentimental poetry. Sometimes even overreading the affec-
tive element, this chapter will excavate some connections that have been

buried by an academic criticism that has as a whole been keen to recuperate the poet's work into a detached, masculine, ironic modern (or even post-modern) tradition. I will compare his poetry with the work of several well-known nineteenth-century sentimental poets and trace the structural and gestural echoes that emerge, in the process complicating the partially accurate assessment by some of Frost's contemporaries (and given the length of his career this assessment takes place over many years and undergoes many variations) that some (or much, depending on the interpreter) of the poet's work is "sentimental." I want to argue that to situate him in a sentimental tradition is neither to diminish his work nor to suggest that his poetry is not also "modern" or "modernist"; rather, it is to enrich our understanding of this versatile poet's repertoire and to recognize his virtuosity in reshaping a powerful cultural discourse well into the twentieth century.[3]

In spite of Jane Tompkins's *Sensational Designs* and its descendants bringing a modicum of respectability to the genre, sentimentalism (as opposed to reputable romanticism) is a subject that many literary scholars—especially of poetry—still acknowledge and discuss with some reluctance and embarrassment.[4] Although in the mid-nineteenth century a writer could be both "serious" and "sentimental," Tompkins observes, "twentieth-century critics have taught generations of students to equate popularity with debasement, emotionality with ineffectiveness, religiosity with fakery, domesticity with triviality, and all of these, implicitly, with womanly fakery."[5] Fakery is a key, and recent, association with sentimentality. Referring to no less august an authority than the *Oxford English Dictionary,* Fred Kaplan argues: "With slowly gathering force, *sentimentalism* came to denote late in the nineteenth century the misuse of sentiment, 'the disposition to attribute undue importance to sentimental considerations, to be governed by sentiment in opposition to reason; the tendency to excessive indulgence in or insincere display of sentiment.'"[6] In spite of its effectiveness as a tool for social change (particularly in the novel), sentimentalism, at least in its late-twentieth-century sense, has nevertheless come to encode inauthenticity, class consolidation, evasion of social responsibility, (undue) popularity, (false) religiosity, and excessive emotion (vs. reason).[7] These criticisms emerge from "modes of definition and evaluation developed exclusively within the framework of a critical valorization of romantic, individualistic, culturally dissenting, self-consciously artistic aspects of the classic masculine texts."[8]

In continuing to respond somewhat defensively to these criticisms of the mode, we necessarily elide potentially productive discussions. For example, the kinds of poems that we now call sentimental have in common the ambition to express or to evoke emotion. Used merely as a shorthand to signify a response of sympathy or (at its most extreme) weeping, the term, and the history of critical condemnation that surrounds it, inhibits a more capacious and complex understanding of its shifting territory, for the variety, shape, and direction of that emotion can vary widely. As some scholars have begun to do, we need to inquire more carefully not only about the different emotions that various texts elicit but also about the variation in readers' responses, according to gender as well as such variables as age, class, race, and personal experience;[9] the textual or aesthetic qualities that can lead to the perception (or prevention) of "excess" or inauthenticity in affective literature; and the historical and generic variations that occur. Perhaps because nineteenth-century poetry has elicited some of the most severe criticism for emotionalism and conventionalism, it has fostered important revaluations by feminist critics whose recent work reveals that it is far more diverse and complex than earlier accounts acknowledge.[10] Nevertheless, because the term *sentimental* remains contaminated by its critical history and because it reduces this diversity and complexity to homogeneity, I will frequently use less loaded (if similarly imprecise) terms to signify this body of work, such as *mainstream nineteenth-century poetry, popular nineteenth-century poetry, conventional nineteenth-century poetry,* and *affective nineteenth-century poetry.*[11]

"Rational" critical dismissals of the sentimental mode, at least in poetry, are not merely recent. Published in the prestigious *Century Magazine*, poet and literary scholar Helen Gray Cone's 1890 essay "Woman in American Literature" is representative of the mood in the closing decades of the nineteenth century; Cone remarks disparagingly that "sentimentalism has infected both continents," and she bemoans "the flocks of quasi swansingers!"[12] The tone differs very little when Amy Lowell, writing in the *New Republic* in 1923, looks back to the nineteenth century as "a world of sweet appreciation, a devotee of caged warblers, which species of gentle music-makers solaced it monthly from the pages of the 'Century' or the 'Atlantic Monthly.'"[13] (It is interesting, to say the least, that one of the magazines that Lowell accuses of treacle had three decades earlier printed a denouncement of the sentimental style.) This denunciatory vein runs through virtually all accounts of nineteenth-century American poetry from Cone to the present.[14] Louise Bogan, invited to edit a collection of women's poetry, announced famously that "the thought of corresponding with a flock of female songbirds made me acutely ill." In a strongly gendered remark Roy Harvey Pearce describes the work of Edwin Arlington

Robinson as "coming out of a time of sentimentalists, poetasters, androgy-nous Adams, and their bluestocking Eves—a barren time for the life of American poetry." More recently, Rita Felski has remarked generally upon "the regressive, sentimental texts of mass culture."[15] Directly or indirectly, all of these remarks intimate the association of sentimentality with women and hence with "femininity." But, however much they might try to hide the fact, plenty of men cry at the movies.

While Frost's foes would invoke sentimentality as a term of disparage-ment, his sympathetic critics have been eager to defend him by segregating him from the "flocks of quasi-song singers." In a 1934 discussion of the poet's early work Cornelius Weygandt affirms that "it were better for poetry everywhere had it this right hardness I talk of, but in America, where everything must run the gauntlet of ridicule, poetry has been done a great disservice by the sentimentalists who write rhetorical verse and by the fee-ble souls who do attain to poetry of a sort" (Frost, in contrast, has this "hardness"). More recently, in an important account that situates the poet in the context of popular voices as well as those of his New England pre-cursors, George Monteiro compares "The Oven Bird" to Mildred How-ells's "And No Birds Sing" in order to distinguish him from an earlier poetic tradition: "There can be no doubt, of course, that in quality, no matter what yardstick we use, Miss Howells's autumn poem does not measure up to Frost's. For one thing, it lacks immediate force and overall resonance. Its images too evidently belong to the pale, late Victorian poetry of nature. They remain static and generalized." Writing in the authoritative *Columbia History of American Poetry* Jay Parini affirms that "the quest for 'ulteriority' is all part of the Frostian world. On the surface one finds the sentimentalized view of New England embodied in familiar images. . . . But only a very superficial reading stops there." Randall Jarrell falls into this posture too: "Frost's best poetry . . . deserves attention, submission, and astonished awe that real art always requires of us; to give it a couple of readings and a rib-bon lettered First in the Old-Fashioned (or Before 1900) Class of Modern Poetry is worse, almost, than not to read it at all." Finally, like other critics emphasizing the modern element and constructing the modernist Frost, John Evangelist Walsh implicitly compares one of the poet's early efforts, "Ghost House," to his later work, observing that, "though graceful, the poem is unoriginal and rather too much on the sentimental side. Yet one whole stanza . . . virtually leaps out of its context, speaking almost a differ-ent tongue from the rest of the poem."[16]

Perhaps critics should begin focusing on the doughnut ("the rest of the poem") and not on the hole ("one whole stanza"). Indeed, contemporary critics have been so determined to reinvent Frost as a participant in a cosmopolitan masculine twentieth-century literature that they have not even given him "a couple of readings" in the "Before 1900 . . . Class of Modern Poetry." As these defenses of Frost suggest, however, the application of the term *sentimental* to the poet possesses an exceedingly complex texture with strands of tension arriving from several angles. For example, although sentimentalism has been retroactively and essentialistically assigned to the category of feminine (here meaning women's) discourse, this categorization has an element of accuracy, in that sentimental poetry often incorporates the culturally feminine voice theorized in the introduction: it possesses a dispersed subjectivity, establishes a connection of empathy with a reader, and addresses feminine subjects, including emotion itself.[17] Frost invokes such elements of nineteenth-century tradition, elaborating on and reinventing this feminine voice balanced with his own intonations while retaining the tradition's cultural power.[18] The fabric of his history becomes even more tangled when we recognize that, unlike his other books, *A Boy's Will* (a principal target of the label "sentimental") was written and assembled without a prior critical context for the poet's work: that is, critics had no direct role in its creation, even though they would have fundamental parts to play in its reception and eventual integration into the Frost canon.

After I contextualize the poet's early work more specifically in its nineteenth-century cultural context, I will pick up the first two of these strands, namely, Frost's affirmation of a feminine voice in poetry and the echoes, sometimes clearly deliberate, that this voice elaborates of a prior sentimental tradition. The speaker's stance—of romantic "autonomy" and "authority," or sentimental dispersed subjectivity—provides an important touchstone for discussion.[19] In the context of this discussion I will touch upon the amenability of his poems to recuperation into modern poetry by a later critical tradition that would come to assess mainstream nineteenth-century poetry in overwhelmingly negative terms. Moving to further appraisals of the poet by himself and others, I will suggest that a selection of his "good" poems for academic anthologies may be predicated in part on invisible and unconscious gender norms. Finally, I will attempt to revise and complicate contemporary readers' notion of the sentimental by indicating echoes of its attitudes in a poem that seems highly resistant to this reading, as I discuss how a balanced and reinvented affective discourse, a modern sentimentality, empowers and in some measure defines Frost's complex feminine measures.

The central problems on which I hope to shed some light are: the availability of cultural ideologies and aesthetic modes to male as well as female writers; the detachment by modern and contemporary critics of emotional from intellectual and aesthetic modes and the limitations of critical appropriation of Frost into a lyric romantic subjectivity; and the amenability of many of Frost's poems to parallel interpretation as both sentimental and modern—the presence, even in texts that display what I will call "ironic sentimentalism," of a concurrent, or echo, text that retains empathic force. My goals are to de-essentialize, complicate, and transvalue Frost's affiliations with mainstream nineteenth-century American poetry, recuperating as a strength its emotional content. At the same time, I will suggest that affective response should be an important element of critical— as well as popular—understanding of American poetry. From this dual standpoint Frost's pronouncement of poetry as providing a "momentary stay against confusion" can be elaborated in two directions. For the modernist reader and her or his offspring *confusion* and *momentary* are where the stress of the phrase falls, while for the popular reader *stay* is its central emphasis. Not a "caged warbler," Frost nevertheless writes poems that situate him in eventually uncomfortable proximity to Pearce's "androgynous Adams." In the process he engages in a discourse of continuing cultural power and complexity that often negotiates in order to transcend gender.

### Contexts: "That stinking sugar teat"

Sometime in the late winter of 1890 a fifteen-year-old youth began canvassing door to door. In his reading of a youth's magazine he had discovered an offer for a telescope powerful enough to let the viewer see the rings of Saturn; the telescope would be sent free to anyone selling several subscriptions. As a new resident of his neighborhood, the boy met with enough resistance to discourage him from his plan, but his mother completed the sales and the longed-for device arrived shortly afterward. The magazine was the *Youth's Companion*. The boy was Robert Frost.[20]

By locating Frost's early published work in its cultural contexts, we gain insight into the development of his feminine voice, particularly its affirmative initial alliances with and transformations of nineteenth-century emotion-centered poetry. The *Youth's Companion* is an important resource for this contextualization. Founded in 1827, this popular magazine traditionally directed at young people included stories, advice, and poetry. A survey of a typical issue from the same period that Frost discovered the telescope offer reveals the diversity of these materials, including stories such as the thrilling serial "Through Thick and Thin" and the domestic drama "Mrs. Darrow's Poorhouse"; "history" such as "Reading Indian 'Sign'"; advice such as "Directions for a Trip to Europe" (subtitled "The Outfit Needed"); and poetry such as "The Path of Peace" by Celia Thaxter. Accompanying the prose and poetry was a range of illustrated advertisements for products like Ayer's Sarsaparilla ("Has Cured Others Will Cure You"), Puritan Cookers ("No Need to Watch the Most Delicate Food . . . Ladies! This cooker is a real labor-saver"), and Pearline Soap ("['Washing is] 'Play' for some women—hard work for others"); these advertisements, like health columns such as "Contagiousness of Diseases," were clearly aimed at mothers, not the youths for whom the magazine was ostensibly intended. The enormously varied writing included several poems, of which "One Day in June" is representative:

> A bride went forth with her flowery train,
>     One rose-hung day in June,
> And the birds and sea and the pealing bells
>     Seemed singing the same glad tune;
> And the young bride, seeing but hours of bliss,
> Said, "Who could weep in a world like this!"
>
> A widow went forth with her mourning train,
>     On the selfsame day in June,
> And the wind and the sea and the tolling bells
>     Seemed chanting the same sad rune;
> And the widow, seeing but desolate years,
> Said, "Who could laugh in this world of tears!"[21]

When Robert Frost read the *Youth's Companion,* it is likely that he did not merely read the advertisements: he probably also read the poetry.[22] Representing the "poem of secret sorrow" that Cheryl Walker indicates featured regularly in nineteenth-century women's poetry, "One Day in June" was written by a *male* poet, the kind who continued to write verses as sentimental as those that appeared in the *New England Magazine* alongside one of Frost's earliest publications, "Into Mine Own."[23] When Frost published "Ghost House" (1906), "October" (1912), and "Reluctance" (1912), the *Youth's Companion* published sentimental poems like "Why the Spring Was Late" and "Your Mission" and humorous ones like "The Good Old Firm" on the same pages as his own.

Frost was over thirty years old when the first of these poems appeared in this popular serial, which had by then become a family magazine.[24] The context for "Ghost House" included not only "Why the Spring Was Late" but also short fiction like "Grief," about a woman whose husband had vanished nine years earlier (and which immediately followed Frost's poem); "'The Girls,'" about two childhood friends who rediscover each other in old age; and a "new woman" story, "Kate's Matriculation," which featured a rebellious heroine being reunited with her stubbornly traditional father via her self-renunciation. The issue also featured stories and articles that would interest boys, such as "Harry Harding's Last Year," "Learning to Shear Sheep," and "Johnny Barsand's Great Wolf Fight."[25] As the advertisements make apparent, however, the *Youth's Companion* remained a periodical that was overwhelmingly purchased and read by women: Rumford Baking Powder occupies the entire last page of the issue, and advertisements for Quaker Oats, New York City's Latest Models (of clothing), and American Radiators and Ideal Boilers ("snug for child and grandma") figure prominently. That Frost chose to situate three of his earliest publications in this venue raises a number of questions: Did he regard his work as sentimental? Was it consciously aimed at a predominantly female audience, or was he simply writing out of the American poetic tradition as he understood it?[26] How did he intend this audience to interpret these poems? Was he publishing in the *Youth's Companion* merely for the sake of publishing or for the sake of the income?

The editor who selected "Ghost House" would have sought appropriate family entertainment, not a radically new or individual perspective or an experimental structure; he accepted it based on its accessibility to his readers and its confirmation, not interrogation, of cultural norms, knowing that his readers would value it for precisely these features. In this domestic and didactic context the opening stanza of "Ghost House" resonates with its nineteenth-century precursors:

> I dwell in a lonely house I know
> That vanished many a summer ago,
>    And left no trace but the cellar walls,
>    And a cellar in which the daylight falls,
> And the purple-stemmed wild raspberries grow.
>
>                            (CP 15)

Focusing on isolation and loss ("lonely," "vanished," "no trace," "falls," "wild"), Frost's poem evokes the ambivalently pleasurable absence of death as the poem conjures the ghosts ("mute folk") who visit from the nearby graveyard. The narrator's "strangely aching heart" and the dead lovers, "as sweet companions as might be had," recall the mourning verses of his antecedents at least as much as they anticipate the alienation and anxiety of a modernist vision figured in "the black bats" that "tumble and dart" later in the poem.

Although Frost, of course, affirmed that "a poem is best read in the light of all the other poems ever written,"[27] his work has not been studied in the context of the popular feminine (which in the parlance of the day meant female) predecessors whose work filled the pages of serials like the *Youth's Companion* and *St. Nicholas*. Instead, he has been read exhaustively and exhaustingly in terms of the ostensibly more manly traditions of Virgil and the Romantic poets who filled the last (and by far the longest) chapter of one of the poet's favorite volumes, Francis Turner Palgrave's *Golden Treasury of the Best Songs and Lyrical Poems in the English Language:* Wordsworth, Keats, Shelley, and Scott.[28] Following the line mapped out by his critical predecessors, Jeffrey Meyers emphasizes Frost's participation in a tradition of male poetry, especially from "the Bible, the Latin poets, the ballads, Shakespeare, the English Romantics and the Victorians," and he affirms that "the *Golden Treasury*, a lifelong source of inspiration for his prose, his poetry, and his life, had a greater influence on Frost than any other book."[29] Although Frost never claimed to read or to be influenced by earlier American women poets, it is highly unlikely, given his mother's regular reading to him and his sister Jeanie as well as the proliferation of anthologies of feminine verse during the late nineteenth and early twentieth centuries (and his own voracious reading habits), that he did *not* read such New England writers as Lucy Larcom and Celia Thaxter or, for that matter, their earlier counterparts, Elizabeth Oakes Smith and Lydia Sigourney.[30] But, even if he did not read their verse himself or hear it read, he came of age during a period when it was still highly visible, popular, and esteemed by many. We cannot assume that he was unfamiliar with their work merely because he does not tell us he knows it; in the context of his growing desire to be seen as part of a larger and more masculine American tradition, it would perhaps be more surprising if he did choose to identify their writing as a source of inspiration.[31] To do so would have been as daring (and fool-hardy) as admitting that one's new car design was based on the Edsel.

The barrier between the mainstream American poets of the *Youth's Companion* and the Romantic poets of Frost's beloved Palgrave is not as great as some would have it, and, in spite of attempts by critics to segregate between the two on the basis of the latter's rational control of emotion, we can understand the distinction as a matter of degree rather than kind;

indeed, modernist critics regarded both as feminized.[32] As its subtitle announces, the *Golden Treasury* attempts to represent "the best songs and lyrical poems in the English language." The "best" turns out virtually to exclude women, even though British (as well as American) women poets had been writing prolifically and well for some time.[33] Yet a closer inspection of the *Golden Treasury* yields the observation that there appears to be little difference between, say, Shelley's "Dirge" and Elizabeth Oakes Smith's "Dream"; Charles Lamb's "On an Infant Dying as Soon as Born," Thomas Hood's "Death Bed," and Lydia Sigourney's "Death of an Infant"; Wordsworth's "Daffodils" ("I wander'd lonely as a cloud"), and Helen Hunt Jackson's "Poppies on the Wheat"—or, for that matter, Tennyson's "Tears, Idle Tears" (not included in Palgrave) and any number of poems by nineteenth-century writers, male or female.[34] If William Dean Howells would reflect upon "the sentimental response of passive sympathy" as "tears, idle tears," then modernist Ezra Pound would characterize Palgrave more bluntly as "that stinking sugar teat."[35]

Let's preface more detailed attention to Frost with a glance at one or two poems that represent for contemporary readers some of the most extreme and uncomfortable versions of the sentimental. An exemplary early, "transparent" (or unironic) sentimental poem, "The Light of Home," is as good a place as any to begin suckling:

> My boy, thou wilt dream the world is fair,
>   And thy spirit will sigh to roam,
> And thou must go;—but never when there
>   Forget the light of home.
>
> Though pleasure may smile with a ray more bright,
>   It dazzles to lead astray;
> Like the meteor's flash it will deepen the night,
>   When thou treadest the lonely way.
>
> But the hearth of home has a constant flame
>   And pure as the vestal fire;
> T'will burn, 't will burn for ever the same,
>   For nature feeds the pyre.
>
> . . . . . . . . . . . . . . . . . . . . .
>
> The sun of fame, 't will gild the name,
>   But the heart ne'er feels its ray;
> And fashion's smiles, that rich ones claim,
>   Are like the beams of a wintry day

And how cold and dim those beams would be,
    Should life's wretched wanderer come:
But my boy, when the world is dark to thee,
    Then turn to the light of home.[36]

The author of this poem is Sarah Josepha Hale, for many years the editor of
*Godey's Ladies' Book* and an important cultural arbiter; the poem itself
appeared in Rufus Griswold's enormous popular anthology, *The Poets and
Poetry of America,* which went through seventeen editions (and many more
printings) between 1842 and 1893.[37] I have spared colicky contemporary
readers a rehearsal of the entire poem, but the sections cited provide a
glimpse into a prototypical nineteenth-century poetic project: couched in
images of a heroic struggle with nature, the maternal and antiworldly values
of the bourgeois Christian family are safely ensconced here. Performing an
oblique counterpoint to the journey of Ishmael in *Moby-Dick,* who seem-
ingly, like Emily Dickinson, "never had a Mother," the poem offers affec-
tive goals: inasmuch as it addresses the son himself, to cement imaginatively
his relationship with his mother, and, as it addresses the mother, to console
women whose sons have departed for the world of "pleasure," "ambition,"
and "fame" and to inspire empathy in those who have not had this experi-
ence. "The Light of Home" speaks intimately and directly to the reader;
fundamentally feminine in attitude and voice, the poem calls on and creates
a community of emotional support, desiring and offering the self-in-rela-
tion, seeking to elicit emotion, and embracing a wide and receptive audi-
ence at a time of intense westward migration and cultural dislocation.

    But it is not only on cultural and substantive grounds that contempo-
rary readers might find this poem repugnant but also on aesthetic ones: not
only are its rhythms and rhyme scheme appallingly, not appealingly, "regu-
lar" and "unsurprising," but its images are "conventional" and "clichéd"
and its voice "undistinguished":[38] in practice the "wide audience" becomes
so inclusive as to suggest Groucho Marx's witticism that he wouldn't belong
to any club that would have him as a member. These qualities were (and
are) gendered feminine and marked as deficient by an emerging modernist
critical tradition[39] that would apply the same standards to the opening lines
of "The Mother Perishing in a Snow-Storm" by Seba Smith, published on
the same page as Hale's poem:

The cold winds swept the mountain's height,
    And pathless was the dreary wild,

And mid the cheerless hours of night
    A mother wander'd with her child:
As through the drifting snow she press'd,
    The babe was sleeping on her breast.

And colder still the winds did blow,
    And darker hours of night came on,
And deeper grew the drifting snow:
    Her limbs were chill'd, her strength was gone;
"O GOD!" she cried, in accents wild,
    "If I must perish, save my child!"[40]

The poem progresses with an account of the mother removing her own coat to cover the child, and it concludes predictably when she is found frozen at dawn by a traveler, as "the babe look'd up and sweetly smiled!" In "The Mother Perishing in a Snow-Storm" the speaker's authority is displaced onto the mother, with her plea to God (who is a version of the poet, deciding whether the child will indeed "live" or "die"), as death and rescue combine with a portrait of maternal selflessness in a poem that advances the same virtues and values advocated by Hale's.

Feminist critics might easily and reasonably point to Smith's (and Hale's) investment in a patriarchal and capitalist family unit centered and dependent on the self-sacrifice of the mother, but that is not the point. What *is* at issue is the availability of cultural ideologies, aesthetic modes, and epistemological stances to both male and female writers. If anything, Smith's poem is "more sentimental" than Hale's, attempting to evoke emotions of fear, pain, and reassurance. Moreover, in both poems the strong, individuated self of canonical lyric as Pearce outlines it is absent, relinquished to a broader and more inclusive cultural collectivity (circumscribed, of course, by class, race, and language). As Paula Bennett has argued, "Such poetry is not meant to be a vehicle for the poet's idiosyncratic psyche or uniquely personal vision, nor does it claim to be. Rather, it speaks in the unified voice of a single cultural point of view, a view that addresses, as it were, in public language the values and concerns of women's 'private' sphere."[41] The *point* of these speakers is that they are *not* individual and *not* innovative—and *not* hierarchical in their displacement from the reader.

Although contemporary academic critics may find "The Mother Perishing in a Snow-Storm" repugnant because it transparently manipulates the emotions of the audience and because it elevates "public, communally shared values such as religion and family love,"[42] this response does not take into account the continuing power of this mode, evident in the popularity of poets like Rod McKuen or the huge market for films like *Sleepless in Seattle*. An elite masculine Western perspective that values reason over emotion will always decertify popular art because it is contaminated by affiliation with feminized mass culture and "excess" emotion, yet we can speculate that it is not emotion per se that alienates many contemporary readers but, rather, emotion unsteadied by rhetorical, structural, or stylistic features that inhibits for those contemporary readers the empathic response sought by many nineteenth-century poets. In poems like "The Light of Home" and "The Mother Perishing in a Snow-Storm" the balance tips decisively and precariously, for the contemporary reader, toward the overstated and saccharine. In contrast, Frost, often able to discover precisely this balance, elaborates upon and reinvents the feminine voice that resides in nineteenth-century sentimentalism: its appeal to the values of a broad audience, attempt to engage the reader in a relation of empathy, and invocation of familiar images and forms.

## "You come too": Home, Nature, God, and the Sentimental

Before we look at specific instances of Frost's feminine voice we need to explore his attitude toward sentimentality and emotion, which are clearly not the same. While, on the one hand, he and Louis Untermeyer share repeated jests about excessive, false sentiment in poetry, on the other hand, they include in their group of friends Sara Teasdale, a woman writing emotionally inflected poetry clearly in the mainstream nineteenth-century tradition.[43] One element of Frost's attitude toward feelings is suggested by his famous affirmation, "No tears in the writer, no tears in the reader" (*CP* 777). Similarly, in an early letter to Untermeyer, Frost praises one of his friend's poems for first provoking feeling and then thought, concluding: "That's what makes a poem. A poem is never a put-up job so to speak. It begins as a lump in the throat, a sense of wrong, a homesickness, a lovesickness. It is never a thought to begin with" (*LU* 22). In 1923 he implicitly criticizes Amy Lowell for engendering insufficient emotion: "The water in our eyes from her poetry is not warm from any suspicion of tears; it is water flung cold, bright and many-colored from flowers gathered in her formal garden in the morning" (*CP* 712). The remarks to Untermeyer represent an implicit response to a prior tradition—to its excess and its potential for manipulation. On the other hand, Frost suggests that emotion must be central to the finest poetry, for Lowell's work (he feels) performs a detachment that eventuates in a merely intellectual response. This emotion must be genuine and intimate, and it must be evoked from a stance of empathy with the reader.

Frost elaborates this position of empathy in the familiar 1910 poem that frames all of his collected and selected poems after 1930: "The Pasture."[44] This "tender and gentle" poem bespeaks an unabashed appeal to emotion.[45] Focusing on small tasks, the opening stanza depicts the events of everyday life in a way that we might call domestic, especially in view of what follows. For example, Frost's invocation of the mother is a clear appeal to the cultural icon of the mother caring for her offspring—a figure as appealing to popular audiences in the twentieth century as in the nineteenth. Just as the mother in Hale's poem acts as the safe haven for her son and the mother in Smith's poem covers her baby with her cloak, Frost's cow licks her calf, also depicted as entirely vulnerable in the lines "It's so young / It totters when she licks it with her tongue."[46] Beyond the appeal to the image of the mother is the use of nature, for the mother inhabits this poem in the unspoken but intensely present image of Mother Nature. No flowers here, but they're scattered around the edges.

Readers might argue that Frost's poem displays an individuality of voice more typical of romanticism or Frost's own modernism; performing the particular actions of an individuated lyric speaker, he represents "the poet's uniquely personal vision" or "privileged central self," and he is decidedly not erased from the poem. Simultaneously, and at least as strong in "The Pasture," is "the unified voice of a single cultural point of view, a view that addresses . . . the values and concerns of women's 'private' sphere" characteristic of mainstream nineteenth-century American poetry.[47] From this perspective his self-presentation is decisively, unapologetically, and overtly feminine (and again, some might say, sentimental). We should recall Frost's affirmation to his friend John Bartlett that he seeks an appeal beyond "the critical few who are supposed to know . . . I must get outside that circle to the general reader who buys books in their thousands. I may not be able to do that. I believe in doing it—dont you doubt me there. I want to be a poet for all sorts and kinds. . . . I want to reach out" (*CP* 668). Embracing a broad audience in "The Pasture," Frost melds the individual speaker with the collective perspective and concerns of mainstream nineteenth-century poetry to authorize his feminine voice. Intimacy is the key to maneuvering between the critical rock of excess emotion, or fakery, and the hard place of ostensible manipulation of the reader; by personalizing his appeal, he paradoxically makes it more accessible, inviting readers to hold emotional and intellectual responses to the poems that follow in productive equilibrium.

This balance reappears in different form in "Wind and Window Flower," in which the poet skillfully negotiates among a number of different cultural discourses, one of which is plainly that of his mainstream American precursors:

> Lovers, forget your love,
>     And list to the love of these,
> She a window flower,
>     And he a winter breeze.
>
> When the frosty window veil
>     Was melted down at noon,
> And the cagèd yellow bird
>     Hung over her in tune,
>
> He marked her through the pane,
>     He could not help but mark,
> And only passed her by,
>     To come again at dark.
>
> He was a winter wind,
>     Concerned with ice and snow,
> Dead weeds and unmated birds,
>     And little of love could know.
>
> But he sighed upon the sill,
>     He gave the sash a shake,
> As witness all within
>     Who lay that night awake.
>
> Perchance he half prevailed
>     To win her for the flight
> From the firelit looking-glass
>     And warm stove-window light.
>
> But the flower leaned aside
>     And thought of naught to say,
> And morning found the breeze
>     A hundred miles away.

(CP 20)

On the surface an old-fashioned ballad of love lost—reminiscent of a Tennysonian song[48]—the poem resonates in a variety of directions: the mismatch between lover and beloved, who inhabit entirely separate spheres; the hardness and coldness of the male and the softness and ostensible vulnerability of the female; the rejection, silence, or ineptitude of the female; and the betrayal by a not-too-persistent lover. At one level the poem, like most of those in *A Boy's Will,* is written for an audience that we might call "Elinor," or, more broadly, "Beloved," as it intimates the pain implicit in the lovers' separation by "the pane." Poirier describes the poem as part of a larger story depicted by *A Boy's Will,* focusing on the young man/lover as the central organizing consciousness that he describes as "the isolated 'I.'" As part of this overriding narrative, "Wind and Window Flower" and the poems that surround it indicate "that the threat to love [that shapes the volume] has been gradually internalized by the young poet and that the landscape is an imaginary one of those moods, depressions, and melancholies which threaten their love with devastation and aridity." Troublingly, "the poet has himself been seen as a force for frigidity working in conjunction with the most malevolent aspects which he selects or imagines in the natural environment."[49] To be sure, the central self invokes the scene in the opening stanza, and the narrator's focus and sympathies are to a degree with the excluded "he."[50]

Bearing these insights in mind, we might easily be tempted to elide its popular genealogy and ask: Does the poem (and *A Boy's Will* more generally, with its glosses on individual poems) simply use the appurtenances of a sentimental plot to. convey a modernist message of the isolation and self-alienation of the individuated poet? Is Frost ironic here, poking gentle fun at an earlier poetic sensibility?[51] While it is easy to acknowledge Frost's narrator's self-awareness, especially over the course of *A Boy's Will,* it is important to note also his sympathy for the female flower, a sympathy for femaleness that recurs and is elaborated even more fully elsewhere. At the same time, the speaker figuratively disperses his own authority in the closing image as well as in the poem's title: "wind" is incorporated into "window flower." Even if we choose to read irony and poking fun, there is a coexisting or echo text that retains sentimental and empathic force, paralleling "the poem of secret sorrow" exemplified in "One Day in June."[52] In its anxiety about loss "Wind and Window Flower" also echoes Hale's "Light of Home," though the former is considerably more delicate in its expression and provides no overt consolation for the ultimate separation that occurs. Readers who interpret the poem solely from a modern, ironic perspective risk losing the deep emotional resonance of separation and loss that constitutes a fundamental part of its meaning.

Frost's familiarity with the work of his popular nineteenth-century precursors also emerges in his striking invocation of "the cagèd yellow bird," an avatar of the flower/woman and a familiar image in mainstream nineteenth-century poetry.[53] Rose Terry Cooke's "Captive" provides another touchstone for "Wind and Window Flower":

> The Summer comes, the Summer dies,
>     Red leaves whirl idly from the tree,
> But no more cleaving of the skies,
>     No southward sunshine waits for me!
>
> You shut me in a gilded cage,
>     You deck the bars with tropic flowers,
> Nor know that freedom's living rage
>     Defies you through the listless hours.
>
> What passion fierce, what service true,
>     Could ever such a wrong requite?
> What gift, or clasp, or kiss from you
>     Were worth an hour of soaring flight?
>
> I beat my wings against the wire,
>     I pant my trammeled heart away;
> The fever of one mad desire
>     Burns and consumes me all the day.
>
> What care I for your tedious love,
>     For tender word or fond caress?
> I die for one free flight above,
>     One rapture of the wilderness![54]

Clearly more passionate, intense, and unrestrained than Frost's, Cooke's poem possesses an intensity in part due to the presence of an explicit first-person narrator purporting to be the bird herself. Nevertheless, the popular ballad form enhances the storytelling, representative, parable-like quality of each. "Captive" also falls into the category of "the poem of secret sorrow," for, like "Wind and Window Flower," it relies on nature to tell a story of a vulnerable betrayed female, though it addresses the loss of female voice as well as female freedom. Although from one perspective Cooke's first-person narrator seems to invoke the strongly individuated self of romantic lyric, from another we can read this voice as a representation of collective "womanhood."

Two much earlier Frances Osgood poems, "The Daisy's Mistake" and "A Cold, Calm Star," echo the betrayal theme with inflections similar to Frost's. The first is a dialogue between an underground daisy awaiting spring and the sunbeam and zephyr who attempt, and finally succeed, in luring her from the ground prematurely, against her better instincts; the result of their betrayal, and her foolishness, is death:

> And so she lay with her fair head low,
>     And mournfully sigh'd in her dying hour,
> "Ah! had I courageously answer'd 'No!'
>     I had now been safe within my native bower!"[55]

Like Frost's, Osgood's poem shows the female beloved as betrayed and affirms the "safety" and comfort of her "native bower" (imagined in Frost's poem as "the firelit looking-glass / And the warm stove-window light"), but "The Daisy's Mistake" writes beyond the ending of "Wind and Window Flower" in that it imagines the daisy succumbing to the allure of the tempters. Providing a revealing look into the perspective of the daisy, which Frost withholds in the case of the window flower, Osgood's poem antici-pates the narrative of temptation performed by her successor. Part of what allures is the freedom that Cooke's bird seeks, for, responding to the lies of the ambiguously gendered sunbeam and zephyr, the daisy "sprang to the light, as she broke from her chain, / And gayly she cried, 'I am free! I am free!'" For contemporary readers the potential for sentimentality in this poem and Cooke's arises from the lack of balance in this kind of exuberant language. Another poem by Osgood enacts a similar drama, with the same relaxation of selfhood on the part of the narrator that we have seen in "Wind and Window Flower" and "The Daisy's Mistake":

> A cold, calm star look'd out of heaven
>     And smiled upon a tranquil lake,
> Where, pure as angel's dream at even,
>     A lily lay but half awake.
>
> The flower felt that fatal smile
>     And lowlier bow'd her conscious head;
> "Why does he gaze on me the while?"
>     The light-deluded lily said.
>
> Poor dreaming flower!—too soon beguiled,
>     She cast not thought nor look elsewhere;
> Else she had known the star but smiled
>     To see himself reflected there.[56]

"A Cold, Calm Star" again figures the distant masculine figure attempting to lure a vulnerable female to her ruin. Like the "cold, calm star" depicted here, the wind in Frost's poem is both severe, cold, and remote, "a winter wind, / Concerned with ice and snow, / Dead weeds and unmated birds, / And little of love could know." The ending of "Wind and Window Flower" reflects what we might call a modernist ambiguity in that the resolution is unclear, while in "The Daisy's Mistake" the woman-daisy plainly dies. In spite of the hint that the relationship is "fatal" in "A Cold, Calm Star," the lily's fate is not clear; beyond the male star's narcissistic betrayal, we are not told whether she dies or simply learns a lesson about distant maleness.

Like Frost's, these nature poems depict a "secret sorrow"; they debate the nature of "freedom"; they are "regular in meter and rhyme scheme . . . operating within the fixed boundaries of a shared discourse";[57] they call upon familiar cultural images and stereotypes; they seek empathy from the reader; and, most significantly, they perform a different, more dispersed subjectivity than romantic lyric subjectivity.[58] Frost's speaker fosters the illusion of this "shared discourse" by calling on readers directly in an old-fashioned and conventional language ("Lovers, forget your love, / And list to the love of these"), and he encodes nineteenth-century strictures about the danger of the worldly male to the warm, domestic female. While "Wind and Window Flower" is far more restrained in tone than "Captive" and "The Daisy's Mistake," it is only slightly more so than "A Cold, Calm Star," whose only linguistically emotional excess from a contemporary perspective are such word choices as "fatal," "deluded," "poor," and "beguiled." In spite of his third-person narrator, Frost's self-presentation in "Wind and Window Flower" incorporates a striking sense of emotional longing and vulnerability, but, at the same time, by retaining a level of detachment that anticipates his later lyrics, he constrains the potential for emotional excess and manipulation of the reader for which contemporary critics have attacked popular nineteenth-century American poetry.

My own response to this poem is less intense and appreciative than to "The Pasture," whose first-person intimacy evokes a willingness to share the speaker's experience, allowing emotional and intellectual responses to work in evocative balance. Nevertheless, in both "The Pasture" and "Wind and Window Flower" Frost calls upon familiar cultural themes and forms to advance a feminine voice that establishes a connection with an audience like that of the *Youth's Companion*. Written in the late years of the nineteenth century or the early ones of the twentieth, the latter poem imagines an audience represented by the editor and publisher of his first paid publication ("My Butterfly"), Susan Hayes Ward, to whom he sent a collection of seventeen pieces of his early work for Christmas 1911. Only two months later he would acknowledge to his lifelong friend and supporter, in a joking and somewhat embarrassed fashion, that "[I am] something of a sentimental sweet singer myself" (*SL* 45).[59] The poems that accompanied "Wind and Window Flower" in this Christmas gift included "October" and "Reluctance," both published in the *Youth's Companion* in 1912. By this point Frost was apparently becoming alert to the dangers of such an identification and the limitations of such an audience, in spite of his reconstruction of a feminine voice from components of his predecessors' work.

The alliances of Frost's work with the conventions of mainstream nineteenth-century American poetry emerge repeatedly in *A Boy's Will.* Although he minimizes these alliances, Clement Wood disparages them in his 1925 *Poets of America,* citing "remembered excrescenses like *fain to list . . . wist, alway, hie me, 'neath, 'wildered, whelming . . . didst, wended me,* and even *asphodel.*"[60] That is, only ten years after publication of the American edition of Frost's first book, critics were already engaged in the work of reconstructing him in the context of "the new poetry." Calling upon the image of the flower to structure a romantic encounter whose potential tenuousness is reiterated, in different ways, in poems like "Waiting," "Going for Water," and "Love and a Question," Frost's feminine voice resonates powerfully again in the delicate and exquisitely lovely "Flower-Gathering":

> I left you in the morning,
> And in the morning glow,
> You walked a way beside me
> To make me sad to go.
> Do you know me in the gloaming,
> Gaunt and dusty gray with roaming?
> Are you dumb because you know me not,
> Or dumb because you know?
>
> All for me? And not a question
> For the faded flowers gay
> That could take me from beside you
> For the ages of a day?
> They are yours, and be the measure
> Of their worth for you to treasure,
> The measure of the little while
> That I've been long away.

(CP 22)

While we might associate the elegiac tone with a modernist sensibility, we should recall that mainstream nineteenth-century American poetry rehearsed the elegiac mode again and again. Retaining the accessibility of its popular precursors, the poem's language includes conventional images such as "the morning glow," "the gloaming," and "the faded flowers gay"; and its simple diction ("sad," "gaunt," "dumb," "treasure"), which employs words of only one and two syllables, focuses the effect more on the emotional weight that the language bears. Paradoxically, the speaker relies on a delicate restraint of emotion to evoke an affective connection with the listener, who can share in the anxiety and potential isolation engendered by his departure (figured in "left," "go," "from beside you," and "long away"). Shirley Samuels has observed: "Sentimentality is literally at the heart of nineteenth-century American culture. . . . As a set of cultural practices designed to evoke a certain form of emotional response, usually empathy, in the reader or viewer, sentimentality produces or reproduces spectacles that cross race, class, and gender boundaries."[61] "Flower-Gathering" exemplifies Frost's brilliant ability to create a feminine voice that engages elements of the sentimental tradition to cross gender boundaries.

Written during the summer of 1896, "Flower-Gathering" accomplishes in exemplary fashion the transcendence of such gender boundaries in part because of its embeddedness in the poet's own experience. At this time the Frosts were staying in a cottage in Allenstown, New Hampshire, and Elinor, nearly seven months pregnant, insisted that Frost continue alone the outdoor explorations that he loved so much. His late return on several occasions prompted Elinor's anxiety that he might be stuck in a swamp. Conceived as an apology for this behavior, "Flower-Gathering" responds to the characteristic withdrawal into which she would fall at such times; as an "apology," it was aimed at creating precisely the kind of emotional response that would enable renewed connection between them. In spite of the (distancing and rationalizing) interpretive apparatus that he placed on *A Boy's Will,* "Flower-Gathering" emblematizes Frost's willingness to be vulnerable, a stance that would be embarrassing to later critics eager to represent poetry principally as an aesthetic object.

In its evocation and valorization of the heterosexual domestic romance "Flower-Gathering" represents an even closer proximity to the nineteenth-century cultural norms also invoked by "Wind and Window Flower." While we could choose to read the former ironically (i.e., from a modern perspective), it seems to me that to do so is, once again, to erase the intense vulnerability that the poem evokes, the feminine fragility of the male speaker ("Do you know me in the gloaming . . . ?"). By recovering its affiliations with nineteenth-century precursors, we are able to retrieve the poem's representation of a voice that skillfully appeals to emotion as well as to intellect. A similar appeal occurs in the writing of an earlier, immensely popular New England poet whose work would have been difficult for Frost to avoid. Celia Thaxter shares with him an interest in region and nature; with more overt intensity, her poem "Alone" also recalls the distance of the beloved and the central floral metaphor that we see expressed in "Flower-Gathering":

> The lilies clustered fair and tall;
> I stood outside the garden wall;
> I saw her light robe glimmering through
> The fragrant evening's dusk and dew.
>
> She stopped above the lilies pale;
> Up the clear east the moon did sail;
> I saw her bend her lovely head
> O'er her rich roses blushing red.
>
> Her slender hand the flowers caressed
> Her touch the unconscious blossoms blessed;
> The rose against her perfumed palm
> Leaned its soft cheek in blissful calm.
>
> I would have given my soul to be
> That rose she touched so tenderly!
> I stood alone, outside the gate,
> And knew that life was desolate.[62]

Leaving aside the possibility that this poem might enact a desire for lesbian relationship, we see the emotional workings of the narrator more directly than in "Flower-Gathering," especially in the last stanza. At the same time, the language retains the overt intensity and the gorgeousness that Frost's poem mutes, as Thaxter calls on conventional images such as "the fragrant evening" and "the rich roses." But Frost's poem takes place in the evening as well, and "the faded flowers gay" evoke in more restrained form Thaxter's "unconscious blossoms."[63]

From another angle Thaxter's poem promises even more stringent isolation and alienation than Frost's, which, however anxiously, nevertheless traces the return of the speaker to the beloved. In addition, the rhetorical positioning of the narrator in relation to the reader differs fundamentally.

Speaking directly to a beloved whose position the reader must also assume, "Flower-Gathering" pursues an imaginative and retrospective trajectory of togetherness to separation to reunion. We can read the ending as a form of consolation and the poem itself as a bouquet of flowers presented to us as a token of the poet's intimacy with and love for our presence. In contrast, the beloved of Thaxter's similarly retrospective poem is described in the third person to a reader imagined as a sympathetic friend; we could read it even more severely as a meditation of the self to the self. Ultimately "alone," "outside," "desolate," her narrator returns to no consoling vision of reunion, as the language and formal regularity of the poem war with its narrative. To say that Frost's poem is "more sentimental" than Thaxter's, however, does not indicate with sufficient clarity the nature of that excess. The "happy ending" of the former occupies one node of that affiliation, allied with the poem's comforting formal regularity.[64] Perhaps it is his evocation of speaker-reader intimacy, in which he crosses the boundaries of selfhood as he does in "The Pasture," that best encapsulates the poem's emotional resonance, as it anticipates the dramatic monologues, and vulnerable feminine voices, of *North of Boston*. For some contemporary readers the emotional intensity of "Flower-Gathering" may threaten to overflow into excess, but I find it one of Frost's most moving, expressive, and delicately balanced works.

As evocative as "Flower-Gathering" may be for some readers, "some of the loveliest of Frost's poems, especially in *A Boy's Will,* are in the forms of prayers, petitions, instructions to the seasons." Exploring the literary antecedents of "A Prayer in Spring" and noting that it has not "the slightest hint of country speech," Poirier argues that both it and "Rose Pogonias" are " 'literary' by design . . . not because they belong to any earlier selfconsciously poetic period. The two poems constitute a choice to write poetic exhibitions rather than dramas; he designed them to be conspicuously evocative of familiar poetic sounds and traditions, especially of English poetry from Spenser to Marvell and the early pastorals of Pope."[65] While these connections with "high art" are inevitable and illuminating, they obscure the links of "A Prayer in Spring" with less illustrious feminine antecedents, concealing the poet's affiliation with and contribution to another American tradition than the one to which Poirier is in fact attempting to link him: "These poems have to be called 'learned' with respect to both traditions of poetic style and religious and romantic metaphysics especially of the seventeenth and nineteenth centuries. They are not unmistakably American poems in their tone or movement." Poirier finds Frost's

Americanness elsewhere, in the concerns and tones of "Putting in the Seed."[66] In comparing Frost to Thaxter, however, I mean to highlight an element of "Americanness" in the poems of *A Boy's Will*. Ironically, Thaxter's "Alone" is in some sense atypical of her work, which is fundamentally invested in an American regional and natural project, from her (still) popular "The Sandpiper" to poems like "Land-Locked" and the moody protomodernist "Remembrance."

To this point I have attempted to recuperate the value of the emotional-sentimental matrix as a resource for reading Frost's early lyrics, but, as I suggested with "Flower-Gathering," some poems may elicit more resistance to this approach than others, possibly because of their apparent unwillingness to hold emotional and intellectual responses in equilibrium. "A Prayer in Spring" connects not only with Gray's "Ode on Spring" but also, like other poems of *A Boy's Will* upon which I have focused, with the American tradition of the feminine nature poem; here Frost exceeds the use of conventional images and dispersed subjectivity to include the substantive and structural gesture of the turn to God:

> Oh, give us pleasure in the flowers today;
> And give us not to think so far away
> As the uncertain harvest; keep us here
> All simply in the springing of the year.
>
> Oh, give us pleasure in the orchard white,
> Like nothing else by day, like ghosts by night;
> And make us happy in the happy bees,
> The swarm dilating round the perfect trees.
>
> And make us happy in the darting bird
> That suddenly above the bees is heard,
> The meteor that thrusts in with needle bill,
> And off a blossom in mid-air stands still.
>
> For this is love and nothing else is love,
> The which it is reserved for God above
> To sanctify to what far ends He will,
> But which it only needs that we fulfill.

(CP 21–22)

Loaded with flowers, bees, trees, and love (and anticipating a poem like "Good-by and Keep Cold"), the poem extends beyond the others that I've cited from *A Boy's Will* to incorporate the tradition of sentimental femininity in at least two ways. First, as I indicated, it moves from nature and humans to link love and God in the closing stanza; this rhetorical gesture was commonplace in mainstream nineteenth-century verse.[67] Second, the stance of the speaker betrays considerably less ambiguity than "Wind and Window Flower" at its conclusion. As with "The Pasture," I believe that Frost intends for us to engage with this poem transparently and empathically, to take its "prayer" at face value and to share his reverence; "it should be noted that the pleasure and happiness are not for the speaker alone but are for 'us'—the lovers."[68] Nevertheless, what comes to my mind as I read the ending are the bumper stickers proclaiming, "God is my copilot."

Indeed, this early (1903) poem's language and images embody what contemporary academic readers might regard as a cloying quality, with its emphasis on "pleasure," "flowers," "the orchard white," "the happy bees," "the perfect trees," "the darting bird," and "love"; reflecting "an intensification of the familiar aspects of life" rather than "aiming at surprise."[69] Some might ask, can we excavate any modernist language beneath this wagonload of flower petals? Perhaps we can locate it in the image of the bird as a "meteor" with a "needle bill"—reminiscent of Emily Dickinson's "Meteor of Birds," the oriole—but the weight of the images falls decisively into the feminine sentimental tradition.[70] Expressing "the unified voice of a single cultural point of view," the poem "addresses . . . in public language the values and concerns of women's 'private' sphere":[71] the loveliness of nature, the loveliness of love, the reliance on religion as love's counterpart. Depending on my mood, this poem evokes a sense of peaceful celebration and comfort, or it provokes the discomfort of a modernist-trained sensibility in the face of explicit religiosity. But I believe that the latter response represents my misapprehension rather than Frost's ironic intention; to the contrary, whether we choose to locate it in the high art or popular verse tradition, we are, I think, meant to take it "seriously."

While Frost more often expresses a modernist skepticism in his later work, "A Prayer in Spring" invokes the same rhetoric and movement as many of his popular predecessors. Elizabeth Oakes Smith's "Strength from the Hills" provides a starting illustration:

Come up unto the hills—thy strength is there.
   Oh, thou hast tarried long,
Too long, amid the bowers and blossoms fair,
   With notes of summer song.

> Why dost thou tarry there? what though the bird
>     Pipes matin in the vale—
> The plough-boy whistles to the loitering herd,
>     As the red daylights fail—
>
> Yet come to the hills, the old strong hills,
>     And leave the stagnant plain;
> Come to the gushing of the newborn rills,
>     As they sing to the main[.][72]

The poem begins with an invocation to nature, and it continues by praising the strength of the hills and their inhabitants, "the denizens of power": "the eagle" and "the shattered tree." Invoking images of freedom that recall "Captive," combined with a rejection of "bowers and blossoms fair," Oakes Smith may be repudiating domestic norms for women. Indeed, as my account so far suggests, much sentimental poetry is *itself* not sentimental, containing elements of other, yet-to-be-defined forms and attitudes. Read as a call to independence, this poem also anticipates Whitman's outdoor rebellion, yet Oakes Smith, when she is read at all, is customarily seen within a tradition of transparent or unironic sentimentalism.[73] In this context we might emphasize the poem's concluding stanza, in which she attributes the source of this freedom to the affiliation between nature and God:

> Come up to the hills. The men of old,
>     They of undaunted wills,
> Grew jubilant of heart, and strong, and bold,
>     On the enduring hills—
> Where came the soundings of the sea afar,
>     Borne upward to the ear,
> And nearer grew the moon and midnight star,
>     And God himself more near.

In spite of the dramatically different tone of this poem from Frost's, the rhetorical gestures are essentially the same: a description of the natural world and a summoning at the conclusion of the association between that world and the divine. Although Frost issues a disclaimer about humans' ability to "sanctify" the love expressed in nature, he indicates human participation in an inclusive realm that echoes that of Oakes Smith. In both poems we see the poet creating a community of individuals, of selves-in-relation whose relationships are essential for human happiness: that is, both articulate feminine voices. The romantic audacity, intensity, and exalted tone of "Strength from the Hills" translate into a muted, quiet celebration in "A Prayer in

Spring" that, in its implied relationship with the reader and its willingness to disperse the self, is no less—and perhaps even more—sentimental.

At this point I should confess that I find reading much conventional nineteenth-century poetry difficult, even sickening. The problem is not simply that the cultural and aesthetic norms encoded in that earlier poetry have been superseded or that we have not yet formulated interpretive criteria capable of understanding and appreciating these poets' (and, hence, their successors') achievement. Revulsion for their language and form emerges from academics' inability to integrate feeling into critical response, to achieve the kind of skillful balance that Frost accomplished and for which many of his poems reward us. For "you come too" is surely meant to appeal beyond the intellect, whether or not we welcome—or can even hear—his invitation.

## "To ask if there is some mistake": Frost and His Reader(s)

> Both academics and the public love [him], but it should surprise no one that the academy and the public admire him for different reasons. In fact, the images the two groups have created . . . differ so greatly that they seem to describe two different men, or, rather, two different cultural icons.
> —Gregg Camfield, *Sentimental Twain*

This observation about the "twoness" of Mark Twain could as easily apply to Frost. For example, very few of the poems dotting the Robert Frost Interpretive Trail figure as objects of sustained admiration in critical accounts of the poet's work. In the same vein of bifurcation, many academic readers will no doubt protest at this point that I have purposely focused on some of Frost's "weaker" and "less representative" poems and elided discussion of his "stronger" ones. Or argue that I could, for example, have chosen to emphasize the kind of radical transformation that Frost makes in "Birches" (originally titled "Swinging Birches") of a poem like Lucy Larcom's sentimental "Swinging on a Birch-Tree."[74] But the lexicon of the protest is itself, I think, revealing, for it encodes the investment of contemporary readers in interpretive practices and norms that deflect our attention from resonances that emerge not only here in Frost's work but elsewhere, even in his putatively stronger poems. This investment represents a direct inheritance of gendered New Critical standards. Suzanne Clark locates the demonizing of the sentimental in the hands of New Criticism, and she points out the collaboration of women writers, especially poets like Louise Bogan, in inaugurating the dominance of modernism.[75] Timothy Morris agrees, noting that "poetry criticism by the 1910s had decisively entered highbrow and academic realms where there were either no women listening or where the listening women were aggressively unfeminine, like Harriet Monroe and Amy Lowell." He adds, "In these realms the 'feminization' that had been seen by progressive males as sapping American literature of vitality was finally marginalized."[76] The final goal of the war on sentimentalism was to consolidate cultural authority over and against a dangerous feminine and feminizing mass culture. Ostensibly excluded from modernism is the sentimentality that resides within it, for (feminine) emotion remains transgressive in a culture structured by (masculine) rationality.[77] Nevertheless, as my discussion of Frost's poetry so far indicates, to characterize the sentimental as defined solely by the emotional realm oversimplifies at best. What we need to interrogate more narrowly are *kinds* of emotion, the *means* for their evocation in *all* poetry, and the interaction of appeals to feeling and intellect, along with the relative position of narrator, author, and reader.

With these ideas in mind we should notice the gendered quality of the language that protests my choice of weak over strong poems, with *stronger* being a code for "more masculine" and detached and *weaker* invoking "more feminine" and "sentimental." Frost's use of the images, rhetoric, and structures of his mainstream nineteenth-century American precursors is embarrassing because he crosses an invisible line into feminine territory— problematic for any male modernist (and for many female ones as well) but especially for Frost, who constructs himself as so publicly and rigidly masculine. Professional readers disregard these echoes in Frost's poetry because we are trained to be uncomfortable with "excessive" emotion—that in men and in ourselves as "critical" and "objective" readers. *A Boy's Will* is in fact resolutely floral and often unapologetically sentimental, but, as my own language indicates, it remains difficult to interrogate the negative valuation of the tradition that precedes him. As we have seen, later modern-minded readers could easily ignore the feminine echoes in these poems, dismiss many as Hallmark efforts, or, alternatively and more customarily, associate them with a male poetic tradition or recuperate them within the "harder," skeptical modernism of his later work, in effect retaining the distinction between highbrow and lowbrow (and in the process reinforcing their own epistemological and cultural authority).

In this context we might consider "Stopping by Woods on a Snowy Evening," which intimates the affiliations in Frost's "better" poetry with the nineteenth-century feminine poetic tradition. I will cite only its conclusion, which focuses first on the speaker's "little horse":

> He gives his harness bells a shake
> To ask if there is some mistake.
> The only other sound's the sweep
> Of easy wind and downy flake.
>
> The woods are lovely, dark and deep,
> But I have promises to keep,
> And miles to go before I sleep,
> And miles to go before I sleep.

(CP 3)

The poem as a whole, of course, encodes many of the tensions between popular and elite poetry. For example, it appears in an anthology of children's writing alongside Amy Lowell's "Crescent Moon," Joyce Kilmer's "Trees," and Edward Lear's "Owl and the Pussy-Cat."[78] Pritchard situates it among a number of poems that "have . . . repelled or embarrassed more highbrow sensibilities," which suggests the question: "haven't these poems ['The Pasture,' 'Stopping by Woods . . . ,' 'Birches,' 'Mending Wall'] been so much exclaimed over by people whose poetic taste is dubious or hardly existent, that on these grounds alone Frost is to be distrusted?" The views represented—and the representations of the poem itself, affiliated with the work of Dickinson, Longfellow, Dante, and the Romantics—range from emphasis on its gentility to its modernist ambiguity. Nevertheless, more than one critic underscores its threat to individualism, its "dangerous prospect of boundarilessness," which suggests the masculine conception of poetic selfhood with which the poem is commonly framed.[79]

In apparent harmony with these views the poem appears almost entirely restrained in its emotion; we are given only glimpses: "the darkest evening of the year," "the woods are lovely, dark and deep." It is not from the poem's language—or, for that matter, structure, which is as predictable as Thaxter's "Alone"—that the stream of emotion flows. Rather, as in "My November Guest," the season and the elegiac tone provide the link with Frost's antecedents. Walker observes of nineteenth-century women writers that "at mid-century the seasons were especially popular with Indian Summer a particular favorite, perhaps because its juxtaposition of different seasonal moods helped a poet to illustrate her mixed feelings about so much in her life and culture."[80] Seasons were a conventional means to illustrate feelings, as in Helen Hunt Jackson's " 'Down to Sleep' ":

> November woods are bare and still;
> > November days are clear and bright;
> Each noon burns up the morning's chill;
> > The morning's snow is gone by night;
> > Each day my steps grow slow, grow light,
> As through the woods I reverent creep,
> Watching all things lie "down to sleep."
>
> I never knew before what beds,
> > Fragrant to smell, and soft to touch,
> The forest sifts and shapes and spreads;
> > I never knew before how much
> > Of human sound there is in such
> Low tones as through the forest sweep
> When all wild things lie "down to sleep."
>
> Each day I find new coverlids
> > Tucked in and more sweet eyes shut tight;
> Sometimes the viewless mother bids
> > Her ferns kneel down full in my sight;
> > I hear their chorus of "good night,"
> And half I smile, and half I weep,
> Listening while they lie "down to sleep."
>
> November woods are bare and still;
> > November days are bright and good;
> Life's noon burns up life's morning chill;
> > Life's night rests feet which long have stood;
> > Some warm soft bed, in field or wood,
> The mother will not fail to keep,
> Where we can "lay us down to sleep."[81]

Jackson's poem relies on associations with the mother as well as the seasonal metaphor to make its point, making explicit what Frost's intimates: his speaker's desire to merge with the lovely, snow-clad woods suggests a desire to merge with the mother (Mother Nature) as strong as Jackson's. Having removed the traces of religiosity encoded in the refrain "down to sleep," a child's nighttime prayer to God, Frost's speaker nevertheless evinces his prayerful attitude in "the woods are lovely, dark and deep," as well as in the hymnlike regularity of the stanzas. And, in the affectionate reference to "my little horse" reminiscent of the cow-calf image in "The Pasture," he suggests the connection between human and animal parallel to Jackson's explicit observation: "I never knew before how much / Of human sound there is in such / Low tones as through the forest sweep / When all wild things lie 'down to sleep.'" "Sweep," of course, recurs in Frost's quiet poem: "The only other sound's the sweep / Of easy wind and downy flake." Though probably accidental, Frost's echoing of the sweep-sleep rhyme indicates some of the emotional resonances and connections, especially with "weep," itself embedded in "sweep," that are explicit in Jackson. Finally, Jackson's narrator acknowledges only slightly more directly the movement toward age and death that Frost's suggests: "Each day my steps grow slow, grow light / As through the woods I reverent creep." The subjectivity of both Frost's and Jackson's poems is simultaneously individual and representative, suggesting that "Stopping by Woods on a Snowy Evening" is a feminine poem with close connections to its popular antecedents.[82]

Once again we can trace the emotional resonance of Frost's poem back to the concrete situation that helped engender it. Shortly before Christmas of 1905, Frost had made an unsuccessful trip into town to sell eggs in order to raise money for his children's Christmas presents. "Alone in the driving snow, the memory of his years of hopeful but frustrated struggle welled up, and he let his long-pent feelings out in tears."[83] The intensity of this tearful moment translates into the affective content that permeates but never overwhelms "Stopping by Woods on a Snowy Evening." The fact that the poem would be written seventeen years after the moment that it reflected testifies to the deep suffering that this experience engendered; too painful to be dwelt upon, it would be only with time and distance that the emotions of that awful moment could be balanced, in a "momentary stay against confusion," by the comforting restraint of formal expression.

"Stopping by Woods" provides a doorway into an understanding of the poet's great popularity with "ordinary" readers. Jarrell observes, "ordinary readers think Frost the greatest poet alive, and love some of his best poems almost as much as they love some of his worst ones. He seems to them a sensible, tender, humorous poet who knows all about trees and farms and folks in New England." This view clashes with that of "intellectuals," who have "neglected or depreciated" him: "the reader of Eliot or Auden usually dismisses Frost as something inconsequentially good that *he* knew all about long ago."[84] Slightly later poems like "The Onset" and "Evening in a Sugar Orchard" would do nothing to alleviate this polarization. Put plainly, professional and nonprofessional readers admire poems like "Stopping by Woods" in different ways and for different reasons. Let me digress here briefly to reemphasize that, as my occasional interpolations discussing my own responses to individual poems suggest, this distinction is not a secure one; in fact, it is wholly created by a professional elite that requires for its survival the perception that readers need special knowledge to read poetry.[85] Though they frequently left no written record, I suspect that Frost's contemporary "amateur" readers responded less to his irony, playfulness, and modernist ambiguity and sophistication than they did to his accessibility and appeal to domestic, familiar, and emotional values reiterated from mainstream nineteenth-century poetry.

The implication of Frost's popularity (and his image as the Poet) in these values is as evident today as it was during his lifetime. As a lecturer for New England Humanities Councils, I have given a variety of public talks on Frost, but the one that leaps to mind I gave at the Frost Farm in Derry, New Hampshire, a number of years ago. I was discussing early portions of this work, focusing on the female voices in the early dramatic poems, and at one point I lingered on the subtextual violence in "Home Burial," mentioning the famous (and contested) episode described by Thompson in which Frost, brandishing a gun, dragged a sleepy Lesley out of bed and ordered her to choose between himself and her mother.[86] Listeners in the audience, many of whom knew Frost's poetry as well as I did, were uncomfortable, even dismayed, with this story. The reason: it cast a shadow on their reverent image of the poet as kindly, avuncular storyteller-sage whose poetry confirmed some of their deeply cherished values not only about Frost but also about the family, New England, and the United States. I could see from the faces of more than one or two in the audience that they doubted my veracity—didn't I, perhaps, have it wrong?

I tell this story not to cast aspersions on popular readers—for, as I have suggested, everyone, myself included, is to a degree such a reader—but, rather, to underscore the continuing fissure between academic and nonprofessional readers. We can trace this split, perhaps, to Lionel Trilling's description of Frost as "a terrifying poet," an observation he made, to the shock of many listeners (including the poet's own), at Frost's eighty-fifth birthday party.[87] The approval that this view has won in academic circles is perhaps most evident in anthologists' choices of his work for student consumption. In addition to the usual suspects, such as "Design," "Directive," "Desert Places," "Stopping by Woods," "The Road Not Taken," "Mending Wall," "Provide, Provide," "The Oven Bird," "Once by the Pacific," and "'Out, Out—,'" the forward-looking *Heath Anthology of American Lit-*

*erature,* volume 2 (1st ed.), includes "The Fear," "The Axe-Helve," "The Investment," "A Line-Storm Song," and "The Pasture."[88] While the two dramatic poems incorporate some of the themes of the longer, better-known ones, their selection, along with "The Investment" and "An Old Man's Winter Night," confirms our view of Frost as a "dark poet," however witty. Only the last two seem to veer from this portrait, with "The Pasture" chosen, presumably, because of its prominence in Frost's work, not for its "quality." In this company "A Line-Storm Song" seems at first glance peculiarly misplaced, inasmuch as it is (at least to me) overtly sentimental. Accessibility and representativeness are, of course, always considerations for the anthologist, but as a whole these choices seem to reflect an academic rather than popular view of the poet.[89]

While some might quibble over my reading of the selections, I think that virtually everyone will agree that even the more famously "dark" poems, however, can be (and are) read differently by academic and popular audiences, with "Stopping by Woods" being perhaps the most obvious example; as Frank Lentricchia notes of "The Road Not Taken," "it remains a famous poem, one of the 'best loved of the American people,' not for its irony, but for the sentiments that make its irony hard to see."[90] As Mark Richardson has observed, "throughout his career, Frost would resist the seductions of a [Poundian] sort of condescension" toward the public.[91] What I have tried to do here is to suggest the possible resonances, conscious or unconscious, for ordinary readers of the poem, readers like my great Aunt Fanny and great Aunt Sarah, who read it as a New England pastoral ending with an affirmation of life. This kind of reader is conjured, interestingly, on the closing page of my tattered edition of *The Poetry of Robert Frost,* by no less a personage than the himself-mythical President Kennedy: "His death impoverishes us all, but he has bequeathed his nation a body of imperishable verse from which Americans will forever gain joy and understanding."[92] The values of this traditional reader are informed by the sentimental tradition, as Kennedy's rhetoric underscores. And this reader has culturally feminine, not masculine, values—among them home, family, nature, community, and country.

In Frost's era at least this reader actually *bought* poetry books; the huge sales of Palgrave's and Jessie Rittenhouse's anthologies indicated that the market for poetry (at least of a certain kind) was thriving, constituted by much more than (as is true today) students and other poets. Frost's attitude toward sales and popularity was unabashed. In 1915 he wrote to Unter-meyer that "a thousand copies is a lot of any book of poetry to sell. Five

hundred is more of an edition than many a good man sells in England. Big
reputations are made on smaller sales." To this he added: "Do you know, I
think that a book ought to sell. Nothing is quite honest that is not com-
mercial. Mind you I don't put it that everything commercial is honest" (*LU*
8–9). The critical responses to *A Boy's Will* seemed to promise good sales at
the same time that they inaugurated disagreements about Frost's "simplic-
ity" and his status as a poet (*CR* xi–xii). His ability from early on to sell and
to attract a wide market for poetry was related not only to his energetic self-
promotion but also, if more covertly, to his affiliation with feminine voices.

This affiliation changed form and direction as he shaped his career with
different audiences in mind. In a 1916 letter to Untermeyer, Frost high-
lighted his self-consciousness about marketing (though as with all Frost pro-
nouncements we have to remain somewhat skeptical about his stance):

> The poet in me died nearly ten years ago. Fortunately he had run through sev-
> eral phases, four to be exact, all well-defined, before he went. The calf I was
> in the nineties I merely take to market. I am become my own salesman. Two
> of my phases you have been so—what shall I say—as to like. Take care that
> you don't get your mouth set to declare the other two (as I release them) a
> falling off of power, for that is what they can't be whatever else they may be,
> since they were almost inextricably mixed with the first two and only my
> sagacity has separated or sorted them in the afterthought for putting them on
> the market. (*LU* 29)

Most significant here is Frost's assertion that he has "separated or sorted"
poems written at the same time in anticipation of the demands of "the mar-
ket." Given his desire to be successful in these terms, the lessons of nine-
teenth-century sentimental poetry's popularity and healthy sales were prob-
ably not lost on him, however unconscious such an understanding may have
been. The irony, of course, given Frost's concern for the masculine business
of economic success in the face of his de facto working-class identity and for
his literary reputation, is that many of the nineteenth-century women poets
whom he does not acknowledge directly wrote not for recognition but to
feed themselves and their families: Sigourney is in this instance, as in so
many others, emblematic.

Another letter is also helpful. Writing to Thomas B. Mosher about the
responses to *A Boy's Will,* Frost observes:

> I am made too self-conscious by the comment on my first book to think of
> showing another like it for some time. If I write more lyrics it must be with no

thought of publication. What I *can* do next is bring out a volume of blank verse that I have already well in hand and won't have to feel I am writing to order. . . . I dropped to an everyday level of diction that even Wordsworth kept above. I trust I don't terrify you. I think I have made poetry. The language is appropriate to the virtues I celebrate. (*SL* 83–84)

Here the poet appears to contradict his statement to Untermeyer; there *is* a "self-conscious" "development"—at least in relation to form—and he may have moved from the sentimental inflections of *A Boy's Will* to the dramatic voices of *North of Boston* as a kind of defensiveness about readers' character-ization of the former's "simplicity." But the worry remains about whether or not he had "made poetry," as an unsent letter-poem to Ezra Pound demonstrates. Poignantly and revealingly, Frost affirms: "All I asked was that you should hold to one thing / That you considered me a poet."[93]

## "My heart and soul to share their depth of woe": The Politics of Sentiment

> Even an Indian trail
> Would swerve to a haunt so fair!
> One used to—there were the ferns
> And the falls came down there.
> —Robert Frost, "The Falls"

What remains in the present glance at Frost's early oeuvre is to acknowledge the presence of poems with less obvious affinities with sentimental feminin-ity, to explore other forms of emotional engagement with the reader, and to highlight the fact that many popular nineteenth-century poems, emerging from a bourgeois Christian domestic ideology, often made forays into the "public" and "political" world. There are many variations on these poems, from "nature" poems like Sigourney's "Niagara" to those of advocacy like Frances E. W. Harper's "The Slave Mother." Mainstream poetry at its strongest was not simply a celebration and affirmation of bourgeois values; it was also, as Nina Baym convincingly indicates in relation to Sigourney, a site for contestation within historical and political debates, a mode of activism.[94] Arguing that Sigourney's reputation is based on only a small pro-portion of her writing, Baym maps out how a large portion of her work, mistakenly stereotyped as limited to death and mourning, actually engages with European Americans' collisions with and betrayal of Native Ameri-cans.[95] Employing history to attempt to provoke activism on behalf of

Native Americans, this work "enacted womanly behavior that in many ways nullified the distinction between public and private that operated so crucially in other contexts." One of the poet's most important efforts in this vein, *Traits of the Aborigines of America* (1822), is a five-canto, four thousand–line blank verse poem "structured from the Indian point of view" that in Baym's opinion "ought to be considered a belated entry in the competition for 'the' American epic."[96]

But Sigourney also wrote many shorter poems mourning the demise of Native Americans in the face of predatory European American practices and advocating a different relationship with the latter. "Indian Names" confirms (as it paradoxically enacts) the betrayal and erasure of Native Americans by their white counterparts; I cite the poem in full because a large measure of its impact and effectiveness relies on the sweep and intensity of the lines:

> Ye say they all have passed away,
>     That noble race and brave;
> That their light canoes have vanishéd
>     From off the crested wave;
> That, mid the forests where they roamed,
>     There rings no hunter's shout:
> But their name is on your waters—
>     Ye may not wash it out.
>
> 'Tis where Ontario's billow
>     Like Ocean's surge is curled;
> Where strong Niagara's thunders wake
>     The echo of the world;
> Where red Missouri bringeth
>     Rich tribute from the west;
> And Rappahannock sweetly sleeps
>     On green Virginia's breast.
>
> Ye say their conelike cabins,
>     That cluster'd o'er the vale,
> Have disappeared, as withered leaves
>     Before the autumn's gale:
> But their memory liveth on in your hills,
>     Their baptism on your shore,
> Your everlasting rivers speak
>     Their dialect of yore.
>
> Old Massachusetts wears it
>     Within her lordly crown,

And broad Ohio bears it
 Amid her young renown;
Connecticut has wreathed it
 Where her quiet foliage waves,
And bold Kentucky breathes it hoarse
 Through all her ancient caves.

Wachusett hides its lingering voice
 Within its rocky heart,
And Allegany graves its tone
 Throughout his lofty chart.
Monadnock, on his forehead hoar,
 Doth seal the sacred trust:
Your mountains build their monument,
 Though ye destroy their dust.[97]

In restrained and indirect fashion Sigourney invokes the conventional language of Christianity ("baptism," "sacred," "dust") in the radical service of consciousness-raising. Yet, to borrow from Philip Fisher's work on the American sentimental novel, if the poem on one level "soothed by means of the familiar"—here, form, language, image, and diction—on another, that very familiarity made possible the capacity for "feeling in entirely new directions": the commonplace, in effect, enables the controversial.[98] Despite the ethnocentrism uncomfortably evident today in this poem, "Indian Names" is an elegy, a tribute, and an intensely political work arguing for European Americans to take responsibility for their injustices and the erasure of a people. Although the narrator apparently accepts the Indians' ultimate disappearance, the poem indicates their presence through the rhetorical device of apostrophe ("Ye say"), as, distancing herself from this view, she highlights their omnipresence in the land and in the language surrounding the colonizers. As Baym notes, "unwilling to adopt a tragic or ironic stance toward history (though she could not always avoid doing so), Sigourney could not accept the palliating conviction found in so many writings of the time that the destruction of the Indians was merely inevitable."[99] In the apocalyptic closing lines of the poem, in fact, the speaker seems implicitly to curse the would-be destroyers. The moderated or absent subjectivity of much mainstream nineteenth-century poetry is transformed here into a perspective that is at once a nonspecific individual and a collective, responsible—and presumably, because of the moral stance, female—citizen-poet.[100] Furthermore, the effect of its apostrophe is not embarrassment about the audacious romantic/lyric claim of the narrator to embody the spirit of poetry,[101] but embarrassment of a different sort, originating in the complicity and guilt that the narrator projects onto her putatively Christian readers. Too overtly didactic for most modern tastes, too invested in the business of history, "Indian Names," like Lucy Hooper's "Oseola" and Whitman's "Osceola," represents a powerful precursor to Frost's "The Vanishing Red."[102]

We are not accustomed to regarding Frost as a political poet; in fact, many professional readers seem to regard his overt efforts in this direction, such as "Kitty Hawk," with a heaping measure of embarrassment or criticism.[103] This embarrassment may emerge in part from such poems' inception in and affiliation with poetry that consciously exercises the historical power of sentimental writing for the kind of moral and cultural transformation elicited by *Uncle Tom's Cabin*. At first glance "The Vanishing Red"— which rarely figures in any discussion of the poet and is certainly not seen as one of his "important" poems—seems quite remote from these links, especially in the context of Louis Untermeyer's remark that Frost "was always against 'movements,' 'causes,' cliques, groups, social workers of any kind— he called them 'gangs of do-gooders'" (*LU* 55; see 372). As Untermeyer's description indicates, however, this attitude of Frost's related more to institutionalized or even communal morality than to any absence of an ethical stance; as the poet's "Introduction to Sarah Cleghorn's 'Threescore'" indicates, Frost admired reformers like Cleghorn, "the complete abolitionist," who had "all her life long pursued the even tenor of her aspiration."[104] Confronted with the poet's occasionally blatant and unappealing conservatism, we can easily forget his capacity for empathy with the disadvantaged, a capacity that I shall explore in more detail in the next chapter but that is forecast by the touching uncollected poem, "My Giving," which begins: "I ask no merrier Christmas / Than the hungry bereft and cold shall know / That night. / This is all I can give so that none shall want— / My heart and soul to share their depth of woe" (*CP* 518).

If one letter is any indication, then, while Frost did not believe that poetry and politics were comfortable sharing the same sphere, he did not believe they were necessarily incommensurate. Commenting on an article by Archibald MacLeish, he observes: "Wordsworth and Emerson both wrote some politics into their verse. Their poetic originality by which they live was quite another thing. So of Shelley. His originality was sufficient to give him his place" (*LU* 255). Politics are on a "lower plane" and cannot be the center of good poetry; on the other hand, as Frost's work repeatedly indicates—and the work has to be the final arbiter of belief in any dispute—

personal ethical beliefs, what we might interpret as a different form of "politics," can inflect and lend force to poetic expression, as in the early uncollected poem "The Sachem of the Clouds (A Thanksgiving Legend)."[105] Published in the Lawrence *Daily American* on 2 November 1891, the poem dramatizes a mood that is ultimately embodied in the vision of the Native American sachem-wizard's invocation:

> "Come, O come, with storm, come darkness! Speed my clouds on Winter's breath.
> All my race is gone before me, all my race is low in death!
> Ever, as I ruled a people, shall this smoke arise in cloud;
> Ever shall it freight the tempest for the ocean of the proud.
> 'Thanks!' I hear their cities thanking that my race is low in death,
> Come, O come, with storm, come darkness! Speed my clouds on Winter's breath!"
>
> (CP 495)

Sharing the apocalyptic tone of "Indian Names," and published the year following the Wounded Knee massacre,[106] the poem envisions an ominous scene of racial conflict transposed to the natural domain, where winter represents the sachem's ultimate revenge. Within the framework of accessible, conventional diction and a familiar dramatic situation Frost provides the powerful sachem with a voice of "vengeance" that the poet, like the lone traveler in the poem, hears but cannot judge. The poem's conclusion aims to shock the reader with a subtle inverted representation of the Wounded Knee disaster ending, as that one did, with "ashes," "smoke," and "Winter":

> Thus his voice keeps ringing, ringing, till appears the dreary dawn,
> And the traveler, looking backward, sees the ashes on the lawn,
> Sees the smoke crowd to the hilltops, torn away, and hurried south,
> Hears a shrieking answer speeded from the Winter's snowy mouth.

The austere sympathy for and awe of the sachem that appear here are echoed (if transfigured) in both the exquisite, delicate poem "The Falls" (1894) and the comic "Genealogical" (1908).[107]

But, unlike these poems, "The Vanishing Red" (CP 136) takes the political content of its subject both seriously and explicitly:

> He is said to have been the last Red Man
> In Acton. And the Miller is said to have laughed—
> If you like to call such a sound a laugh.

But he gave no one else a laugher's license.
For he turned suddenly grave as if to say,
"Whose business—if I take it on myself,
Whose business—but why talk round the barn?—
When it's just that I hold with getting a thing done with."

Both the title and the image of "the last Red Man," highlighted by the cap-italization, evoke the conception of the Vanishing American. Yet this image reduces John in its very self-restraint and absence of remark; the narrator refuses to depict him as a noble savage. In this vein Frost highlights the poem's "made" quality, its legendary framework, by opening as he does ("He is said") and by reiterating this phrase on the next line. At the same time, this locution suggests at least the possibility of an ironic skepticism that John could ever attain this status, a skepticism embodied in the pseudo-laughter that echoes in these opening lines and that signifies the Miller's power and authority over all his auditors, from whom he ominously with-holds his "business." Told and retold many times, this story is, the opening stanza chillingly suggests, a familiar one of deliberate, cool dispossession and death, of "getting a thing done with," in Frost's vernacular, minimalist, and modern reinvention of Sigourney's accusation of genocide.

The lines that follow appear to make an implicit advance apology to the reader for the violence that is about to occur:

You can't get back and see it as he saw it.
It's too long a story to go into now.
You'd have to have been there and lived it.
Then you wouldn't have looked on it as just a matter
Of who began it between the two races.

This story that is "too long" "to go into now" is in fact what the poem unfolds, as it also invokes the long history of white-Indian brutality and the equally lengthy literature surrounding that history. In fact, Frost's narrator is overtly concerned with attempting to sort out truth from fiction, experi-ence from story, and, at least at first, he seems eager to divest the Miller for responsibility for his brutality:

Some guttural exclamation of surprise
The Red Man gave in poking about the mill
Over the great big thumping shuffling millstone
Disgusted the Miller physically as coming

From one who had no right to be heard from.
"Come, John," he said, "you want to see the wheel-pit?"

He took him down below a cramping rafter,
And showed him, through a manhole in the floor,
The water in desperate straits like frantic fish,
Salmon and sturgeon, lashing with their tails.
Then he shut down the trap door with a ring in it
That jangled even above the general noise,
And came upstairs alone—and gave that laugh,
And said something to a man with a meal-sack
That the man with the meal-sack didn't catch—then.
Oh, yes, he showed John the wheel-pit all right.

Speaking from the point of view of someone who has not only heard the story but also been present during its actual enactment, the narrator intimates the responsibility of the voyeuristic audience, himself included, in the murder that transpired. This murder, which remains painfully unspoken, is not simply the death of an anonymous man but of a people.

Beyond the implicit accusation of genocide the story reflects unspoken but evident sympathy for the murdered man and horror at the Miller's deed. Again, in spite of the narrator's pronouncement that one had to be there to understand the Miller's actions and his rhetorical affiliation with the latter ("you can't get back and see it as he saw it"), he invites us to reread the narrative from a perspective that is ironically more sympathetic to John than to the Miller. The description of John in the third stanza confirms his antagonist's stereotypical view of him as inarticulate and ignorant, for we hear him speaking in a "guttural exclamation" that "disgusted the Miller physically." One of the poem's primary issues is John's—and by analogy all Indians'—power to influence the world through language, for the Miller interprets John's exclamation "as coming / From one who had no right to be heard from." Similarly, one of Sigourney's concerns in "Indian Names" (as in Frost's "The Sachem of the Clouds") resides in the ability of Native Americans to speak; encoded in the title and theme of Sigourney's poem is the inescapable residue of Indian language in the landscape, as she tells us: "Your everlasting rivers speak / Their dialect of yore." The pun on this final word of her third stanza mocks European Americans' attempts to silence, for what is "their" language has become not extinct, "of yore," but "your" language as well. Evoking the Indians' affiliation with nature in Sigourney, the image of the river is repeated indirectly in Frost, as the Miller gives John a glimpse of the nature to which he is inevitably and retroactively joined: "The water in desperate straits like frantic fish, / Salmon and sturgeon, lashing with their tails."

Engaging powerful if unspoken emotions in such images, the ultimate horror of the murder is its concealment, both concretely and linguistically. The speaker himself intimates and covers the violence with ostensibly detached and shockingly ironic language like "a *manhole* in the floor" (emph. added). Next it is muffled by the noise of busyness, of business, and then the final line of the poem buries the Miller's guilt in a metaphoric and linguistic hole that renders it even more abhorrent because of the vacuum of moral responsibility it conceals: "Oh, yes, he showed John the wheel-pit all right." The auditor inside the poem—like the speaker and the reader— shares the Miller's guilt, for he "didn't catch" what the latter tells him until much later. Similarly, though more explicitly than Frost's "He is said," the apostrophe of Sigourney's poem excavates the complicity of language in the Indians' erasure by emphasizing the first lines of stanza one and three: "*Ye say* they all have passed away"; "*Ye say* their conelike cabins . . . Have disappeared" (emph. added). That Frost's narrator is as serious as Sigourney's emerges, paradoxically, from the Miller's irreverent and utterly misplaced and recurrent laughter that, like the "trap door," "jangled even above the general noise" of the poem itself.

From one perspective "The Vanishing Red" represents the antithesis of sentimental femininity, for it suggests where Sigourney's makes explicit, and it evinces the utter control of emotion that we can call modernist where Sigourney's displays her anger. Yet Sigourney's poem *itself* is not sentimental in the sense that twentieth-century critics have constructed the term, for it performs a kind of strong selfhood, however different from the autonomous self of traditional romantic lyric. Furthermore, "Indian Names" is not merely implicated in the nostalgic construction of the noble savage described by Roy Harvey Pearce in his discussion of Sigourney's *Traits of the Aborigines of America* and a matrix of similar works: "the inevitable destruction of the noble savage is not explained; it is merely accepted. The fact of destruction serves only further to ennoble the savage."[108] As I have suggested, "Indian Names" is also intended to be an intervention in a disgraceful history via the moral authority of a feminine voice that values community; unlike other poems that seek merely to establish empathy, "Indian Names" levels an accusation that raises its speaker to a level of higher authority as it aims to engage white readers in a collective project of self-examination and, if less obviously, amelioration of the situation.

Frost's poem reinvents this project on modern territory. If in "The Vanishing Red" John is hardly noble, then, in a supremely ironic twist, the Miller becomes the savage; the shifting stance of the speaker indicates his uneasiness about his own complicity in the genocide that the poem describes in miniature. Frost's appeal to the reader is less direct than Sigourney's but equally evocative and perhaps even more painful because he balances the poem's affective content with its putative rationality.[109] In spite of the narrator's attempts at a reportorial detachment, the subject matter, the title, and the brutal murder that the poem both depicts and shrouds—all aimed at producing nothing if not an empathic emotional response of anger, fear, and shame in the reader—indicate that we can categorize "The Vanishing Red" as a powerful political poem with its roots in a varied, rich, and still largely misunderstood feminine American tradition.[110]

## Chapter 2

# "The Feminine Way of It"
## Frost's Homely Affiliations

"I'd like to know if you think it's fair. Had I ought to have
been born with the wantin' to write poetry if I couldn't write
it—had I? Had I ought to have been let to write all my life,
an' not know before there wa'n't any use in it? Would it be
fair if that canary-bird there, that ain't never done anything
but sing, should turn out not to be singing? Would it, I'd like
to know?"[1]

In Mary Wilkins Freeman's short story "A Poetess" (1891) Betsey Dole
offers both herself and the reader this series of questions after the obituary
verses that she has composed for a neighbor's son have been relegated to the
realm of "not poetry"; the gossipy and insensitive neighbor for whom she
has written the poem, Mrs. Caxton, tells Betsey that *"Sarah Rogers says that
the minister told her Ida that that poetry you wrote was jest as poor as it could be."*[2]
Judged by a male authority to be inauthentic, illegitimate, Betsey cannot see
either the function or the value of her work, which offers women a sense of
community and understanding. Yet, as Betsey herself acknowledges, in spite
of her own lack of children and hence her unfamiliarity with Mrs. Caxton's
kind of loss, "I guess I can enter into her feelin's considerable." Noting that
"Betsey in this room, bending over her portfolio, looked like the very
genius of gentle, old-fashioned, sentimental poetry," Freeman intimates the
faded quality of her heroine's work: "It seemed as if one, given the premises
of herself and the room, could easily deduce what she would write, and read
without seeing those lines wherein flowers rhymed sweetly with vernal
bowers, home with beyond the tomb, and heaven with even." Unlike
Twain's Emmeline Grangerford, however, Betsey engages our respect and
sympathy, giving of her limited means to ensure the happiness of others.
Freeman makes evident the potential limitations of the minister's judgment,
for, in comforting Betsey, Mrs. Caxton points out, "I don't care if he does

write poetry himself, an' has had some printed in a magazine. Maybe his ain't quite so fine as he thinks 'tis."[3]

Writing about "A Poetess," Linda Grasso makes an observation that is relevant to Frost as well: "by making a link between the economic and social status of the writing woman and a sentimental ethos, Freeman compels a reexamination of a sentimental legacy that brings the function of sentimentality in America—including the question of aesthetics—into full view. . . . [She had an] acute awareness of literary sentimentality as a highly gendered, specifically female tradition."[4] As in Freeman's story, who evaluates poetry, what constitutes sentimental poetry, and what is the proper function of poetry are all questions addressed by Frost, both directly and indirectly, in his earliest narrative as well as lyric verse. William Pritchard has observed of the *North of Boston* poems as well as of "The Tuft of Flowers" that we often find the poet "breaking down the barrier between 'lyric' and 'narrative' verse."[5] This elision of barriers emerges in part from the poet's embeddedness in the tradition of women-authored New England regionalist fiction that forms another important strand of his early published work. Not only does the poet draw from a background of sentimental poetry, he also elaborates a feminine voice via his connections with this popular fiction, especially in his attitudes toward the often poor and disadvantaged women who people his narrative poems. His feminine voice also emerges from the intimate dialogical relationship that he imagines with a reader; sometimes this dialogue is structured rhetorically into the poem, and sometimes it is performed more circuitously, via the sympathies that he conveys. Here the appeal to emotion and the encouragement of empathy that shape the lyrics of *A Boy's Will* mute and change form but remain important.[6]

If Frost's critics have regarded *North of Boston* as a significant transformation of the poet's voice, in which "a harder broken speech replaces the language of flowers," suggesting his rejection of a genteel and feminine tradition, a number of them have also connected his narrative verse with women-authored New England regionalist writing like Freeman's.[7] For supportive present-day critics this connection often causes anxiety and necessitates a transvaluation. For example, John Kemp attempts to define New England regionalism, to suggest some affiliations, and to assess Frost's developing participation in the tradition. Finally, however, Kemp argues that the poet's "best New England poems *transcend* the *limitations* of local-color writing and attain a *complexity* and *universality* not inherently regional."

Viewing regionalism as something from which critics need to rescue the poet in order to recuperate him for a greater modernist tradition, he points to *Mountain Interval* as the "first collection to show the *debilitating* influence of his *regional* commitment."[8] Focusing on particular influences, Perry Westbrook offers a similar perspective. He suggests that we cannot know with certainty how much the poet read of writers like Jewett, Freeman, Cooke, or Brown, but, "since they published prolifically in periodicals and in book form, it is hardly likely that he did not have an acquaintance with the work of at least some of them. Indeed, only a determined nonreader—which Frost was not—could be entirely ignorant of their work." Westbrook concludes, "But even if he had read nothing by any of them, he is of their company—though admittedly his work as a whole *transcends* their 'local-colorist' limitations."[9]

Many of Frost's professional readers after *North of Boston* would not be able to get beyond the romp the poet enjoyed in works like "Brown's Descent" or "The Gum Gatherer," while earlier critics were quick to establish Frost's qualifications as a "New England" poet, to associate him with women's writing, and to assess his importance in relation to what he called *A Book of People* (*CP* 759). Just as sympathetic critics of *A Boy's Will* would minimize his sentimental femininity, so too readers of *North of Boston* and many of his other volumes have transformed an equally feminine and presumably debilitating association with regionalism into a more palatable and masculine "universality." Yet the regionalist settings and voices that propel these poems contribute to an achievement of unequaled power and authority; rather than representing the dilution of "poetry," they reconfigure its margins in a far more capacious and inclusive manner, inviting readers to acknowledge the poetry of everyday life and to feel the emotional power resident in plain talk, whether coming from a husband and wife at odds over the death of a child or from a wife who feels like a servant.

As with sentimentalism, regionalism resides in Frost's *North of Boston* poems both as an internal impetus expressive of a feminine voice and as a feminizing critical reconstruction. This chapter will trace the metamorphosis of Frost's feminine voice into narrative and dramatic forms in *North of Boston* and *Mountain Interval*. Indicating the continuation of the poet's relatively relaxed and dispersed poetic self, it aims to outline both imagined and real readers' responses and their implication in Frost's continuing self-representations for the market. It also explores Frost's recognition that in some ways the normative masculine self, with its impulse toward autonomy, is destructive to the creation of "home" as both literal and psychic region, for masculine men in the home may be emblematic of or even sources of the mental disorder afflicting their female counterparts.[10] The problematic situation of the masculine self "at home" is analogous not only to that of the masculine writer, who balances the pressures of tradition with individual talent and history, but also to that of a masculine reader (male or female), who may erase a feminine voice or translate that voice into tones that are, on aesthetic, psychological, and historical grounds, gendered masculine. The first section, which follows, maps out the theoretical and historical context within which this engendering occurs. While both the term *regionalism* and its valuation represent sites of contest, recent feminist critics have clarified the gender inflection of the term and have sought to recuperate it as a source of merit for late-nineteenth- and early-twentieth-century American women writers; their work helps indicate the benefits and costs of Frost's feminine affiliations.

Section 2 discusses Frost's continuing connection with sentimental antecedents and the overlap of this tradition with regionalist fiction, with "Home Burial" offering the exemplary case. Section 3 centers more specifically on the physical and psychological hardships endured by rural women as it maps out the structural performance of the important feminine voice and subjectivity of Len's wife; the empathy that the poet is able to engender in "A Servant to Servants" emerges in part from the delicately balanced, interactive relationship that he establishes between the narrator and her implied auditor. The discussion of "The Death of the Hired Man" that follows indicates a more affirmative vision of rural life and women's roles in that life. Calling upon the resources of regionalist fiction that emphasizes the self-in-relation and social connection, Frost elicits a concern for Silas that enables even masculine "readers" (like Warren) to understand and revalue such connections. The next short section traces briefly the critical responses of Frost's contemporaries to his ambitious genre (and implicit gender) mixing. Finally, a critically neglected but important poem, "In the Home Stretch," indicates the tensions within Frost's project, anticipating the more anxious poems that I discuss in chapter 3 and raising significant questions about subjectivity, genre, and gender. Though in different ways than their precursors in *A Boy's Will,* many of the narrative and dramatic poems of *North of Boston* and *Mountain Interval* continue the dispersal of subjectivity that distinguishes much of Frost's early work, as he creates an innovative poetics of empathy.

## Reading Regionalism

> You can't be universal without being provincial, can you? It's
> like trying to embrace the wind.
> —Robert Frost, *Interviews with Robert Frost*

*Regionalism* is an imprecise and contested term.[11] Whether applied in relation to the late nineteenth and early twentieth century or to contemporary literature, however, the difference between regionalism and local color concerns a number of readers, principally as a means of assigning or determining aesthetic value.[12] Recent attempts to reclaim a privileged space for regionalism emerge from the minimization that the label "regionalist" engenders, for "the term *regional* has so predictably been employed as a term of relegation that serious writers have been less than eager to be identified with it."[13] In relation to critical practice, "finding region an important factor in literary studies is now usually seen as the equivalent of being an over-enthusiastic salesman with a special marketing territory. Regionalism, it seems, is often next to boosterism, a fatuous puffing of merely local talent."[14] At the other end of the spectrum regionalism can represent a powerful conceptual category: "the reassessment of literary regionalism . . . goes hand in hand with the reconsideration of space as an analytical category, itself a compelling exercise in revision, and a major project of our *fin-de-siècle*."[15] Part of the negative construction of both regionalism and local color is due to their perceived potential for nostalgia, sentimentalism, and naive idealism.[16] But it is also the affiliation between local color and femininity that destined the genre to marginalization early in this century; "the connection between local color and femininity is so well fixed in critics' minds that when they wish to reclaim particular writers for more serious treatment, they often adopt the strategy of arguing that the writer is not a local colorist after all." Another way of dismissing women writers was "to divide local color itself into its masculine and feminine practitioners; predictably, it is women writers who are found guilty of domesticity and effeminacy."[17] As Kemp's and Westbrook's comments on Frost exemplify, the goal for many critics has been to explore how a writer simultaneously "transcends" as he embodies regionalism and how his work is *not* "local" but "universal," representing a manly (and even nationalist) present rather than a nostalgic past.[18]

Distinctions such as these erase important and valuable connections between male and female writers as well as elide crucial questions about subjectivity. More practical distinctions in relation to regional writing relate to the positionality of the narrator and author: whether she or he is visitor or native, critic or supporter makes a difference, for, "although the visitor may render tragic events or conditions in his or her writing, his or her stance as outsider tends to exoticize such events."[19] In this connection Judith Fetterley and Marjorie Pryse offer an important theoretical context in which to appreciate the relationship between Frost and the regionalists. Acknowledging that the women of whom they write would not necessarily have perceived themselves to be part of a tradition or that they would have defined themselves in other terms than (the diminishing) "local color," Fetterley and Pryse argue that these women nevertheless created a distinctive regionalist tradition characterized by a form (the sketch), in which character development rather than plot remains central;[20] by a focus on the relationship of identity to place and to other people; by an emphasis on community, connection, and inclusivity; and, most significantly, by a narrator who attributes subjectivity and power to the voices of regional characters rather than regarding them from an ironic distance.[21] The last quality "fosters *an empathic connection* between the reader of the work and the lives the work depicts"; "because regional narrators *identify with rather than distance themselves from* the material of their stories, regionalist texts allow the reader to view the regional speaker as subject and not as object and to *include empathic feeling as an aspect of critical response.*"[22] This emotional investment required by the reader of regionalist fiction is aligned with, though it formally translates, the goals of sentimentality. Joanne Dobson formulates the connection most precisely: "Connection, commitment, community: out of these priorities spring both domestic sentimentalism and a realist/regionalist aesthetic."[23]

While the regionalist writers with whom we might associate the poet sometimes relied on nostalgic scenes and attitudes, they equally often depict a harshly realistic vision of rural life. Like his predecessors, Frost uses as subjects the lives of what Frank Lentricchia calls "the suffering rural poor" that we see in poems like "An Old Man's Winter Night" and "The Self-Seeker," "lives that are by turns lonely and boring and horrifying and dull; relationships that bespeak little relating; tales of coldness of the heart, stupefying routine, sexual betrayal, and madness."[24] Frost's early economic disadvantage surely helped to elicit his evocation of these difficult lives; this disadvantage applied (at least) as stringently to the women in his life: his mother, Jeanie, and Elinor, upon whom he had to call at various times not only to advance his poetic ambitions but simply to survive.[25] Many of his most moving poems—"Home Burial," "A Servant to Servants," "The Housekeeper," "The Fear"—bear witness with dazzling intimacy and directness to the pinched and strained circumstances of his female protagonists, not only to combat idealization of them but also to provide them with recognizable identity and agency in a culture that diminished them or obscured them entirely. As Robert Faggen has observed, "Frost's domestic dramas present women as powerful ethical figures, not merely representatives of frustrated desire or wild sexuality."[26] In these early narrative poems, as in regionalist fiction, character fuels plot, not vice versa, and it often does so through the "poetic" and "everyday" medium of women's language. Relinquishing his own identity as an autonomous male poet, Frost enters into the psyches of these women, representing female voices and women's subjectivities in explosive detail. Even when he "enters" the poem as an understood listener, this listener—sometimes the narrator—often has an empathic and engaged perspective that echoes those of woman-authored regionalist narratives.

At the same time that we accept the capacity of narrators or listeners for empathy, however, we have to remember that positionality is not always a simple matter and that one—whether the poet or the reader—can be simultaneously "inside" and "outside," sympathetic and critical.[27] Given many feminist critics' idealizing accounts of female-authored regionalism, we need to be cautious about assigning a purely "empathic" perspective to women writers and readers, which risks essentializing and utopianizing both, for, as Frost's narrative poems amply demonstrate, male writers can also "bear witness" to cultural disadvantage among what Frost called "the ordinary folks I belong to."[28] Moreover, many New England regionalist fiction writers emphasize the judgmental and detached ("masculine") perspective of certain *women* characters. Like his female counterparts who wrote fiction, Frost exposes the reality of rural life and dismantles the critical myth of the regional as ideal at the same time that he affirms the potential strengths and tensions of that life for modern persons.[29] As the next section explores, in accomplishing these tasks he draws upon the resources of two very different feminine literary traditions—nineteenth-century affective poetry coupled with regionalist fiction—that in his hands enable the emotional power of his materials to be both felt and held in creative, thoughtful synthesis.

## "I guess I can enter into her feelin's considerable": Reinventing Death

> Whatever general hardships, such as poverty, isolation, lack of
> labor-saving devices, may exist on any given farm, the burden
> of these hardships falls more heavily on the farmer's wife than
> on the farmer himself. In general her life is more monotonous
> and the more isolated, no matter what the wealth or the
> poverty of the family may be.
> —*Report of the Commission on Country Life,* 1911

From one angle Frost's "Home Burial" explores a wife's "suffocation," "the limits . . . of 'home,'" and, ultimately, "poetic form seen in the metaphor of domestic form."[30] But, in addition, the poem reveals a deep, "insider's" understanding of women's subordinate position in a male-dominated culture, explicating a profoundly social drama informed by Frost's own experience, from his courtship of and marriage to Elinor to the loss of their young son Elliott in 1900 and infant daughter Elinor in 1907. In the former instance he blamed himself for not calling the doctor, who might have saved the boy's life.[31] We see this guilt refracted through the wife's eyes in the poem, for she blames her husband for his detached self-reliance; from my perspective her anguish motivates the poem and engenders its piercing, painful authority, for "Home Burial" brings to the surface the potential hostility between men and women that earlier poems like "Going for Water" and "Love and a Question" only intimate.

The "plot" is straightforward: the poem opens with the husband discovering his wife peering out a window in order to see the grave of their dead son. While in a happy marriage this moment could offer the opportunity for emotional reunion, Frost has another project in mind. Using stage directions and description as well as dialogue, the poet outlines and underlines the cultural power relations shaping the characters' perspectives; paralleling regionalist narrative practice, Frost underscores character development and the deteriorating relationship between the married couple at least as much as plot. From one perspective he indicates his sympathy for the wife and criticism of the husband by emphasizing and even overwriting the husband's potential brutality; male physicality, he suggests, translates into menace at best, as the poem opens with a stark representation of bodily power hierarchy emphasized by the speakers' anonymity.[32] At first the female protagonist occupies a physically superior position, at the top of the stairs, but her husband soon remedies their inverted status, "advancing toward her," while she "sank upon her skirts," and, as "her face changed from terrified to dull," we see him "mounting until she cowered under him" (*CP* 55). The language of the phrase underlines the specifically sexual, even bestial, nature of the threat he poses to her. When she challenges his vision, he quickly dominates her again: the graveyard is full, he tells her, of "'my people,'" and the view from the window, symbolic of her entrapment, is "'not so much larger than a bedroom.'" Much more than "dangerously thoughtless," reflecting "a kind of stupidity,"[33] this metaphor underscores the husband's earlier unspoken sexual threat. Even his ostensibly pained words— "'Can't a man speak of his own child he's lost'"—echo this threat in their thrusting, piercing power to wound in spite of his wife's plea: "'Don't, don't, don't, don't'" (*CP* 56). Her tangible anguish invites an emotional response from the reader; as Frost's contemporaries Amy Lowell and Jessie Rittenhouse indicated, it is difficult to engage with this poem as an outsider.[34] Although the husband also makes claims on our sympathy, Frost continues to reveal extraordinary empathy for and insight into the wife's perspective. When she says, "'I must get air.— / I don't know rightly whether any man can,'" she asserts knowledge beyond the loss of a child, knowledge of her woman's place. Dramatizing the wife's extremity, Frost enables "the reader to view the regional speaker as subject and to include empathic feeling as an aspect of critical response."[35]

Interestingly for our purposes, a central source of friction between the couple is the divergence between their self-conceptions, expressed in their different attitudes toward grief; while he mourns inwardly, she affirms the necessity of its outward expression. In her pain and anger she threatens him with her physical absence (her emotional absence is only too evident), yet, when she makes this threat, his real fears of sexual inadequacy surface: "'Amy! Don't go to someone else this time.'"[36] What stands out for me at this moment—and elsewhere—is the duplicity of the language in which the husband couches his desire, for this line represents both plea and command. Furthermore, his words exhibit a wide veering from his behavior: "'Listen to me. I won't come down the stairs.' / He sat and fixed his chin between his *fists*. / 'There's something I should like to ask you, *dear*'" (*CP* 56; emph. added). Throughout the poem a language of endearment masks and conventionalizes the subverbal menace emblematized in his physical gestures. Echoing an issue that emerges differently in poems like "The Housekeeper" and "The Fear," Frost understands—only too well, perhaps—the psychic weight carried by the threat of physical violence embodied here by the husband, and he is deeply sensitive to the wife's vulnerability. If masculinity requires bodily supremacy, it also colludes, however unwittingly, with psychological dominance. Yet the consequence of this dominance seems to be only greater alienation, sexual as well as emotional. As I will discuss in more detail in chapter 4, the portrait of the husband on the verge of a violent brutishness both reflects and interrogates early-twentieth-century notions of muscular masculinity.[37]

Part of the wife's sense of his sexual and emotional inadequacy arises, the husband acknowledges, from the fact that, although they use the same language, the words mean differently:

> "My words are nearly always an offense.
> I don't know how to speak of anything
> So as to please you. But I might be taught,
> I should suppose. I can't say I see how.
> A man must partly give up being a man
> With womenfolk. We could have some arrangement
> By which I'd bind myself to keep hands off
> Anything special you're a-mind to name.
> Though I don't like such things 'twixt those that love."
>
> (CP 57)

Maddeningly condescending, this offer emphasizes his power—it is not simply bonnets or even conversation that he offers to "keep hands off"; it is also her body. When he begs her not to go, he seems to Poirier "not without gentleness."[38] Yet the voice of power can afford to be gentle. If language and communication fail the couple in this poem,[39] the *poet's* language does *not* fail to communicate with the reader—not only the threat to masculinity engendered by the wife's attitude but, as important, the damaging limitations imposed on her by patriarchal culture. And, if the wife cannot communicate with her husband, her voice is certainly efficacious for many readers, as it invites us to understand as much by empathy as by judgment.

In contrast to this view, Joseph Brodsky has asserted that in the poem Frost evinces "an extremely wide margin of detachment"; he adds, "where does he go . . . with all that detachment? The answer is: utter autonomy." This assertion of masculine autonomy echoes the familiar narrative of the lyric poet, but, when we view Frost's narratives in the context of popular nineteenth-century poetry and regionalist fiction rather than the mythical one of the Pygmalion story or the Virgilian eclogue, we tell a different story in which self-dispersal, rather than detachment, figures centrally.[40] Enabling an intimate "connection between the reader of the work and the lives the work depicts,"[41] Frost imagines Amy's burden vividly: women's imprisonment, not only in the literal home but also in the often-silent inner room of feelings, rather than the outdoors of concrete action and verbal expression, causes all emotions to intensify as if under pressure, becoming hypercharged. The husband, after all, can obtain physical release in the work of digging the grave, as the wife implies:

> "I saw you from that very window there
> Making the gravel leap and leap in air,
> Leap up, like that, like that, and land so lightly
> And roll back down the mound beside the hole."
>
> (*CP* 57)

Even though she blames her husband for his apparent inability to feel or to express grief, the wife suggests that there is something transcendent—leaping and light, airy—in his labor, while her own "labor," her literal creativity, is lost when her son dies. This situation parallels Frost's early married life when both Frost and Elinor had to work hard to survive, yet the release of poetic labor was reserved for Frost, in spite of the fact that, as editor of the high school newspaper, Frost published Elinor's poetry and that he recognized that she "not only wrote poetry, but knew many good poems new to him" (*CR* 61).[42]

In "Home Burial" we are left a capacious space in which to imagine the transformation of a prior intimacy into an utter fracture of relationship. As the husband reflects on his wife's kind of grief, he pleads, "You'd think his memory might be satisfied—," and she responds,

> "There you go sneering now!"
>        "I'm not, I'm not!"
>
> (*CP* 57)

Frost breaks this line in the middle to suggest how profoundly at odds they are, how much psychic as well as literal space separates them. Once again, the relationship between the husband and wife's creativity emerges most clearly in language: his language wounds powerfully, and, however unwittingly, he, not she, is the metaphor maker, the poet who speaks of fences when his heart aches. When the wife accuses, "'You can't because you don't know how to speak,'" she is unable to hear the pain and beauty in his lament: "'Three foggy mornings and one rainy day / Will rot the best birch fence a man can build!'"[43] We see a moment in which the poet urges and

encodes the efficacy of language but only to an audience that can under-
stand it—the reader willing to respond emotionally as much as intellectu-
ally. Frost acknowledges that Amy—like Elinor, perhaps—is confined by
the literal creativity that her role as wife demands and by the emotions that
such limitation imposes. Being *only* a place of "confinement" for her, home
is too much where the heart is.

Working against the stereotype of the nostalgic regionalist idyll, Frost
is especially critical of representations of home as merely a source of renewal
and refuge. Amy is home-less, and the tension that sometimes filled the
Frost household is echoed in her circumscription, in her repeated affirma-
tions that she has to escape, get out, go, "'Somewhere out of this house.'"
She wonders, "'How can I make you—'" understand, we assume, but she
is inadequate even to complete her sentence. The husband's "sentence" that
concludes the poem—"I'll follow and bring you back by force. I *will!*" (*CP*
58)—represents both desperate plea and the final, overt expression of the
menace that has underscored his speech throughout the poem. Structurally
as well as semantically, the poem enacts the enclosure of the feminine self
and feminine speech; to read this last line as merely desperate is seriously to
underread the danger that the husband poses. Echoing the voice of cultural
authority, he becomes both judge and author of his wife's fate: house arrest.

Like other narrative poems by Frost, "Home Burial" participates in and
transforms the feminine literary traditions of his precursors, but it offers a
particularly vivid example of the convergence of two traditions. The death
of children figures largely not only in affective nineteenth-century Ameri-
can poetry but also in a number of important New England regionalist texts,
Freeman's "Poetess" among them.[44] Betsey Dole seeks to assuage the grief
of Willie Caxton's mother through sentimental poetry that Freeman repre-
sents vividly as an echo of Betsey's bodily sympathy. When Mrs. Caxton
asks her friend if she would "be willin' to—write a few lines" memorializ-
ing her son, "Betsey looked up inquiringly, throwing back her curls. Her
face took unconsciously *lines of grief* so like the other woman's that she
looked like her for the minute" (emph. added).[45] This empathy contrasts
starkly with the minister's woodenness and conventionality on the occasion
of Betsey's own death and, moreover, with his utter obliqueness about his
role in that death: upon learning of his authoritative, masculine criticism of
her mourning verses for Willie, she burns all her poetry and goes into a
rapid decline. In the closing image of the story, Freeman affirms the affec-
tive and empathic mode of Betsey and her poetry: Betsey's canary "chirped
faster and faster until he trilled into a triumphant song."[46]

With Betsey's "triumphant song," "Home Burial" has as its precursor the numerous mainstream nineteenth-century poems about dead children to which Frost plainly alludes. The prototypical American example is Lydia Sigourney's "Death of an Infant":

> Death found strange beauty on that polished brow,
> And dashed it out. There was a tint of rose
> On cheek and lip. He touched the veins with ice,
> And the rose faded. Forth from those blue eyes
> There spake a wishful tenderness, a doubt
> Whether to grieve or sleep, which innocence
> Alone may wear. With ruthless haste he bound
> The silken fringes of those curtaining lids
> For ever. There had been a murmuring sound
> With which the babe would claim its mother's ear,
> Charming her even to tears. The spoiler set
> The seal of silence. But there beamed a smile,
> So fixed, so holy, from that cherub brow,
> Death gazed, and left it there. He dared not steal
> The signet ring of Heaven.[47]

In spite of the restrained, even austere mood evoked by Sigourney's pentameter lines and the relative detachment of the narrator, what seems most striking to contemporary readers is Frost's *difference* from such poems: his focus on the parents rather than the dead child, his dialogical form, his removal of religious "platitudes."[48] Nevertheless, he calls upon the conventional and familiar motif of the mother's grief, often expressed in similar nineteenth-century poems written from the mother's perspective; more broadly, he, like Sigourney, "spoke for affect along with rationality, for working people . . . and for women."[49] These poems are themselves grounded in an earlier tradition of American women's poetry framed by Anne Bradstreet's "In Memory of My Dear Grandchild Elizabeth Bradstreet, Who Deceased August, 1665, Being a Year and a Half Old" and "On My Dear Grandchild Simon Bradstreet, Who Died on 16 November, 1669, Being but a Month, and One Day Old." What Paula Bennett has observed about another poet's child-death poems is equally true of "Home Burial": "sentimentalism turns in upon itself," and "child-death does not lead to reform or redemption."[50]

Nevertheless, a poem in the same tradition as "Death of an Infant," Charles Lamb's "sentimental yet moving" poem from Palgrave's *Golden Treasury,* was important for the poet: "'On an Infant Dying as Soon as Born' consoled him after the death of baby [daughter] Elinor."[51] It is instructive to pause for a moment to juxtapose this poem with Sigourney's. Lamb's (longer) poem begins much as does his American counterpart's, with the depiction of the dead child's body:

> I saw where in the shroud did lurk
> A curious frame of Nature's work;
> A flow'ret crushéd in the bud,
> A nameless piece of Babyhood,
> Was in her cradle-coffin lying;
> Extinct, with scarce the sense of dying;
> So soon to exchange the imprisoning womb
> For darker closets of the tomb![52]

Using the conventional language of flowers to describe the dying child, the poet goes on to question the meaning of the child's death, to justify it inasmuch as it may have enabled the mother to survive, and to curse the "Heaven" that would deny life to the infant yet grant life to "shrivell'd crones," who "stiffen with age to stocks and stones." The poet also imagines the impossible future:

> —Mother's prattle, mother's kiss,
> Baby fond, thou ne'er wilt miss:
> Rites, which custom doth impose,
> Silver bells, and baby clothes[.]

Like Sigourney's poem recalling the innocence of the child and the relationship between mother and child, Lamb's feminine verses enter into empathic relationship with their readers. Poems like "Death of an Infant" and "On an Infant Dying as Soon as Born" recognize shared experiences and create a community that enables suffering to be both publicly acknowledged and dispersed. However cloying these lines may seem to a modern sensibility, they apparently offered Frost some consolation.

By fusing the feminine tradition of popular poetry with elements of realist prose fiction, and, in particular, of an often self-critical and dystopian late-nineteenth-century New England women's regionalist writing, Frost achieves in "Home Burial" a modern permutation of such work, in which he balances emotional intensity with a dramatic presentation that enables empathy for modern readers. Although Frost's poem does not offer the same consolation as its predecessors, it nevertheless enables readers to feel the suffering of its characters and to understand the sources of this conflict and alienation in a modern world in which males—including male poets—had access to fewer emotional outlets like the sentimental poems of Lamb and those cited in the previous chapter by Seba Smith and Harrison H. Harkesheimer. The simultaneous hospitality of "Home Burial" to analytical interpretation and affective engagement is achieved via its weaving together of an explosively emotional subject with the formal strategy of dialogue, paradoxically enabling the emotion to be felt even more powerfully. Moreover, in spite of the intensely personal resonances for the poet of this encounter between husband and wife, we do not see an individualistic consciousness mediating the events and ultimately centering them on itself; instead, Frost's perspective and his sympathies are widely dispersed and openly available.

As Pritchard notes about North of Boston, "Frost's poetics was intimately connected with his increasing responsiveness to other people."[53] "Other people" includes not only the characters of the narrative poems but readers as well, for we are invited less to judge this "poetry of experience"—to initiate "critical" activity—than to "respond" with empathy. Invoking the communal power of the sentimental image of a child's death, Frost's work rewards, though it does not require, exegesis. If this generosity of access has alienated some intellectual readers, it has endeared the poet to "ordinary" men and women whose experience it seems often to echo. In speaking of Frost's women, we can borrow from Betsey Dole's assertion: "I guess I can enter into her feelin's considerable."[54]

## "I can't express my feelings": Speaking of Silence

> The farmers' wives! what monotonous, treadmill lives! Constant
> toil with no wages, no allowance, no pocket money, no vaca-
> tions, no pleasure trips to the city nearest them, little of the
> pleasures of correspondence; no time to write, unless a near rel-
> ative is dead or dying. Some one says that their only chance for
> social life is in going to some insane asylum!
> —Kate Sanborn, Adopting an Abandoned Farm, 1891

By 1914, when such poems as "Home Burial," "The Housekeeper," "The Fear," and "A Servant to Servants" were published, Elinor Frost had borne six children and buried two of them within nine years. She had also labored teaching school to help support the family, moved countless times, and seen Frost through multiple job changes, from teacher to factory worker to student to farmer back to teacher, at which he finally became successful.[55] She had visited Frost's grandfather to arrange that he buy the Derry farm for the family; they had hopes for a new financial start as well as for the improvement of Robert's health. Yet, when her mother visited several weeks after the move, she found her daughter "too busy caring for the baby, too busy getting meals and washing dishes for three hungry men," to have spread rugs or hung curtains. Although there is no evidence that Elinor herself ever feared insanity—indeed, the poet's family history engendered this worry about *himself*—in view of Robert and Elinor's domestic situation, it is ironic that Frost locates the source of his poem "A Servant to Servants" in a stranger he encountered during a summer in Vermont (*CR* 115, 118, 143), for his wife's experience surely formed a significant if invisible thread in the narrative.

Working in the vein of Patricia Wallace's depiction of "woman" in Frost as a fearful outsider,[56] and underscoring how the poet writes as if women's "capacities tend toward hysteria and irrationality," Katherine Kearns re-creates this poem as a story of a disturbed wife whose very womanness engenders in men a fear of madness. We can as readily understand "A Servant to Servants," however, from a perspective that emphasizes Frost's empathy for the woman narrator and his ability to enable that empathy in a reader, for the violence that Frost portrays in "Home Burial" as inherent in masculinity and related to male sexuality emerges even more dramatically here. If we can read the narrator as "miserable," confused, and possessing a "disunified consciousness,"[57] we can also identify her self-awareness and her desire to communicate her pain, for, in spite of the outsider status of the botanist-auditor, the rhetorical structure of the poem invites us to an emotional "engagement," to use Frost's term, even more than "Home Burial."

"A Servant to Servants" echoes the domestic landscape of "Home Burial," and this narrator is also imprisoned in home, but her view seems more cheering, "a fair, pretty sheet of water" (*CP* 65); unlike Amy, she seems able to effect a temporary, if troubled, release from the cares of housekeeping for her dense (if sympathetic) husband and his hired men by scanning the prospects outside of her home. Speaking "glad[ly]" to a visiting botanist who camps on their property, she explores with him her interior as well as exterior landscape. The landscape of the psyche at first unrolls flat and clipped as a meadow or, as she describes Lake Willoughby: "'long and narrow, / Like a deep piece of some old running river / Cut short off at both ends'" (*CP* 66). In other ways she acknowledges that the constriction of her life demands a certain repression, as she gestures toward a meaningful female silence for which conventional language is no longer adequate or possible. Intending to have visited her auditor before their "conversation," she says:

> but I don't know!
> With a houseful of hungry men to feed
> I guess you'd find. . . . It seems to me
> I can't express my feelings, any more
> Than I can raise my voice or want to lift
> My hand (oh, I can lift it when I have to).
>
> (*CP* 65)

Her physical impotence mirrors her linguistic powerlessness; the men she "mothers" seem predatory, as if "feeding" from her saps not just her will and energy but her voice itself. Here, as in "Home Burial," the matter of labor shapes her perspective, as the title suggests and as she acknowledges: "'It's rest I want—there, I have said it out— / From cooking meals for hungry hired men / And washing dishes after them—from doing / Things over and over that just won't stay done'" (*CP* 66). Anyone who has been part of such a routine—or who can imagine it from the inside—will feel the wife's nearly tangible pain, frustration, and exhaustion, rather than simply judging her to be on the verge of madness (to which such conditions could understandably drive her).

Routine kills the spirit, but, although her ostensibly good-natured husband offers a change of scenery, this change is as irritating and inefficacious as his platitudes: "'one steady pull more ought to do it'" (*CP* 66). Suppressing her anger and frustration, the narrator nonetheless lets escape the painful vision of a domestic economy in which Len can *choose* to work, but she cannot:

> His work's a man's, of course, from sun to sun,
> But he works when he works as hard as I do—
> Though there's small profit in comparisons.
> (Women and men will make them all the same.)
>
> (*CP* 67)

She possesses the knowledge of an irrevocable difference between women and men without the power to change it in the poem's postlapsarian world. In some sense Frost seems to me almost to overemphasize the woman's perspective in order to make his point. In my own recollection of growing up on a New England farm with my great aunt and uncle, both worked very hard: the former cooking with an old Glenwood wood-fired stove well into her seventies as well as making butter, preserving food, and fostering orphaned animals; the latter milking the cows twice daily, feeding and caring for them and the other animals, and attending to the births of calves and piglets. Just as she could not choose whether or not to cook supper, so he could not decide whether or not to milk the cows.

If physical labor is important to "A Servant to Servants," here, as in "Home Burial," sexuality and sexual labor also simmer as subtext, but we can invert Kearns's story of "women [who] may bring men to madness" to hear another narrative.[58] In this retelling, it is not the *woman* who is powerful; it is the *men* who bury her alive. Len's wife is, she tells us, ignorant of the names or characters of the boarders or "'whether they are safe / To have inside the house with doors unlocked'" (*CP* 67). What inhabits the inner rooms of "home," of the psyche, are men, alien to her sensibility, emblematic of disease, dis-ease, and engendering a fear of rape. This meditation about her boarders initiates a "mad" verbal wander, conjuring up a foreign, disturbing image of home, her insane uncle lurking above in the attic, poisoning the sexual connections in her mother's marriage: "'She had to lie and hear love things made dreadful / By his shouts in the night.'" On a deeper level, the madman evokes an image of all men, the narrator's father and husband included with her uncle, who is made crazed and bestial by love: "'he was crossed in love, / Or so the story goes. It was some girl. / Anyway all he talked about was love'" (*CP* 68). At issue, however, is not love but sexuality, particularly unsatisfied male sexuality. Here, as he does somewhat differently in "The Subverted Flower," Frost demythologizes and deromanticizes such social institutions as love, marriage, and home: from one angle the poem intimates that these institutions privilege the satisfaction of male lust. Ultimately, the poem suggests, the culturally sanctioned image of males as uncontrollably sexual has been the rationale for violence, rape, sexual abuse, and, conversely, marriage, for all are sanctioned by male power.

Of course, we should notice that the narrator affirms her affinity with, not her difference from, her uncle, suggesting that her own female sexuality troubles her as well. Surprisingly, this highly charged and sexual poem makes no mention at all of children, and we are left to wonder if the narrator has chosen childlessness or if she suppresses their presence. Certainly, Elinor did not have such a choice. Thompson speaks of Frost as intermittently guilt-ridden by his own sexual drives and notes that his guilt was intensified by his feeling that "his passionate demands had brought six children upon a woman whose heart was weak, and therefore that he had, in a sense, killed her."[59] The scenario for rural childbearing at the beginning of the twentieth century remained physically and psychically grim. As Adrienne Rich suggests, centuries of women's and infants' deaths from puerperal fever and misused forceps influenced women's experience of pain and fear of death:

> even in a place and time where maternal mortality is low, a woman's fantasies of her own death in childbirth have the accuracy of metaphor. Typically, under patriarchy, the mother's life is exchanged for the child; her autonomy as a separate being seems fated to conflict with the infant she will bear. The self-denying, self-annihilative role of the Good Mother . . . will spell the "death" of the woman or girl who once had hopes, expectations, fantasies *for herself*.[60]

As an educated daughter from a well-to-do family, Mrs. Frost surely had to confront both the partial knowledge and genteel ignorance about childbirth required by that background.[61] If we add to these circumstances the imagination of a poet, we can understand more vividly, perhaps, the psychic "issue" of labor. Yet, if Elinor's repression in some ways helps to engender Frost's poetry, the narrator's repression in "A Servant to Servants" engenders not children but, as we shall see in "The Witch of Coös," poetry, as if speaking the words Elinor herself cannot say.[62] Deeply rooted in rural life, Frost ultimately mourns the trials and "solitary confinement" that give birth to such a painful version of the self, and he invites readers to share this feeling. As Poirier observes of one passage, it "might bring anyone to tears."[63]

Beyond considerations of setting and subject "A Servant to Servants" expresses a culturally feminine sensibility and uses an important rhetorical stance of women's regionalist fiction in the relation of its narrator to the listener-reader. The narrator spends much of her time in the feminine labor of forging a relationship. Take, for example, the "trivial" discussion concerning the listener's arrival at the lake:

> Our Willoughby! How did you hear of it?
> I expect, though, everyone's heard of it.
> In a book about ferns? Listen to that!
> You let things more like feathers regulate
> Your going and coming.
>
> (*CP* 66)

While the narrator may seem merely voluble, her primary, even desperate, concern is to establish a link with the listener—the reader's alter ego—and

thus to engage and draw us into relation with her via the intimacy of gossip.[64] What vibrates beneath the content here is an almost electrical connection between speaker and listener. The narrator of "A Servant to Servants"
allows us, with the botanist, to "answer," to occupy our own space in the
poem, and she gently teases us for the apparently whimsical nature of our
"wandering," making us feel at ease. Part of this openness results from a
need to share, to be "confidential," with someone who might understand
her predicament as her practical husband cannot. In some sense her open
speech represents a "betrayal" of Len because she reveals his shortcomings
while reflecting his impotence both as husband and as speaker. Although,
like the muse-wife of "Home Burial," her labor is lost—here in repetition
and lack of meaning—this apparent "lack" of meaning is especially important because she evinces the sensibility of the poet in her description of the
lake ("To step outdoors and take the water dazzle") and in the distorted
"poetry" of her tales of madness (*CP* 66). We may wonder how much of
her tale about her uncle is fact and how much is invention, but we are compelled by its power.

That she represents a specifically feminine poet, however, emerges in
her rhetorical gestures of intimacy and inclusion: questions, teasing, and
painful frankness. Scarcely a proxy for the masculine, magisterial "I" of the
traditional lyric poet, the speaker attains the kind of dispersed subjectivity
that Fetterley and Pryse highlight in woman-authored regionalist fiction
(and that Bennett and others underscore in sentimental poetry); furthermore, while there is a male auditor, his relationship with her is not merely
voyeuristic, nor is he simply an outsider. In "A Servant to Servants" the
poet invites us to share a dialogue with the feminine voice of the narrator as
she elaborates her vision with a clarity that she cannot perform with Len.
This dialogue involves a willingness to empathize, to expand our own ego
boundaries as feminine readers willing to forgo judgment for participation
in a process, as Frost signals by repeatedly invoking the "you."[65] In the first
six lines a version of "you" occurs four times; slightly later, after the narrator scans her exterior "prospects," she turns again to the botanist-reader,
five times in lines 33–35, as if to prepare us for the meditation that follows.
In a final gesture of courtesy, as if to confirm our intimacy, she returns to
the "you" near the end:

> I've lain awake thinking of you, I'll warrant,
> More than you have yourself, some of these nights.
> The wonder was the tents weren't snatched away

From over you as you lay in your beds.
I haven't courage for a risk like that.
Bless you, of course you're keeping me from work,
But the thing of it is, I need to *be* kept.

(*CP* 69)

In some sense our presence enables a delivery from the "pregnancy" of pain, madness, and repressed speech that she perceives to be her lot in life, and we do not simply keep her from her work; we enable a different "labor" of the tongue. Unlike the hired men who are "'no more put out in what they do or say / Than if I wasn't in the room at all'" (*CP* 69), we endow her with substance and voice. Blurring the boundaries between insider and outsider, Frost de-emphasizes his own poetic selfhood to enable the "servant" to tell her own story, and the poem provides for the listener—who simultaneously internalizes and enacts the voice of the poem's speaker—a kinetic sense of feminine presence. In an essay on Sarah Orne Jewett that resonates for much of Frost's early work, Marcia McClintock Folsom highlights the writer's empathic style; she argues that "'self-forgetfulness' [Jewett's word] allows the narrator freedom to enter other lives even as it denies her full fictional presence in the book," and she points out that "the artist relinquishes a personal point of view in order to enter into the spirit of other people or even of objects."[66] By endowing Len's wife with a subjectivity and a voice in "A Servant to Servants" the poet also "relinquishes a personal point of view" and engages in a "'self-forgetfulness'" that enables him to "enter into the spirit of other people" just as many of his regionalist and sentimental forebears had done.

The sympathy for feminine presence and voice in "A Servant to Servants" finds a parallel in a story like Rose Terry Cooke's "Mrs. Flint's Married Experience," in which the central character, the widow of a kind and much-loved husband, decides to remarry because she fears she is a burden to her daughter and son-in-law. Her new spouse is an infamous pennypincher; as one of the secondary characters, the wise and independent "village fool," observes, "A wife's a lot cheaper than hired help, and this one's got means." Described by Widow Gold's son-in-law as "town-talk for nearness and meanness," Deacon Flint essentially works and starves his new wife to death as he has his first.[67] Far from representing the rural utopia imagined by many modern and contemporary critics, stories like "Mrs. Flint's Married Experience" take the study of gender-power dynamics to an extreme, expressing the suffering of rural women in traditional married relationships much like that of the narrator of Frost's poem. Significantly, Mrs. Flint has no voice of her own once she is married; "she toiled on dumbly from day to day, half fed, overworked, desperately lonely, but still uncomplaining." Her perspective is expressed by a poor young woman who is a relation of the Deacon's, but such expression comes far too late. The all-male members of the local church hierarchy conspire with Deacon Flint to confine Mrs. Flint to a traditional female role and to deny her subjectivity, for, when she leaves him shortly before her death, they call on her to repent and return to him, whom they read as "resigned, pious, and loftily superior to common things." With irresistible irony Cooke's narrator continues: "then he was a man, and a deacon! Is it to be wondered at that their letter to the church at Bassett was in the deacon's favor?"[68]

Like Cooke, Frost exposes the hardships and pain of a rural New England wife, and he highlights the social structures that work to suppress her subjectivity and her voice. Like Mrs. Flint, the narrator of the poem is surrounded by men, and, like her, the wife is controlled by them and their demands. Hunger occupies a central position in both narratives; where Deacon Flint takes the best portions of food and leaves his servantlike wife to starve, the hired men in "A Servant to Servants" devour the wife's labor and energies along with her food. The only escape possible for Len's wife is her plain talk to the sensitive, even effeminate, auditor who is willing to shape his life by ferns, "things more like feathers." Far from being "hysterical" and "irrational," "Much Madness is Divinest Sense" here:[69] Len's wife articulates a wholly reasonable response to the psychological violence that she endures in a home haunted by strange and crude male boarders, a dull husband, and a mad uncle. Here in Frost, as in much regionalist fiction, it is the males who embody and engender dis-ease with their brutish power.[70]

Both of these regionalist texts provide, directly in Frost's case and indirectly in Cooke's, a consciousness for the marginalized woman protagonist, not "undermining them with the ironic perspective characteristic of 'local color' writing" but, instead, "bearing witness" to their circumscribed lives by giving voice to a poor rural woman's marginalized experience.[71] As Fetterley acknowledges elsewhere, "In seeking to empower persons made silent or vacant through terror to tell stories which the dominant culture labels trivial, regionalism seeks to change our perspective and thus to destabilize the meanings of margin and center."[72] In this fiction Frost empowers the woman simply by allowing her to tell her own story. As "Home Burial" and "A Servant to Servants" tell it, "her story" reflects the disabling limitations and frightening expectations imposed by traditional gender roles, limitations and expectations that are exacerbated by his protagonists' rural existence. The loss and silence at the heart of the wife's experience in the former translate in "A Servant to Servants" into a liberating self-voicing that forestalls the madness that threatens her. "The Death of the Hired Man," the focus of the next section, explores a more affirmative, while more sentimentally inflected, vision of feminine experience and voice.

## "The feminine way of it": Women and Men at Home

Discussing "The Death of the Hired Man" in an interview, Frost says Mary's view of home is "the feminine way of it, the mother way. You don't have to deserve your mother's love. You have to deserve your father's. . . . One's a Republican, one's a Democrat. The father is always a Republican toward his son, and his mother's always a Democrat. Very few have noticed that second thing; they've always noticed the sarcasm, the hardness of the male one."[73] Indirectly affirming his engagement with a feminine perspective, the poet's comments reveal a strikingly politicized sense of gender relations, and they emphasize his sympathies: "The Death of the Hired Man," at least, epitomizes the ethic of connection and nurturing that undergirds mainstream nineteenth-century poetry and regionalist fiction. The "child" who requires this nurturing is the dying hired man Silas, who left the protagonists' farm during the busy haying season only to return when the work was completed. The poem's drama hinges upon Mary's ability to reconcile her husband, Warren, to Silas's return to the place he calls home. Yet, although the poem addresses the definition of home, it elaborates at a more profound level the emotional conversion of a masculine listener-reader-critic, figured by Warren, to a feminine vision of home and its proper relations.[74]

Mary's perspective echoes that of Sarah Orne Jewett's narrator in "The Town Poor," in which two women, one affluent, one poor, visit two elderly sisters (the Bray "girls") who have "gone on the town."[75] Because of the selectmen's penurious attitudes, the sisters live in extremely pinched circumstances with a family that is responsible (and paid) for sheltering and feeding them. The visitors' relative economic standing is crucial to the story, because, while the affluent woman, Mrs. Trimble, has been unable to recognize the poverty endured by her youngish traveling companion, Rebecca Wright, when confronted with the genteel and previously independent elderly sisters, she is stunned into acknowledgment. In spite of reduced economic circumstances that leave them hungry and cold, the Bray sisters exemplify self-respect, treating their guests to the best of their small possessions, such as the last of their homemade jelly. In this portrait of Mrs. Trimble, who is blind to the less fortunate and, hence, who shares the responsibility for the Bray girls' condition with the "selectmen," Jewett prohibits easy or essentialized affiliations between women and sympathy; the portrait of Mrs. Trimble may also implicate the imagined (female) reader of the story, herself in comfortable circumstances. Similarly, in Freeman's story "A Mistaken Charity," Harriet and Charlotte are sent to the poorhouse by the "mistaken" sympathy and "charity" of two comfortable neighbor women. Although it idealizes its central female character in a way that the fiction writers frequently do not, Frost's poem shares many of the attitudes of these stories: an acute awareness of rural poverty, a depiction of women as mediators in ameliorating the situation, an appeal to emotion, and a narrator who values and enables the perspectives and subjectivities of his female characters. It is ultimately through the force of Mary's character that she effects an affirmative change in Warren and, by proxy, in the reader.

At the opening of the poem, Mary waits for Warren in order to forestall his anger at Silas, urging her husband to "'be kind.'" In contrast to Warren's emphasis on economic concerns—"'Who else will harbor him / At his age for the little he can do?'"—is Mary's emotional, relational concern: "'Sh! not so loud: he'll hear you'" (*CP* 40, 41). Yet, in the face of Mary's gentle reminiscences, even Warren must admire Silas's knowledge of facts that books can't teach. In an extended monologue on another, more "successful" of their "children," Harold Wilson, Mary emphasizes Silas's strengths, among which is a different way of knowing. If Harold is, according to Silas, "'daft on education,'" even "'the fool of books,'" Mary seems to share the latter's perception that practical learnedness outweighs theoretical knowledge, and her nostalgic, even sentimental, recollection inspires agreement from Warren. Mary juxtaposes Harold's love for Latin to Silas's "body language," capable of "divining" water with a hazel prong, images that suggest the relative sterility and fertility of each pursuit. Like Silas attempting to convert Harold, Mary claims she has little skill with words: "'I sympathize. I know just how it feels / To think of the right thing to say too late'" (*CP* 42, 43). Feeling and thinking, culturally feminine and masculine tasks, are set apart not only here, in the lines and content of the poem, but between the lines as well in the dialogue between wife and husband. Mary underlines her value system when she affirms, "'Poor Silas, so concerned for other folk'" (*CP* 43).

Kearns acknowledges that the poem "represents one of the most sustained visions of an apparently noncombative male-female relationship to be found anywhere in Frost's work," but she confines this insight within the boundaries of her argument about Frost's drive for masculine power and autonomy and the threat that women pose to both, arguing that "implicit in Mary's great power to move Warren toward empathy is an equivalent power to remove him from control." But I see Mary's power not only as *not* malign, affiliated, as Kearns intimates, with Frost's witches, but affirmative and desirable.[76] Mary seems to gather part of her quiet power and care from her affiliation with nature, yet she exceeds this affiliation in her visionary power:[77]

> Part of a moon was falling down the west,
> Dragging the whole sky with it to the hills.
> Its light poured softly in her lap. She saw it
> And spread her apron to it. She put out her hand
> Among the harp-like morning-glory strings,
> Taut with the dew from garden bed to eaves,
> As if she played unheard some tenderness
> That wrought on him beside her in the night.

> (*CP* 43)

Almost angelic in gathering in the moon's light and playing on the "harp-like morning-glory strings," her music represents and engenders "tenderness" in Warren, as Frost orchestrates explicitly the power of the wife in relation to her husband. Most important to notice is the stylistic transition at this moment, for Frost distills the "poetry" of Mary's presence and signals that presence in the most conspicuously poetic language of the poem; it is in such moments of overt self-awareness and self-declaration that Frost makes most audible to the reader his own alliances. This language—not only self-consciously lyric but highly sentimental, feminine—incorporates the immanent "language" of gesture, for Mary gathers the moon to her lap as she would a child. In spite of her protests to the contrary, her own efficacious language distinguishes her from the muse-wife of "Home Burial," who is obsessed with the literal language of the body, as well as from Silas himself. Able to assume the ancient responsibility of the poet, to speak for those who, like Silas, cannot speak for themselves, she achieves more than momentary transcendence of her routine through language, for she effects a moral change upon her listeners. Her most important task in the poem is to teach Warren and, by extension, the reader, especially the masculine reader, the value of sustaining relationships.

Mary's affirmation that one should not have to deserve a home leads Warren to consider what the term means, and she fosters his awakening by extending her perspective to include his own, agreeing that Si's "'brother ought to help'" with the financial burden and echoing Warren's earlier remark, "'What good is he?'" with a comment about Si's status: "'Worthless'" (*CP* 40, 44). Of course, by all financial standards, the standards with which Warren and the masculine reader begins, the old man *is* worthless, but Mary has led him to reconsider the meaning and implications of his term, and he responds to her comment, "'*I* can't think Si ever hurt anyone'" (*CP* 40, 44). Given Warren's assent, Mary reverts to her ethic of nurturing: she confesses to being hurt by Si's debilitated condition, she makes up a bed for him, and she arouses in Warren the empathy that is necessary before the two men meet: "'His working days are done; I'm sure of it.'" Warren's conversion to his wife's value system emerges again in his response: "'I'd not be in a hurry to say that.'" When the revelation of Silas's death occurs, Warren provides it in the gentlest manner; echoing her own facility with a gentle language of the body, he "slipped to her side, caught up her hand, and waited" (*CP* 45). Warren's transformation mirrors the reader's own, as the dialogue of the poem teaches us to value relationships over autonomy, compassion over economics, and feeling over thinking.[78]

The final conversion of Warren and the masculine reader appears at the end of the poem, where Frost symbolizes Mary's facility with language after she cautions Warren a final time:

> "I'll sit and see if that small sailing cloud
> Will hit or miss the moon."
>                                    It hit the moon.
> Then there were three there, making a dim row,
> The moon, the little silver cloud, and she.
>
>                                    (*CP* 45)

Explicitly symbolic and attentive to sound ("sit," "if," "will," and "miss," as well as the monosyllabic spondaic conclusion, "It hit"), these lines evoke Mary's own ability to express in poetic terms the violence of nature—of the moon being "hit," of Silas dying—and the violence of normative culture, which would erase Silas as a meaningful presence. Into the breach, the absence in the middle of these lines, arrives the other presence that haunts the poem, that of Frost himself; yet Mary, the explicitly feminine poet, becomes his proxy in the process of engendering "tenderness" in Warren and the reader. As the poem's primary speaker, Mary enables us to experience a conversion through persuasive poetic speech enabled by her evident love for Warren himself. Home is less problematic, less confining, in "The Death of the Hired Man" than in "Home Burial" and "A Servant to Servants" in part because of its revision of the role of the husband. Where in the former the husband is at times a whining and obtuse brute and in the latter a sympathetic but uncomprehending dullard or, more frighteningly (if metaphorically), a madman in the attic, here Warren's ultimate openness and flexibility husband Mary's voice. Frost's delicate withholding of a masculine "I" permits the narrative to oscillate between the two points of view and finally to culminate in Mary's "Democratic" feminine vision.

To some readers this story of Frost's poem will certainly be too affirmative and even syrupy. To be sure, we could read the lyrical passages in the poem as comical—they incorporate the usual characters of romance, namely, clouds, the moon, morning glories like harp strings—and as such they not only intimate a portrait of Mary's affiliation with sentimental poetry but also potentially gloss that tradition as limited. This reading is possible in part because of professional readers' sense that they pander to a false emotion. For example, Poirier points to home as "a dangerous subject for [Frost]. It can encourage his tendency to wax idyllic about the possibilities of marital relationships." He asserts that "Frost is close to selling out to his popular audience when he, or his characters, speak as if the environment around them adequately sustains their aspirations to hygienically fine feelings. 'The Death of the Hired Man' has that touch of gentility which is even more obnoxiously at work, for me, in . . . 'The Generations of Men.'"[79] But I have suggested that Frost also invites us to read these lyrical lines from "The Death of the Hired Man" seriously—that is, sentimentally—in his overt sympathy for Mary's perspective, certified by the poem's romantic yet realistic conclusion: death and love converge. In the tradition of female-authored regionalist texts Frost's poem explores the characters' search for an identity that is "collective, connected, and collaborative," and it "allow[s] the reader to view the regional speaker as subjects and not object and to include empathic feeling as an aspect of critical response."[80] While "The Death of the Hired Man" attempts to highlight character over plot and, for the reader, empathy over critical detachment, such detachment arrives with the "sophistication" of a modernist and masculine perspective that is often allied with the repression of emotion—and, again, with the segregation of elite from popular readers.[81]

But there is another way to interpret Warren's (if not the reader's) detachment, one that he would probably be loath to acknowledge. Such detachment can in fact be willed, achieved, for a variety of practical reasons, at a price. Here a personal account may help: in their later years my great aunt and uncle's farm had shrunken to a size where hired help was no longer a necessity or financially a possibility. While they willingly and unstintingly gave of their meager resources to help the local Congregational Church, they could not have supported a hired man, even one who *was* able to help on the farm, no matter how close a friend; they had suffered silently the indignity of having to sell off bits of land to sustain their diminishing home life. To use another, even harder analogy: once or twice a year my great uncle would be forced to drown a litter of kittens from the half-wild cat who earned her keep by terrorizing the local rat and mouse population. He did not, however, enjoy it: such farm work had its own costs.

## "Go get a reputation": (Re)Reading Frost's Regionalism

> The thing which makes Mr. Frost's work remarkable is the fact that he has chosen to write it as verse. We have been flooded for twenty years with New England stories in prose. The finest and most discerning are the little master-pieces of Alice Brown. She too is a poet in her descriptions, she too has caught the desolation and "dourness" of lonely New England farms. (*CR* 18)

In this review of *North of Boston* Amy Lowell celebrated Frost's connection with place, specifically New England, and praised the poet for creating "the most American volume of poetry which has appeared for some time," adding, "I use the word American in the way it is constantly employed by contemporary reviewers, to mean work of a color so local as to be almost photographic" (*CR* 18). Describing the poems as "stories," Lowell goes on to connect *North of Boston* explicitly with women's regionalist writing. She was not the only contemporary of Frost's to observe this affiliation.[82] Given his desire to be seen as a poet, Frost was predictably anxious about the kinds of connections made by these reviews, even though (or perhaps because) Lowell highlighted the contiguity between prose and poetry. As the unsent letter-poem to Pound cited in the preceding chapter reveals, these fears of being seen as less than a poet framed Frost's work and his self-presentation virtually from the beginning. The gender of genre is illuminated in a differ-ent way by Frost's newly acquired friend, William Dean Howells, in a review of 1915 that also depicts the poet's investment in regionalism and his alliance with Jewett, Wilkins Freeman, and Brown: "His manly power is manliest in penetrating to the heart of womanhood."[83] The self-consciously heterosexual language illuminates Howells's interpretation of the complicated relationship between poetry, gender, and culture and the danger that feminine affiliations posed for masculinity.

The threat that these precursors posed to Frost's reputation as a poet, rather than "merely" a prosaic regionalist, recurs repeatedly in early Frost criticism. In his own review of *North of Boston* Louis Untermeyer characteristically comes to his friend's defense: "I have little respect—literary respect—for anyone who can read the shortest of these poems without feeling the skill and power in them. But I have far more respect for the man who can see nothing at all in this volume than for him who, discovering many other things in it, cannot see the poetry in it" (*CR* 24). Acknowledging that "there is, for instance, a lack of 'poetic' figures and phrases in this volume," Untermeyer asserts that, although "Mr. Frost neglects" "the property and perquisites of even the greatest poets," he "still writes poetry"; "the effect rather than the statement is poetry; the air is almost electric with it" (*CR* 25). The reviewer's focus on this issue indicates both the heatedness of the debate and, by one remove, the intensity of Frost's anxiety on the matter, for shortly after the publication of *A Boy's Will* Frost writes to John Bartlett that "I expect to do something to the present state of literature in America" (*SL* 88). To Thomas Mosher he claims, "I have not strength to batter out against the indifference of those who will meet me with 'Who are you?' or 'Go get a reputation,'" (*SL* 96), though his letters to Untermeyer indicate considerable feistiness and combativeness.

Soon after *North of Boston* was published, he wrote to a literary acquaintance, John Cornos, "My versification seems to bother people more than I should have expected" (*SL* 128); in another letter the same month to Cornos he observes:

> I am not bothered by the question whether anyone will be able to hear or say those three words ("If—you—do!") as I mean them to be said or heard. I should say that they were sufficiently self expressive. Some doubt that such tones can long survive on paper. They'll probably last as long as the finer meanings of words. And if they don't last more than a few hundred years that will be long enough for me—much longer than I can hope to read. (*SL* 130)

Ironically, in view of the debate outlined by Untermeyer, Frost acknowledged that many reviews of the book were "ridiculously favorable" (*SL* 132 [to Sidney Cox]). When Frost returned to the United States from England, attending both a lunch with the editors of the *New Republic* and a dinner meeting of the Poetry Society of America, he was lauded as "America's newest poetic discovery" (*SL* 153). Part of his success with reviewers was due to his own "public relations campaign," starting with *A Boy's Will*. Thompson notes that "by the time *North of Boston* was published, in May of 1914, he had become so skillfully enterprising as his own promoter that some of the best reviews reflected his careful coaching" (*SL* 51).

The poet must have felt considerable relief, for such recognition promised at least a modicum of economic success and relief from the financial pressures that he had been suffering for some time. In March 1914 he wrote to Sidney Cox requesting what was for that time the fairly sizable loan of "twenty-five or fifty dollars (if fifty is too much, twenty five) to help me out of a tight place" (*SL* 118). A few days later the poet's sister Jeanie interceded on the poet's behalf with the executor of their grandfather's estate: "My brother is, I am afraid, embarrassed for money this spring, (I am afraid he would be very much displeased if he knew that I was writing to you)"; she added, "I have reason to know that he needs $75 at least. Of course he hasn't the slightest idea that I am writing to you. I am in hopes that he will realize rather more from his new book 'North of Boston' than from his first book of poems" (*SL* 119). Given that this theme of economic hardship reverberates throughout the letters of the period, it is little wonder that Frost had deep sympathies with the rural underclass or that poverty is a regular subtext of his early work. Perhaps it was in part the fear of this end that kept him so attuned to his readers' responses, most notably the debate over whether or not his regional writing was "universal" or, indeed, even poetry.[84]

## "Dumped down in paradise": Realism and Sentimental Romance

> Some day, in the middle of it all, I shall write another kind of
> poem like ["The Death of the Hired Man"]—and I'm afraid
> that it will be a little less innocent, a little more argumentative
> and authoritative. When I wrote the "Book of People," *North of
> Boston,* it was in innocence of heart—no implications.
>                                        —Robert Frost, *CP*

Along with poems like "The Telephone," "The Fear," and "The Exposed Nest," "Home Burial," "A Servant to Servants," and "The Death of the

Hired Man" enact in various ways Frost's proximity to female and feminine voices and his affiliations with mainstream nineteenth-century poetry and regionalist fiction. A discussion of "In the Home Stretch" is a good place to suggest some of the tensions in this group of poems and the ways in which they not only work within but also complicate the New England regionalist tradition. The poem was included in *Mountain Interval,* which itself reflects a variety of pressures, both internal and external, on the poet. According to Thompson, when Frost first returned from England, he overcommitted himself to "noncreative activities"; *Mountain Interval* was "hurriedly and somewhat resentfully assembled due to pressure from the poet's publisher." Thompson also observes that, at nearly the same time as the book's publication, Frost accepted a position at Amherst College, "hoping that his presence there might resolve his precarious financial position" (*SL* 154). Whether Frost wrote "In the Home Stretch" earlier with the *North of Boston* poems or whether (as the poem's rough quality suggests) he composed it quickly in an effort to reproduce his earlier successes is uncertain.[85] We can, however, regard it in the thread of Frost's unfolding self-presentation—here as one of the few dramatic poems in a volume that incorporated some masculine lyrics that exemplify the self-centered subjectivity of the romantic tradition, most notably, "The Road Not Taken," "Meeting and Passing," and "Birches." Although *North of Boston* inaugurated this stance with "Mending Wall" and "After Apple Picking," *Mountain Interval* anticipates Frost's final departure from the prosaic, realistic dramatic poems for which he had become famous.

Unlike "The Death of the Hired Man," which successfully melds the two voices, "In the Home Stretch" retains traces of Frost's conflict between the ordinary speaking voice that he attempts to elevate to the status of poetry and the long tradition of canonical, masculine lyric. Moreover, while "The Death of the Hired Man" investigates Mary and Warren's self-definitions via their relationships to another person—and, by extension, to a community of other persons—"In the Home Stretch" focuses more narrowly on a husband-wife relationship, evoking Elinor confronting her husband, who had himself initiated countless relocations and redefinitions of home. Once again, the plot is straightforward and less central than character: an aging couple leaves the city in order to farm, a move the husband has wanted for many years. We see them amid jumbles of furniture and comical yet brutish moving men as they discuss their past, present, and future. The poem's central tension resides in the husband's guilt that perhaps he has imposed the move on his wife, but, in spite of the ostensible disparity in their experiences and attitudes, their perspectives ultimately do not conflict but come together.

Most readers of Frost ignore or pass very quickly over this poem, but I am assuming here as elsewhere that exploring a poet's "less good" work can help to clarify the attitudes, gestures, and goals that she or he performs more "gracefully" and invisibly on more "perfect" occasions; in the case of Frost "In the Home Stretch" offers a glimpse at the ambivalences of his public self-representation. The poem's narrative focuses on the unnamed and emblematic woman's perspective, as it opens with a snapshot that might depict generations of women: "She stood against the kitchen sink, and looked / Over the sink out through a dusty window / At weeds the water from the sink made tall" (*CP* 108). The poignancy of this image bespeaks the sympathy of the poet for this wife, who mirrors the speaker in "A Servant to Servants." If the sink seems like a hole into which she might fall, the windows are always in need of cleaning; the residue from the dishwater grows weeds that seem internal as well as external.

At the wife's back the moving men heap furniture in "confusion," asking her where to locate things, and she replies with good-humored laughter, for they insist on calling her "lady." When her husband comes in and "gently" asks, "What are you seeing out the window, *lady?*" her response indicates the playful tone of their relationship:

> "Never was I beladied so before.
> Would evidence of having been called a lady
> More than so many times make me a lady
> In common law, I wonder."
>
> (*CP* 108)

Although she knows that in this context "lady" means "boss," she deliberately misinterprets the word to underline women's normative roles and the class structures inherent in gendered selfhood; the wife does not consider herself a lady because she has to labor to keep house, here literally to *make* a home.[86] Frost's poem points to his understanding of the discrepancy between the way women are often viewed and the way they see their lives from the inside.

In Frost's own life Elinor's move to the country as a young wife meant her transformation from a genteel and ladylike woman to a hardworking farmer's wife.[87] When the husband of "In the Home Stretch" pursues his question, his wife hedges in terms that Elinor herself might have used: "'What I'll be seeing more of in the years / To come as here I stand and go the round / Of many plates with towels many times.'"[88] The wife perceives a cycle ("round") of repetitious and ultimately meaningless actions figured in the repetition of "many"; women's circle of existence is circumscribed by social and cultural rules/roles whether one is a lady or a laborer. When her husband persists that he has not received an answer to his question about what she sees, she pushes the metaphor further:

> "Rank weeds that love the water from the dishpan
> More than some women like the dishpan, Joe;
> A little stretch of mowing field for you;
> Not much of that until I come to woods
> That end all. And it's scarce enough to call
> A view."
>
> (CP 108–9)

The baldness of the language here highlights the presence of the poet and his alliance with the wife's perspective. Explicit about women's cultural role, Frost externalizes the limitations of her and their life, and with this vision the poem's "seer" forecasts only her labor, their confinement and their impending mortality as they give up "lighted city streets" for "country darkness" (CP 109).[89] Interestingly, Frost transposes the traditional association in much canonical American literature between women and nature, men and culture, for it is *Joe* who desired the move into the country; furthermore, the poet flattens the figurative impact of the metaphor by contextualizing it in the wife-poet's clearly pragmatic vision. Both of these gestures prefigure the convergence of apparent opposites at the end of the poem.

Joe is Frost's narrative and rhetorical response to the vision of dead endings. He clearly loves the place and the rural surroundings, and, amid the bumps of the movers above their heads, he tries to provide her with a comforting view of the present—"'Come from that window where you see too much, / And take a livelier view of things from here'"—embodied in the benign figure of one of the movers lighting his pipe. Making the effort to see from Joe's perspective, but still burdened by her vision of light and "dark," she discovers the lovely, evocative—and poetic—new moon:

> "A wire she is of silver, as new as we
> To everything. Her light won't last us long.

It's something, though, to know we're going to have her
Night after night and stronger every night
To see us through our first two weeks."

$$(CP\ 110)$$

Recalling the moon in "The Death of the Hired Man," the poem evokes the hospitality of nature in this lonely country place and the strength its recurrence bestows on human beings, for, in contrast to her earlier vision of repetition, the wife discovers (or the poet discovers for her) a healing wholeness in cycles. This healing is inspired by the transformation of nature into the language of romantic poetry; as the wife's perspective metamorphoses from the quotidian to the extraordinary, Frost underscores her visionary power.

Perhaps what makes modern readers—myself included—uncomfortable with this poem is that here at least it seems to cross the boundary from evocative to excessive (as the language of my own narrative suggests). Perhaps Frost himself was aware of this tone and its effect on readers—or perhaps he too was uncomfortable, for the wife continues in language that jars with the self-consciously metaphoric diction that immediately precedes it:

"But, Joe,
The stove! Before they go! Knock on the window;
Ask them to help you get it on its feet.
We stand here dreaming. Hurry! Call them back!"

$$(CP\ 110)$$

Juxtaposing a lyric voice with this pragmatic language without the marker of a stanza or even a line break, the poem highlights the collision and discontinuity between romantic and quotidian, lyric and narrative, perspectives—or possibly, from another perspective, their convergence. The narrative tensions enacted here between husband and wife are reiterated within the wife's language. In her lexicon a "window" becomes a tangible, useful object, not only a frame for dreams; her grounding in the literal enables the pragmatic vision she elaborates throughout the poem. An emotional, nostalgic voice affiliated with nineteenth-century affective poetry ("a wire she is of silver") enters into dialogue with the realistic perspective of regionalist fiction ("we stand here dreaming") to provide readers with a complex understanding of this experience.

The description that follows evokes both the wife's double vision and that of a shadow narrator, the poet, in excessive metaphoric weightiness that is conspicuously comic:

> The house was full of tramping, and the dark,
> Door-filling men burst in and seized the stove.
> A cannon-mouth-like hole was in the wall,
> To which they set it true by eye; and then
> Came up the jointed stovepipe in their hands,
> So much too light and airy for their strength
> It almost seemed to come ballooning up,
> Slipping from clumsy clutches toward the ceiling.
>
>                                        (CP 110)

Revising the threat of too many men in the home that we saw in "A Servant to Servants," this passage balances menace with comedy. The men "tramp" in, "dark" and looming enormous; they "seize" the stove violently and fill up an aggressive "cannon-mouth-like hole." Yet, because the hole is only *like* a "cannon-mouth," the threat dissipates into the humor of their fumbling. Representing Frost's fears about his status as a real poet, the tension between the ordinary speech of regionalist fiction and the language of lyric reemerges in this passage. The narrator so clearly delights in the language of poetry—"clumsy clutches," for example—that the effect of the whole passage mimics the lifting of the heavy stove and then the ballooning of the images and sounds with the oxygen of the narrator's voice. If the heavy stove figures the literal, associated with the bulky men who move it, the stovepipe evokes, with a laugh, the metaphorical ("light and airy") and feminine. While in "Home Burial" Frost confirms the traditional association of male with figurative and female with literal, here he inverts it to playful effect, an effect emphasized by the mundane domain that the narrative describes. Of course, from another angle we might read the stovepipe as a phallic image and the hole as a vagina, in which case the passage regains an edge of menace balanced once again by the comedy of its excessive figurative display.[90] To underscore these tensions, and their momentary balance, Frost gives us the words of one of the moving men: "A fit! . . . It's good luck when you move in to begin / With good luck with your stovepipe" (CP 110). This remark gestures comically toward the end of the poem, when the couple go beyond linguistic foreplay actually to make love.

The protagonists engage in verbal interplay with the moving men that precedes a narrative movement in which Joe acknowledges his wife's point of view, and we see here a sharing of her perspective that enables him to gain insight and sympathy. Joe's questions about the wife's vision are informed by his prior knowledge of and concern for her answer and especially by his concern that she has regrets: "'Did they make something lonesome go through you? / It would take more than them to sicken you— / Us of our bargain.'" The linear fragmentation of "you" and "us" represents Joe's anxiety about the distance between their desires, but, although she briefly echoes his sense of the mood, she confirms their shared desires: "It's all so much / What *we* have always wanted" (*CP* 111; emph. added). They come together first by their shared labor of getting a fire and a meal and then by the invocation of another cycle, the anticipated visit of their adult son, who will share the love and labor of their new home, lending it a continuity it lacks. Frost's apparent desire here is to tell a story that reaches toward a conventional and emotional conclusion based in a family reunited. For me, at least, this desire highlights his own presence, which is much more evident than in "The Death of the Hired Man," in which he leaves more room for the reader and balances more skillfully the emotional and intellectual, lyric and narrative, concerns of the poem.

   "In the Home Stretch" zigzags between these poles.[91] Another playful moment on the idea of "lady" elicits from the wife an "unpoetic"—and ambivalent—affirmation of their happiness: "'Dumped down in paradise we are and happy.'" The dialogue that follows may be too baldly emotional for some readers' taste, but it clarifies Frost's debt to sentimental poetry as it exposes the framework of potentially conflicting desires that structures much of Frost's work but especially his dramatic poems. When Joe asks his wife, "'I'd like to know / If it is what you wanted, then how much / You wanted it for me'" (*CP* 113), cognizant of his worry, she generously assumes his attitude for her own and enables him to discuss his fears openly; furthermore, in naming the fears, she confirms her role as poet-visionary. When he tries to remember who first spoke of making a new home, her response again relieves him of responsibility:

> "My dear,
> It's who first thought the thought. You're searching, Joe,
> For things that don't exist; I mean beginnings.
> Ends and beginnings—there are no such things.
> There are only middles."

(CP 113)

As a proxy for the sympathetic poet, the wife rearticulates the tension that has circumscribed and structured the poem—between sentimental-romantic and realistic views of human existence. The couple have explored both: she, with her reflections on the numbing repetition of female chores and on the landscape that begins at her window and ends with the blank impassivity of the woods but that also offers the healing moon; he, with his insistence on who spoke first but with his recollection of the continuity provided by their son, Ed. If she is touched by sadness at the loss of a home, with his loving play he assures her of the continuity of their relationship: when she notes all that is not new around them, ending with "'you are not [new] to me, / Nor I to you,'" he teases, "'Perhaps you never were'" (*CP* 113). That is, he takes her wisdom about middles and accepts it to form an intercourse that prefigures the gentle sexual gesture he makes toward her at the end of the poem, as he invites her outside "'to grope / By starlight in the grass for a last peach / The neighbors may not have taken as their right / When the house wasn't lived in.'" Ultimately, as he confirms his own nurturing, feminine role, she recognizes and accepts his invitation to embrace the farm's bounty, an invitation that invokes the plenitude of their love: "'I know this much: / I'm going to put you in your bed, if first / I have to make you build it'" (*CP* 114). Accepting his sexual invitation, the wife confirms her—their—synthesis of apparent polarities, a synthesis that ultimately requires what the husband in "Home Burial" acknowledges, though from a wholly different perspective: "A man must partly give up being a man / With womenfolk."

Finally, though thematically the poem leaves unanswered the tension between realism and nostalgia, Frost wants to celebrate both the vitality of the pair's dialogue, in which each is able to share the other's point of view, and the renewing intimacy that speaks through and beyond ordinary words to a healing and mysterious body language:

When there was no more lantern in the kitchen,
The fire got out through crannies in the stove
And danced in yellow wrigglers on the ceiling,
As much at home as if they'd always danced there.

(*CP* 114)

While the narrative tension remains unresolved, the structural, figurative, and rhetorical movements of the poem achieve a kind of closure, resting between two points of view. The self-consciously and perhaps excessively figurative language in this last section forms a dialogue with the flattened and everyday language elsewhere of stoves, chairs, and weeds, affirming in effect the continuity between the two. At last, like Mary and Warren and unlike the pair in "Home Burial," the protagonists are "at home." Especially noteworthy is the role that the unnamed wife plays: poet-visionary, capable of seeing, articulating, and interpreting experience for her husband. Nevertheless, while the poem establishes her as its central character, the comfort and love achieved at the end are not possible without the husband's loving presence, just as a poem is not possible without the "husbandry" of the reader; if the poet shares the wife's realistic feminine perspective, he cannot imagine the home or the poem without the complementarity of a generous, loving other. Frost attempts to reinvent traditional oppositions— city and country, female and male, figurative and literal—into an inclusive, nonhierarchical, and dialogical "marriage." Here the wife is not only poet-speaker but also "reader" of past, present, and future, and Frost's portrait of her expresses hope that, for the feminine self, the home of the poem need not always be a place of silent confinement.[92]

As with "The Death of the Hired Man," we might end feeling skepticism for the apparent ideality of farm life that contrasts with the critique expressed by writers like Freeman, Cooke, and Frost himself; the conclusion seems to be located outside the worldly tensions of which gender relations were an integral part. We might also question the wife's apparent "conversion" to a utopian point of view, especially in the light of the poet's personal experience, as an example of wish-fulfillment. Sandra Katz suggests that Frost and Elinor's attitudes were the inverse of those expressed by the couple in the poem, which was published the year after the family moved into their Franconia, New Hampshire, farm. Katz affirms, "the first summer on the farm was perfect," and she describes in idyllic terms the activities in which the family participated: gardening, "picnics, botanizing excursions, blueberrying expeditions, and the neighborhood baseball games." But the idyll turned to nightmare in the face of renewed financial difficulties, a dangerous seventh pregnancy for Elinor, ending in miscarriage, and the severe winter weather conditions.[93] Given these circumstances, the affirmative ending of "In the Home Stretch" at least partly reflected desire rather than reality, and in this context the wife's affirmation, "dumped down in paradise we are and happy," acquires a painful irony.

In this light my initial story of "In the Home Stretch" reflects a utopian perspective fostered, perhaps, by the poet's conclusion that echoes his earlier-published sentimental poems like "Waiting," "Flower-Gathering," "A Line-Storm Song," and "A Prayer in Spring." This affirmative coming together of male and female perspectives is extremely rare in Frost's work, and in the formal and tonal tensions enacted by the poem we see him moving toward the disjunctions explored much more fully and dramatically in "The Witch of Coös" and "Maple," on which I will focus in the next chapter. In its very diction the poem not only performs a conflict between nostalgic and realistic constructions of the world but encodes the questions that, in the light of reviews of his work and a developing modernist critical practice that would value detachment over commitment and the aesthetic over the actual, would come to concern Frost ever more intimately (if not always consciously): How can I be a strong, recognizably masculine poet (a Poet, not a poetess like Freeman's Betsey Dole, doomed to oblivion) if I imagine subjectivity for others and de-emphasize myself? How can I achieve the authority of the male poet speaking in a (reconstructed, retrieved) male poetic tradition without erasing my understanding of the norms, including the emotional and economic norms, that regulate femininity? Can I accomplish these goals and still be popular, avoiding the intellectual classism of much modernist poetry and its accompanying criticism?[94]

In spite of the affirmative story that I have told about these narrative-dramatic poems, the problem of subjectivity in relation to audience sometimes resides uncomfortably within them, especially since regionalism, like sentimentalism, is often construed by feminist critics as a mode in which "the self exists . . . as part of the interdependent network of the community rather than as an individualistic unit."[95] This view of the fluid self and the supportive community seems to problematize the relationship that I have outlined between Frost's dramatic poems and New England regionalist fiction, inasmuch as the former often manifest an appalling *absence* of community. The husband and wife pair in each of the four poems that I have discussed in this chapter are effectively or literally alone with each other—the wife of "Home Burial" so desperate that she has to leave the house, the wife of "A Servant to Servants" so isolated that she tells the most intimate details of her life story to a stranger. Mary and Warren, on the other hand, are able to talk and, hence, to come together in a community of two. From one angle Mary's success in converting Warren to her perspective is related to her imaginative verbal creation of a community that includes Silas, Harold Wilson, and even Silas's stingy brother. "In the Home Stretch" portrays a community more directly, though ambivalently, in the persons of the (presumably local) moving men as well as the expected presence of the couple's son. If the reader represents another implied community for each of the poems, then we can conclude that in some sense Frost is attempting to situate these characters in a "narrative of community."[96] In the absence of the reader's presence, however, what we must notice is how often this attempt at community building *fails,* how isolated many of Frost's characters are, and (hence) how modernist is his vision.

But a response to this observation is, as my account has repeatedly suggested, that the regionalists *themselves* do not unanimously or uniformly portray rural life or community in the affirmative manner described by many feminist readers. Cooke's Mrs. Flint is worked to death not only because of the parsimony of her husband but also because the patriarchally defined local community refuses to assist her; in Freeman's "The Revolt of 'Mother'" the community rejects Sarah's self-assertiveness and sends the minister to intervene between her and her husband; the community members in the latter's "A Mistaken Charity" think it best to send the indigent heroines to an "old ladies'" home. Even when the result is favorable, as when Hetty, in Freeman's "Church Mouse," wins the right to remain as church deacon, she must triumph as an individual over the stubborn, jealous, and tradition-bound community, embodied in particular by the women. Not only are communities not always beneficent in female-authored New England regionalist texts; they are also often absent. The characters are frequently as secluded as were the Frosts themselves at times in Franconia, whether on failing farms (Freeman's "Taste of Honey") or in tidy town homes (her "New England Nun").[97]

What, if anything, redeems the grimness of this vision, both in Frost and in the regionalists? Whether directly or indirectly, both Zagarell and Fetterley point to the importance of storytelling as a means, in the latter's words, "to include rather than exclude, to heal rather than to harm": "In regionalist fiction, the impulse to dissolve binary oppositions and destabilize the definition of margin and center through shifting our perspective begins with a feeling that can best be described as empathy."[98] Zagarell takes a slightly different route toward the same destination: "only one with a distancing, interpretive 'seeing eye' and 'feeling heart' can identify the women's valor fully, and the defamiliarization to which such analysis gives rise is as essential to narrative of community as is the identification facilitated by empathy."[99] In the end we can choose to emphasize how, like their forebears in regionalist fiction, Frost's feminine-voiced narrative poems bear witness to the privations and necessities of rural female experience as they acknowledge "the feminine way of it, the mother way"[100] and engage the reader, however temporarily, in the necessary creation of a community, offering *both* a seeing eye *and* a feeling heart.

Invoking this complicated attitude, Frost's female voices dramatize what Rose Terry Cooke elaborated in her short story "The West Shetucket Railway." Cooke discusses the pressures of isolation, overwork, and "underfeeding" on rural farmers, and she highlights the consequences of these forces on their wives, in a description both sentimental and realistic that can serve as a frame for many of Frost's narrative poems:

> When you bring to bear on these poor, weak souls, made for love and gentleness and bright outlooks[, the effects of] the daily dullness of work, the brutality, stupidness, small craft, and boorish tyranny of husbands, to whom they are tied beyond escape, what wonder is it that a third of all the female lunatics in our asylums are farmers' wives? that domestic tragedies, even beyond the scope of a sensation novel, recur daily in these lonely houses, far beyond human help or hope?[101]

In sharp contrast to this insider's perspective offered by Cooke, "Local Color and After," a 1919 editorial in the aptly named *The Nation,* castigated the "strongly, often stiflingly domestic atmosphere which hangs over most of these [local color] stories"—their debilitating femininity. Sensing the mood of literary studies articulated in this essay and anticipating the diminishment of local color, with its vivid and empowering representations of feminine orality, Frost would move from a poetics of empathy toward a poetics of presence embodied in a manly and detached lyric poetry that would secure his situation in a tradition of national and international, not simply regional, literature.[102]

## Chapter 3

# "Lightning or a Scribble"
## Bewitched by the Mother Tongue

In "Christmas Trees" Frost acknowledges "the trial by market everything must come to" (*CP* 104). With the market in mind he must have been delighted with some of the reviews of *New Hampshire*. John Farrar observed:

> Quaint, genial, humorous, wisely tolerant, he is not only a writer of grim, dramatic portraits but of lyrics whose precision and beauty are overpowering, and of bits of Yankee whimsicality that are irresistible because they are both funny and true. As a man he is gentle, humorful, and kindly. It is difficult for me to write sanely of Robert Frost; for, in my opinion, he is one of the few great poets America has ever produced. (*CR* 55)

In similar terms Untermeyer claims that "[the poet's] work is distinguished—even impelled—by a rare and fantastic mind" (*CR* 64), and he concludes his review using superlatives that rival Farrar's: "With absolute freedom from contemporary fashions, technical trickery, or the latest erudite slang, Frost has created a poetry which is at one time full of heat and humor, a poetry that belongs not only to the America of our own day but to the richest records of English verse" (*CR* 65). Even more interesting for the present discussion is Untermeyer's observation of the shift in Frost's poetry from predominantly narrative in *North of Boston* and predominantly lyric in *Mountain Interval* to a mixture in *New Hampshire* (*CR* 62), for the portrait that Frost forwards is of a poet who is advancing, developing, yet retaining all his old virtues.[1] As Linda Wagner points out, Untermeyer reassures readers that they will find in the new volume the Frost with whom they had become comfortable: "Nothing, really, has changed. The idiom is clearer, the convictions have deepened—the essential things, the point of view, the tone of voice, remain the same" (*CR* 63).

But something *has* changed. For one thing Frost's lyrics more often represent a masculine speaker; poems like "Fire and Ice," "The Aim Was Song," and "For Once, Then, Something" transform the hospitable and affective access of his more sentimental lyrics to a harder, more intellectual challenge. In spite of the poet's indirect claim via the girl speaker at the end of "Wild Grapes," that "nothing tells me / That I need learn to let go with my heart," (*CP* 185), this kind of tenacity must more and more be masked. Perhaps most vividly, the radical, empathic recognition of the circumstances of rural people's lives and, especially, the appreciation of women's perspectives and powerful use of women's voices in many of the narrative-dramatic poems are being replaced by a more ambivalent and occasionally even hostile attitude, prefigured by the husband's words to his wife in "Snow":

> "You like your fun as well as anyone;
> Only you women have to put these airs on
> To impress men. You've got us so ashamed
> Of being men we can't look at a good fight
> Between two boys and not feel bound to stop it."
>
> (*CP* 140)

In *New Hampshire* Frost more often imagines himself in more problematic relationship to women characters and feminine voices, and after this point he censors them almost entirely, with the exception of the witty and ambiguous *Masques*.[2]

This chapter studies Frost's shifting alliances and their relationship to his self-conception and situation vis-à-vis readers, implied and real. While his self-transformation is scarcely linear or unequivocal, *New Hampshire* highlights it most plainly. Focusing on two matrices, "Two Witches" and "Maple," which review uneasily his participation in gender and genre hierarchies and his assumption of feminine voices, I argue that at some level Frost ultimately understood these voices as unmanning, circumscribing him into amateur literary circles. Framing Frost's gendered concern for professional status, section 1 addresses the relationship in the poet's mind of masculinity to popularity and gender to genre. In the context of a feminized popular oral literature, or "gossip," Frost's regionalist poetry evinces less a tension between oral and literate speech than between feminine and masculine kinds of orality. The next section explores his layering of perspectives in "The Witch of Coös," indicative of his unease about what is possibly his most powerful feminine voice and his parallel discomfort about poetic legitimacy; at the same time, it underscores the continuity of his earlier feminine affiliations in the poignant performance of "The Pauper Witch of Grafton." "The Tutelory Genius of the Nation" focuses on the poet's self-transformation from farmer-gossip to bard, suggesting the implication of genre (regionalism) in the poet's development of a national or even "universal" voice. In the discussion that follows we see how "Maple" reconfigures the poet's relationship to his regional subject matter and characters, stripping the feminine voice of its subjective authority and substituting a detached masculine presence. Interrogating once again the idea of strictly linear development in the poetry, the concluding section ("My best bid for remembrance") outlines the *overlay* of feminine and masculine, sentimental, regionalist, and modernist voices/stances in the poems of *New Hampshire*, inviting readers to acknowledge their continuity as much as their difference, as we preview the poet's ultimate departure from a poetics of empathy.

### "The cave of the mouth": Orality and Gender

No wonder poets sometimes have to *seem*
So much more business-like than business men.
Their wares are so much harder to get rid of.
                                        —"New Hampshire"

The relationship in Frost between form and gender remains a complex and circuitous one inflected by his attitude to the literary marketplace. The title poem of *New Hampshire,* which appeared a full seven years after *Mountain Interval,* makes explicit his concern—revealed in the letters as an obsession—with popularity and sales, which measured his ability to support his family and, hence, his masculinity.[3] We cannot take at face value (nor, of course, are we meant to) the narrator's claim in the first stanza that "the having anything to sell is what / Is the disgrace in man or state or nation," though Frost would certainly have understood Emily Dickinson's "Publication—is the Auction / Of the Mind of Man."[4] While presented in a witty and playful voice, the poem worries repeatedly about the idea of sales and financial gain, suggesting the poet's profound anxiety about such matters. His ultimate desire is to *appear* "to be a plain New Hampshire farmer / With an income in cash of, say, a thousand / (From say a publisher in New York City)" (*CP* 151, 162). But how to earn such an income? By confirming the public opinion, providing a commodity that is valued, familiar? Yet how to ensure one's longevity within a nascent poetic (and critical) tradition formed by an elite community that "respected the dramatically inventive rather than the subtle kind of experimentation that suffused Frost's poetry" (*CR* xiv), especially given the reductive critical accounts of women-authored regionalism that framed his writing? Finally, Frost wanted it both ways: to be a poet for all Americans, not only "those who read the *Atlantic* with pleasure" but also "the emerging avant-garde" who read Harriet Monroe's *Poetry*.[5]

An ambition for such a dual audience in the modernist era must inevitably precipitate an anxiety about form in a poet as putatively "traditional" as Frost. If, as Sandra Gilbert notes of Whitman and Dickinson, "lapses of gender, indeed, seem to occur because of lapses of genre rather than the other way around," we can invert this idea in the case of Frost and his own "not poetry," which, as we have seen, the earlier narratives appeared to many readers to be.[6] In the same year that *New Hampshire* was published, Frost himself assessed with prescient accuracy his claims on a future literary canon, writing to Untermeyer, "Stopping by Woods on a Snowy Etc. is my best bid for remembrance" (*LU* 163). More obviously "poetic" than, say, "Home Burial," it evoked the nostalgic and even sentimental attitude for the country desired by popular readers while concealing beneath its snowy surface enough irony to please "intellectual" readers, though even many of *them* would miss it. That Frost's assessment was correct is indicated by Farrar's comment in the review cited earlier: "Turn to these lyrics and you find half a dozen poems that you'll remember forever. 'Stopping by Woods on a Snowy Evening' is as simple as nature herself—as inevitable—as beautiful" (*CR* 58).

We can trace in the poet's letters about his poetics the gender dispute that is elaborated partly in genre terms. In an early (1914) letter to Sidney Cox, for example, he emphasizes the necessarily conversational element of "living" poetry; without the "tones" of contemporary "talk" (not "Greek and Roman talk") the language becomes a dead language, the poetry dead poetry (*SL* 107). Writing to John Bartlett a month later, Frost famously reiterates and develops these ideas; about the "sentence sound," he writes, "They are apprehended by the ear. They are gathered by the ear from the vernacular and brought into books. . . . The most original writer only catches them from talk, where they grow spontaneously." The genderedness of this familiar idea appears in the next two paragraphs:

> A man is a writer if *all* his words are strung on recognizable sentence sounds. The voice of the imagination, the speaking voice must know certainly how to behave how to posture in every sentence he offers.

A man is a marked writer if his words are largely strung on the more strik-
ing sentence sounds. (*SL* 111)

"A man . . . a man": these words are not neutral for Frost; language "caught
fresh from the mouths of people" is engendered by male writers (*SL* 113).
At the end of the same year Frost again asserts to Cox: "I want the unmade
words to work with, not the familiar made ones that everybody exclaims
Poetry! at. Of course the great fight of any poet is against the people who
want *him* to write in a special language that has gradually separated from
spoken language."[7] Perhaps most striking is his remark to Walter Pritchard
Eaton in 1915 (note the characteristic economic reference): "All I care a
cent for is to catch sentence tones that haven't been brought to book. I dont
say to make them, mind you, but to catch them. No one makes them or
adds to them. They are always there—living in the cave of the mouth. They
are real cave things: they were before words were" (*SL* 191). "Brought to
book" or brought to bed with child, "living in the cave of the mouth" or
the cave of the womb, the poet's creativity parallels procreativity—and
hence, perhaps, another need to identify as masculine.

In tandem with his reliance on formal written traditions, Frost's insis-
tence on spoken language and the vernacular redefines, wittingly or unwit-
tingly, a binary that resonates throughout American poetry and American
literature more generally: the relationship between the oral and the written,
their gender affiliations, and their investment in matters of popularity and
canonicity. For example, whereas Whitman's brawny "barbaric yawp"—
which Frost, following such precursors as Longfellow and Oakes Smith,
makes suitable for genteel audiences—claims oral speech for men, in *Walden*
Thoreau envisions such orality as an uncivilized "mother tongue":[8]

> there is a memorable interval between the spoken and the written language,
> the language heard and the language read. The one is commonly transitory, a
> sound, a tongue, a dialect merely, and we learn it unconsciously, like the
> brutes, of our mothers. The other is the maturity and experience of that; if that
> is our mother tongue, this is our father tongue, a reserved and select expres-
> sion, too significant to be heard by the ear, which we must be born again in
> order to speak.[9]

Unlike Frost, Thoreau insists on the father tongue apprehended in the liter-
ate languages of Greek and Latin. Feminizing oral speech, and by extension
storytelling, Thoreau effectively, if unwittingly, marginalizes all those who
carry their traditions on their tongues.

Ironically, the sentimental, mainstream poets of the nineteenth century, many of them women, forwarded this "literate" art in contrast to the profoundly oral Whitman, whose own work is mediated and sometimes moderated by his self-conception not only as a *man* but also (what we would today call) a *gay* man.[10] Nevertheless, however much Whitman's practice was informed by orality, it was also shaped fundamentally by an acute awareness of his place in a male-authored literary tradition and the charge of "effeminacy" that he, like Frost—as we will see in chapter 4—would have to guard against. Writing himself into literary history as a professional *male* poet, Whitman's task was one that the insistently oral Frost would also have to accomplish, Thoreau notwithstanding, in order to achieve self-defined manhood.[11] If writing poetry in the late nineteenth and early twentieth centuries had become, in the view of many male modernists, a decidedly "lady-like," or soft, occupation, it was up to Frost to make it hard and immediate once again. What is a poem, anyway? And what kind of a person is a poet, especially one who emphasizes spoken language? As Walter J. Ong underscores, New Criticism was deeply invested in a literate, text-based method that "insisted that the poem or other literary work be regarded as an object, a 'verbal icon'"; in spite of this criticism's focus on vernacular (rather than Latin) discourses, it shifted earlier criticism away from "a residually oral (rhetorical, contextual) mentality."[12]

Within this developing interpretive matrix Frost's response (in 1918) to Thoreau (whether conscious or not) was to emphasize the poetry of the elevated everyday and vernacular:

> There are two kinds of language, the spoken language and the written language—our everyday speech which we call vernacular; and a more literary, sophisticated, artificial, elegant language that belongs to books. . . . we rather expect people to write in a literary, somewhat artificial style. I, myself, could get along very well without this bookish language altogether. . . . We've got to come down to this speech of everyday, to begin with . . . but there is some sort of obligation laid on us, to lift the words of every day, to give them a metaphorical turn.[13]

If Whitman's effort was to free himself and poetry from the indoor language of the parlor (which he nevertheless, characteristically, does not reject), Frost's was to make rugged outdoor talk poetic. As the preceding discussion indicates, any critical generalization that we might attempt to make between gender and genre is problematic without a historical and biographical context in which to situate it. And, as I observed in chapter 1, for example, nineteenth-century popular poetry was practiced by male as well as female writers; consequently, we can speak of cultural affiliations and the "feminization" of lyric in this period only by acknowledging the non-sex-specific application of the term. In the context of the present discussion it becomes important to reemphasize that *sentimental writer* and *regionalist,* like *feminine* and *masculine,* can be seen as metaphors for ways of imagining and representing the self in relation to others and that their historical manifestations determine their gender affiliation at a particular moment. These affiliations often shift, as we have seen, within the framework of a later critical or cultural paradigm; hence, the "orality" explored by Thoreau, Whitman, and Frost himself is neither identical nor intrinsically gendered.

One strand of orality woven thick into the texture of regionalism, and in particular the New England regionalism with which Frost was often associated, is private conversations, often between women:

> "I must say that with all her virtues she never was a first-class housekeeper, but I wouldn't say it to any but a friend. You never eat no preserves o' hers that wa'n't commencing to work, an' you know as well as I how little forethought she had about putting away her woolens. I sat behind her once in meetin' when I was stoppin' with the Tremletts and so occupied a seat in their pew, an' I see between ten an' a dozen moth millers come workin' out o' her fitch-fur tippet. They was flutterin' round her bonnet same's 'twas a lamp. I should be mortified to death to have such a thing happen to me."
>
> "Every housekeeper has her weak point; I've got mine as much as anybody else," acknowledged Mercy Crane with spirit, "but you never see no moth millers come workin' out o' me in a public place."[14]

As this passage from Jewett's "The Passing of Sister Barsett" intimates, a central feature of much of this vernacular fiction resides in its alliance with a form of gossip (and, thus, with lowbrow art). Sarah Ellen Dow, a poor woman who has gone to watch during the illness of a friend, is angry over being displaced by the friend's sisters, of whom she says to her friend Mercy Crane, "now they thought she was re'lly goin' to die, they come settlin' down like a pair o' old crows in a field to pick for what they could get." At one point she tells Mrs. Crane: "I set there in the kitchen within call an' waited, an' . . . I heard 'em sayin', 'There, she's gone, she's gone!'" Rushing out of the house, she goes to Mrs. Crane's on her way home, and the two have a lively discussion about the merits and faults of their friend, only to learn rather awkwardly that she has not died at all. Sarah Ellen is "dazed": "'I don't know but we might as well laugh as cry,' she said in an aimless sort of way. 'I know you too well to think you're going to repeat a single word.'"[15] The pleasure of the gossip lies in large measure in the intimacy that develops between the two women, mirrored in their actions of sharing food as well as in the reader's access to their intimacy.

With Jewett, Freeman, Brown, and others, Robert Frost's regionalist writing shares this pleasure in gossip that in some sense is a defining feature of the genre. The poet acknowledges his stance when he writes to William Braithwaite in 1915: "I like the actuality of gossip, the *intimacy* of it. Say what you will effects of *intimacy* and actuality are the greatest aim an artist can have. The sense of *intimacy* gives the thrill of sincerity" (*SL* 159; emph. added). Frost's critics have noted this quality in his writing: "[His] anecdotes are told in a discursive, racy way, which may cause us to overlook their psychological penetration, the technical skill of their verse . . . and the economy of means behind their apparent ranginess." More recently, William Pritchard has observed that "no poet I can think of, with the possible exception of Oscar Wilde, put forth 'gossip' as an ideal vehicle to express those qualities [of actuality and intimacy]."[16]

An important feature of gossip, especially in relation to Frost's work, that these readers' accounts elide becomes clear in Patricia Meyer Spacks's *Gossip:* its genderedness. Spacks highlights a number of significant features that offer useful contexts for a further discussion of Frost's regionalism and his gendered transformation from what we might call "gossip" to "bard." Certainly, gossip's quality of playfulness recalls one of the poet's familiar modes, and its ability to call "attention to ambiguities of facticity and interpretation" as well as to raise "questions about boundaries, authority, distance, the nature of knowledge" seems readily applicable to poems like "The Housekeeper," "A Servant to Servants," "The Fear," and many other dramatic-narrative poems.[17] Four features of gossip seem particularly pertinent at this juncture: its creation of intimacy with an auditor and its ability to create, for positive or negative uses, a community; its uses of power; its alliance with the erotic; and its affiliation with women.

Of the first of these features Spacks observes, "Surfaces are not superficial: talk that dwells on the surfaces of life, even talk that sounds like mere chatter, may constitute a form of intimate relationship."[18] She identifies two ends of a continuum, the hurtful kind of malicious gossip that "damages reputations and hurts feelings" and that actually enables gossipers to detach themselves from intimacy with one another via a focus on others. At the other end lies a "serious" and intimate gossip that "takes place in private, at leisure, in a context of trust, usually among no more than two or three people. Its participants use talk about others to reflect about themselves, to express wonder and uncertainty and to locate certainties, to enlarge their knowledge of one another."[19] The potentially harmful consequences of gossip suggest its potential power. One of gossip's traditional arenas is that of sexuality, but it turns out that the activity itself is eroticized, becoming a form of voyeurism.[20] As we see in "The Passing of Sister Barsett," the exploration of Sister Barsett's character involves an intimate, even secretive, attention to her body, with the moths evoking a revolting staleness, not simply of her clothing but of her corporeal self. Spacks notes that "gossip, like sexual intercourse, belongs to a hidden life. Sex and gossip alike comprise modes of intimate communication; both epitomize the unpredictable and uncontrollable. Like sex, gossip serves impulse and has explosive potential. Passionate attacks on the secret life of words parallel warnings about the secret life of the body."[21] And not just any body, but women's bodies, for it is women who must guard their words as zealously as they do their physical selves. Regionalist writers like Jewett, Freeman, and Brown explore the dimensions of gossip and the sanctions placed on women, often in a realm apart from men: "Now we've got red [rid] o' the men-folks," said Mrs. Robbins, "'le's se' down an' talk it over."[22] Orality, at least in this form and from this (female) source, engenders suspicion at the least or, more stringently, censure and silencing. Spacks observes that gossip occupies "the borderlands of socially sanctioned oral discourse," and she constructs an analogy between gossip and indeterminate literary genres, such as biography, autobiography, published letters, and published diaries, asking, "where do we draw the line—and what line, exactly, do we draw?"[23]

This interstitial generic situation of gossip corresponds to and forms a paradigm for Frost's "not poetry," located by contemporary critics somewhere between a feminized kind of literature and a kind of feminized everyday speech. Struggling to revise his public image, Frost attempts to remake his voice into the professional, canonical, and national—not local—one of bard, which in his rendition encompasses not only "the ancient oral tradition" but also "the refreshing legend of the 'dry' Yankee sage."[24] Leading ultimately to the more masculine voice explored in chapter 5, both the identification of gossip with femininity and the poetic selfhood required of the retailer of gossip provoke Frost's discomfort, figured in the layered perspectives and shifting voices in "The Witch of Coös," to which I will turn in a moment. To be a gossip was not only to be (once again) feminized; it was also to be part of lowbrow rather than highbrow art. Ironically, for many critics Frost's image as bard represented a cheap imitation of the "real" poet revealed in *North of Boston,* and the potential (and actual) commercialism of much of his work in *New Hampshire* and afterward thrust him back into the realm of merely popular versifier (in one sense a contemporary manifestation of a writer like Lydia Sigourney) who could later write in "On Being Chosen Poet of Vermont":

> Breathes there a bard who isn't moved
> When he finds his verse is understood
> And not entirely disapproved
> By his country and his neighborhood?

> (*CP* 477)

## "They did all the talking": Conjuring the Poet

> Social unacceptability and political censorship, personal prohibitions and cultural conventions, the literary market and language itself all contribute to the shaping of stories. Yet untold stories press for a hearing.
> —Priscilla Wald, *Constituting Americans,*
> *Cultural Anxiety and Narrative Form*

Both Ann Douglas Wood and Josephine Donovan have argued that the local color writers regarded themselves in opposition to their sentimental precursors, that they attempted to create a countertradition to a weak and melodramatic past.[25] The desire of these writers to separate themselves from an earlier tradition is ironic in Frost's historical moment, when female-authored regionalist fiction had itself come under fire as modernist writers (both male and female) endeavored to re-create literature, to "make it new." Disparaging realist practice—not only by writers like Jewett, Freeman, and Deland but also by a feminized Howells—as actually sentimental, the modernists attempted to reinvent both fiction and poetry as masculine *and* to claim for themselves professional status, abetted in this project by the incipient professionalization of literary studies and masculinization of the academy. Yet earlier male poets had also had to assert their masculinity in the face of a sentimental tradition: in 1900 Stedman affirmed protectively (in the introduction to his canon-making anthology of American poetry ) that "the work of [women's] brother poets is not emasculate, and will not be while grace and tenderness fail to make men cowards, and beauty remains the flower of strength."[26] And we should recall that Howells, after

linking Frost with the regionalism of Jewett, Freeman, and Brown, found it
necessary to highlight the poet's masculinity. Frost's continuing link with
regionalist fiction was not unproblematic, for "the masculine status of realist
fiction was itself made suspect by its investment in the domestic and by the
fuller emergence of fiction by women."[27] However much it might have
endeared him to popular readers, making poetry from gossip was not likely
to render his affiliations less suspect to increasingly powerful academic critics.

The continuum of gossip from harmful to serious suggests a parallel
with the analytical paradigms for regarding regionalist fiction reviewed in
the previous chapter, inasmuch as those who engage in the former are more
likely to consider (or construct) themselves as *outside* a community—
whether or not they are literally or physically detached from it—rather than
*inside* it. Yet "stranger" and "native" are unstable categories; and the
"ambivalence about belonging to the community and being a stranger to it,
and to oneself, operates as one of the most important strategies of regional
writing."[28] The poems at the center of discussion in chapter 2, as well as
many of Frost's other dramatic poems, either incorporate the literal figure of
an external listener to local gossip or enact a contiguous role, making the
stranger familiar and hence eliciting empathy in the reader-"listener." The
issues of perspective and self-representation, and Frost's consequent status as
a professional, "legitimate," and masculine poet, blister forth in two transi-
tional poems, "The Witch of Coös" and "Maple." Here the poet makes,
respectively, his most intimate and sustained foray into, and most self-con-
scious discussion about, those voices, imagining them not simply as power-
ful but overwhelming: the erotic magic of a mother tongue, enacted in the
uncivilized terms elaborated by Thoreau, bewitches the poet and the reader
with its presence or numbs with its absence. Both poems rehearse the dan-
gerous, sexualized, and seductive gossip of rural life along an uncertain con-
tinuum of intimacy with the reader, as the events described are bordered by
a reporter whose desires are frequently ambivalent and guarded and whose
situation as outsider or insider is in question.

As it has threatened to do in "A Servant to Servants" beneath the
weight of men in the home, the feminine voice erupts into putative mad-
ness in "The Witch of Coös," while in "Maple" Frost's presence manifests
itself not in empathy and engagement, but as a more detached, more indi-
vidualized speaker and implied "reader" of his own work, engendering a
similar situation in actual readers. The tension between inside and outside
readers and speakers matters, for, "in its figuration of the narrator, regional-
ism highlights and affirms the cultural authority of a narrator to represent

and interpret the inhabitants of a region, and makes certain decisions about who may have what we would call psychological ful[l]ness, a textual convention which realism rarely questions. In turn, this convention allows us to look at who was granted character, personhood, status, and individuality."²⁹ We could say that "The Pauper Witch of Grafton," for example, grants its narrator "psychological fullness," performing serious, intimate gossip, and that it represents a liberation of the sexual forces that the narrator attempts to circumscribe in "The Witch of Coös"—but we could as easily regard the poem as voyeuristic. Nevertheless, with such poems as "The Fear," "The Housekeeper," and "Snow," "The Witch of Coös," "The Pauper Witch of Grafton," and "Maple" represent most overtly the dangerous, repressed feminine voice in Frost's poems and in the canon of Frost's poems, for, if Frost ultimately normalized his own voice, his actual readers, both traditional and feminist, have abetted in that project.

"The Witch of Coös" has generated a wide range of responses, from Clement Wood's curmudgeonly statement that it is "a weird mixture—tepidly interesting, if authentic, but utterly below the rollicking greatness of 'Tom o' Shanter,'" to Bogan's perception that it (with the pauper witch poem) reveals "the utmost insight into, and sympathy with, woman's nature and character beset by time" and Jeffrey Meyers's observation that the poem is "a ghost—or skeleton—story inspired by the heroines in the tales of Edgar Poe who burst the confines of their coffins." Moreover, as Robert Faggen affirms, "The poem can be read, in part, as a satire of the burgeoning spiritualist movement in the late nineteenth and early twentieth centuries in general and the two major forces it became associated with: science and feminism. . . . In 'The Witch of Coös' the pretense of spiritualism hides a visceral game of sexual selection." It is significant that Oster, with her affirmative view of readers' relations with Frost's poems, omits "The Witch of Coös" entirely, while Kearns incorporates it into her story of the threat of a feminine voice, locating Frost's voice in the poem in the "brief, dry voice of the 'visitor'" as well as the son's voice, "as [the poet] translates himself out of complicity in this tale of sex and violence by making his 'story' about strangers."³⁰ Perhaps this repudiation is necessary because in "The Witch" questions about sexuality and power are linked so intimately with those of cultural and psychological gender.³¹ Patricia Wallace centers on the witch's "power to trespass boundaries," which include the limits of "imagination," for she is "an entertainer, a *story teller,* a *magician,* a *conjurer,*" and an outsider who renders problematic the nature of "truth" and of power itself.³²

The tension over issues of home, labor, sexuality, and, most significantly, poetic identity are chillingly conjured in the regionalist-inflected "Witch of Coös," whose narrative is at once lurid and banal: a visitor to a farm records a dialogue between the witch-narrator and her son in which they remember her adultery, the murder of her lover by her and her husband many years before, and the subsequent "fantastic" "resurrection" of the lover's bones come back to haunt her. The thematics of love and betrayal shade into the poem's more important business: via the characters that it imagines, we find an implicit, performative account of a masculine (self-centered, detached, autonomous) poet's place in a poem, of his voice married to or embedded in the witch's and, finally, of a (male) reader's role in the creative drama, which in the retelling invokes gossip's uses of power, its alliances with the erotic, and its affiliation with women. The shaman-storyteller witch's voice, as both subject and object, surpasses that of the ostensible poet-speaker and brings into question his (and our) relation to her and, ultimately, his own legitimacy: Is he merely engaging in the titillation of gossip as it is purveyed by a male outsider?

Eventually inhabiting all of the poem's slippery subjectivities, from the husband to the witch herself, this poet-speaker tries to distance himself from the beginning:

> I stayed the night for shelter at a farm
> Behind the mountains, with a mother and son,
> Two old-believers. They did all the talking.
>
> (CP 187)

Detaching himself from the irrationality and mysticism of mother and son, he invites us to "forget" that it is *he* who actually does "all the talking." Inspired by their speech, he makes us wonder if the witch takes on a traditional role as Muse or whether the poet-speaker himself is not thrust into the background as mere mouthpiece or ventriloquist. His banality contrasts vividly with the electric and intimate quality of her speech, a speech that is emphatically oral, nonprofessional, and threatening. Indeed, as Gilbert and Gubar note in another context, "Even when the female imagination is incarnated in a nonprofessional teller of tales . . . its newly established primacy seems able to rob the male interlocutor of his ancient potency."[33]

From this perspective one of the many roles that the visitor-poet enacts is that of the son; serving as a catalyst for her charismatic voice, he initiates his controlling mother's revelation: "'You wouldn't want to tell him what we have / Up attic, mother?'" (*CP* 188). Acting as intermediary between the visitor-speaker and his mother as well as between the reader-listener and his mother, he dramatizes the incestuous intimacy that he shares with her by revealing that he knows both her psychological torment ("'Mother hears it in the night, / Halting perplexed behind the barrier / Of door and head-board'") and the details of her betrayal of her husband. Furthermore, his language confirms the vision of the witch-poet, for he describes the lover's removal from cellar to attic in words as confidently (if comically) poetic as her own: "'It left the cellar forty years ago / And carried itself like a pile of dishes / Up one flight from the cellar to the kitchen.'" Yet his speaking power largely exhausts itself by line 35, for he admits his perspective is infantile in comparison with the mother's: "'I was a baby: I don't know where I was'" (*CP* 188). That he has been privy to her most intimate secrets, however, is evident. At this point we might gather that he is the "illegitimate" product of the unholy union of the mother and her lover, a socially subversive "utterance" of her body—but he inherits her "knowl-edge" without her vision and remains silent until the end.[34]

From this moment the licentious mother gives birth to her own narra-tive, bewitching her son, the traveler, and the reader with a voice that mar-ries free orality and free sexuality. In the face of her uncivilized power the narrator must relinquish his own control and open ("the cave" of) his mouth to her voice, as his already feminized gossip becomes translated into her intimate story. As she reflects first on her sexual detachment from her inadequate husband, we wonder: Are we to feel sympathy here or anxiety? Are all external readers invited to respond in the same way? As transsexual speaker and paralyzed listener, the narrator-poet rehearses her self-alienation as lover and wife, empowered speaker and silent partner. In the social struc-tures of which she is presumably a part, the witch chooses to be an outsider, chooses her "vision" of "madness," which fascinates as it repels the narrator-reader. The madness incorporates a projection of her deviant pregnancy ("The bulkhead double-doors were double-locked / And swollen tight and buried under snow"), a conception that echoes and figures her facility with language while it once again confirms her sexual (un)availability. Carried away by her vision, both in the moment of its occurrence and in its reen-actment for the speaker-poet himself echoing her voice, the mother mar-ginalizes her dead lover (just as she herself is culturally marginal), symbol-ized by her rejection of his bones. He seeks an emotional and physical proximity with her that, in her story of appropriation by the cultural norm of monogamy, she must deny. First, "'the bones didn't try / The door; they halted helpless on the landing, / Waiting for things to happen in their favor'" (*CP* 189). Passive, longing, when she "'flung the door wide on him,'" making him vulnerable, "'a moment he stood balancing with emotion, / And all but lost himself'" and then "'he came at me with one hand outstretched, / The way he did in life once'" (189). Appearing to external readers to be gentle, caring, ghastly, hilarious, the dead lover intimates the wife's repressed sexual and emotional longing, while he embodies her powerful rejection.

The witch's vision of the silent lover reverberates in the poet-speaker, who by virtue of his own gender is allied with an unholy trinity of father-husband, son, and ghost lover, for whom the most frightening knowledge remains that of the untamable mother tongue in his own mouth, in a self-effacing, adulterous, and incestuous coupling of his "I"/eye with that of the cultural and poetic other. All the males in the ostensibly real world, the world that the poem seems to mimic yet really only shadows, possess power over the mother tongue, yet only by imagining himself as a version of the murderous husband can the speaker retain his power over her, for, under her spell like the dead lover, he too is dismembered from culture and divorced from his voice, so that the poetic lines of his bones look like "'lightning or a scribble.'" Even as a mirror of the husband, however, the visitor-speaker-reader is alienated from the radical verbal and erotic power that the witch represents, unless he accepts her weird gossip as his own. Lajway has no vision to compare with hers; she has to conjure up for him the image of the dead lover: "'It's the bones.' / 'What bones?' 'The cellar bones—out of the grave.'" She imagines the lover singing then orchestrates his entrapment: "'The steps began to climb the attic stairs. / I heard them. Toffile didn't seem to hear them'" (*CP* 190). This moment represents not the wife's hallucination but the *husband's* radical lack of imagination, a lack he shares with the son. (And by proxy, Frost invites us to ask, with the male narrator? With a resisting reader?)

Perhaps the most troubling relationship in the poem is that between mother and son, suggesting Frost's unease with his own upbringing. Thompson argues that, reared in a predominantly female context, Frost revered his mother's struggle to sustain the integrity of the family but also saw her as frighteningly powerful. As a boy, he often felt himself possessed by the same mystical voices and visions that she revealed to him, and, as an adolescent, he felt that his life was too heavily subjected to feminine influence.[35] A part of this influence was her poetic and storytelling abilities; hence, Frost's search for affiliation concerns itself not simply with his literary precursors but with literal, familial ones. The inspired presence of Frost's mother reverberates in his re-creation of the witch. Whether Toffile's or the lover's, the son is an *illegitimate* extension of either when compared with the bewitching power of the feminine voice, which commands him at the end, "'Tell the truth for once'" (*CP* 191). Though it is unclear whether or not *she* tells the truth, the witch's complicity with the son, their "lying" together, suggests once again the incestuous relationship between a mother-muse and son-poet:

> "Son looks surprised to see me end a lie
> We'd kept up all these years between ourselves
> So as to have it ready for outsiders.
> But tonight I don't care enough to lie—
> I don't remember why I ever cared.
> Toffile, if he were here, I don't believe
> Could tell you why he ever cared himself. . . ."

(CP 192)

Both linguistic and psychic, her structural "return" to the husband mocks his specious control over her tongue as it emphasizes her control over the illegitimate son's—and narrator-poet's—speech. In part, perhaps, she exorcises her ghosts by sharing their presence in language like the wife in "A Servant to Servants," but, more important, the narrator-listener has acquired the status of captivated if unwilling intimate in the "inadvertent" telling of the tale. We must ask a question that will secure more direct attention in the next chapter: Is he repeating this gossip to engender an intimacy with a *male* listener-reader, objectifying the witch as a means of homosocial and patriarchal empowerment?

In some sense the narrator-poet or the listener-reader provides the occasion that enables the tale to be told. But, if the last four lines emphasize the masculine outsider's desire for ultimate control over the mother tongue, they also underline his alienation and detachment from that voice and its explosive erotic potential:

> She hadn't found the finger-bone she wanted
> Among the buttons poured out in her lap.
> I verified the name next morning: Toffile.
> The rural letter box said Toffile Lajway.

(CP 192)

In the wonderful/awful pun "to file away," the narrator quietly questions the truth of her story and, while affirming the husband's name, suggests that this name may have been *all* that was true. Appropriating the speaking power of the witch, he attempts to domesticate it at the end with the button box and the "rural letter box"; both images suggest womblike enclosure. What seems odd about this conclusion is that the narrator tries to verify only the witch's *husband's* name, as if he—and the mailbox, their link to the (rational) outside world—is complicit in silencing her. In the traditional terms of the patriarchal family, "translated" onto and into a masculine lexicon, her story is after all the story of the cuckolded Toffile.[36] In this drama "home" signifies a disruptive place to be feared, for it represents the scene of betrayal—in the wife's adultery, in her linguistic exposure of Toffile as a cuckolded husband, and in her ambiguous "betrayal" of feminine power and masculine impotence: the narrator's gesture of control at the end seems trivial and anticlimactic when compared to her voice. As in "A Servant to Servants," home conveys both the potential for madness and for potent poetic intercourse. "The Witch of Coös" imagines violent male intervention and sexual jealousy as the source of the former, while it lacks—and this point is crucial—the deep sympathy that fosters and surrounds Len's wife's tale and the subjectivity that the poet enables there. That is, the witch is what Len's wife becomes without the emotional husbandry of the reader.

Her imagined relationship with the reader is perhaps the most complex and problematic element of this narrative. While feminine readers may find themselves sympathetic with the witch, the initial rhetorical positioning of the narrator as reader, and his fear-awe of her, make such sympathy more difficult to achieve. From one perspective giving us only a peephole through which to view the show, he invites us to become masculine voyeurs regarding a strange and objectified woman as outsiders. In envisioning us as intimate with or identical to the narrator, Frost requires that immasculated readers enter the poem as spellbound as he, for the witch and the poem make love to language itself, highlighting its compelling grasp of all who come near. The intensity of this grasp is potentially terrifying to the male reader-narrator, for it offers not understanding but violent appropriation, posing a threat to his coherent identity. In contrast to the more benign access of the poems in chapter 2, "The Witch of Coös" provides a deranged double vision that distances as it compels attention.

One measure of this distancing resides in the tone. We are invited to wonder if the witch is speaking simply, with the transparency of unambiguous orality, or if she instigates a subtextual comedy that questions our gullibility and the tale's veracity.[37] One place we might locate this comedy is at the beginning, after the visitor's opening lines:

> Folks think a witch who has familiar spirits
> She could call up to pass a winter evening,
> But won't, should be burned at the stake or something.
> Summoning spirits isn't "Button, button,
> Who's got the button," I would have them know.
>
> (*CP* 188)

"Button, button" represents a child's game; is the witch then saying that her story is "child's play" and questioning whether the narrator—and maybe the reader—is simply too dense to get the joke? Or is the narrator attempting to subvert the witch's charisma? Where does Frost stand in relation to this potential comedy, and does the humor direct itself differentially to insiders who get the joke and to outsiders who do not? Frost himself acknowledges "this question of who has the right to do what he pleases with my poetry—the right kind of people that can take it their way." But who are "the right kind of people"?[38]

Like its predecessor "A Servant to Servants," "The Witch of Coös" emphasizes the subversive power of a domesticated discourse based in a kind of "plain speaking"—"simple" language and "transparent" meaning—that structures itself in narrative poetry, poetry that tells a story. More vividly than in the earlier poems, however, Frost confounds such polarities as literal and figurative: whimsically yet gruesomely, buttons and bones are mixed up, language signifies something other than it appears to, something adjacent to but not symbolic of "reality," as figure is detached from ground. While in "The Death of the Hired Man" and "In the Home Stretch" this domesticated discourse appears benign (and even at times morally efficacious), here it resurfaces Medusa-like, and neither the masculine speaker nor his implied double (the reader) can close his eyes to the truth and power it evokes and, more threateningly, embodies. Frost emphasized the plasticity, duplicity, and power of the mother tongue and its intercourse in his readings of the poem: by omitting the final words of the "visitor" in the Library of Congress recording, he leaves his listener spellbound.[39]

Having explored all this rhetorical positioning from a relative distance, my own emotional response to "The Witch of Coös" is difficult to pin down, and in this very difficulty lies the point. It is related, I think, to the distanced and voyeuristic stance that the narrator assumes. Is the witch a crazy woman? Perhaps, but, read in the context of empathy-producing poems like "A Servant to Servants," "The Housekeeper," and "The Fear," the witch's story becomes more accessible—in fact, it makes perfect sense. Like her counterparts, she is isolated in the home. Work is primary: I can imagine her peeling potatoes, husking corn, putting up beets for the winter—anything to forestall the boredom and, conversely, the sexual intensity, that flare up and drive her out into the weather. This reading is willed, not invited, by the poem, and it is enabled in part by my training as a formalist reader, in part by my experience of growing up female on a (not very isolated) New England farm. Such a reading, I think, cuts against the grain of the rhetoric and structure that Frost creates here. What, I want to ask, does the ordinary reader make of this poem and, more precisely, of its real narrator, the witch?

The issue of speaking power coalesces in the shape of this narrative, as it asks some painful questions about the legitimacy and the sources of this power. Masculine, detached, the speaker attempts to focus where the witch wanders; he elaborates on orality and its meanings where she meditates on a domestic drama. Nevertheless, like the witch, he is (however unwillingly or unwittingly) a storyteller. As his proxy, the witch speaks from a maddened and maddening "I" that simultaneously concerns itself utterly with relationships—to the lover, the husband, the son, the visitor, the reader—and situates herself as their confounding matrix of meaning. Poised on the threshold of identity, crushed by what he dramatizes as the mutual exclusivity of his alternatives, Frost places feminine and masculine voices in competition. The winning mother tongue is at once seductive and forbidden, engendering a dead husband and lover and an illegitimate son who can only retell a kind of captivating gossip.

But this affiliation of the poem with gossip extends beyond the metaphoric level. As another kind of institutionalized gossip, stories about witches have long been an important part of New Hampshire folklore, and they continued to occupy this role during the poet's lifetime. Their affiliation with another feminine and feminizing form of oral literature is evident in volumes like the popular *New Hampshire Folk Tales,* compiled by Mrs. Moody P. Gore and Mrs. Guy E. Speare and published by the New Hampshire Federation of Women's Clubs. Overwhelmingly the work of women, *New Hampshire Folk Tales* devotes an entire chapter to "Witchcraft in New Hampshire." The introduction to the chapter, which indicates the gossipy tenor of the longer stories, provides a brief account of how "in 1656 a woman at Little Harbor, Piscataqua, was accused of being a witch. A neighbor charged that the witch caused her to suffer severe illness because she refused to lend her a pound of cotton; and testified that the accused vanished toward the waterside in the shape of a cat." Another story from 1860 tells of Hampton being "thrown into a state of alarm. A man affirmed that he had seen a company of witches on the marsh, seated about a cake of ice and comfortably taking tea," while still another relates how elderly "Granny Hicks had come as a woodchuck," sat on her neighbors' threshold, and bewitched their youngest child, who died soon afterward.[40]

The reviews of *New Hampshire* must have intensified Frost's anxieties about his affiliations with such "literature," for they rehearse yet again the debate about his "not poetry." Robert Littell's commentary in the *New Republic* highlights this debate. In discussing the title poem, he observes, "the voice which talks to us does so in an easy, unhurried monotone, never dull, never lifted, never strained: now it is speaking prose, now doggerel, now verse, now poetry"; a bit later, after citing a passage, he announces, "Maybe this is not poetry. But does that matter? Or does it matter very much that so many of Mr. Frost's lines sound as if they had been overheard in a telephone booth[?]" (*CR* 58–59). Perhaps it didn't matter to Littell or to many of Frost's readers, but it mattered a great deal to the poet himself, because such remarks both threatened his future reputation and endangered his current livelihood. In spite of the success of *North of Boston* and *Mountain Interval,* he was forced to borrow large sums of money to keep his household afloat—including a princely loan of a thousand dollars from Untermeyer in 1920. Of this loan Frost notes to his friend, "we have had one of the great affairs of the purse that will go jingling down through Am lit. . . . In the supreme hour of trial you proved generous—you gave me all you had offered—and I proved grateful and honorable—I paid you back with thanks" (*LU* 108). Not only were reputation and literary longevity at stake in reviews like Littell's, so was financial security, something that Frost still felt to be elusive. Borrowing from Untermeyer must have required a considerable sacrifice of pride and engendered further concerns about manliness, represented by his ability to provide for his family. Not inconsequentially, the title poem of *New Hampshire* reiterates in outrageously comic, if bitter, form the alliance between gender and money, for the poet-speaker cites two witches that he knows, the modern one a psychic who can read "letters locked in boxes" and whose "husband was worth millions. / I think he owned some shares in Harvard College" (*CP* 154).

Echoing other discussions about the forms in *North of Boston*, Littell's review highlights for us the poet's internal conflict, finally enacted in the generic affiliations, subjective positions, and rhetorical stances of many dra-

matic poems. The shape of *New Hampshire* itself marked this conflict and
pointed toward the future: the title poem remained alone in the first sec-
tion, with the narrative-dramatic and lyric poems essentially segregated into
"Notes" and "Grace Notes." In an ironic twist the poem that initiates the
latter section ("Fragmentary Blue") was written, Frost tells G. R. Eliott, "to
tease . . . my personal friends who want me to stop writing lyrics" (*SL* 248).

Paired with "The Witch of Coös," "The Pauper Witch of Grafton"
forms a noteworthy twin and counterpoint. While it also may express some
anxiety about a strong feminine voice—and I will explore this anxiety in the
poem more fully in the next chapter—the older note of sympathy never-
theless remains. Readers may argue about the degree of voyeurism invited
by the poem's ending, but Randall Jarrell's famous remark still seems accu-
rate: "I sometimes murmur to myself, in a perverse voice, that there is more
sexuality there than in several hothouses full of Dylan Thomas; and, of
course, there is love, there."[41] Here we see a positive enabling of a woman's
voice, frank, strong (in spite of the ending line), and intense. Frost's invest-
ment in a poetics of empathy here is most evident when we consider how
he transformed the original folk material. *The History of Warren, A Mountain
Hamlet, Located among The White Hills of New Hampshire* by William Little
contains "A Gay Little Chapter about Witches," in which the author
describes the unsurpassed power of Mrs. Sarah Weeks, who is a seductive
subject for "the gossiping slanderers of that day": "invisible on her good
steed, a broom-stick, she rode all the country round and was a sort of
revenging angel for her husband." In both this chapter and the following
one about the lawsuit mentioned in Frost's poem, the overall tone is jocu-
lar and condescending, as Little observes that "the hallucinations of other
generations are passing away and few are the persons at the present time
who indulge in the belief of goblins, ghosts, and witches. True it is that the
mediums, clairvoyants, and cabinet gentlemen bring to mind the diabolerie
of old Salem, when our fathers, the good puritans, made fools of themselves
and hung thirty old women as witches." He concludes the first chapter by
asserting, "No more do we see the individuals who indulge in such fancies,
and although there were such [fancies] . . . we have little right to laugh at
them."[42]

Little's description of Sarah Weeks's feats of bewitchment makes for
interesting reading, conveyed in a narrative that resembles nothing more
than printed gossip, including the story about the man biting a bedpost that
Frost reshapes in his poem. The most striking aspects of Frost's transforma-
tion of the original materials are his assignment of subjectivity (and sympa-

thy) to Sarah Weeks, his emphasis on her sexuality, and his attention to her distressing poverty. If Little approaches the material more as an outsider—as his critical assessment of the subject of witchcraft suggests—Frost engages in gossip of a different sort, imagining the reader as a confidante of the witch: "Now that they've got it settled whose I be, / I'm going to tell them something they won't like: / They've got it settled wrong, and I can prove it" (*CP* 192). While the poem vibrates with the revelatory details of "The Witch of Coös," the witch's tone is for the most part more daring and saucy than that of her twin. Echoing his concern for the laboring woman in "A Servant to Servants," Frost enhances the subjectivity, and hence the power and pathos, of Sarah Weeks, and he underscores not only the gender disadvantage under which the pauper witch labors but also the parsimony of New Hampshire towns and their inhabitants. The wrenchingly poignant closing lines of this regionalist tale seem to me to secure the poem from charges of voyeurism and situate it in the realm of affirmative, intimacy-creating gossip between two people, the narrator and the reader:

> All is, if I'd a-known when I was young
> And full of it, that this would be the end,
> It doesn't seem as if I'd had the courage
> To make so free and kick up in folks' faces.
> I might have, but it doesn't seem as if.

> (*CP* 194)

## "The Tutelory Genius of the Nation": Frost, Regionalism, and Nationalism

> The clouds look low and heavy, as if there would be rain;
> It always means bad weather when you hear the brook so plain.
> The wet won't make much trouble now, for all the crops are in,
> And yet I somehow hate to see the long fall rains begin.
>
> I couldn't sense the half I read, the air is close and still,
> If I were young as once I was, I'd go up on the hill.
> It isn't as it used to be when I could come and go,
> And keep upon my feet all day, now I am stiff and slow.
>
> There's nothin' in the paper; you can take it if you choose;
> I can't make head nor tail of half they nowadays call news.
> I use to think the *Farmer* was head of all the rest;
> 'Twas full of solid common sense; I tell you that's the best!
>
> What does a plain, old-fashioned man care whether stocks go down?
> My stock is all four-footed!—but 'twill please the folks in town.

Here's new machines preached every week, to help the folks that sell;
And fashions for the women folks, and other trash as well.[43]

In "A Farmer's Sorrow" Sarah Orne Jewett offers readers a dramatic mono-
logue that tells the story of an aging farmer whose son has left the farm to be
educated and returned virtually helpless for outdoor work: "he looked just
a white-skinned birch, and I felt like an oak." Anticipating Harold Wilson
in "The Death of the Hired Man," the farmer's son Dan is feminized by his
mind-work, for his father says, "Farmin's the honest work of men," and
highlights the fact that it is his wife, along with the local minister, who col-
laborated in Dan's departure: "pretty soon I see / The book fools and the
women folks would be too much for me." In a striking echo of the image
of stacking hay in Frost's poem, the narrator points out that a man's work
and book work are incommensurate: "Folks talk of edication as if the Latin
showed / A farmer how to cast accounts or how to stack a load." Equally
striking, the hardworking second cousin whom the narrator favors as his
replacement on the farm is named Silas. While Frost may not have read this
poem of 1884, "A Farmer's Sorrow" not only anticipates his examination of
New England decline and dramatizes the voice of the rural working poor;
it also rehearses a hidden conflict that resides at the heart of much of this
earlier poetry, a conflict between rural and urban, regional and national per-
spectives, embodied perhaps most ironically and poignantly in its place of
publication: *Manhattan* magazine.

Jewett was not the first to publish regionalist poetry, especially about
New England. In "If and If" Alice Cary had given a vivid account of rural
life as early as 1855, as had Lucy Larcom in her Cape Ann poems, Elizabeth
Stuart Phelps in poems like "The Stone Woman of Eastern Point," and Celia
Thaxter in virtually all of her oeuvre.[44] Regionalist poetry is plainly repre-
sented at the turn of the century in Stedman's anthology, from Helen Hunt
Jackson's "Poppies on the Wheat" and Thaxter's famous "The Sandpiper" to
the work of Edwin Arlington Robinson. But Jewett's poem represents a
moment when the tension between rural and urban, regional and national
identities emerges explicitly via a dramatic regional voice; as June Howard
points out in the introduction to her recent collection of essays, newer work
highlights "[Jewett's] implication in the process through which, at the turn
into the twentieth century, a national culture was constituted."[45] Echoing
the nostalgia of much regionalist writing, "A Farmer's Sorrow" may exceed
the boundaries of such nostalgia and tip into sentimentality, suggesting once
again the possibility of an alliance between the two modes.[46]

By 1915 regionalism had achieved its reputation as narrow, provoking Fred Lewis Pattee, in reviewing the common comparison of Jewett with Hawthorne, to observe that "she is a writer of *little* books and *short* stories, the painter of a *few* subjects in a *provincial little* area, but within her *narrow* province she has no rival nearer her own times than Mrs. Gaskell." Given this diminishment, it should be no surprise that Pattee acknowledges that "during all the period [beginning in 1868] the work of women dominated to a large degree the literary output."[47] Granville Hicks expresses a similar attitude, allowing that Jewett "rose . . . far above the merely nostalgic, sentimental regionalists" but highlighting her "limitations" as "a master of a tiny realm." Without directly pointing to Frost's smallness, Hicks implies that he shares with Jewett a myopic narrowness: "One not only realizes that life in New Hampshire is not altogether representative of life in the United States as a whole; one has to admit that Frost disregards many elements in New Hampshire life, and especially the elements that link that state with the rest of the country. . . . [such as] the growth of industrialism." In a similar vein Amy Lowell had also minimized Frost's achievement, arguing that "his canvas is exceedingly small, and no matter how wonderfully he paints on it, he cannot attain to the position held by men with a wider range of vision."[48]

In all of these observations we can trace an affiliation (as well as an antagonism) between regionalism and nationalism. In 1938 Donald Davidson observed: "We cannot define regionalism unless at the same time we define nationalism. . . . Regionalism is the name for a condition under which the national American literature exists as a literature: that is, its constant tendency to decentralize rather than to centralize; or to correct over-centralization by conscious decentralization."[49] Davidson's point was echoed only two years later by Van Wyck Brooks, who affirmed that "writers come to know the general by knowing the particular"; Brooks saw "no more American writers, and none more *universal,* than those who were Southerners, Westerners, New Englanders first. The widest American visions had been village visions" (emph. added). Unlike Hicks, Brooks makes clear Frost's universality ("Frost carried with him an aura as of infinite space and time"), affirming that it was "Frost's function to mediate between New England and the mind of the rest of the nation. . . . In him the region was born again,—it seemed never to have lost its morning vigour and freshness; and one felt behind his local scene the wide horizons of a man whose sympathies and experience were continental."[50] Anticipated and echoed elsewhere by Frost's supporters,[51] this statement must have pleased the Frost who surely read Edmund Clarence Stedman's observation in 1900 that "the method and spirit peculiar to a region make for 'an addition to literature,' but a work conveying them must have the universal cast to be enduring, though its author waits the longer for recognition."[52] As Jac Tharpe was to note on the centennial of the poet's birth, "Robert Frost had to wait for recognition as a poet"; earlier "reactions were often either prejudiced or emotional; and they were based in great part on the perception of Frost as a popular regionalist who had no more than pretensions to artistry."[53]

In taking to task the "metropolitan critics" who, he says, have constructed a false dichotomy between regional and national, Davidson takes issue with Hicks's view that "regional art is necessarily at odds with national art, or is at best subordinate, minor and petty," and hence, indirectly, with Hicks's representation of Frost's regionalism as narrow sentimentalism.[54] Recent discussions of regionalism highlight its implication in both national and international concerns.[55] Frost was certainly not indifferent to ostensibly "larger" concerns than nature seen through a New England lens, and we could cite as examples of his investment in broader modernity poems such as "A Lone Striker," "Out, Out—" "The Vanishing Red," or "The Self-Seeker," which, as Louise Bogan observed in 1962, confront the dire consequences of modern industrialism. If Frost was less concerned with "the blighting results of industry upon human beings in general" and more with "a personal feud, with the machine as adversary" and a mostly affirmative view of "a vanished way of rural existence" that provoked nostalgia in the transitional generation of people, "it cannot be truly said of Frost that he catered to this nostalgia. . . . If a large proportion of his readers preferred to separate out from his work those poems which satisfied their yearning for some version of a lost American Golden Age, the fault was theirs."[56] We need to acknowledge Stephanie Foote's observation that "our historical position may *intensify* the nostalgic effect of regional fiction precisely because we are so much more innocent of the urgent material and social history that produced it, but so much more inundated with the effects of that material history."[57]

Frost surely did not want to be remembered as a poultryman-farmer or a New England storyteller but as a poet—and a good one at that. If being affiliated with female regionalist writing—admittedly dominant in the late nineteenth and early twentieth centuries—was to be considered "effeminate" and merely local, then that affiliation would have to be broken.[58] The institutional acceptance of this regional, feminized view of Frost appears in an unexpected source. In 1930 Stanley T. Williams and Nelson F. Adkins

published *Courses of Reading in American Literature with Bibliographies,* which
"was begun with the purpose of aiding the work of assignments and con-
ferences in a course in American literature at Yale University." As the proj-
ect developed, they tell us, "it has taken the form of a guide to the reading
and study of this subject, within or without the college classroom"; and "the
grouping [of writers] is based . . . upon principles of association derived
from the experience of the classroom."[59] This text is striking for many rea-
sons, not least because of the degree to which it includes women writers
from all periods, including in the chapter preceding Frost such writers as
Rose Terry Cooke, Helen Hunt Jackson, Louisa May Alcott, Emma
Lazarus, Jewett, Brown, and Freeman. The poet himself is studied in con-
junction with regionalist writing by Edith Wharton, Willa Cather, and
Robinson. As late as 1951, when Perry Westbrook first published *Acres of
Flint,* the affiliation between Frost and female predecessors and contempo-
raries like Larcom, Thaxter, Brown, and Jewett remained strong, and West-
brook announced that, with Frost's appearance, local color writing "was to
make a death-bed recovery into a life fully as vigorous as its former one and
perhaps more important for the *nation* as a whole. . . . [T]he almost exclu-
sively *feminine* monopoly on this type of writing had been broken; and a
*broader* background of experience was being brought to bear on the inter-
pretation of New England life."[60]

Once again, Frost's affiliation with regionalism was feminizing and
localizing because it engendered a disabling disqualification from the world
of serious art; to be a retailer of gossip was, perhaps, merely to please those
in one's "neighborhood," not in one's country, which now had to come
first. Lionel Trilling's birthday remarks encoded this tension, and his
description of Frost as "a terrifying poet" paved the way for a broader
understanding of the poet's ironic complexity as it confronted the notion of
him as merely rural. Even though Trilling acknowledged Frost's vast popu-
larity at this time, depicting him as "a national fact," "virtually a symbol of
America," "a tutelory genius of the nation," he intimated the disaffection
and misunderstanding of an urban critical elite, himself included, with the
poet's work. The antidote to this view was a recognition or recovery of
Frost's (modernist) darkness: "when ever have people been so isolated, so
lightning-blasted, so tried down and calcined by life, each in his own way,
to some last irreducible core of being. Talk of the disintegration and slough-
ing off of the old consciousness!" He concluded, "The manifest America of
Mr. Frost's poems may be pastoral; the actual America is tragic."[61] With the

transformation to "tragic" poet, Frost could move from local to universal and from lowbrow (merely popular) to highbrow. The affiliation of this transformation with genre (and indirectly, with gender), however, emerged considerably earlier, for in 1943 Henry W. Wells of Columbia University, observing in *The American Way of Poetry* that "Two Witches" is the only piece in *New Hampshire* that "makes extensive use of dialogue and dialect," had affirmed: "In becoming more thoughtful and less dramatic or sentimental, Frost's poetry tends steadily to become more cosmopolitan and less provincial."[62] By this point, however, the transformation was not only under way but nearly accomplished.

## "Dangerous self-arousing words": Fathering the Self

"Who was Mrs. Captain Tolland?" I asked eagerly, to change the current of our thoughts.

"I never knew her maiden name; if I ever heard it, I've gone an' forgot; 'twould mean nothing to me," answered Mrs. Todd.

"She was a foreigner, an' he met with her out in the Island o' Jamaica. They said she 'd been left a widow with property. Land knows what become of it; she was French born, an' her first husband was a Portugee, or somethin'."[63]

In "The Foreigner" Jewett's sibylline and maternal Mrs. Todd from *The Country of the Pointed Firs* is prompted to tell a story—to gossip—about the mysterious Mrs. Tolland, a racially and nationally ambiguous woman who enters and disrupts a Maine seafaring community via marriage to one of its sea captains. One of the most delicious moments of revelation occurs when Mrs. Todd delineates how Mrs. Tolland not only sings and dances in the meetinghouse vestry but also inspires her listeners to participate: "'You could n't help seein' how pretty 't was; we all got to trottin' a foot, an some o' th men clapped their hands quite loud, a-keepin' time, 'twas so catchin, an' seemed so natural to her. There wa'n't one of 'em but enjoyed it."[64] The result of these actions is "an awful scandal," the pleasure of which is recuperated in the retelling. Creating intimacy with both her immediate and external listener, intimating an erotic female energy, "The Foreigner" also represents the alienation of a woman outside the community as it attempts (and fails) to assimilate her into an American national identity. In its concern for who is an insider and who is an outsider, situated in the context of an explicitly New England locale, Frost's "Maple" recapitulates many of the tensions explored here and elsewhere by Jewett, including a search for an absent or endangered mother and for her mysterious language. Published only three years after the struggle for women's rights had (ostensibly) climaxed with women's suffrage and in an era of women's increasing sexual freedom, *New Hampshire,* not *Mountain Interval,* represents the place at which the poet's voice turns irrevocably to that of the bard, recalling Whitman's self-transformation into the Good Gray Poet.[65]

This change in self-representation is reflected in a more detached stance and an attitude of authority. The mechanisms and tensions of gendered poetic identity, and the concerns of a professional poetic speaker, become most visible and concrete in "Maple," one of Frost's critically neglected poems.[66] What situates the poem in this "less good" category is precisely its excess: its excessive self-consciousness, its (possibly self-consciously stiff) efforts to be poetic, and its overt didacticism—all qualities that make it revealing in the present context. "Maple" is an important marker of the end of Frost's fruitful feminine narrative/dramatic mode, because the poet indicates that he can no longer afford to identify with the kind of voice embodied in the witch of Coös or enacted in "A Servant to Servants"; moving through the relative distancing of "West-Running Brook" to the erasure of feminine subjectivity in "Paul's Wife," he commits himself explicitly in "Maple" to transformation. "Maple" articulates the problems of identity for the poet who seeks at once to incorporate and to repress a powerful feminine voice; as in "The Witch of Coös" reading itself is again gendered—here, it is literally female. Finally, the elements of positive gossip that fuel "A Servant to Servants" and even "The Pauper Witch of Grafton"—the creation of intimacy, the affirmation of female erotic power—are transformed into a detached and aggressive self-announcement. The poem recounts the lifelong search of a girl named Maple for her identity. In this parabolic narrative, when the mother assumes the Adamic function of naming at the birth of her daughter, she dies, as if for her impudence. Maple's teacher denies that such a name exists, while the other representative of culture, her father, finds the mother's words inscrutable:

> "I don't know what she wanted it to mean,
> But it seems like some word she left to bid you
> Be a good girl—be like a maple tree.
> *How* like a maple tree's for us to guess."

> (*CP* 169)

The structural gestures of the poem highlight a detached, masculine, professional speaker who shapes and guides the narrative from beginning to end.[67] In fact, what is remarkable about this poem is the degree to which we feel the poet's presence. "Maple" is less a story (or a poem, for that matter) and more a harangue in which he challenges readers to make any sense at all.[68] His distance, even hostility, emerges in the first section that is dominated by the father's story, a twin of the poet's, about his daughter's identity. Not simply expressing confusion about "meaning," the story fosters it: we must "guess" the mother's intention. More confusingly, even ominously, he tells Maple that he is *purposely* withholding meaning: "By and by I will tell you all I know / About the different trees, and something too / About your mother that perhaps may help" (*CP* 169). Unlike in "The Witch of Coös," the narrator depicts the *daughter,* not the son, as illegitimate, and this daughter is silent because of her separation from her mother('s) tongue. Like Jewett's Mrs. Captain Tolland in "The Foreigner," she is defined by those external to her, possessing no subjectivity of her own.

The dominance and exposure of the father-narrator's voice emerge in the next, very self-conscious comment: "Dangerous self-arousing words to sow" (*CP* 169). Sexuality permeates this "sentence," from the autoerotic "self-arousing" to the phallic "sow"; it seems as if the father desires and instigates an incestuous covenant. Words appear to have natural lives of their own, independent of the intentions of their speakers; part of their danger, however, must lie in the gender of their auditor, for they threaten to make Maple self-conscious and perhaps, via her female sexuality, a potentially powerful speaker like her mother. What is the place for female/feminine readers of the poem? It is the *father's* words more than the mother's that engender Maple's (self-)difference. Ominously, this father guards against the communion between mother and daughter: *he* occupies the bedroom that was once her mother's, in "her mother's childhood home" (*CP* 170), suggesting that such self-knowledge can come only through her incestuous relations with him. Home, and the sexual self-definition it encodes, threatens as it defines women's identity. The "seed" he plants lies buried for many years:

She all but forgot it.
What he sowed with her slept so long a sleep,
And came so near death in the dark of years,
That when it woke and came to life again
The flower was different from the parent seed.

(*CP* 169)

Again Frost intimates his (the father's, the poet's?) incestuous relations with the daughter, resulting in a kind of illegitimate pregnancy, whose "issue" is a false kind of "knowing." What is striking about this passage is its excessive self-consciousness, its straining toward poetic language, that renders the poet's presence almost oppressive. It is as if Frost is telling us that his figures must *mean,* although he withholds the meaning from us just as the father does from Maple. Or, more ominously, perhaps the father himself does not know its meaning because he has killed the mother tongue, leaving Maple effectively without a voice. In either case the implied reader is left to "make sense" the best she or he can, as is evident by Frost's rhetorical positioning of us with Maple.

Growing up without a legitimate interpreter of the mother's language, Maple feels her name's "strangeness lay in having too much meaning. Other names, / As Lesley, Carol, Irma, Marjorie, / Signified nothing" (*CP* 169–70). In an ominous echo of Macbeth, the child-killer's assessment of life as "a tale told by an idiot, full of sound and fury, signifying nothing," the narrator points to anxiety about his own loss of authority. Two other elements of these lines deserve attention. First is the fact that the names to which "Maple" assigns *no* meaning are those of the poet's own children, as if to suggest that his own naming has none of the frightening, mysterious, apparently self-destructive, and figurative power of the mother tongue. These names do not signify *nothing,* but they *signify* nothing. This affirmation seems disingenuous at best in view of the explicit metaphor of Maple's father planting a "seed" that "flower[s]": that is, in view of the poet's self-conscious use of figurative language. The overlay of the poet's "real life" with imaginative work indicates his mixing of boundaries and implies not only the unknowability of the truth but also his privileged relation to it compared to the reader's ignorance: go ahead and guess what something means—at your peril.

What the naming mother tongue seems to signify, however, is not "too much meaning," meaning that exceeds the boundaries of language but, instead, pure difference: "This difference from other names it was / Made people notice it—and notice her. / (They either noticed it, or got it wrong)" (*CP* 170). Frost's revision of the measure and form of his own discourse underscores this excess, for the lines in the first edition, "What was it about her name? She saw its strangeness / Lay in its having meaning," become in subsequent editions "What was it about her name? Its strangeness lay / In having too much meaning" (*CP* 169). For Maple, as for her mother, the important fact is that of difference, for that fact incorporates all meaning. Frost's omission of "She saw" in later editions underscores the fact that the narrator's discourse in these and subsequent lines overlays Maple's indirect interior monologue. In musing about meaning, the duplicitous poetic speaker appropriates Maple's dilemma rather than dramatizing it; he emphasizes his omniscience, defining himself in effect as an interpreter. This gesture of covert detachment, like the father's earlier promise to reveal to Maple her meaning, effectively distances readers from the narrative and from Maple's subjectivity. In some sense this gesture of distancing may also encode the poet's concept of the critic as masculine, stern, and judgmental, and it may represent his increasing attempt to circumvent or frustrate judgment. If so, it worked: "Maple" is to my mind one of the most irritating, though most interesting, poems that Frost ever wrote.

From this angle of vision we can see that Maple herself represents an attempt to read from a masculine perspective. Her self-alienation and loss of the mother tongue (and its interpreter) emerge most strikingly when she discovers her mother's Bible with a maple leaf pressed between the pages:

> She read every word
> Of the two pages it was pressed between,
> As if it was her mother speaking to her.
> But forgot to put the leaf back in closing
> And lost the place never to read again.
> She was sure, though, there had been nothing in it.
>
> (*CP* 170)

Not only does Maple find her mother's words opaque (perhaps because they are cloaked in the potent sounds and images of the patriarchal Bible), but she accepts the sentence of the culture on such language: "sure . . . there had been nothing in it," just as Betsey Dole, Freeman's sentimental poetess, on one level accepts the minister's "sentence" and burns her poems. A masculinized Maple reads her name and herself from the perspective of the culture that, finding the mother tongue uncivilized and untranslatable, erases it. We do well to recall here Elaine Showalter's caution in another context, "Women are estranged from their own experience and unable to perceive its shape and authenticity . . . they are expected to identify as readers with a masculine experience and perspective, which is presented as the human one."[69]

The effect of this moment reverberates again from Maple to the reader, and, whether wittingly or unwittingly, Frost requires that we question masculine systems of interpretation. He underlines this issue in revision; in the first edition of the poem line 68 reads, "And lost the place never to find again," while subsequent editions substitute "read" for "find." Like the containment of Maple's thoughts and feelings within the voice of the detached masculine narrator, repeating "read" twice in the space of five lines implicates it in a self-conscious gesture toward interpretive systems. While from one perspective we might see here "the voice of the poet intruding to criticize inability to be figurative enough, to allow metaphor some flexibility, some openendedness,"[70] the poet's heavily accented voice intimates his own overriding knowledge as an insider, in contrast to our Maple-like ignorance and incapacity.

The inscrutability of Maple's mother's text to her daughter derives in part from the latter's immasculation, her conversion to a narrowly patriarchal perspective, but Maple does not merely misread the words; she reads the wrong language. Instead of studying the Bible, she should be reading the "text" she puts aside, the maple leaf. Not surprisingly, when she turns from the Bible in the adolescent search for self, and particularly for sexual identity, she looks again in the wrong place: "So she looked for *herself*, as everyone / Looks for *himself*, more or less outwardly" (*CP* 170; emph. added). The pronoun slippage marks the narrator's—and, hence, the poet's—divided, or "different," consciousness, and it seems remarkable in view of the fact that feminine identity is at issue; whether aware of this shift or not, again Frost indicates the way in which a masculine "norm" circumscribes Maple's life. As gesture toward the reader, it demands continued attentiveness to his and to our difference from Maple, and it requires our own immasculation. This story embodies a narrator detached from and critical of his characters; the poet's subjectivity and his forceful shaping of the story prohibit the identification, empathy, and, finally, emotional response that empower dramatic poems such as "A Servant to Servants" and "The Death of the Hired Man."

Adulthood further enforces Maple's circumscription into masculine systems of meaning and interpretation, for, like many middle-class American women at the time that Frost was writing, Maple becomes a secretary in an artificial male world. Maple is part of a cohort that would be "still huddled within the 'feminine' ghettos of the employment world,"[71] confined to taking shorthand, which figures a cryptic, debased feminine language that services a male economy; this language parodies the authentic feminine language that her mother would have taught her. Is the narrator, or the poet, sympathetic? It appears not, for, as cultural text or body, Maple's first clue to her meaning arrives through the mediation of a young *male* interpreter, who "recognizes" her as Maple even though others in her office misname her, to her powerless dismay: "'I have to let them call me what they like'" (*CP* 171). In spite of this appropriation, or because of it, his naming her encodes the larger appropriation by masculine culture of female identity, and it inspires kinship:

> They were both stirred that he should have divined
> Without the name her personal mystery.
> It made it seem as if there must be something
> She must have missed herself.
>
> (*CP* 171)

Ironically, though she has "missed" her mother's tongue and her own female-centered, sexual self, she has "found" her social self as wife and, ultimately, mother, as the "divine" and "divining" husband confirms her female role as cultural mystery. This role is one in which she becomes an object for study—both for herself and her husband, the poet and the reader—rather than the subject of her own narrative like Len's wife or even the witch of Coös, whose selves are vigorously revealed.

To discover the secret of Maple's identity the couple must look to her "father's" house; by this point Maple's *mother's* childhood home has been completely redefined in terms of the father, completing Maple's circumscription in and by masculine language. Maple's husband seems as naive as she in the absence of the mother and the mother's language. Their willed ignorance of adult passion is figured by the images of the maple trees they choose to associate with Maple—not the sap-bearing ones of spring but the dying ones of autumn. These trees have a "fire," a passion that leaves their central selves untouched. Another tree, lovely with a bed of red and pink leaves about its feet, seems as though it has some words to speak:

> They hovered for a moment near discovery,
> Figurative enough to see the symbol,
> But lacking faith in anything to mean
> The same at different times to different people.
> Perhaps a filial diffidence partly kept them
> From thinking it could be a thing so bridal.
> And anyway it came too late for Maple.
> She used her hands to cover up her eyes.
>
> (*CP* 173)

Both this passage and the activity it encodes are problematic, for we dis-
cover a fundamental disjunction between language and experience. In its
patently unpoetic and self-conscious shape the passage underlines the chasm
between figure and ground, or perhaps the absence of one of the pair, since
both Maple and her husband are too literal in their search: they both look
for a particular tree, and they both assume the father has "the answer." But
Frost indicates that, without a mother tongue, language has no pregnancy;
it confounds with sheer surface. Lacking a mother, both the young man and
Maple suffer for their inability to interpret the natural, numinous, and
"figurative" language that she bequeaths them. Their "filial diffidence,"
their loyalty to the father/Father, and their own innocent brother-sister
relationship ensure their ignorance of the mother tongue in all its uses.

Frost makes plain Maple's deliberate and complicitous unknowing of
her achieved social identity, for, like Elinor herself, Maple is both wife and
mother, but her relationship with her husband represents presexual affilia-
tion. In making this gesture, Frost circumscribes the sister into the brother's
system of meaning and representation, just as he himself did, directly and
indirectly, with Elinor in such poems as "Meeting and Passing" and "The
Subverted Flower." This translation of the "sister" into the Beloved or the
Mother began in high school when Rob insisted with "mixed feelings of
delight and jealousy" that Elinor be named co-valedictorian.[72] Though she
completed her college education in spite of his repeated attempts to prevent
it, in their marriage he succeeded in displacing her as the family intellectual,
in spite of his failure to complete his education at Dartmouth or Harvard.[73]
Frost's surpassing of his wife is figured in the narrator's gesture at the end of
"Maple." In the last stanza the narrator draws back, as he has periodically,
but this withdrawal seems emotionally and sexually charged, accusatory,
and, ultimately, bitter:

> Thus had a name with meaning, given in death,
> Made a girl's marriage, and ruled in her life.
> No matter that the meaning was not clear.
> A name with meaning could bring up a child,
> Taking the child out of the parents' hands.
> Better a meaningless name, I should say,
> As leaving more to nature and happy chance.
> Name children some names and see what you do.

> (CP 173)

This stanza echoes with more than Frost's habitual love of play and ambi-
guity. In his anger at and resentment of the father's loss of control of his

Adamic power of naming, the narrator-poet, who specifies his difference explicitly, condemns Maple to spend her life obsessed with her absent mother's meanings while she unwittingly enacts those of the father. The poem repeatedly evokes another, feminine way of knowing, seeing, and speaking that includes but exceeds words; this visionary language is another kind of poetry that seeps out around the margins. Yet, by illegitimately appropriating the father's power of naming, by claiming a figurative status as a poet, the mother condemns her own story, encoded in the metaphoric name of Maple, to obscurity.

The subjectivity that Frost has permitted to women elsewhere—as characters, as readers—is entirely suppressed, making an external reader's relationship to this poem problematic at best: the gossipy intimacy that empowers many of his finest and most sympathetic regional poems has vanished entirely.[74] Although the poem mimics third-person narratives like "Home Burial," "The Death of the Hired Man," and "In the Home Stretch," "Maple" contains a preponderance of narrative, emerging from the organizing consciousness of an omniscient and ostensibly professional narrator, in contrast to the earlier poems' more generous diffusion of self into female characters and investigation of feminine voice. This stylistic change parallels a less hospitable attitude toward the reader, as the detachment of the narrator's voice thrusts us apart from Maple's drama, looking— as spectators—as she does, "more or less outwardly." In "Maple" the poet's voice shadows the narrator's until the two converge at the end. While the poem's conclusion also points to the self-deception, even collusion, of women in claiming a patriarchally defined identity (Maple "used her hands to cover up her eyes" and affirms, "'We would not see the secret if we could now: / We are not looking for it any more'" [CP 173]), the "secret" of identity is available only via the perspective of the (professional) speaker-father-bard. From another angle the poem is self-subversive because it gestures toward the speaker's silences, especially toward the mute power of nature's meaning and what he cannot say about intimacy and about female sexuality: to his own unintelligibility. Part of this unintelligibility derives from his own withdrawal—his movement toward a self-conception as detached, masculine (lyric) professional poet, rather than dispersed, feminine (narrative) storyteller-gossip. As "Maple" concludes, the father-poet resists violently what he has enacted, that the erasure of the uncivilized mother tongue represents a loss. This knowledge comes at the cost of his own power: at the end of the poem his only words to the absent and unnamable mother are a curse.

The story that I have just told about "Maple" is vulnerable to a number of complaints, but I will respond to only a few. First is that I idealize and sentimentalize a feminine voice, perhaps as an antidote to Frost's own sentimentalization (and then obliteration) of it. Is "Maple" a "good" poem, I ask again, even worth the discussion space that I have allotted it? For me it is "less good" not because it is self-conscious or didactic but because it fosters a distance that its precursors do not. The story that I have told of the poem is not one that Frost would likely acknowledge; he would probably insist that "Maple" is simply a bit of fun and that I'm missing the point. (It recalls the old [anti-] feminist joke: *Q:* How many feminists does it take to screw in a light bulb? *A:* That's not funny.) "Maple" also recalls for me one of Judith Fetterley's conclusions about "The Legend of Sleepy Hollow":

> In his postscript to this story Irving suggests that the quintessential American story will be a tall tale circulated among men for the purpose of establishing dominance. The good reader is the one who gets the joke; the bad reader is the one who doesn't get it or refuses to find it funny, perhaps because the joke is on her or him; and telling stories about winning and losing becomes in itself an act of winning and losing, of inclusion and exclusion.[75]

While I acknowledge "Maple's" wily humor and its joke on those who would worry an interpretation to death, I believe that, unlike "A Servant to Servants" or "The Housekeeper," it pivots on this dynamic of "winning and losing, of inclusion and exclusion." At the same time, it unwittingly reveals Frost's anxiety about and experimentation with a gendered poetic self—as does "Wild Grapes" in a more affirmative way—and an equally gendered reader. Their interplay, as represented here in genre, alters dramatically and permanently in and after *New Hampshire*.

One subtext of the gender tensions enacted in "Maple" and the accompanying alterations in genre may have been the very concrete pressures of competition with female modernist poets. Frost's complex relationship with Amy Lowell, and his occasional nastiness toward her in the letters to Untermeyer, suggests such an explanation. In one written the year before *New Hampshire* was published he describes Lowell's poetry reading at the University of Michigan—part of a series that he had sponsored and in which Untermeyer had also participated—in ostensibly comic but subtly hostile and combative terms:

No, Amy didn't displace you in our affections. You still hold the top of both the batting and fielding lists. Amy upset a lamp and a water pitcher. . . . As a show she was more or less successful. . . . Her speaking and reading went well considering the uproarious start she made with the lamp and water. I never heard such spontaneous shouts of laughter. Out in front she took it all well with plenty of talk offhand and so passed for a first class sport.

I give you all this to give you an idea of what you were better than. (*LU* 148–49)

The jocular tone and grudging admiration conceal the threat Frost felt at Lowell's success. Two years earlier he tells Untermeyer, "I don't believe she is anything but a fake, and I refuse longer to let her wealth, social position, and the influence she has been able to purchase and cozen, keep me from honestly bawling her out—that is, when I am called on to speak!" (*LU* 106). Speaking about a comment (inaccurate, he believes) that Lowell made about "periodic sentences," Frost observes:

She couldn't get away with that if she hadn't us all corralled by her wealth and social position. . . . Nonsense and charlatanry—that's all that kind of talk amounts to. I'm sure she guessed without looking it up that there must be something recurrent like beat or pulse implied in periodic. She knew ladies were periodic because they recurred monthly. She's loony—and so periodic by the moon herself. Feeling as I do don't you think it would be honester for me to refuse to be bound between the covers of the same book with her, do you? (*LU* 107)

This entirely problematic comment, steeped in sexual anxiety ("between the covers of the same book"), indicates the depth of Frost's concern about Lowell's power, social and economic as well as literary, and it recalls Hawthorne's famous remark about the "damned mob of scribbling women" who sold very well. Ironically, of course, Lowell had been one of Frost's early supporters, helping to launch his career with her laudatory review of *North of Boston* in the *New Republic* in 1915, and the two at times enjoyed a productive and sometimes even friendly relationship.[76]

His keenness for public acclaim and his sensitivity to the debates about his standing as a poet are enacted in part in the changing, and more masculine, bardic stance of *New Hampshire*. Frost himself points indirectly to his genre transformation at this time, as he observes humorously to Untermeyer shortly before the volume's publication: "I'll tell you about my next book in the letter when I write it. Already some of my staider friends have stuck at the levity of the title and the forced use of notes. They say it doesn't seem like me but (with a sigh) after all they had felt I was changing. O gee" (*LU* 165). In another, famous letter to his friend only a few weeks after the book's publication, he highlights his increasing practice of detachment from his readers:

> I own any humor shows fear and inferiority. Irony is simply a kind of guardedness. So is a twinkle. It keeps the reader from criticism. Whittier, when he shows any style at all, is probably a greater person than Longfellow as he is lifted priestlike above consideration of the scornful. Belief is better than anything else, and it is best when rapt, above paying its respects to anybody's doubt whatsoever. At bottom the world isn't a joke. We only joke about it to avoid an issue with someone to let someone know that we know he's there with his questions: to disarm him by seeming to have heard and done justice to his side of the standing argument. Humor is the most engaging cowardice. With it myself I have been able to hold some of my enemy in play far out of gunshot. (*LU* 166)

Conceptualizing his readers as potential "enemies," Frost distances himself from them via humor—and irony. Both in its content and its rhetorical structures, "Maple" exposes the process of self-transformation in which he was engaged. No longer is the reader part of a community of empathic listeners to a story of disadvantaged rural women and men but, instead, an adversary to be held "in play far out of gunshot"—in Fetterley's terms, positioned either conspiratorially, as a masculine "good reader" "who gets the joke," or adversarially, as "a bad reader . . . who doesn't get it or refuses to find it funny." The feminine voices incorporated literally into many important dramatic poems via character and figuratively via rhetorical stance, and generically in the poems' affiliations with regionalist, woman-authored fiction (and mainstream nineteenth-century poetry), become muted in virtually all of Frost's subsequently published work.

## "My best bid for remembrance": Genre Crossings

> The question is whether [the times have] reached a depth
> Of desperation that would warrant poetry's
> Leaving love's alternations, summer and winter,
> Our age-long theme, for the uncertainty
> Of judging who is a contemporary liar—
> Who in particular, when all alike
> Get called as much in clashes of ambition.
> —Robert Frost, "Build Soil"

And what about the poem in *New Hampshire* that Frost thought was his "best bid for remembrance"? If, as I observed in chapter 1, "Stopping by Woods on a Snowy Evening" invokes its sentimental roots, it also invites an entirely different relationship with the reader than the narrative poems on which I have focused. Echoing and transforming the feminine genre of sentimental poetry, Frost reconstructs the wild mother tongue of the witch poems into a safely civilized account by a male speaker (who else would be out driving around alone in a sleigh late at night?) of a Close Encounter with deathly Mother Nature. In spite of my tone, this gesture is intensely conventional both in literary and psychological terms, for it is through his stance as Poet that we see Frost's difference from both his sentimental and regionalist forebears. The "I" of "Stopping by Woods" is at once more intimate with and more detached from us, more diffused and more individual than theirs often is.

This convergence of sentimental-feminine and modern-masculine modes emerges in other poems in *New Hampshire*. "Our Singing Strength," a pastoral, regards the returning spring birds with whimsical pleasure: "The road became a channel running flocks / Of glossy birds like ripples over rocks." The intensely self-aware narrator imagines their "talking twitter" (*CP* 221), and his imagination takes delightful flight as he startles them out of the road. The poem's affirmative conclusion offers an intimation of its sentimental roots that bring to earth the levity of the preceding lines:

> Well, something for a snowstorm to have shown
> The country's singing strength thus brought together,
> That though repressed and moody with the weather
> Was nonetheless there ready to be freed
> And sing the wild flowers up from root and seed.
>
> (*CP* 221)

"The Onset" accomplishes a similar concluding gesture, affirming spring in the face of death. The snow will melt, the narrator affirms, and "all go down hill / In water of a slender April rill"; finally, there will be resurrection: "Nothing will be left white but here a birch, / And there a clump of houses with a church" (*CP* 209). While the poem can be read—against the grain, I think—in darker fashion, the implicit reference to God at the end affirms a faith more typical of sentimental and genteel than modernist poetry. On a slightly different note but with an analogous closing gesture, the witty, moody "Good-by and Keep Cold" envisions the danger of too much heat to the narrator's apple orchard and acknowledges his powerlessness with the seasons by concluding, "something has to be left to God" (*CP* 211). The rhetorical force conjures and depends upon precursor sentimental poems' supposedly "pat" invocation of the divine. Whether one is a popular reader and accepts the statement at face value or a critical reader who overlays it with irony is not the point: surely, Frost (who, again, wanted to be "a poet for all sorts and kinds") relied on making both interpretations available.

The muted feminine voices of *New Hampshire* find a less equivocal articulation in "The Runaway," in which a passing couple see a Morgan colt frightened by his first snowstorm. The depiction of "the miniature thunder" the colt causes in bolting is the only real moment in the opening lines in which the narrator's voice departs from realistic description reminiscent of regionalist fiction. Like "The Pasture," the lines that follow invoke the conventional icon of the mother, as the protagonists seek to calm and protect the terrified colt:

> "I think the little fellow's afraid of the snow.
> He isn't winter-broken. It isn't play
> With the little fellow at all. He's running away.
> I doubt if even his mother could tell him, 'Sakes,
> It's only weather.' He'd think she didn't know!
> Where is his mother? He can't be out alone."
>
> (*CP* 206)

"The Runaway" possesses a sentimental residue that is more audible than most of the poems of *New Hampshire,* and it signals the poet's unwillingness to relinquish this voice entirely. Combining sentimentalism with the language of regionalist/local color fiction, the poem marks out the spaces that Frost has already moved to abandon in favor of the canny and supposedly more "characteristic" voices of "Nothing Gold Can Stay" and "The Need of Being Versed in Country Things."

The quirky, dazzling pastoral "A Hillside Thaw" bespeaks this movement, with its gorgeous "ten million silver lizards out of sun" conjured not by "some magic of the sun" but by the poet's own audacity (*CP* 218). Playful, humorous, the first stanza elicits delight and amusement; the poem's humor accomplishes its purpose, of "disarming" the poet's enemies. But the second stanza tells a somewhat different, and more ominous, tale:

> It takes the moon for this. The sun's a wizard
> By all I tell; but so the moon's a witch.
> From the high west she makes a gentle cast

And suddenly, without a jerk or twitch,
She has her spell on every single lizard.

(CP 219)

Chilling the lizard engendered by the sun, the moon casts a spell that "held them until day, / One lizard at the end of every ray. / The thought of my attempting such a stay!" (*CP* 219). Confirming the traditional affiliation between moon and witch and transplanting the witches of Coös and Grafton from their places on earth to a safe distance in the sky (and in lyric poetry), the visionary, masculine, self-centered poet can affirm the power of this witch, which in the final line he appropriates ironically as his own. Am I taking the gendered rhetoric of this poem too "seriously"? Perhaps, from one perspective, the perspective that sees jokes about women funny but jokes about men not, the perspective that ignores gender relations almost entirely in Frost's work. But then again, and in another mood, perhaps not.

The gendered self-reinvention that climaxes in *New Hampshire* has ramifications for Frost's standing as a regional poet; by detaching himself from the domestic realm peopled by self-empowered women who tell their own and others' stories in compelling fashion, he indicates his designs on a larger canonical terrain: if the gossip has claims to a local audience, the bard seeks a national hearing. (Ironically, the matter of reputation, closely affiliated with women's sexuality, is deeply embedded in gossip itself; indeed, "fame," usually personified as female, itself embodies reputation in a larger sense.)[77] Even though Frost's increasingly lyric poems continue to focus on (another regionalized version of) nature, they indicate his participation in a version of American culture that we can say on the one hand stubbornly affirms the value of the natural world at the time of its ostensible disappearance and that on the other questions that affirmation. In one sense Frost continues the "nostalgic" tradition of regionalism (valued more by his popular readers), while he enters the realm of modernism (invented, or finally acknowledged, in the Trillingesque, urban, academic view of the poet)—although, as I have indicated, regionalism/local color is itself anything but monolithic in its attitudes and ambitions, and the "dark" Frost is almost everywhere present in the dramatic regionalist poems. In turning to lyric, however, Frost engages in another, more masculine version of national reinvention, with all the resonances of the frontier, on at least two levels. He appears to erase or subdue the increasing cultural heterogeneity of and conflict (about gender, race, ethnicity, class) in the United States in the early twentieth century, reinventing an idealized natural past for all Americans. At the same time, his ironic subtexts indicate anxiety about, or perhaps even a critique of, such a unifying project. It may be that the poet, riddled by ambivalence, wanted it both ways.

Regardless of his desires, Frost's movement toward lyric and away from narrative-dramatic modes (revisited in very different form in the *Masques*) emblematizes one of the continuing tensions in American literature and criticism: between popular writing affiliated with prolific, "scribbling women" who nevertheless could write "as if the devil was in [them]," and elite writing, associated with serious, intellectual men.[78] Paradoxically, his popularity was not compromised by such a move, for Frost went on to become America's unofficial poet laureate in spite of criticism by the cultural elite for his regressive, anti-modern formality, and to attract scorn from leftist critics for his ostensible detachment from—or, worse, his antediluvian attitudes toward—the crushing issues of modern life. Given the residue of its affiliation with women in the nineteenth century, this popularity would necessitate further proofs of masculinity, for, even though his newly hardened lyrics could be affiliated with a (male-but-feminine) romantic tradition, they also echoed and paralleled the work of female premodernists like Lizette Woodworth Reese and Louise Imogen Guiney, as I discuss in chapter 5. That these concerns about popularity and, indirectly, about gender were very near his thoughts is revealed in a journal entry of about 1919–21: "Is poetry highbrow or lowbrow. The ballads are one and Comus is the other. The distinction in poetry has no significance. Poetry may be either but it doesn't matter so long as it is spirited. Nor ouht [*sic*] it to matter to anything else which it is so long as it is spirited."[79]

The "more lyric" poems of *New Hampshire* discussed in this final section, many of which echo gestures of sentimental poetry, point again to the artificial critical distinction that segregates the two genres. At what moment does sentimentalism turn to "genuine" lyric, or, more menacingly for modernist poets and their allies, at what point does "real poetry" return to "verse"? Why is it difficult to see "The Death of the Hired Man" not only as lyric (another spurious distinction) or oral narrative but also as sentimental poem? (And, while we are at it, what about Pound's "The River-Merchant's Wife"? Eliot's "Prufrock"?) Similarly, the dramatic poetry more generally can be read as stories or lyrics or as a combination of (borrowing the terms from Littell's review of *New Hampshire*) prose, doggerel, verse, and poetry. The Western cultural prohibition against mixing has problematized our ability to hear multiple genres at work in single texts, especially by canonical authors. As Sandra Zagarell points out in another context, "individual literary works participate in genres rather than belong to them, and a number of genres are often present in a given work."[80] Elaborating the gendered inflection of multiple and sometimes competing genres, Frost's work exemplifies a distinguished and innovative mixing. Poems like "The Witch of Coös" and "Maple" express most interestingly and overtly his trepidations about poetic selfhood as it is formally elaborated; moreover, the same poem, as Frost's work amply illustrates, can occupy different generic and emotional territory for different readers, however much he might have wished to have been seen "simply" as a poet. As the next chapter explores in relation to sexuality and its connections with gender identity, how *we* define the tones and gestures of that work determines in large part how it is (and will continue to be) read.

## Chapter 4

# "Button, Button . . ."
## Becoming a Man's Man

Bradford and I had out the telescope.
We spread our two legs as we spread its three,
Pointed our thoughts the way we pointed it,
And standing at our leisure till the day broke,
Said some of the best things we ever said.
　　　　　　　—Robert Frost, "The Star-Splitter"

In a letter of about 1938 to R. P. T. Coffin, Robert Frost wrote: "A real artist delights in roughness for what he can do to it. He's the brute who can knock the corners off the marble block and drag the unbedded beauty out of bed" (*SL* 465). Frost (the "real artist") foregrounds the "real man" metaphor, here in an envisioned scene of projected rape of the virgin by the "brute" defined by his "delight in roughness." In anticipation of the discussion to follow, we might note this observation's striking resemblance to Whitman at moments in "Children of Adam" ("I press with slow rude muscle, / I brace myself effectually, I listen to no entreaties, / I dare not withdraw till I deposit what has so long accumulated with me").[1] Frost's self-assertive "display of prowess" also presupposes the kind of regulative drive for autonomy and independence that is part of the inheritance of white male poets of the United States at this time, as he evokes a muscular and highly differentiated version of masculinity and, by extension, sexuality in a remark that unwittingly highlights the relatively recent necessity for (hetero)sexual self-definition.[2]

"Prowess" has other resonances in connection with World War I, at the time when Frost was just beginning to publish—to engage in the "effeminate" work of poetry and, at the same time, to inaugurate his career as a self-made man, capable, he hoped, of being a breadwinner by virtue of his muscular poetry alone. World War I marked an intensification not only of gender tensions but also of sexual ones; "as Wilfred Owen's poems testify again and again . . . the Great War produced for many men a 'front-line experience replete with what we call the homoerotic.'" In contrast to women writers' frequent experience of sisterhood, "the combatants' comradeship 'passing the love of women' was as often energized by a disgust with the feminine as it was by a desire for the masculine."[3] A corollary to these observations was the tenuous quality of manhood itself: a soldier might be lucky enough to survive the crushing dangers of technological warfare only to arrive home missing a limb, an eye, or other member; or be paralyzed, unable to "perform" not only sexually but economically.

What might it mean to be a man in such provisional and awful circumstances? As a poet, Frost's masculinity was under fire in analogous (if far less bodily threatening) ways; his display of prowess is poetic, not sexual, although the two often come together in his work—whether quietly, in the climax of "The Silken Tent," or somewhat more flamboyantly, in that of "In the Home Stretch." In "Maple" the poetic connection, like the sexual one of Maple and her husband, fails—no matter that she is reported to be pregnant. Similarly, Frost himself remains intact, refusing connection with Maple and waging war on feminine speech even as he admires its immediacy and power. The result is not a gossiping regionalist narrative that enables the reader to enter and empathize with multiple perspectives but one that holds us at arm's length. The voice that Frost obliterates in "Maple" encodes another kind of dissolution of boundaries that was potentially terrifying for the self-defined masculine poet: the boundary between the feminine and the homoerotic. The poems of *North of Boston, Mountain Interval,* and *New Hampshire* reveal Frost's working out of (in both senses) a tenable sexual identity and working through the idea of masculinity, not only in marriage poems like "The Death of the Hired Man," "A Servant to Servants," "In the Home Stretch," and "Home Burial" but also, perhaps more radically and affirmatively, in poems of same-sex relations such as "The Tuft of Flowers" and "To E. T." Frost's work reminds us that "masculinity is no more natural, transparent, and unproblematic than 'femininity.' It, too, is a socially constructed role, defined within particular cultural and historical circumstances, and the *fin-de-siècle* also marked a crisis of identity for men."[4]

In this chapter I will trace the outlines of Frost's conversion of sexualized discourse to gendered discourse and, in particular, of a rhetoric and posture centered around (homo)erotic relations to those framed by the ideas of masculinity and femininity. From one perspective the complex issue of femininity in the tradition of American poetry and the anxieties that such femininity engenders about one's legitimacy is elaborated in the ostensible and excessively assertive heterosexuality of Frost's poetic self, in his explicit self-connection with canonical male (and presumably masculine) poets like Wordsworth, and in his self-separation from nineteenth-century mainstream poets and New England regionalist writers. Read in the context of contemporary gay theory, however, Frost's increasingly insistent masculinity over the course of his career also cloaks an earlier alliance between femininity and the homoerotic, both of which voices and attitudes the poet ultimately minimizes.[5] Outlining how he represents and represses these alliances, I suggest that Frost affirms his manliness via a voice that is sometimes homophobic but at other times homosocial or even homoerotic and that the latter inflection emerges from his echoes of Whitman.[6] Frost has been aided in this project of repression by contemporary critics, and I remain concerned with critics' creation of Frost's persona (and repressions of his voice), both as it may have shaped the poet's own self-construction and as it continues to inform our understanding of his relation to masculinity.[7]

In turning to this angle of Frost's self-engendering, I will rely on more general historical discussions of masculinity than in previous chapters. Part I traces some historical, biographical, and critical contexts for the discussions that follow, making more explicit the concepts of masculinity represented in some of the heteroerotic poems of *North of Boston, New Hampshire,* and *Mountain Interval,* in which we have seen the speaker-poet struggling to locate a happy and productive middle ground between men and women in heterosexual marriage and in which contemporary manliness is often portrayed problematically. In the section entitled "Soon satisfied for the time being" I explore Frost's elaborations of and responses to a lesbian homoerotic self; homophobic male bonding and exaggerated claims of masculinity are one means to corral this dangerous self and to distinguish his manly poetry from the effeminizing sentimental and regionalist traditions. The third section maps out the dangerous allure of a masculine homoerotic self by suggesting Frost's echoes of Whitman, while the concluding remarks raise questions about the categorical construction of desire and resituate the tension between gender and (homo)sexuality in the poet's historical and biographical moment. Ultimately, I will suggest that, just as humor or irony was for Frost a form of "guardedness," or defense, another wall that the poet erected between himself and his readers was that of the gendered self—a wall that he hoped would never be penetrated.

## Sissy Poems and Poetic Boys: Sexuality and Poetry

> A man with feminine traits of character, or with the frame and
> carriage of a female, is despised by both the sex he ostensibly
> belongs to, and that of which he is at once a caricature and a
> libel.
>
> —Dr. Alfred Stillé, *A History*
> *of the American Medical Association*

Let me be clear at the outset: I am not suggesting that Robert Frost was
homosexual. What I will delineate is the way in which Frost's gender iden-
tity was fundamentally mediated by sexuality, his own and others, especially
in the cultural context when the early stages of his career took shape. In
addition to the war this context included the hardening of a specifically
homosexual identity in contrast to earlier concepts of particular *practices* not
constitutive of social identity. Citing the trial of Oscar Wilde, various writ-
ers' attempts to normalize homosexual identity, and sexologists' "question-
ing the moral censure and censorship with which their society surrounded
homosexuality," Gilbert and Gubar suggest that one result of such cultural
transformations was a linking of "social change with sexchange, feminism
with lesbianism."[8] E. Anthony Rotundo highlights not only the sexologists'
roles in the creation of a homosexual identity and the development of a
concept of homosexuality as a "condition with natural causes" (rather than
"unnatural" ones) but also the investment of homosexual individuals them-
selves in self-creation: "men and women whose sexual desires focused on
their own sex began to think of themselves as separate social groups."[9] In a
patriarchal setting female sexual self-sufficiency or independence, some-
times embodied as "lesbian," was marked as a threat not only to men but
also to mainstream culture itself. Moreover, homophobia directed against
women sometimes metamorphosed into a homosocial bonding among men
that may or may not have had a homoerotic component but that was, how-
ever expressed, appropriative and misogynous.[10] In this context D. H.
Lawrence's affirmation is exemplary: "Ego-bound women are often les-
bians, / perhaps always . . . of all passions / the lesbian passion is the most
appalling, / a frenzy of tortured possession / and a million frenzies of tor-
tured jealousy."[11] While (as Lawrence's own celebrated self-obsessiveness
indicates) *self-centeredness* represents a value term for many male writers, and
for masculine poetry in the romantic tradition, this same self-focus was
demonized when embodied in and engendered by women writers.

Masculinity, an important subtext of such reflections on lesbianism, appears as an important concern in a large number of Frost's earlier poems. Revealing great sympathy for and understanding of women's position in marriage, Frost's powerful heterosexual dramatic poems also display a profound uneasiness about masculinity and, not unrelatedly, about sexuality. We have seen how, in poems like "Home Burial" and "A Servant to Servants," heterosexual masculinity easily spills over from strength and prowess to brutality—a brutality that is not celebrated but problematized. In this positioning Frost affirms earlier attitudes toward masculinity and at the same time questions contemporary ones. Late in the nineteenth century "there was a growing tendency to look at men as creatures of impulse and passion, even as animals or savages." If a feature of middle-class masculinity throughout the nineteenth century was "passion," by the turn of the century the valuation of this association had changed from negative to affirmative, as ideal manhood became more bodily strenuous. Whereas earlier men regarded the expression of primitive passion as uncivilized and improper, by the turn of the century they were more likely to believe that the "'brutish' side of [a man's] nature . . . expressed his manliness."[12] In contrast to the stance he adopts later, which is reflected in Frost's remarks to Coffin cited at the beginning of this chapter, the poet often appears ambivalent about this form of masculinity in the early heterosexual dramatic poems.

"The Death of the Hired Man" and "In the Home Stretch" articulate a more affirmative perspective of masculinity in which the heterosexual couples come together by means of a wife's mediation and a husband's understanding and self-sublimation; masculinity is muted and transformed within a domestic economy of emotional concerns.[13] Both poems reaffirm the relationship of the couples at the end, but the bonding in "In the Home Stretch" is explicitly sexual, and this sexual connection is also enabled by the husband's reinvented, emotional—feminized—masculinity. Throughout the nineteenth century, as well as in our own, Rotundo explains, "boyhood experiences were teaching a youngster to master his inner world of emotions. . . . As boys learned to master pain, fear, and the need for emotional comfort, they were encouraged to suppress other emotions of vulnerability, such as grief and tender affection." What boys learned, men put into practice. The "tender, reflective male" "bore the social stigma of male femininity in a society that elevated gender separation to the highest level of principle,"[14] and he came to be affiliated with the homosexual male. In the face of these social constructs Frost's creation of the tender male in "In the

Home Stretch" is both daring and unusual. The normative detachment of middle-class men from emotional experience and, furthermore, from the ability to talk about that experience in meaningful ways results in utter frustration: emotional hardness represents, ironically, a kind of impotence that renders the men unable to perform in other ways. At one extreme of heterosexual relations, then, we see the alienation of "Home Burial" and, at the other, the working through to connection and consummation in "In the Home Stretch," in which the physical dominance of the male partner is muted, and more delicate emotional concerns, rather than economic or merely pragmatic ones, acquire potency. A version of this reinvented masculinity, which reveals a relatively dispersed subjectivity in both his characters and in the poet himself, emerges more readily and even more explicitly in some of Frost's homoerotic poems.

At this point I want to focus briefly on a critical comment that seems particularly resonant both in relation to "Maple" and "The Witch of Coös" and to the present discussion. Emphasizing Frost's (masculine) autonomy and individuality, Kearns remarks: "the mother co-opts one into a barrierless, empathetic chaos of contradictions."[15] An earlier observation may serve as a gloss: "Being 'mentally agape' is a clear perversion of the intact self, an invitation to violation, a dissolution of the virile tension between appetite and self-control. It also suggests, in the pun on *agape,* the 'open-mindedness' of liberal, collectivistic love that is nonexclusionary and undisciplined; *agape* becomes another kind of promiscuity."[16] In its reference to the dissolution of boundaries this observation points us back not only to feminist psychologists' depiction of feminine selfhood[17] but also to the important judgments on Walt Whitman rendered by D. H. Lawrence and F. O. Matthiessen. Lawrence, of course, mourned what he believed to be Whitman's loss of self: "Your mainspring is broken, Walt Whitman. The mainspring of your own individuality. And so you run down with a great whirr, merging with everything . . . [Y]our own individual self . . . sounds as if it had all leaked out of you, leaked into the universe." Or, alternatively: "Everything was female to him; even himself. . . . Always wanting to merge himself into the womb of something or other."[18] Given his aggressively individualistic self-representation, Frost himself might have authored Lawrence's modernist horror about merging. Yet, as his rhetorical stance in "The Witch of Coös" indicates, in spite of the horror, he finds such merging with a female alter ego seductive.

A second, more ominous (from Frost's perspective) affiliation between him and Whitman appears when we pair Kearns's remark that "the mother co-opts one into a *barrierless*, empathetic chaos of contradictions" with Matthiessen's accusation of Whitman: "in the passivity of the poet's body there is a quality vaguely *pathological* and homosexual. This is in keeping with the regressive, infantile fluidity, imaginatively polyperverse, which breaks down all *barriers*, a little further on in 'Song of Myself,' to declare that he is 'maternal as well as paternal, a child as well as a man.'"[19] The loss of selfhood, especially the individuation culturally assigned to masculine self-hood, implies not only the feminization of such a process but also its homo-sexualization.[20] In his discussion of Whitman, Matthiessen attempts to recapture for poetry an essentially defined masculinity that is all hardness, or, as Kearns puts it in discussing Frost, inadvertently echoing one of Matthiessen's keywords: "One who is compact, taut against himself, is mas-culine; to become loose, soft, and flaccid is to be feminized and to make manifest the female *pathologies* this state invites and proclaims."[21]

The conjunction between femininity, homosexuality, and pathology is no accident in conjunction with modernist discourse; it runs as a virulent sexist and homophobic subtext through the comments of many male mod-ernists, Frost included. Here we might recall Eliot's description of "the Feminine in literature" and of Stevens's notion that the making of verses was "a positively lady-like" habit as well as Joyce's remark that *The Waste-Land* "ends [the] idea of poetry for ladies."[22] These comments mirror the mood not only of the age but also of Frost himself as he praises a poem sent by his son Carol in a striking remark that resonates with sexualized as well as gendered terms: "No sissy poem such as I get from poetic boys" (*SL* 390). We might well wonder if Frost could have said the same, say, of Eliot's "Love Song of J. Alfred Prufrock." Frost's choice of language is telling and possibly self-conscious, for "the homosexual male and the man who were insufficiently manly were understood in the same figures of speech," and *sissy* was a term that commonly linked the two to suggest this effeminacy.[23]

This relationship between homosexuality and femininity has a long and complex history. Commenting on the "historically specific overlaying of the question of sexuality and the question of gender in modern Western cultures," Lee Edelman highlights "the way in which the issue of sexuality has been ideologically constructed upon a naturalized gender binarism that not only allows but, implicitly, requires that the image of a 'womanly' or 'feminine' man be interpreted within the field of associations that radiate from the culturally endorsed interpretation of male homosexuality."[24] Edelman takes on Lentricchia's conceptualization of Wallace Stevens (in an article that forms the basis for the chapter on Stevens in *Modernist Quartet*), which he suggests obscures the sexual component of what Lentricchia describes as the modern poets' feminization.[25] Interestingly, in the space between the precursor essay in *American Literature* and *Modernist Quartet* itself Lentricchia actually *erases* an earlier reference to gayness in Frost, in spite of the publication, four years earlier, of Edelman's penetrating (the pun is irresistible) remarks. What is left out in this case is as instructive as what finally makes it in *Modernist Quartet*. Citing Frost's letter of praise for his son Carol's poem ("No sissy poem such as I get from poetic boys"), Lentricchia observes in both the article and the full-length study: "(And note 'poetic boys': the provocatively gendered responses of Frost, Pound, and other male modernists were to a literary style, a cultural feminization, at work in the writing of both sexes)."[26] But in the earlier essay Lentricchia allows the idea he has introduced to peep briefly out of the closet of his parentheses only a few sentences later, specifying what has been lingering around the margins of his discussion: "Frost's sexual self image" was simultaneously "phallic inseminator" and "radical female creator," which combined permitted him to "penetrat[e] down—now the homoerotic image—into a man's depth."[27]

In the case of Frost surely part of the reason for the foreclosure of discussion on sexuality has been the poet's own obliteration of this subject by his self-creation as "manly"; critics have tended to foreground the obvious, to take him at his word in this case as they might not in others. The virtual absence of this discussion results in part from Frost's coded expression of a homoerotic subtext that transfigures itself into gendered discourse as a form of defense and, ultimately, as a means of reappropriating to himself heterosexual masculine power. That is, just as *class* in the United States is often a cover term for *race* (*welfare mother,* with its constellation of associations, is perhaps the most obvious example), so too is gender often represented as a translation of homoerotic preoccupations: for *feminist* many read *lesbian*. In this situation the aggressive self-representation of a male poet as manly or masculine should more often spark readers' response that perhaps the poet's anxieties lie elsewhere than with gender identity. Between Lentricchia's story of Frost as strong, manly (if socially and economically disadvantaged) modernist and Kearns's as threatened masculine poet lies a closeted middle term, such as gayness or effeminacy—a charge to which many male poets of the period are vulnerable, in sexual terms as well as in their aesthetic and generic affiliations with sentimental poetry.

## "Soon satisfied for the time being": Poetic
## Masculinity and Lesbian Power

> Be a man—that is the first and last rule of the greatest success in
> life.
>
> —Albert J. Beveridge,
> "The Young Man and the New World"

Paradoxically, as this section will explore, a harder and more authentic man-
liness that could resist an endangering and independent (lesbian) female sex-
uality runs the risk of engendering an equally dangerous homoerotic bond-
ing. Returning to "The Witch of Coös," the subtextual drama that we
might read, then, would not focus on the difference between the witch's
husband and her lover but, rather, asseverate their *identity*.[28] Their war for
the witch's favors—another front on which men come together not only in
cooperation but also deadly competition—unmans them, quite literally, by
assuring their deaths. In this reading Frost's narrative becomes homophobic,
and the witch's excessive femaleness catapults them toward a more "inti-
mate" relationship with the other than either might have wished.

This excessive femaleness is *itself* homoerotically coded in the image of
the button. Here Paula Bennett's discussion of Emily Dickinson is helpful;
Bennett argues that Dickinson's use of "small, round objects" indicates the
poet was "replacing the hierarchies of male-dominated heterosexual dis-
course—hierarchies that disempowered her as woman and poet—with a
(paradoxical) clitorocentrism of her own, affirming her specifically female
power."[29] This association has endured over a long period of time, for,
"according to Robert Scholes, 'jewel' or 'gem' is the clitoris's only sec-
ondary meaning in classical Greek."[30] Like the metaphor of gems, "the Lan-
guage of Flowers has been Western culture's language of women. Most
specifically, it has been the language through which woman's body, and
even more particularly . . . women's genitals have been represented and
inscribed."[31] Frost's history in a family of poetic women and his growing up
in a period rich in women's poetry suggest the likelihood that he was famil-
iar with the language of gems and flowers and, possibly, with its elaboration
in the earlier Amherst poet's work.[32]

Seen in this context, the clitorocentric button dominates and focuses
"The Witch of Coös." The witch evokes her power and control in the
opening lines of the narrative: "Summoning spirits isn't 'Button, button, /
Who's got the button'" (*CP* 188). A womblike image of self-containment

and independence if there ever was one, the "button box" is, ironically, what also (reputedly) contains the remains, the bones, of the witch's lover, as if to signify that female sexuality also comprehends the dead residue of his own depleted and impotent passion. The opening passage anticipates the witch's search in her button box halfway through the poem; she breaks off her narrative in a parenthetical aside that is ostensibly spoken to herself or to the son but which, in its gruesome dailiness and its request for complicity, highlights for the listener the intense drama and co-optive power of her tale: "(Where did I see those pieces lately? / Hand me my button box—it must be there)" (*CP* 190). Afterward she continues her narrative of being haunted by the dead lover's bones, and the sounds that she makes echo as background noise beneath her own voice until the end, when the male narrator describes her final gesture: "She hadn't found the finger-bone she wanted / Among the buttons poured out in her lap" (*CP* 192). Not only is the phallic residue of the lover missing; it is magically transformed into a flood of buttons. The witch's clitoral sexuality, significantly located "in her lap," is not singular but multiple, both comical and terrifying in its excess. As Robert Faggen observes (though with a different emphasis), "Coös is not only a county but a New England slang word that means 'whore' and that echoes the ancient Greek *chaos,* meaning primal chasm and source of disorder."[33] Speaking and licentious female sexuality converge in the telling and acting out of this poem, and what makes this convergence even more significant is its autoerotic component, as if the lover—like the speaker of the poem—is inessential in the witch's sexual economy. If a woman is sexually independent, where does that leave a man? With other men, is perhaps the answer. From this perspective one link between homophobia and patriarchy becomes readily visible, and enforced heterosexuality not only ensures the continued availability of women's bodies; it also provides a necessary means of self-identification for the "normal" "straight" man.[34]

From this perspective we need to backtrack for a moment and trace the concern with female erotic self-sufficiency in Frost's earliest published work, for the sentimental "Wind and Window Flower," for example, gains another resonance. The wind is unable to capture the window flower; he is "concerned with ice and snow, / Dead weeds and *unmated* birds" (emph. added) in part because the remote beloved is identified with a warm, self-sufficient environment, and she is unwilling to leave "The firelit looking-glass / And warm stove-window light" (*CP* 20). Heat, and its mirror image, is self-contained, and the flower needs nothing or no one to generate warmth (or, for that matter, "light"); in fact, the arrival of the wind signals the loss of her erotic self-sufficiency and anticipates her death. "Flower-Gathering," too, bespeaks the impotence of the male lover in the face of the beloved's self-sufficiency, in spite of his picking the flowers, and his poetic performance (Was it any good? he seems to be asking the beloved in his assertion at the end that these flowers "are yours, and be the measure / Of their worth for you to treasure, / The measure of the little while / That I've been long away" [CP 22]. Did I measure up?).

"Rose Pogonias" represents another example of Frost's familiarity with the language of gems and flowers:

> A saturated meadow,
>     Sun-shaped and jewel-small,
> A circle scarcely wider
>     Than the trees around were tall;
> Where winds were quite excluded,
>     And the air was stifling sweet
> With the breath of many flowers,—
>     A temple of the heat.
>
> There we bowed us in the burning,
>     As the sun's right worship is,
> To pick where none could miss them
>     A thousand orchises;
> For though the grass was scattered,
>     Yet every second spear
> Seemed tipped with wings of color
>     That tinged the atmosphere.
>
>                                   (CP 22–23)

In the language of the opening stanza we have a highly coded drama of female sexuality. The wet, "saturated meadow" is "sun-shaped" and "jewel-small"; its reiterated roundness ("a circle") is self-contained and self-complete. In contrast to "Wind and Window Flower"—or in hothouse parallel to it—we see that winds are quite excluded. The effeminate or feminine lushness and gorgeousness of the imagery link this poem not only with the language of gems and flowers but also with its generic vehicle, the sentimental poem. The "temple" is a conventional nineteenth-century image for women's bodies, externalized here in the sun-shaped, sun-filled circle that is warm to the point of being overheated: the speaker comments on being "in the burning"; and in a kind of pagan ritual to summer, the protagonists "worship" the sun by gathering flowers. This scene becomes further complicated when we acknowledge that the flowers themselves ("orchises") are at once representations of female eroticism and coded metaphors for male sexuality: according to Kearns, in Greek *órchis* means "testicle."[35] From one perspective we could read this poem as a reference to the appropriation of male sexuality by female sexuality (with men picking "female" flowers); from another, as a representation of the transformation of male body parts into female ones. This subtle form of fooling represents Frost at his most elusive.

The closing stanza projects and even purports to invoke the "confusion" engendered upon mowers (most likely men, as "Mowing" suggests) in the face of powerful female sexuality figured by the flowers and their "jewel-small" setting:

> We raised a simple prayer
>     Before we left the spot,
> That in the general mowing
>     That place might be forgot;
> Or if not all so favored,
>     Obtain such grace of hours
> That none should mow the grass there
>     While so confused with flowers.
>
>                                   (*CP* 23)

The narrator seems to approve the isolation of this sexuality provided that he (and his partner, whose sex/gender is never identified) has access to it. This access is reaffirmed in "In a Vale," in which he describes his nighttime meetings with "maidens pale," who embody "every kind of bloom" and who vanish in the mornings, having given the narrator the ability to assert that he "know[s] so well / Why the flower has odor, the bird has song." Highlighting his "display of prowess" he claims, "No, not vainly there did I dwell, / Nor vainly listen all the night long" (*CP* 24). The tale of dominance—by "God" or the narrator or the poet or all three—culminates in "My Butterfly," in which the speaker envisions the butterfly as "a *gem-flower* waved in a wand" (emph. added). In one of its manifestations the "wand" is the poet's pen(is) by which the delicate sexual power of the butterfly is ultimately dismembered: "I found that wing broken today! / For thou art dead, I said" (*CP* 37). In the saying he makes it so.

However conscious or unconscious it may have been, Frost's understanding of the language of gems and flowers becomes more charged and emotional when female sexuality and textuality get out of hand, so to speak. The highly erotic "wet snowberries" in "The Pauper Witch of Grafton" intimate another perspective on self-directed female sexuality than longing, passionate affirmation, or arrogation—fear. Of Arthur Amy the witch famously confides:

> Up where the trees grow short, the mosses tall,
> I made him gather me wet snow berries
> On slippery rocks beside a waterfall.
> I made him do it for me in the dark.
> And he liked everything I made him do.
>
> (CP 194)

With its wetness, darkness, and clitoral snowberries, this passage intimates a feminine landscape over which men have no control. Arthur Amy aside, witches were traditionally women who represented independent sexuality,[36] and, as the Pauper Witch's ostensible "promiscuity" suggests, men were simply means to an end: pleasure. In the context of the present discussion femaleness, when it rejects or dominates masculinity, enforces a trajectory toward male helplessness (seen homophobically as "effeminacy" and, hence, "homosexuality") in the males that it encounters—whether they be the town fathers in Warren and Grafton, or the poet-listener in "The Witch of Coös."

On the other hand, it may also require a homosocial (and potentially homophobic, misogynous) bonding among males to confine or repress the independent feminine power that vibrates in these witch poems. In "A Fountain, a Bottle, a Donkey's Ears, and Some Books" the speaker provokes a male acquaintance to take a pilgrimage to an outdoor "baptismal font" that predicts, among other things, the creative self-baptism and self-authorization that the speaker conducts in the progress of the poem. A precursor to "Directive" and, in its worrying about female speaking potency, an affiliate of "Maple" and "The Witch of Coös," with which it appeared in *New Hampshire,* "A Fountain" is conducted by Old Davis, another avatar of the poet, who "only has at heart [our] getting lost." This lostness is cannily purposeful, preparing the narrator (and reader) for a descent to a deserted house (women's realm) whose most remarkable feature is its dereliction: "I never saw so good a house deserted" (CP 199), the narrator tells us. What is abandoned is the House of Poetry; Old Davis says:

> I want to introduce you to the people
> Who used to live here. They were Robinsons.
> You must have heard of Clara Robinson,

The poetess who wrote the book of verses
And had it published. It was all about
The posies on her inner windowsill,
And the birds on her outer windowsill,
And how she tended both, or had them tended:
She never tended anything herself.
She was "shut in" for life. She lived her whole
Life long in bed, and wrote her things in bed.

(*CP* 199)

Echoing Old Davis's scorn for both books and female poets, these remarks encode, in the language of gems and flowers, what the "guide" regards as her sterile sexuality. In an early reading of this neglected poem Robert P. Tristram Coffin highlights the poetess's smallness and limitations: "It is poetry *inside,* from in bed, poetry at two removes from life."[37] Although it mirrors the view of Emily Dickinson (as well as of Barrett Browning and Rossetti) at the time "A Fountain" was published,[38] this stereotypical image of the poetess comes undone when we restore the context of the language of gems and flowers. The conjunction between poetry, "posies" ("poesy," a snide reference to sentimental "verses" written by a "poetess"), and "bed" is hardly accidental. The woman writer whose sexuality is self-directed, self-confined, independent, is represented as ultimately self-defeating, sterile, helpless, sick, "shut-in," dead. Or perhaps, from another perspective, murdered.

This portrait of Clara Robinson transports us back to Mary Wilkins Freeman's Betsey Dole. The drama of Freeman's story—the rural female poetess unwittingly killed by the educated male poet, the minister—is reenacted in Frost's own "memorial poem," but the feminine voice that frames "A Poetess" and the sympathy of the author for her protagonist are erased. Although her income is exceedingly meager, Betsey is entirely self-sufficient, and her poetry substitutes for nearly all bodily and emotional needs, including food and love. Indicating again that regionalism is not inherently feminine and that its characteristic attitudes need not be those of empathy, Frost transforms this regionalist drama into an intensely sexualized and appropriative one explored from a masculine perspective, as gossip mutates into malicious and destructive action. The narrator's avowed fascination with books finds its outlet in the attic, the place of madness and sexuality in "A Servant to Servants." No lover here, though, but daunting female self-love embodied, as the narrator describes, in a proliferation of books:

the poetess's poems.
Books, I should say!—if books are what is needed.
A whole edition in a packing-case,
That, overflowing like a horn of plenty,
Or like the poetess's heart of love,
Had spilled them near the window toward the light,
Where driven rain had wet and swollen them.
Enough to stock a village library—
Unfortunately all of one kind, though.

(*CP* 199–200)

Again the affiliation between the poetess, poetry, love, and sexuality (the books are "wet," "swollen," pregnant as the "swollen" "bulkhead double doors" in "The Witch of Coös") ends in autoerotic satisfaction and a severely limited, almost unnatural progeny—the books are (alas!) "all of one kind." We know, or should know, that they are the *wrong* kind, at least according to the narrator-poet. To apply Coffin's reading in another context and with a different inflection: "these books are a small elegy of a whole world, a whole body of poetry."[39] This poem is a willed "elegy" for a woman whom the speaker identifies physically, bodily, with her books.

The narrator ostensibly reproves "boys and bad hunters" for "their outrage," their attempt to destroy the verse, but this attempt fails because the poetry is "invisible for what it was" or because it has "some remoteness that defied them / To find out what to do to hurt a poem" (*CP* 200). Utterly alien to them, it is familiar to, usable by, and vulnerable to the narrator, who ultimately pockets (and hence conceals, makes "invisible") a copy. Frost's own voice seems to emerge audibly here in the narrator's comic yet menacing exclamation:

Yet oh! the tempting flatness of a book,
To send it sailing out the attic window
Till it caught wind, and, opening out its covers,
Tried to improve on sailing like a tile
By flying like a bird (silent in flight,
But all the burden of its body song),
Only to tumble like a stricken bird,
And lie in stones and bushes unretrieved.

(*CP* 200)

This ostensibly comic passage confines Clara Robinson's verse to a violent and obscure end, conflating Clara's desire to have the poems soar "like a bird" with the narrator's determination to have them be "silent in flight" and weighted with the "burden of . . . body song." Women poets have the wrong body to write, and any attempt to "fly" ends in a spectacular crash orchestrated by the narrator-poet. We need to recall here an important nineteenth-century convention, the affiliation between women and birds exemplified in Cooke's "Captive," as well as to recognize that birds often figure female sexuality. The imagination of the book as a wounded bird thus encodes both the destruction of the (sentimental) poetess and control of her sexuality.

Not surprisingly, while the bookish narrator's own image takes flight, the sterile, self-satisfying woman poet's verses are abandoned, "rejected," in the attic, not good enough "to sell" or even "to give away." The poem's climax—and I use the word quite deliberately—is stunning in the context of the present discussion. As the two men rummage around the attic, Old Davis urges the narrator to "take all you want. / Good-looking books like that." The narrator highlights the proximity of this language to that spoken by men in collusion for control of women's bodies—here, control by these two men of the same woman:

> He picked one fresh
> In virgin wrapper from deep in the box,
> And stroked it with a horny-handed kindness.
> He read in one and I read in another,
> Both either looking for or finding something.
>
> The attic wasps went missing by like bullets.
>
> I was soon satisfied for the time being.
>
> (CP 200–201)

The terminology ("virgin," "horny," "stroked," "satisfied") highlights the erotic (and patriarchal) collaboration between the two men, while the image of the angry "wasps" evokes the spinster-poetess's clitoral sexuality besieging them ("like bullets") in futile ("missing") self-defense.[40] On this homosocial and potentially homoerotic terrain the two men wage (*really* masculine) war on the poetess's virginity: strikingly, the line about the narrator's satisfaction (which is only temporary—"for the time being"—since a "real man" is never *really* satisfied) constitutes a single stanza. In the end Clara Robinson's sexuality and her textuality are conflated and utterly appropriated:

> All the way home I kept remembering
> The small book in my pocket. It was there.

The poetess had sighed, I knew, in heaven
At having eased her heart of one more copy—
Legitimately. My demand upon her,
Though slight, was a demand. She felt the tug.
In time she would be rid of all her books.

(*CP* 201)

The narrator invents a drama of "satisfaction" for both himself *and* his guide, but his desire is satiated as much by their collaboration in overpowering her as by his "possession" of the poetess's sexual text—the "posies on her inner windowsill." Female erotic self-sufficiency threatens a masculine poet's self-definition, which ironically can be recovered only by his hypermasculine and spurious "rescue" of her, abetted by another man. The voyeuristic component of the poem and its sexualized overtones intimate the males' titillating, fearful homoerotic connection; Frost makes explicit the fact that in the United States "masculinity is largely a homosocial enactment."[41] In some sense the poem represents Frost's larger attitudes toward the work of precursor feminine poets and his disposal of the sexual and textual threat that they necessarily entail.[42] From another perspective, however, "A Fountain" performs a kind of painful self-destruction, as Frost figuratively kills the sentimental poetess in *himself,* the "sweet singer" that he acknowledged to Susan Hayes Ward, making way for a more manly replacement.

But this more manly replacement was not necessarily another man. Particularly challenging to Frost was the work and self-representation of one American woman poet: Amy Lowell.[43] As we have seen, Frost situated Untermeyer in competition with Lowell, and his letters to the former suggest considerable ambivalence for her personally as well as her work.[44] In the vanguard of promoting the new poetry as a masculine endeavor, Lowell argued in *Poetry and Poets* that, "whether written by men or women, [the new poetry] was in essence masculine, virile, very much alive. Where the nineties had warbled, it was prone to shout."[45] Constructing herself as androgynous, Lowell was so influential in poetry circles that she could make or break reputations, possessing an emasculating power to enhance or disable the potential earnings of male poets.[46] The poet recognized this power in his observation: "We all lost a publicity agent when she died. She stomped the country for everyone," while Untermeyer acknowledged in 1919 that "no poet living in America has been more fought for, fought against, and generally fought about than Amy Lowell."[47] Nevertheless, some of Lowell's own books were best-sellers, and there was a keen sense of competition between her and Frost. Probably responding to the publication of *Mountain Interval,* Lowell wrote to a friend, "Oh, I do wish I could beat Frost in having a best-seller just once!"[48]

In this connection Frost was both grateful for Lowell's promotion of his work and angry over her portrait of him in *Tendencies in American Poetry,* believing that she had circumscribed his work too narrowly in the vein of grim New England regionalism.[49] And, in spite of his affirmation to Lowell that "the great thing is that you and some of the rest of us have landed with both feet on all the little chipping poetry of a while ago. We have busted 'em up with cavalry,"[50] he also saw in her (as he did in most other poets) a competitor. Lowell would not only write the famous poem "Lilacs," which affirmed her New England roots, but also a number of powerful dramatic poems that rivaled his own, including "Number Three on the Docket," a monologue spoken by a farm woman who kills her husband because of maddening loneliness; "The Rosebud Wall-Paper," about a man who draws on his walls powerful scenes of apocalyptic destruction of his first wife, who has abandoned him and hence prevented him from marrying a beloved common-law wife; and "The Day That Was That Day," in which a woman intervenes in the suicide attempt of her woman neighbor. These are deeply compelling poems, and an excerpt from "The Day," in which the protagonist tells her neighbor about the grinding routine of her work, indicates the parallels with Frost's dramatic poems:

> "I ain't got no more'n most women,
> I know that,
> But I fuss a lot more.
> There's al'ays th' same things
> Goin' roun' like th' spokes to a cart-wheel,
> Ef one ain't a-top it's another,
> An' th' next comin' up all th' time.[51]

Lowell's dramatic poems—this one clearly recalling both "A Servant to Servants" and "In the Home Stretch," though others are less directly responsive to Frost's work—elicited a sense of threat to his reputation as the great New England poet, and, even though Frost wanted more, he also sought to occupy this territory alone. In one aspect of their rivalry the poets discussed the use of dialect, with Frost criticizing Lowell's isolation from the people that she purported to describe and each "contending that the other did not know true New England speech."[52] Frost's feelings were surely also complicated by the anonymous publication in 1922 of Lowell's "Critical

Fable," in which she conducted an irreverent romp of contemporary poetry that not only included unflattering portraits of Eliot and Pound but also, while seeming to regard Frost affectionately, touched upon several of his sensitive areas:

> There's Frost with all his blueberry pastures and hills
> All peopled by folk who have so many ills
> 'Tis a business to count 'em, their subtle insanities.
> One half are sheer mad, and the others inanities.
> He'll paint you a phobia quick as a wink
> Stuffed into a hay-mow or tied to a sink.
> And then he'll deny, with a certain rich rapture,
> The very perversion he's set out to capture.
> . . . . . . . . . . . . . . . . . . . . . . . . . . . . . .
> He's a foggy benignity wandering in space
> With a stray wisp of moonlight just touching his face,
> Descending to earth when a certain condition
> Reminds him that even a poet needs nutrition.[53]

Although Lowell reiterates here the critical bracketing of Frost as a regional poet that she had constructed in *Tendencies,* she manages also to focus on and expose, however indirectly or unwittingly, Frost's financial vulnerability, to which the poet was acutely sensitive and for which it must have been difficult to forgive her.

Beyond Frost's irritation at what he perceived to be Lowell's lack of understanding and his anxiety about her power in literary circles, a concurrent strain in their relationship may have been Lowell's sexuality, which was to become more and more explicitly articulated in her love poetry. She was in some sense the nightmare of every (heterosexual-identified) male modernist poet: an imposing, rich, well-connected, famous, masculine, cigar-smoking, self-confident lesbian.[54] "The Day That Was That Day" circles around the issue of sexuality, for the neighbor asks the suicidal woman, "Minnie, did you ever love anybody? / Any man, I mean?" (154), to which the protagonist replies: "'No, Rachel, I never did. / I know that sounds queer, but it's a fact. / I've tried to think I did, / But 'twarnt true."[55] Moreover, many of Lowell's best and most famous poems, including "Madonna of the Evening Flowers," "The Garden by Moonlight," "July Midnight," "Venus Transiens," and "In Excelsis," a poem of "complete adoration," were written to and about her beloved friend and companion of many years, Ada Dwyer (Russell); these poems elaborate a powerful and erotic romantic vision that must have shocked the conservative and intensely private Frost.[56] Dwyer was not only Lowell's secretary and research assistant but in most senses her "wife," handling all features of managing a large and complex household, including welcoming guests, among whom were the Frosts. Robert would have been faced with Lowell's lesbianism in the flesh as well as in poetry that expressed "passion and desire for the beloved."[57] Here Lillian Faderman is suggestive: "Throughout the late nineteenth century and the twentieth century, where women's demand for independence was the strongest and when it was most within their grasp, the conviction that female same-sex love was freakish or sick was at its most pronounced."[58]

The response to Lowell by other contemporaries, and especially her male contemporaries, was decidedly mixed. An irritable H. L. Mencken described Lowell's first book as "full of infantile poppycock," and he asserted rather baldly that "her celebrity . . . is largely extra-poetical; if she were Miss Tilly Jones, of Fort Smith, Ark., there would be a good deal less rowing about her, and her successive masterpieces would be received less gravely."[59] Because of her problems with overweight (caused by a metabolic disorder), some viciously called her by Pound's term, the "hippopoetess."[60] Ironically, Lowell herself believed that "I meet no jealousy from men who have arrived, like Frost, Lindsay, and Sandburg, but I meet with nothing else from those of lower rank."[61] For others, like Untermeyer, her physical appearance was less important than her imposing presence and ladylike demeanor; he observed: "One noticed only the marvelous neatness, the fine hands and delicate ankles, the small mobile mouth, the coolly modulated voice, the quick-appraising but not unkind eyes, the fine features and almost transparent skin. One saw a woman who was not only intelligent but— there is no other word for it—pretty."[62] For still others, such as her early biographer Clement Wood, her lesbian identity obliterated all other features of Lowell's life and work; Wood's homophobic diatribe, written only a year after her early death, surely contributed to her disappearance from the landscape of modernist poetry. One section stands out as particularly virulent: "The poet qualifies surely as an impassioned singer of *her own desires;* and she may well be laureate of *as many as stand beside her.* Modern psychology suggests the hypothesis that *this number* is increasing." Comparing Lowell's "blend, of the characteristics of the two sexes" to writers like Shakespeare and Whitman, Wood argues that "these remained predominantly men, with a man's attitude; and in their poetry these poets phrase as a rule *normal* human love in quality, however excessive the quantity may be." Finally, he observes:

Miss Lowell was not predominantly the woman in attitude; she was almost the reverse. Yet she was a woman; which brings up the essential paradox of her being and singing, the essential limitation of *the group for whom she speaks*. What causes achieved *this result* are matters for scientific research, in hers and other cases; the fact is spread publicly throughout her books. It leaves her a singer of *her own type of love,* rather than a tongue for the great desire whose sublimation is civilization.[63]

Decidedly *not* "universal" or representative by virtue of her deviant sexuality, which Wood indicates but never explicitly identifies, Lowell's work is narrowly partisan and, he implies, sickeningly deviant. Whether Frost read this biography or not, its attitudes represented a strong set of cultural norms that may have magnified the need to assert his sexual "normalcy" as well as his generic "difference" from a poet like Lowell.

Many other male poets of the time clearly shared Wood's feelings, complicated by their sense of Lowell's "gendered self-sufficiency" and her power and cultural authority.[64] This sense of her position is best expressed by Van Wyck Brooks, who describes her as "a born promoter": "[She saw] that America was giving birth to a first-rate product . . . put her shoulder to the wheel and pushed it on the market. . . . It was another form of Standard Oil; and Miss Lowell set out to put it 'on the map,' as others had put salvation or women's suffrage." But he launches an even stronger set of metaphors than the financial ones:

> For literary soldiership, or literary statesmanship, America had never seen Miss Lowell's equal. Literary politicians had always abounded, but she was the prime minister of the republic of poets; and under her control this republic rose from the status of Haiti and became an imperial republic of the calibre of France. . . . Her telephone had the force of a dozen Big Berthas; and God might have picked up the fragments of those who opposed her,—there was little left of them for men to bury.[65]

If Frost regarded Lowell with the kind of amused caution that Brooks's comments inspire, he nevertheless may have felt a deep, if ambivalent, sympathy for the poet who could write so passionately about love and, like him, identify it so closely with poetry.[66] Her dramatic self-representation and her overt lesbianism, however, surely had other uncomfortable resonances: a number of other women with whom Frost's work was regularly affiliated, most notably Alice Brown and Sarah Orne Jewett, could also be construed as lesbian writers,[67] a construction that probably inflected Howells's assertion of Frost's masculinity in the review that compared the poet to these women regionalists. Even as late as 1938, when Lowell and Jewett were dead and Brown largely forgotten, Sidney Cox would find it necessary to assert Frost's masculinity, along with his uniqueness: "he's always differentiated himself, though not so much by assertion as by behavior, from the prim and the ladylike and the hyperaesthetic."[68]

## "Men work together": Homoerotic Affiliations

> It's important to know where I got this vers libre
> I dont want you to think I got this vers libre from Whitman
> Or from the French writers who got theirs from Whitman
> I dont want you to know where I got it
> For fear you may not think I am as original as I am.
> Surely I got it from somewhere
> I dont pretend to say I invented it? . . .
> Well let me give you the facts
> I never read Whitman
> Not so's to know it.[69]

If the "ladylike and hyperaesthetic," as Cox indicated, were to be avoided, one way of doing so was for Frost to turn, like Whitman before him, to the bodily masculine man whose commercial image was invented late in the nineteenth century and whose nationalistic ideology was forwarded by no less than Teddy Roosevelt himself. The "aesthetic" man was increasingly, at the end of that period and into the early twentieth century, associated with the dangerous sexual inversion or deviance typified by Oscar Wilde and with an "overcivilized" American culture affiliated with women.[70] "Rather than civilize themselves according to a feminized definition, men took the negative labels affixed to their character and made them into virtues. . . . The obsessions of male writing about manhood in the late nineteenth and early twentieth century—competition, battle, physical aggressiveness, bodily strength, primitive virtues, manly passions—all were inversions of 'feminized' Victorian civilization."[71] Connecting the anxieties about homosexuality in middle-class American culture with those about gender, Rotundo argues that the new definition of *homosexual* at the end of the nineteenth century "was about more than homoeroticism—it was a need to create a category of person who could represent men's unacceptable feminine impulses."[72]

James Gifford identifies paired groups of paradigmatic (and often overlapping) roles into which homosexuals could be sorted in the early years of the twentieth century. One of these groups was indeed the "Aesthete," but the roles as a whole, he argues, "take their meaning within a set of practices we now identify as imperialism, that is, the homosexual as a threat to (male) empire."[73] In its aesthetic form homosexuality became identified with the feminine traits of beauty, culture, and learning, and, after the Wilde trial of 1895, the aesthete was projected onto British men in particular, in one form of American nationalism.[74] At the other extreme was a Whitmanesque, hypermasculine "Athlete" found most readily in the gymnasium and the military. Here, too, we see the crossing over of sexuality and gender, for in the eroticization of a "hard, muscular, athletic body" lies a specifically gendered kind of social power.[75] This section explores Frost's affiliation with Whitman and his performance (like his precursor) of this polarized yet interdependent set of attitudes.

In reflecting on the aesthete-athlete pairing in relation to Frost, two concrete connections are worth noting. The first is the poet's attraction to Willa Cather's story, "Paul's Case," about a sensitive (aesthetic, feminine, homoerotic) young man who, rejecting the mundane ugliness of small-town life, steals money from his employer in order to go to the city, where he can indulge his love for beautiful things. When he is discovered, he commits suicide rather than return to his former life. In some sense, we can argue, Paul has "come out"—not surprisingly in the city, the locus of increased homosexual visibility in the late nineteenth and early twentieth centuries—and this suicide represents an acknowledgment that he can no longer conceal his real self.[76] Frost "expressed rare admiration [for] the fiction of Willa Cather,"[77] who was not only Jewett's protégé but also a lesbian herself. This appreciation extended to his own teaching; his 1924 notebooks include notations about teaching the story to his Amherst students.[78] The other connection between Frost and the aesthete comes not from Frost himself but from Amy Lowell, for her portrait of him in "A Critical Fable" represents him clearly in this vein. Not only does his denial of "perversion" and "phobia" have "a certain rich rapture," but the poet himself is feminized in the description: "He's a foggy benignity wandering in space / With a stray wisp of moonlight just touching his face." Given the regular association of him with women regionalists and Lowell's portrait of the poet as somewhat soft and ethereal, Frost opted to take refuge in the ostensibly more masculine (but ironically ambiguous, at this time) figure of the rugged, outdoor, manly man, a type of athlete attendant to the concerns of men. Moving from a kind of poetry that was both ambiguous in its genre and that frequently used the speaking voices of women, Frost transformed his work in the direction of greater detachment, hardness, as time went on.

Yet the homophobic links between (female) gender, sexuality, and textuality that we see in "A Fountain" are only part of the story. On one level it is true that we can read a poem like "The Ax-Helve" as indicative of the poet's "fear that intimate male interaction can become sexualized and hence destructive," while "Mending Wall" can be read as a map for avoiding this potential disaster: only by keeping the wall between them is it possible for men to have free, even intimate relations.[79] While homophobia certainly figures prominently in the poet's work and is essential for his recovery of a hardened masculinity that impels generic self-transformation, however, it does not represent his attitude as a whole. By reconnecting Frost's explorations of homoerotic themes (and their correlative stances for poetic selfhood) with their historical and biographical contexts, we can see that the same-sex poems in Frost are not always or primarily homophobic. A number of early poems in particular evince a nuanced and delicate masculinity that is much more attractive than the manliness represented in the poems of heterosexual love; they embody a positive account of men together, a homosocial and even homoerotic bonding that is not merely a response to female sexual independence (embodied literally in Amy Lowell) but of primary and autonomous significance in Frost's work. Some display echoes of Whitman. These homoerotic poems remain crucial to an understanding of Frost's complex self-engendering.

With the recognition of what Edelman calls "homographesis"—which is both writing gayness and writing about gayness—"Seeing no longer precedes in order to produce, as by 'nature,' understanding; understanding, instead, becomes the prerequisite for a subsequent act of seeing, conjured as by 'a magician's wand,' that figures the transformative agency of ideological perception."[80] Four examples in Frost's work make this delicate masculinity more visible and more affirmative. The first poem that I will point us toward is, as I suggested earlier, easily conceptualized in the terms of the present discussion as feminine: "The Pasture." The poet urges the reader to blur the margins of the self and share his journey, invoking the mother as a culturally privileged image and means of access. In some meaningful sense this is not merely a sentimental poem but a "sissy poem," just as "The Death of the Hired Man" and "In the Home Stretch," with their affirmation of feminine values of home and emotional connection, are sissy poems. When we regard "The Pasture" from the angle of vision suggested by homographesis, what becomes visible (or, rather, what we consequently *make visible*) is the possible conflation, affirmatively coded here, of gendered and sexualized perspectives. This affiliation becomes more persuasive when we juxtapose the welcoming "You come too" with Whitman's invitations to a reader often conceived of not merely as sentimental and feminine but also as gay:

> To one a century hence or any number of centuries hence,
> To you yet unborn these, seeking you.

> When you read these I that was visible am become invisible,
> Now it is you, compact, visible, realizing my poems, seeking me,
> Fancying how happy you were if I could be with you and become your
>     comrade;
> Be it as if I were with you. (Be not too certain but I am now with you.)[81]

In spite of Whitman's much fuller (and more insistent) articulation of the imagined intimate dynamic between reader and poet, Frost's opening poem elaborates the same gesture, a similar quiet tone, and an awareness of future readers. Both poets speak from a position of vulnerability and intimacy, evincing a willingness to dispense with poetic autonomy and, at least apparently, to relinquish the power of a heterosexual, phallogocentric position.

Both Whitman and Frost have been accused of hyperventilating over their masculinity; both are commonly assumed to have powerful, autonomous selves. But, as Lawrence's comments on Whitman cited earlier indicate, this tightly controlled, well-organized self is at risk, provisional, in connection with cultural femininity; "merging" is not the act of a masculine self, much less a masculine poet in the romantic tradition. The loss of selfhood, and especially of the individuation culturally assigned to masculine selfhood, implies not only the feminization of such a process but also its homosexualization. The self who could speak with a kind of intimacy, invitation, and fluid identity similar to that in Whitman can be read as effeminate.[82] In Frost these tones become most evident, perhaps, when he conceived his reader not as a hard masculine critic, willing and able to deny him access to the canon as a real poet (and real man) but, instead, as a close male friend who shares the same attitudes, values, and goals.

In conjunction with this strand of discussion we should look at another poem that Frost published early in his career, "The Tuft of Flowers." It is worth highlighting an important homosocial context in which the poem was read: the Men's League of the Congregational Church in Derry in

1906.[83] Too shy to speak himself, Frost gratefully allowed a friendly trustee of Pinkerton Academy, Charles Merriam, to read it for him. "The Tuft of Flowers" secured the poet a teaching position that was an important means of providing for his family. The poem would also receive significant attention from none other than (lesbian) Willa Cather, who mentioned it prominently in the introduction to her edition of (lesbian) Jewett's *Country of the Pointed Firs,* as she compared the two texts, possibly with an understanding of the homoerotic subtext that propels both: "It [Jewett's novel] will be a message in a universal language, like the tuft of meadow flowers in Robert Frost's fine poem, which the mower abroad in the early morning left standing, just skirted by the scythe, for the mower of the afternoon to gaze upon and wonder at—the one message that even the scythe of Time spares."[84] Affirming both the affinity between Frost's and Jewett's work and suggesting their shared "universality," Cather was clearly responding to and attempting to intervene in matters of regionalism and canonicity as she invoked Frost's lovely poem:

> I went to turn the grass once after one
> Who mowed it in the dew before the sun.
>
> The dew was gone that made his blade so keen
> Before I came to view the leveled scene.
>
> I looked for him behind an isle of trees;
> I listened for his whetstone on the breeze.
>
> But he had gone his way, the grass all mown,
> And I must be, as he had been,—alone,
>
> "As all must be," I said within my heart,
> "Whether they work together or apart."
>
> (*CP* 30)

Readers steeped in Whitman cannot avoid the echoes of *Leaves of Grass;* to "turn the grass" inescapably suggests Frost's revision of his precursor's "leaves." The sensual details, particularly "the dew before the sun," conjure a scene of hidden climax, the predawn wielding of a "keen blade" that created "the leveled scene." In the apparently satisfying absence of his predecessor, however, the narrator evokes a scene of work that separates him from Whitman's narrator, who is unapologetically unemployed in "Song of Myself": "I loafe and invite my soul, / I lean and loafe at my ease observing a spear of summer grass."[85] Frost's two men, both alone, work not "together *or* apart" but paradoxically together *and* apart; finding an imaginative bond with his precursor, the narrator's voice carries a certain poignant resonance and even feminine vulnerability in the recognition of his own aloneness. In some sense this relationship and the masculinity it somewhat paradoxically confers render Frost's speaker *less* alone than a man like Amy's husband in "Home Burial."

Beyond the imaginative connection between men that Frost shares with Whitman in these opening lines, the stanzas that follow in "The Tuft of Flowers" suggest another parallel between the two poets: "But as I said it, swift there passed me by, / On noiseless wing a bewildered butterfly." In a delicate, redefined masculinity evoked by images that recall Mary's "harp-strings" in "The Death of the Hired Man," Frost transforms Whitman's "noiseless patient spider" into a butterfly, and he traces the earlier poet's "filament" in the circular flight of the butterfly returning to the narrator, for whose imagination it, like the spider, serves as an objective correlative. Both these poems speak of aloneness (Whitman: "I mark'd where on a little promontory it stood isolated")[86] within a larger pattern of imaginative connection, but in Frost's the connection takes an erotic turn as it unfolds and concludes:

> I thought of questions that have no reply,
> And would have turned to toss the grass to dry;
>
> But he turned first, and led my eyes to look
> At a tall tuft of flowers beside a brook,
>
> A leaping tongue of bloom the scythe had spared
> Beside a reedy brook the scythe had bared.
>
> The mower in the dew had loved them thus,
> By leaving them to flourish, not for us,
>
> Nor yet to draw one thought of ours to him,
> But from sheer morning gladness at the brim.
>
> The butterfly and I had lit upon,
> Nevertheless, a message from the dawn,
>
> That made me hear the wakening birds around,
> And hear his long scythe whispering on the ground,
>
> And feel a spirit kindred to my own;
> So that henceforth I worked no more alone;
>
> But glad with him, I worked as with his aid,
> And weary, sought at noon with him the shade;

And dreaming, as it were, held brotherly speech
With one whose thought I had not hoped to reach.

"Men work together," I told him from the heart,
"Whether they work together or apart."

                                                            (*CP* 31)

Ironically, the tender masculinity of this poem seems much more affirmative than the brutish male sexuality appearing in poems like "The Subverted Flower" and "Home Burial" (as well as in Frost's comments about the brute cited at the beginning of the chapter); such tender masculinity can, of course, be judged to border on feminine sentimentality for its "rather saccharine imagery and tidy moral."[87] Among the many resonances of this delicate poem is the fondness for bees and flowers that inhabits Dickinson's work and that often intimates a sexual relationship formed by both desire and resistance; to interpret this poem in these (heterosexual) terms, with the flower representing a female presence and the butterfly a male seeker, takes little effort. More neutrally, we can agree with Robert Faggen's observation that the poem "contains in embryo many of the problems that haunt Frost's greatest pastoral poetry; the tension between work and play, the reconciliation of the individual and the community, and the problem of design and providence in events." We can also read the poem as a measure of Frost's homophobia: "rather than manifesting the consummation of the intimately homosocial, it merely recapitulates the expression of such desire. . . . the fraternal tie in 'The Tuft of Flowers' exists purely at the level of illusion."[88]

At the same time, however, more affirmative echoes of Whitman seem inescapable. The notion of meeting while apart that permeates *Leaves of Grass*—especially of *men* doing so in the "twenty-eight young men" section of "Song of Myself" and *Calamus*—is elaborated here in careful detail. Unlike Whitman, Frost's speaker begins with little confidence in the connections between men for, reflecting the poet's characteristic independence, the speaker focuses on how he is "alone, / As all must be." This acknowledgment comes after the disappointment of the speaker seeking the companionship of his alter ego and failing to locate him; embodying an apparently lost principle of sameness, this other self parallels and affirms who he is. The butterfly enacts the path of the narrator's yearning toward this other self objectified in the "tall tuft of flowers beside a brook," in which the tuft (bunch, knot, head) speaks another erotic language, "a leaping tongue of bloom." I cannot imagine these flowers as other than red, perhaps because

of the poem's connection in my mind with a "children's" poem by Sarah
Orne Jewett that figures "the scarlet tufted flowers" as emblems of Native
American male sexuality.[89] But, even without this admittedly quixotic link,
the push of the flowers and the accident of their location "beside a brook"
echo Whitman's image of the calamus plant:

> In paths untrodden,
> In the growth by margins of pond-waters,
> Escaped from the life that exhibits itself,
> From all the standards hitherto publish'd, from the pleasure,
>     profits, conformities,
> Which too long I was offering to feed my soul,
> Clear to me now standards not yet publish'd, clear to me that my soul,
> That the soul of the man I speak for rejoices in comrades[.][90]

Also rejoicing in "comrades," Frost's speaker hears "a message from the
dawn" and feels "a spirit kindred to my own; / So that henceforth I worked
no more alone." There is also in both poems a shared sense of privacy, even
secrecy, about the encounter between men that suggests another connec-
tion. Robert K. Martin points out the affiliation between "In Paths Untrod-
den" and "one of the most famous of homosexual poems, Virgil's Second
Eclogue," arguing that "Whitman, like [Virgil's protagonist] Corydon,
withdraws from the world to find solitude in dark places and to draw forth
his art from this experience of impossible love."[91] In terms similarly remi-
niscent of "The Tuft of Flowers," Martin affirms, "The plants of Whitman's
pastoral are real not literary, American not Roman; but their use as a love-
token imitates one of the greatest homosexual love poems."[92] As an out-
standing classicist as well as reader of Whitman (all protests like the epigraph
to this section aside), it seems likely that Frost would have been conscious
of this borrowing.[93]

The speaker's rejection of solitude and the "brotherly speech" that
ensues in "The Tuft of Flowers" also echo the perspective of the speaker of
"I Saw in Louisiana a Live-Oak Growing":

> I saw in Louisiana a live-oak growing,
> All alone stood it and the moss hung down from the branches,
> Without any companion it grew there uttering joyous leaves of dark green,
> And its look, rude, unbending, lusty, made me think of myself,
> But I wonder'd how it could utter joyous leaves standing there alone
>     without a friend near, for I knew I could not,

. . . . . . . . . . . . . . . . . . . . . . . . . . . . . . . . . . . .
Uttering joyous leaves all its life without a friend a lover near,
I know very well I could not.

In both poets the "utterance," the "brotherly speech," is in part the labor and love of making the poem itself, a homoerotic birth engendered by their speaking together, however imaginatively: "Men work together . . . Whether they work together or apart," affirms Frost's speaker. Of course, he issues a partial disclaimer of the actual connection—the "mower" left the flowers, he says, "nor yet to draw one thought of ours to him, / But from sheer morning gladness at the brim"—and the "message" is "from the dawn." But the writing implement, which is also the instrument of "labor," is the scythe, whose wordless speech engenders "dreaming" of his other self in an erotic partnership far more affirmative than we see in his poems representing explicitly heterosexual masculinity.[94]

This reading clearly represents one informed by "understanding as the prerequisite for seeing," to echo Edelman again, but I think that the poem sustains it. These connections with Whitman seem persuasive enough, but we might also refer to Kearns's analysis of another Frost poem in which a scythe figures. "Mowing" may represent a fuller (and yet less satisfying) elaboration of the homoerotic display enacted in "The Tuft of Flowers," for here the phallic scythe cuts down its avatar, the tuft metamorphosed into the testicular "spiked orchis."[95] The homoerotic tension of both this poem and "The Tuft of Flowers" is often translated or coded in feminine or heterosexual terms both by the poet and by his critics, who often regard "Mowing" as "a glorification of heterosexual love."[96] Here the speaker has to deny, to cut down this elided drive, figured in the snake and the testicle-flower, with the phallic scythe: "There never was a sound beside the wood but one, / And that was my long scythe whispering to the ground . . . / My long scythe whispered and left the hay to make" (*CP* 26). Why this insistence, bracketing the poem, on the "long scythe"? In comments that are inadvertently telling in this reading, Kearns asserts that "the scythe may always bring the orchis and the bright green snake from underneath the hay . . . if only for the briefest flash of an instant and in *seeming* to repudiate them may illuminate momentarily the interdicted space: that place *between* the lines."[97] If it is through his "infinity of small gestures [that Frost] will inevitably keep one from looking to some main point or toward where the main point should be," then this "interdicted space" is bracketed not only by gender but also by sexuality.[98]

In this space sexual difference becomes coded as gender difference, and, in an era at once more homophobic and yet more open to sexual experimentation than Whitman's, Frost appears to translate images of (homoerotic) sameness into (heterosexual) difference.[99] One problem with this reading of Frost, of course, is that, "as soon as homosexuality is localized and consequently can be read within the social landscape, it becomes subject to a metonymic dispersal that allows it to be read *into* almost anything."[100] Another, more vexed problem is the ready transferability of this story of homoerotic male connection into one of heterocentric and patriarchal male bonding. The same story, interpreted from different perspectives—whether the critic's or the poet's—can mean differently. But the version of male connectedness imagined by "The Tuft of Flowers" seems to me to gesture very differently toward the reader than the voyeuristic and vengeful narrative in "A Fountain." While I grant that we can read "Men work together . . . whether they work together or apart" as an ominous encapsulation of patriarchal threat against women—and, as the next chapter suggests, Frost's later voice invites us *retrospectively* to translate the lines in this way—I think that here the narrative expresses a poignant, revealing reach toward a male other-self that is not invested in, or merely a cover for, the heterosexual, patriarchal, and masculine dominance explored by the poet in "Home Burial" and "A Servant to Servants." Over time the poet repudiates *both* the homoerotic and its cultural ally, the feminine self; reading the transformation of the former here points toward the ultimate erasure of the latter.

If one version of the homoerotic self is the feminized aesthete, another is represented by the athlete, the manly man who loves men, and both "The Tuft of Flowers" and "Mowing" weave together the two postures (and voices that evoke them) in interesting ways. Other poems also display traces of this dualism with a self-conscious and wry emphasis on the manly man. Gifford argues that, "aside from the West, the hypermasculine model of homosexuality owed a great deal to the legacy of Walt Whitman, whose praise of the blue-collar man as the salt of the earth found its object in soldiers, construction workers, and trolley-car drivers."[101] In "A Hundred Collars" we see the athlete seductively opposed to the aesthete in what we can choose to read as the comic triumph of a (homoerotic) hypermasculine over a feminized man.[102] The latter is "Professor Square-the circle-till-you're-tired," a small, delicate academic, while the former is the attractively yet repulsively robust Lafe, "A brute. Naked above the waist, / He sat there creased and shining in the light" (*CP* 51). The moment of highest comedy occurs for me when the two compare "collar" sizes in a classic game of "mine is bigger," which Lafe initiates:

> "I'm moving into a size-larger shirt.
> I've felt mean lately; mean's no name for it.
> I just found what the matter was tonight:
> I've been a-choking like a nursery tree
> When it outgrows the wire band of its name tag.
> I blamed it on the hot spell we've been having.
> 'Twas nothing but my foolish hanging back,
> Not liking to own up I'd grown a size.
> Number eighteen this is. What size do you wear?"
>
> The Doctor caught his throat convulsively.
> "Oh—ah—fourteen—fourteen."

(*CP* 51)

Lafe's backhand bragging (he's a *twenty* now) elicits the Doctor's (possibly exaggerated) admission of his own "size." In the context of the erotic description of brute masculinity that precedes it, this passage engenders laughter in the reader as it affirms a fellowship between the men, yet it also fosters in both the Doctor and the reader an anxiety about violation, in which the directionality of Lafe's sexuality is at issue and one way to read him is homophobically, as a menace. The Doctor's anxiety when Lafe offers to pull off his shoes is both comical and understandable: "'Don't touch me, please—I say, don't touch me, please. / I'll not be put to bed by you, my man'" (*CP* 52). Interestingly, in U.S. culture at the turn of the century, as in our own day, "muscular and sexual power become translated into economic power."[103] In view of Frost's obsession with economic success an ironic feature of the late Victorian concept of masculinity is its class inflection: "wealth and success by American men . . . was . . . producing the very effeminacy that was eroding manhood," and the working classes could presumably take advantage of this weakness.[104] We should not miss the conjunction of "collar" and "dollar" in "A Hundred Collars," for Lafe has ninety dollars, while the Doctor has only five ("that's all I carry," he tells his partner, as if to say that he has much more). Although Frost clearly pokes fun at the Doctor, his wit conceals an ongoing conflict inasmuch as he earned his living both by means of his (aestheticized, feminized) profession of poetry *and* through the enormous physical and manly power of his performances.

Lafe's erotic power is both the mirror image of and antidote to the delicate masculinity embodied by the Doctor, as the athletic and aesthetic ambiguously and deliciously come together. Furthermore, it reiterates the muscular manliness imagined by Whitman in the "Children of Adam" poems that he wrote as a partner to and rebuttal of the "Calamus" poems. If "Song of Myself" mixes the delicate with the firm, imagining "manhood balanced and florid and full," the poet as "the teacher of athletes" who is at the same time the loafer, the "female" viewer of the "twenty-eight young men" bathing section, the lover of opera and the "trained soprano," then "A Woman Waits for Me" invokes the brutal male heterosexual who effectively rapes his partner: "I am stern, acrid, undissuadable, but I love you, / I do not hurt you more than is necessary for you, / I pour the stuff to start sons and daughters fit for these States, I press with slow rude muscle."[105] In this ambiguous America "the insistence on Victorian ideals of virility looms large when it is linked with a more suspicious sexuality: it is this fundamental alliance that underlies the Athletic notion of homosexuality."[106] As "A Hundred Collars" recapitulates, muscular manliness promised a duplicitous sexuality that could be regarded from either homophobic or homoerotic perspectives.

## "I slumbered with your poems on my breast": Reading Manhood

> I wish Edward Thomas (that poet) were here to ponder gulfs in general with me as in the days when he and I tired the sun down with talking on the footpaths and stiles of Leddington and Ryton.
> —Robert Frost, "A Romantic Chasm"

Earlier in this chapter I pointed to the presence of "a closeted middle term, such as gayness or effeminacy," that shadows some current accounts of Frost. Before we move to a discussion of the poet's intimate friendship with Edward Thomas and the poetry that it evoked, it may be useful to complicate this account of masculinity and sexuality by blurring the distinction or polarization between *homosexual* and *heterosexual*, inasmuch as these terms represent a categorical convenience rather than an actual bifurcation of human behavior or identity, and by introducing another candidate for this middle term, *bisexuality*. Of recent theorists Marjorie Garber has written in the most thorough and persuasive manner on the subject. Charting the attempts by contemporary culture to normalize bisexuality into a narrative of one or the other, heterosexuality *or* homosexuality, Garber underscores the erratic and constantly changing temporal topography of the erotic in juxtaposition to the diachronistic narrative that mainstream culture reductively constructs for desire. That is, in normative narratives of sexuality—whether from nineteenth-century sexologists or from contemporary popular culture—one "identity" or another must finally be reached for an individual to achieve decisive adulthood, with no account being made of or for changes over time and with the end of the narrative being assigned more weight than earlier moments. The very fluidity of sexuality itself is menacing.[107] Moreover, she suggests that desire itself may be more powerful than its actualization.[108]

Many of Garber's insights about the complexity of sexual desire and its cultural situation resonate in connection with Frost. Even as we acknowledge that many poems we might identify as expressing "homoerotic" or "bisexual" desire were written well before the experimental 1910s and 1920s, before Frost went to England—a perceived locus for same-sex desire and experimentation via the boarding school[109]—we can say that Frost had intense male-male friendships, sometimes expressed in poetry that, echoing Whitman, borders on the erotic. While the mandate in Frost's cultural climate at the time that these poems were written may have been to rigidify desire into one or another channel, "the nature of sexuality . . . is fluid, not fixed, a narrative that changes over time rather than a fixed identity, however complex. The erotic discovery of bisexuality is the fact that it reveals sexuality to be a process of growth, transformation, and surprise, not a stable and knowable state of being."[110] Furthermore, desire itself can contribute to crises of classification, in that it might signify an actual, not just a potential, crossing from one "identity" to another. While it seems unlikely that Frost ever acknowledged his potential desire for Edward Thomas as desire, or that he would ever have identified his sexual energies as multidirectional, such self-consciousness seems as unnecessary as labeling him bisexual (or homosexual) would be, inasmuch as we can acknowledge these extravagant energies without trying to capture and reduce them to homogeneity. What is important is first to acknowledge that what we might call homoerotic impulses and desires do not exclude a more unruly possibility of bisexuality and then to attempt to trace these energies' shapes and patterns, the ways in which they diverge and converge, both in Frost's poetry and in relation to some of the important figures in his life.

That Frost understood at some level the danger of homosocial relationships to masculinity is evident in an early letter to Untermeyer, written in September 1915, only six months or so after their lifelong correspondence had begun:

> Let me call you [Louis] that in the hope of softening a little the light with which you burn too bright for these old eyes. You mustn't be so intellectual with me. I shan't be at ease till we are on emotional terms where there is no more controversy neither is there any danger of crediting one or the other with more or less than we mean. Then we shall know when we are fooling because we shall be always fooling like a pair gay with love. We shan't mean anything too profoundly much except perhaps that we are friends and that nothing else matters between friends. (*LU* 13)

Of course, Frost uses "gay" in the sense of "lively" or "lighthearted," and his tone is jocular, as "these old eyes" suggests, for the poet was barely forty at the time.[111] Yet the letter expresses a striking kind of longing that parallels its humor. In much of the poet's correspondence to his friend—including the remarks on Amy Lowell that create a homosocial bonding—there is a kind of intensity and emotional collaboration that lends resonance to these lines.

An affirmatively homoerotic attitude emerges most explicitly, however, in another relationship. Edward Thomas was "the man who became the most intimate friend [Frost] ever had," and their "daily conversations and intensely emotional friendship" were important in the lives and work of both poets.[112] Thomas's finely nuanced understanding of Frost led him to compare his friend's work to that of Whitman and Wordsworth, as (speaking in terms that evoke Whitman) he emphasized Frost's "healthy natural delicacy."[113] This kind of delicacy emerges in a moving poem that Thomas wrote about their relationship, "The Sun Used to Shine,"[114] as well as in poems that Frost himself composed in connection with this intimate friendship, one of which is "The Road Not Taken."[115] This love between two men is articulated more explicitly in "Iris by Night," which describes an actual event. Out walking in the Malvern hills, the poets came upon a rare and memorable natural phenomenon: a rainbow that, as they approached it, did not recede but instead gathered its ends into a ring.[116] The "misty evening" atmosphere of the poem is erotically charged, with its "last wet fields and dripping hedges":

> Light was a paste of pigment in our eyes.
> And then there was a moon and then a scene
> So watery as to seem submarine;
> In which we two stood saturated, drowned.

In this otherworldly context, the rainbow works a "miracle":

> It lifted from its dewy pediment
> Its two mote-swimming many-colored ends,
> And gathered them together in a ring.
> And we stood in it softly circled round
> From all division time or foe can bring
> In a relation of elected friends.

(*CP* 288)

This friendship occurs in a realm outside of normal human events, in a utopian scene of intimacy that promises an eternal connection. Simultaneously romantic, sentimental, and ironic (with a playful reference to elusive "pots of gold"), the poem suggests a kind of marriage ceremony under "a small rainbow like a trellis gate." Recalling the delicate closeness of the (heterosexual) moonlit "Going for Water" without that poem's ambivalence, "Iris by Night" inverts the hothouse intimacy of "Rose Pogonias" ("the air was stifling sweet / With the breath of many flowers,— / A temple of the heat" [*CP* 22]) as it echoes the drugged mood and urge for privacy of Amy Lowell's homoerotic poems to Ada Dwyer Russell, especially "The Garden by Moonlight": "Moon-shimmer on leaves and trellises / Moon-spikes shafting through the snow-ball bush."[117] We learn early in the poem that Frost and Thomas are "one another's guide" in this moist Arcadian region evoked not only by the landscape but by the poem's reference to the ancient cities of Rome and Memphis. Published nearly twenty years after the events that it memorializes and indicating again the nonlinear movement of his developing masculine self-representation, "Iris by Night" represents one of Frost's most intense, provocative, and moving poems.[118]

Pointing us back to the homosocial proximity engendered by the war, Frost's poems about Thomas must be contextualized within the formation, "between the 1880s and the First World War," of "a sexual minority of sorts" that "elaborated an underground sexual subculture," most often in cities. Social historians John D'Emilio and Estelle Freedman observe that "sex was becoming a marker of identity, the well spring of an individual's true nature," and they add that "nowhere, perhaps, can this change be seen more clearly than in the new definitions and new social experiences that characterized same-sex relationships, especially among men." Perhaps their most significant point for this discussion is "the continuing salience of gender in shaping an individual's sense of sexual meaning, and to how the erotic remained attached to conceptions of gender."[119] The bond between gender and sexuality was still very strong, and any hint of effeminate behavior by men could be affiliated with unpalatable sexual deviance. Increasingly, "the effeminate homosexual provided a negative referent for the new masculinity, with its heavy emphasis on the physical marks of manliness. The emergent homosexual image soon acquired an awesome power to stigmatize."[120] By the early 1920s F. O. Matthiessen, writing to his male lover, would underscore the penalties for overt deviance: "we would be pariahs, outlaws, degenerates."[121] In spite of "the new positive value attached to the erotic" in the 1920s and the increased openness about sexuality in U.S. society, heterosexuality remained a norm, even as boundaries were often crossed and blurred, including the boundary between homoerotic and heteroerotic.

Coming of age and moving toward middle age in these circumstances, surrounded by the textual and sexual experimentation of other modernist writers, Frost could not have escaped engagement with matters of sexual identity; nevertheless, in a 1934 letter to Louis Untermeyer he asserts his innocence about sexual difference (like Whitman before him). Untermeyer does not explain this reference, as he does many others in the letters, perhaps on the principle that silence is the best defense. Here is Frost at length on the subject of female homosexuality:

> Those two girls again. They bother me only a little. From a certain way they had in inquiring about E. T. [Edward Thomas] I am led to wonder if they think all friendships may be like theirs. Maybe I misjudge them. Don't pretend you haven't heard more of such people than I have and even encountered them in polite society. It isn't your fault. You have merely been out around more than I. I am more prepared for them than I was when I went to England in 1911. There I first read of them in The English Review in a series of articles by the heads of the famous public schools—Rugby, Eton, etc. I had just as soon they stayed far from my sphere. It is not my nature to want to slap them in the face. I was tempted to tell them I knew the best poem in the book and would tell them which it was but for the fear of coming between two such with thoughts of rivalry in art. (*LU* 239)

The homophobia and sexism that punctuate this passage need no unveiling, nor does the poet's excessive protestation of naïveté, though Frost was extremely well traveled, being on the road for three or four months a year. Whether Frost's devotion to Thomas had a homoerotic or homosexual component is secondary here. What *is* significant is the recognition of this inflection in the poem by lesbian readers, resulting in the poet's acknowledgment and repression of lesbian identity, figured even in the oblique language of the letter itself; "such people," "public schools," "coming [!]

between two such."[122] We see again that "sexuality is constituted through operations as much rhetorical as psychological"; "as the figure for the textuality, the rhetoricity of the sexual, 'gay' designates the gap or incoherence that every discourse of 'sexuality' or 'sexual identity' would master."[123] Frost's "mastery" emerges in his lexical silencing of identity even as he acknowledges its deviant and threatening presence, which includes a knowing reference to "public schools."

"To E. T.," the poem that evoked the inquiry from the unnamed lesbian women, clearly opens itself to an interpretation of affirmative homoeroticism, offering a stunning echo of Whitman:

> I slumbered with your poems on my breast,
> Spread open as I dropped them half-read through
> Like dove wings on a figure on a tomb
> To see if in a dream they brought of you,
>
> I might not have the chance I missed in life
> Through some delay, and call you to your face
> First soldier, and then poet, and then both,
> Who died a soldier-poet of your race.
>
> I meant, you meant, that nothing should remain
> Unsaid between us, brother, and this remained—
> And one thing more that was not then to say:
> The Victory for what it lost and gained.
>
> (*CP* 205)

These opening stanzas gesture toward Whitman's "Vigil Strange I Kept on the Field One Night" and "As I Lay with My Head in Your Lap Camerado," as images of war, intimate speech, and intimate touch come together as they seldom do in more conventional love poems like "The Death of the Hired Man" and "In the Home Stretch." Moreover, the conjunction of lover and beloved occurs on more equal terms than in such sonnets (however lovely and delicate themselves) as "Meeting and Passing" and "The Silken Tent." In a moment of physical and emotional proximity that parallels the poet who vulnerably "slumbered with your poems on my breast, / Spread open," Whitman's poem begins, "As I lay with my head in your lap camerado, / The confession I made I resume, what I said to you and the open air I resume."

The human, physical link that Frost's speaker desires is transfigured by "the shell's embrace of fire":

You went to meet the shell's embrace of fire
On Vimy Ridge; and when you fell that day
The war seemed over more for you than me,
But now for me than you—the other way.

How over, though, for even me who knew
The foe thrust back unsafe beyond the Rhine,
If I was not to speak of it to you
And see you pleased once more with words of mine?

(CP 205)

Here we might recall that in one early discourse of homosexuality "male homosexuals would have most in common with heterosexual men who shared their delight in male companionship and, to some degree, their disdain for women."[124] Similarly, "many Victorian homosexual men saw the 'exclusion of women from their intimate lives as virilizing them.'"[125] An attraction to military life was a natural outgrowth or expression of this same-sex intensity, coupled with the ongoing emphasis upon a segregated, muscular, and athletic masculinity. If "romantic friendships [between men], idealized in the age of brotherhood, were often a step away from a deeper kind of love," then the military provided a location for the elaboration of an exclusionary (and sometimes misogynous, inasmuch as it was formed as a rebuttal to the charge of effeminacy) masculinity.[126] Both Frost's and Whitman's military images declare their speakers' masculinity, while they gesture equally insistently toward the homosocial and potentially homoerotic structures of military life and the connection between men that is embodied in linguistic as well as physical gesture. For Frost this linguistic gesture embodies the saying of what cannot be heard, the acknowledgment of the sameness of his own and his friend's goals as poets (even, perhaps, "soldier-poets"). Hence, Frost writes that the war cannot be over in the absence of speech: "How over . . . / If I was not to speak of it to you / And see you pleased once more with words of mine?" Ironically (given the poem's subject), this gentle and hospitable ending bespeaks both the dispersed feminine self of "A Servant to Servants" and "The Pasture" and the softer, more delicate masculinity of the aesthete in "Iris by Night."

Thompson points out that "of all the friends that Frost made in England the most important to him was Edward Thomas" (*SL* 51). References to Thomas punctuate the poet's letters to others; he was energetic in promoting his friend's poetry. Writing to Thomas's widow, he observes: "I have had four wonderful years with him. I know he has done all this [going to fight in the war] for you: he is all yours. But you must let me cry my cry for him as if he were *almost* all mine too." He continues:

> I want to see him to tell him something. I want to tell him, what I think he liked to hear from me, that he was a poet. I want to tell him that I love those he loved and hate those he hated. (But the hating will wait: there will be a time for hate.) I had meant to talk endlessly with him still, either here in our mountains as we had said or, as I found my longing was more and more, there at Leddington where we first talked of war.
>
> It was beautiful as he did it. And I don't suppose there is anything for us to do to show our admiration but to love him forever. (*SL* 216)

I find the rhetorical intensity of this letter remarkable, even passionate. The attitudes expressed here continue for several years after his friend's death. Two days after this letter, in another to Edward Garnett, Frost acknowledges that "Edward Thomas was the only brother I ever had. . . . I hadn't a plan for the future that didn't include him" (*SL* 217); nearly four years later the depth of Frost's friendship is still apparent when he writes to John W. Haines: "You and I cared for [Edward] in a different way from the rest of them. We didn't have to wait till he was dead to find out how much we loved him. . . . It is hard to speak of him as I want to yet" (*SL* 262–63). Frost was disturbed when, nine years after Thomas's death, his widow published reminiscences that he interpreted in part as questioning his friend's manhood, and he quickly rose to the defense in a letter to Sidney Cox: "I wondered if she wasnt in danger of making E. T. look ridiculous in the innocence she credited him with. Mightnt men laugh a manly laugh? E. T. was distinguished at his college at Oxford for the ribald folk songs he could entertain with—not to say smutty" (*SL* 351). On the other hand, we might recall that "for a man to be a man's man is separated only by an invisible, carefully blurred, always-already-crossed line from being 'interested in men.'"[127]

The elegy that Frost wrote for this beloved friend enters the genre of homoerotic love poems: "from Robert Graves, who wrote . . . a 'sensuous little ode' in memory of his dead friend David Thomas, to Herbert Read, who wishes one of his dead soldiers to be kissed not by worms 'but with the warm passionate lips / of his comrade here,' to Wilfred Owen, who sends a poem and his 'identity disc to a sweet friend,' imploring that 'may thy heartbeat kiss it, night and day / Until the name grow blurred and fade away.'"[128] A traditional elegy, "To E. T." also recuperates attitudes from the mourning poem in the sentimental tradition, the kind of poem written by Betsey Dole for Willie Caxton and the kind of poem that the Clara Robinson of "A Fountain" probably wrote from time to time. Most strikingly, "uttering" "leaves" (pages, leave-takings) of love, the poem's final question sponsors an ineradicable connection as strong as that created in Whitman's "Reconciliation" as he imagines not his "camerado" but "my enemy":

> Word over all, beautiful as the sky,
> Beautiful that war and all its deeds of carnage must in time be utterly lost
> That the hands of the sisters Death and Night incessantly softly wash again,
>     and ever again, this soil'd world;
> For my enemy is dead, a man divine as myself is dead,
> I look where he lies white-faced and still in the coffin—I draw near,
> Bend down and touch lightly with my lips the white face in the coffin.[129]

The body is a text, just as the speaker's lips iterate a text. In the delicate masculinity evident here, as in "To E. T.," the nurse-poet exposes an erotic link that simultaneously interrogates gender identity.

For Frost, as for Whitman, "the historical positing of the category of 'the homosexual' textualizes male identity as such, subjecting it to the alienating requirement that it be 'read,' and threatening, in consequence, to strip 'masculinity' of its privileged status as the self-authenticating paradigm of the natural or the self-evident itself."[130] Frost's earlier published work as a whole acknowledges, however unconsciously, the "unnatural" status of masculinity. Rejecting or at least problematizing the normative (middle-class, heterosexual) masculinity that he represents in many early dramatic poems, Frost often affiliates himself with culturally feminine perspectives expressed by the emotional weight of such sentimental poems as "The Pasture" as well as by characters like the wives in "A Servant to Servants" and "In the Home Stretch." At the same time, he explores another culturally feminized, "sissified"—though, paradoxically, manly—discourse of same-sex eroticism in poems like "A Tuft of Flowers," "A Hundred Collars," "Iris by Night," and "To E. T." A sense of the menace of both affiliations may have sparked him, as it did Whitman, to reinvent himself as his career progressed. Being effeminate by virtue of vocation, however the term *effeminate* might be defined, could ultimately mean obscurity of the sort described in the problematic poem "A Fountain, a Bottle, a Donkey's Ears, and Some Books," in which the dead poetess's books reside in a dusty attic, "not thrown irreverently about" but "simply lay where someone now and then, / Having tried one, had dropped it at his feet / And left it lying where it fell rejected" (*CP* 200). To rid American poetry of the feminine meant not only to kill the (sentimental, local) poetess herself but also to destroy (or at least confine) the femininity within the male self.

Does being a poet, then, mean being a "man's man"? And what might this, in turn, mean? We return to the impossible question of whether or not this affirmative reading of Frost's homoerotic perspective is "true" or, at least, "truthful." As Edelman points out in another connection, "Like writing, gay male sexuality comes to occupy the place of the material prop, the excessive element, of representation: the superfluous and arbitrary thing that must be ignored, repressed, or violently disavowed in order to represent representation itself as natural and unmediated."[131] Some of Frost's poems ("Snow," "A Hundred Collars," and "A Fountain" among them) court a shadow narrative of homoerotics in their very heterosexual self-assertiveness. At some level the poet may have recognized, circumvented, and encoded this "threat" to sexual identity by assertions of excessive masculinity and an obsession with gender identity; by later affirming his "difference," he acknowledges the "alienating requirement" that male identity "be 'read.'"

The brute, the real-man/real-poet, chest-thumping voice of Frost's letter at the beginning of this chapter had barbaric Whitman as a precursor in more than one sense. Like his predecessor, Frost eventually mutes the affirmative homoerotic perspective. For one thing a homoerotic poet could not be a national poet, as Whitman before him had acknowledged as he moved from "the initial and staunch claims of *Calamus* that homosexual or 'adhesive' affections would bind together the utopian communities he envisioned in North America to the more culturally conservative claims of *Democratic Vistas* that only democracy, religion, and literature would keep America a single and culturally coherent nation."[132] With a different directionality Clement Wood's biography of Amy Lowell makes this disjunction and the exclusion of the homoerotic poet from national status abundantly clear. For Frost the dangers of effeminacy were simply too great, as an ambiguous 1930 letter to Untermeyer indicates. Speaking of his friend's anthology in progress, he observes:

> You can consult with me and when I don't advise you wrong I'll advise you right about Poe Longfellow Bryant and Emerson, those four and no more. You'll have to go it alone on Lowell Whittier Drake Dana Freneau Wigglesworth Barlow Pierrepont and the rest. A lot of them were ladies then as now. I wonder if it wouldn't be found at any time that most of the contem-

porary fit to go into an anthology was feminine. The girls keep it up and every now and then a boy whoops it up. (*LU* 205)

In the midst of these unrelenting "girls," few "boys" were "fit"—or, for that matter, likely—to be heard. Perhaps Frost was thinking not only of another of Untermeyer's anthologies meant to be used as a school textbook but also of his own poetry books when he affirmed on a different occasion, "I should like the books carried away from [school] not to have any dreary ma'amish connotations that would destine them to the attic or the second hand dealer's dump" (*LU* 181). Clara Robinson's fate was one that Frost spent his life attempting to defend against, and part of his defense was his manipulation of his public image via form, voice, and attitude. Like "The Tuft of Flowers" and "Mowing," "To E. T." is at least as much sentimental as it is romantic or modernist; while the former two echo tones of regionalist writing, they also turn from the dramatic/narrative modes and toward more lyric ones. It is noteworthy that the third appeared in *New Hampshire,* the volume that I have suggested represents a turning point in Frost's gendered self-representation. Echoing Whitman's own transformation, Frost's lyrics in future volumes would for the most part abandon the delicate masculinity, the intimate feminine self and voice of "To E. T.," in favor of a bardic or ironic masculinized stance. The loss was great, however: Frost moved from the empowering affirmation that " 'men work together,' I told him from the heart, / 'Whether they work together or apart' " (*CP* 31) to the acknowledgment that "men work alone, their lots plowed far apart, / One stringing a chain of seed in an open crease, / And another stumbling after a halting cart" (*CP* 272). Ironically, in *A Further Range* "The Strong Are Saying Nothing."

## Chapter 5

# "No Sissy Poem"
## Reinventing the (Lyric) Poet

"His whimsical charm drew everyone to him. . . . The dreamer's leisure pervades his speech and manner. As Amy Lowell said of him, he seems enveloped in a beneficent fog. There is nothing sharp, clear-cut, or American about him."[1] These impressions of Frost by anthologist Jessie Rittenhouse in her 1934 autobiography could not have been wholly pleasing to him. For one thing, Rittenhouse goes on to augment what Frost saw as Amy Lowell's mistake, regarding him as essentially a New England poet; for another, the portrait is suspiciously redolent of aestheticism, in spite of Rittenhouse's later reference to "the New England soil" and "the plow." Giving us a portrait of the poet as paradoxically homegrown yet not "American," Rittenhouse also intimates (however unconsciously) Frost's affiliation with the decadence of suspiciously sexualized English poets. As Cassandra Laity has observed in the context of a discussion about male homosexual love, "theorizers of modern poetry such as Eliot, Yeats, and Pound focused . . . on killing off the Aesthete poet and his Platonic doctrine of symbiosis with a spiritual/erotic twin," a twin who appears, in altered form, in Frost poems like "The Tuft of Flowers" and "Iris by Night."[2] Seeking to dispel the image of the "dreamer" as well as that of the limited Yankee poet, Frost assumes other forms and stances as his career progresses beyond *New Hampshire* and *Mountain Interval.* In the later lyrics Frost looks back once again to romantic writing and nineteenth-century nature poetry by women; he participates, however much a "lone wolf," in a new regionalism that claims to be an antidote to urban ills;[3] and he looks forward (in both senses) to a quirky modernist poetic selfhood that engages, however irregularly and differentially, both elite and popular audiences. In addition to the stances cited earlier, we can trace in the later published poems at least four additional, intersecting and interacting voices: the wisecracking Yankee sage, popular and familiar in some sense but detached in another; the political critic, too invested in emotion and personality for high modernist taste; the bard; and the lyricist.

Frost's final major transformation and the voices that emerge from it relate overtly to his concept of the reader and to his early readers' concept of him. In a strain of afterthought he writes to Sidney Cox in 1932: "The *idea* is the thing with me. It would seem *soft* for instance to look in my life for the *sentiments* in the Death of the Hired Man. There's nothing to it believe me" (*SL* 385; emph. added). "Sentiments," by this time, were explicitly coded feminine for Frost, though the "soft" voice persists in scattered echoes until the poet's death. Highlighting detachment, like another New England poet he issues a disclaimer that his protagonist is also "a supposed person."[4] Although we must continue to be cautious about any of Frost's direct statements, as the same letter warns us ("I have written to keep the over curious out of the secret places of my mind both in my verse and in my letters to such as you"), this letter suggests a hostility, even a divorce, between poet and some of his readers, a refusal of intimacy. Randall Jarrell illuminates this change in Frost from one angle, remarking that "Frost *was* radical when young—he was a very odd and very radical radical . . . and now that he's old he's sometimes callously and unimaginatively conservative." This conservatism emerges not only in his overtly political stance but also in the poet's suppression of earlier feminine voices.

Chapter 5 gallops through Frost's work beyond *New Hampshire,* exploring his developing persona and shifting voices and proposing some explanations for his stance as bard and lyricist. I cannot give a comprehensive examination of the remainder of Frost's work in the space that remains, but I will offer a preliminary account of the changes in his attitudes (in multiple senses) and the effects that those changes had on his published performances. In many of Frost's lyrics, I will suggest, the poet is simultaneously absent and present, elusive and rock-hard: absent, for the "sophisticated" reader, and transparently present, for the popular, "naive," mainstream reader. In accounting for his shifting self, I hope to respond both analytically and emotionally, critically and appreciatively, and in the process suggest once again that these attitudes need not be poles of response but can be interdependent. With these aims in mind, section 1 reviews some readers' responses to his self-consciously poetic self, at the same time delineating its masculine contours. The next section explores the continuing, if still buried, alliances with and sympathies for women poets, some of whose work was itself becoming more masculine than that of their precursors, both male and female, while the discussion that follows compares Frost and Millay as a way of refocusing on the relationship between popularity, canonicity, and gender. Section 4 points toward Frost's more masculine, modern subjectivity and puts into play specific examples of this self while highlighting some of its contexts. I continue by tracing some of the conflicting stances of *West-Running Brook* and seek with appreciation Frost's echoes of earlier feminine voices. The discussion of critics' assessment of Frost's increasing guardedness provides the backdrop for the study of "Directive" in section 5, while in the concluding pages I focus on a "lyric" that suggests the nonessential link between gender and genre and offer my responses to a poem that appears in the book that made Frost's reputation—at least at the time—unassailable.

## "The greatest actor in the world": Frost and Audience

> They cannot look out far.
> They cannot look in deep.
> But when was that ever a bar
> To any watch they keep?
> —Robert Frost, "Neither Out Far Nor In Deep"

A continuing source for Frost's increasing detachment from both his implied and actual readers and, ultimately, for the transformation of his voice were the reviews of his early work, though ironically these reviews were almost universally laudatory. As Linda Wagner observes, "In a literary world vehemently divided by controversies over the appropriateness of free verse and common ('antipoetic') subjects, the consistency of favorable response to Frost's work was surprising—even inexplicable" (*CR* xi). In spite of this overwhelmingly affirmative response over a period of many years, Frost was always quick to remember a slight or criticism, whether real or imagined, and he surely found painful the ongoing debate over whether or not his work was "really" poetry. Twenty years after H. L. Mencken had pronounced Frost "a standard New England poet, with a few changes in phraseology, and the substitution of sour resignationism for sweet resignationism" and other critics had debated on the poetic qualities of his work, Cleanth Brooks, an important force in the institutionalization of "the new poetry," would call Frost "a regionalist and a traditionalist," stating that "much of Frost's poetry hardly rises above the level of the vignette of rural New England" and noting of "The Code" what he implies about other work: "Except for the idiomatic and flexible blank verse, Frost makes use of no resources in the poem not available to the accomplished short story writer. The poetry is diluted and diffuse."[5]

If, as we have seen in chapters 2 and 3, regionalism in its nineteenth-century incarnation had been discredited by the early years of the twentieth century for its association with a feminized nostalgia, in the early 1920s another regionalist movement emerged, equally unsystematic but ostensibly more rugged, especially given its connection with the West and the South. The problem for many was how to preserve regional cultures in the face of modernizing pressures, how "to stake out a regional literary position somewhere between the 'Slough of Sentimentality' . . . and [the] modernist Abyss, thus joining a national pattern of regionalist revulsion against modernist styles and, more importantly, its moral relativism."[6] In some quarters this impulse translated to a self-conscious set of political ideas ranging from "liberal" to "conservative," as many writers and artists responded to the accelerating pace of change in America's demographics and its culture. For Frost, who famously disliked "movements" of any kind, the new regionalism was less an opportunity for political change than another impulse toward a new-old aesthetic, an essentially conservative lyricism that would reconstitute an increasingly fragmented American life and culture.[7] Mary Austin's response to Frost indicates one perception of this movement in his work, for she cites his poetry, along with that of Masters and Sandburg, as being "touched with a profound nostalgia for those happy states of reconciliation with the Allness through group communion, which it is the business of poetry to promote."[8] Once again Frost would be amenable to both nostalgic and ironic readings, with the former rendering him vulnerable to charges of a negatively coded, feminized conservatism.

With the publication of the *Collected Poems* of 1939 the issue of Frost's place in a developing American tradition, elite or popular, emerged again when Isdor Schneider noted in the *Nation* "the rivalry of the poetic and the colloquial" and affirmed, "the attempt to fuse the two seems to me doomed to failure" (*CR* 25, 98; see 47–51, 58–60, 98). With *West-Running Brook* we see a new style that "with the exception of the title poem . . . is purely lyrical." The *Dial* reviewer noted, "these are not poems about people" (*CR* 75, 79; see 76). Jarrell, too, recognized the radical shift in Frost's work away from the "extremely rare, extremely wonderful dramatic and narrative element that is more important than anything else in his early poetry" and concluded that an older Frost was alone, no longer sustained by his characters.[9] As Louise Bogan would tell the story in 1951, the gendered (and masculine) nature of this transformation becomes more evident; Frost "restored to a large audience the concept of The Bard. . . . His insistence on uniting his vocation with his avocations . . . reconstituted a simple and self-controlled poetic character which had been attractive to the middle class since the Victorian era. He advocated none but the simplest virtues and expressed the most graspable ideas."[10] And at the end of Frost's life Roy Harvey Pearce described his later work in terms that are virtually constitutive of lyric: "more and more he has chosen to speak only to himself, albeit in public. We listen, we are delighted, we are moved and enlightened; but we are on the outside looking in at a poet who remains resolutely on the inside looking out, telling us what we are not by telling us what he and his special kind are. . . . Frost manages in his poems to create nothing less than an orthodoxy . . . of the self."[11]

What is really at issue here is the engendering (as well as the sexualizing) of modernist aesthetic production as a whole.[12] Lentricchia acknowledges Frost's movement from essentially romantic lyric poetry in *A Boy's Will* to a more overtly modern, if generically mixed, species of writing, and he argues persuasively that this movement originates in Frost's class location, but, in spite of connecting the poet with his Fireside precursors, he repudiates or ignores entirely the feminine work that forms the long background for Frost's. Coupling Frost with Eliot, he comments, in an attitude similar to Kearns's, "they give us their poems as delicious experiences of voyeurism, illusions of direct access to the life and thought of the famous writer, with the poet inside the poem like a rare animal at the zoo."[13] We can read past this account of a poet who increasingly regarded his audience from an ironic and witty distance to identify this distance as masculine and, to a degree, definitive of (one strand of) modernism itself, whether practiced by Frost, Eliot, or (in a very different manner) by Lizette Woodworth Reese, Marianne Moore, Louise Bogan, and others. As Jarrell goes on to observe of Frost's later work: "this poet is now, most of the time, an elder statesman . . . full of complacent wisdom and cast-iron whimsy. (Of course there was always something of this in the official role that Frost created for himself: one imagines Yeats saying about Frost, as Sarah Bernhardt said about Nijinsky: 'I fear, I greatly fear, that I have just seen the greatest actor in the world')" (*CR* 209).

This transformation is partially enacted on the level of genre, for the "acting" that Jarrell observes corresponds to the poet's self-reinvention via a new kind of lyric—the ironic lyric that reflects a masculine strategy not only of rational control but also of self-containment, self-distancing. If we return to a traditional definition of the romantic lyric self as articulated by Sharon

Cameron, we see Frost mirrored as an "I" forcefully and autonomously defined: "Unlike the drama, whose province is conflict, and unlike the novel or narrative, which connects isolated moments of time to create a story multiply peopled and framed by a social context, the lyric voice is solitary and generally speaks out of a single moment in time." Moreover, "its propensity [is] to interiorize as ambiguity or outright contradiction those conflicts that other mimetic forms conspicuously exteriorize and then allocate to discrete characters who enact them in the manifest pull of opposite points of view."[14] If in his dramatic poems Frost crosses genres and reinvents his poetic subjectivity, by the time he writes beyond *New Hampshire* he has returned to the "timeless" lyric, however innovative and diverse, in the process moving toward a more masculine representation and performance of the self.

As we have seen, the effeminate lyric speaker was invented as an aberration and back-formation by such influential critics as T. S. Eliot, F. O. Matthiessen, and Pearce, who sought to locate poetry in a literary tradition that reached back to Emerson and (a manly version of) Whitman rather than, for example, to Lydia Sigourney, Frances Osgood, and Helen Hunt Jackson.[15] As a whole, "male modernists struggled to professionalize literature and literary study in order to create a gulf between themselves and women writers, whom they then labeled as mere amateurs."[16] This reconceptualization of American literary history—one that retains much of its authority in accounts of Frost—was developing just as Frost was coming into his own. As Paul Lauter notes, "a central problem with American literature, or so some seemed to feel, was its 'feminization.'" Lauter gives several examples of the increasingly misogynist and homophobic attacks on feminized men and on women, especially women novelists, whose concerns critics arbitrarily defined as those of the "domestic sphere."[17] One result of these attitudes was a developing emphasis on art *as* art, apart from the tastes and values of a mass culture that was wholly "undistinguished" in its selections. What was under way was nothing less than a wholesale rewriting of American literary history within margins that to a certain degree still prevail. The ramifications for Frost's practice were obvious: with the advent of an aesthetic that valued, among other things, irony, complexity, and ambiguity, the prudent course for an aspiring poet would be to publish poems that accorded with this newly masculinized (and hence newly valorized) form.

Whether Frost actually set out consciously to reform his aesthetic and his voice or whether he participated more indirectly in the general attitudes of the period ultimately makes little difference; what does matter is his situation in this highly gendered historical and critical moment. As Lentricchia points out:

> Frost's ideal audience would not be composed of the Aunt Hepsies contemp-
> tuously alluded to by Pound as the real material base of reception for genteel
> lyric. His ideal audience would be no feminized audience in need of feeling his
> "prowess" (a favorite term with Frost, describing his feats of literary "perfor-
> mance"); it would be, rather, a skeptical and even scoffing *masculinized audience*
> whose American cultural formation had made it resistant to poetic reception,
> but *which might receive him in its depth* if his was the verse of a writer who is all
> man and whose poetry does not present itself under the conventional genteel
> signs of poetry.[18]

Reading, in this gendered account, was to be an entirely masculine occupa-
tion, shared between a strong writer and strong readers who were willingly
"penetrated" by the poet, who is "all man"—and who, by implication,
offered the same kind of engagement in return. Ironically, of course, these
couplings reconstituted the poet as homoerotic, for in American culture a
man can be a man only under the gaze of other men.[19] Perhaps it is worth-
while to recall Frost's remark to Cox: "The idea is the thing with me. It
would seem soft for instance to look in my life for the sentiments in The
Death of the Hired Man. There's nothing to it believe me." The profes-
sional literary critics of both genders who were reading and judging Frost
would, he understood, praise and appraise him not by the measure of soft
sentiment but by the hardness (iron-y) of his tongue. And many critics, male
and female, still do.

## "Plain unmystical decencies": Precursors Encore

Frost's canny pronouncements and published self-representations indirectly
acknowledged critics' power to reconstitute the poet even after his death,
and they frequently revealed an attempt to anticipate (and to inform) the
(gendered) directionality of cultural power. His prescience in these matters
appears not only in the unrelentingly masculine image that has come to
dominate our understanding of the poet but also in the poetic transforma-
tions toward lyric that have invisibly helped to engender that understanding.
In spite of his turn to lyric, however, it is important to acknowledge that
Frost retains connections with women poets who were themselves becom-
ing more masculine in voice, style, form, and subjectivity. Louise Bogan
was both an important observer of and contributor to the masculinization of

American poetry as the century progressed, and, as we have seen, she critiqued "the general leveling, dilution, and sentimentalization of verse, as well as prose, during the nineteenth century," attributing much of this "dilution" to women. Dismissive of the "sentimental poetry on the middle level . . . [that] operates in full and unimpeded force at the present day," she nevertheless located "an authentic current [that] began to run beside it," observing that "the line of poetic intensity which wavers and fades out and often completely fails in poetry written by men, on the feminine side moves on unbroken," and celebrating a new strand of poetry that emerged at the end of the nineteenth century.[20]

This strand has received renewed and more sustained attention with the groundbreaking recovery work of Paula Bennett. Bennett documents a movement of women's poetry, culminating late in the nineteenth century, "toward greater concrete detail, more ambiguous and flexible stylistic expression, and toward a much wider—and more disturbing—range of themes and voices than high sentimentalism." The major shifts that she describes, elaborated in women's nature poetry, are toward a sensibility that we would call modernist, possessing an individualized subjectivity, a sense of nature as "divorced from transcendent meaning" (an "aesthetic object that presents itself as its own excuse for contemplation"), and a sense of poetry itself as "self-consciously art."[21] As both Bennett's and Bogan's observations suggest, there is a movement away from emotion and toward detachment, away from sentimental, collective forms of subjectivity to "the individualized subjectivity that presumably characterizes the modern lyrical voice—a voice that claims to inscribe the uniqueness of a personal, and frequently alienated, vision."[22]

This vision was elaborated in the work of a variety of women poets, many of them from New England, whom Frost knew or most likely knew, either through anthologies or via links with friends: Louise Imogen Guiney, an intimate of Frost's "good friend" Alice Brown, is one example.[23] With an overtly premodernist subjectivity and known connections with Frost, Lizette Woodworth Reese offers the most useful touchstone for comparison. Born in 1856, Reese was a Baltimore writer who worked as a schoolteacher and published prolifically over a period that spanned nearly fifty years, including the early modern era. Frost attended a dinner in December 1926 given in honor of the seventy-year-old poet; Thompson notes that "there were special reasons why he wanted to be present at this dinner, not the least being his admiration for certain of Miss Reese's stubbornly puritanical qualities."[24] Two years earlier, in a letter to Lesley, Frost had described Reese's courageous integrity: "I saw Lizette Reese in Baltimore. She had just been refusing to meet Edna Millais [sic] at the Kingsolvings. She says she is about done with such Churchly toleration for prostitution and hard drinking as some people nowadays go in for." After describing how Reese had made stunningly similar pronouncements in Knopf's New York office, he added: "you can't help being glad that some are sticking to the plain unmystical decencies. It leaves you free to tend to your farming. . . . The thought of Lizette way down below the Mason and Dixon line should reassure us. Something still stands fast."[25]

With the exception of Pearce, virtually every other critic who has noticed Reese has praised her work, and some have noted its anticipation of modernist concerns and styles. In 1919 H. L. Mencken—perhaps with a bit of sectional pride—was as quick to applaud her simplicity as he was to condemn Frost's (limited) regionalism; he affirmed that Reese had "written more sound poetry, more genuinely eloquent and beautiful poetry, than all the new poets put together." Unlike many who followed him, Mencken placed Reese somewhat aside from "the new poetry," while he labeled much of the latter uninspired and second-rate.[26] Others acknowledged not only her "straightforward undidactic speech" but also, like Louise Bogan, her rejection of sentimentality: "She conveyed her emotions by means of an almost weightless diction and by a syntax so natural that its art was very nearly imperceptible. The romantic locutions and faded ornaments of the nineteenth-century lyric here drop away."[27] In 1929 Kreymborg pointed out the interest of both Reese and Frost in country figures, while Untermeyer, writing in 1936, foregrounded the "undercurrent of intensity beneath . . . the quiet contours" of her work.[28] Recently, Alicia Ostriker and Cheryl Walker have also situated her directly in the modernist tradition. Ostriker celebrates a style that was "artistically self-conscious, highly crafted, and musical. Abstractions wane—or are retained for questioning and definition. Clarity and irony replace the ornate fogginess of the mid-century."[29]

Like Frost, Reese wrote carefully crafted, traditionally structured poems about nature, the country, and its people, and it seems likely that she was a significant even if subconscious influence. Early seasonal poems such as "Mid-March" and "August" (both 1887) reflect the growing tendency for a detached, unemotional, and what I have called masculine subjectivity that is quintessentially modern in its attention to image, intensity, and more or less objective individual perception. The latter offers a striking antecedent to much of Frost's work:

No wind, no bird. The river flames like brass.
On either side, smitten as with a spell
Of silence, brood the fields. In the deep grass,
Edging the dusty roads, lie as they fell
Handfuls of shriveled leaves from tree and bush.
But 'long the orchard fence and at the gate,
Thrusting their saffron torches through the hush,
Wild lilies blaze, and bees hum soon and late.
Rust-colored the tall straggling brier, not one
Rose left. The spider sets its loom up there
Close to the roots, and spins out in the sun
A silken web from twig to twig. The air
Is full of hot rank scents. Upon the hill
Drifts the noon's single cloud, white, glaring, still.[30]

With extraordinary restraint of emotion, the poet conveys a disjunctive, postlapsarian, almost claustrophobic state that conjures absence ("no wind, no bird," "silence," "shriveled"), heat ("torches," "blaze," "hot"), and menace ("smitten," "spell," "web," "rank," "glaring"). The feminized spider, with its "loom" and "silken web," seems to suggest an eroticized nature "full of hot rank scents," while the poem's severe enjambment contributes to a sense of breathlessness and anticipation.[31] Most significantly for our purposes, the subjectivity of the poet becomes a central feature, which is, as much as the scene it depicts, an object presented for our aesthetic contemplation. At the same time, the resolutely simple diction of predominantly monosyllabic and quotidian character anticipates Frost's forays into everyday language. If "Mid-August" forecasts poems like "Range-Finding" and "The Oven Bird," it also seems more modern in some ways than later Frost poems such as "Moon Compasses " or "Unharvested," in which the speaker seems more emotionally invested in the people or natural scenes that he describes; or than comic-ironic poems like "Our Hold on the Planet" or "Fire and Ice."

From another perspective Reese's poems like "Emily" (1923) or "Nina" (1930) echo Frost's interest in women, especially those who are strong or disadvantaged. And "A Flower of Mullein" (1926) also parallels Frost's virtuoso ability to ventriloquize:

I am too near, too clear a thing for you,
A flower of mullein in a crack of wall,
The villagers half-see, or not at all,
Part of the weather, like the wind or dew.

You love to pluck the different, and find
Stuff for your joy in cloudy loveliness;
You love to fumble at a door, and guess
At some strange happening that may wait behind.
Yet life is full of tricks, and it is plain,
That men drift back to some worn field or roof,
To grip at comfort in a room, a stair;
To warm themselves at some flower down a lane:
You, too, may long, grown tired of the aloof,
For the sweet surety of the common air.[32]

Hostile yet restrained, the narrator confronts her beloved's love of the "strange happening," the "tricks" of exotic relationships, while she affirms the value of "comfort in a room, a stair," "the common air." Once again we feel a sense of the poet's detachment from the speaker as she creates a dense dramatic monologue that creates the reader as unobservant other and, potentially, as thoughtless critic. That is, once again the poet's aesthetic self-consciousness emerges, here in the representation of the sonnet itself as an embodiment of "the sweet surety of the common air," as distinguished from the surprise and potential danger of a new poetry that may risk more but which is "aloof," less "near" and familiar. Mullein, a common weed in the eastern United States, embodies this familiarity that an audience would "half-see, or not at all." Bold, tenacious, ordinary like the language of the poem itself, the mullein represents not obscure "cloudy loveliness" but bare, clean, hard, everyday reality. The speaker of the poem suggests, though she does not promise, the continued availability of this consolation; in some sense for the adventurous reader-beloved to return home to familiar things may mean both to lose them and to appreciate them more fully, as necessary as "air" to human survival.

Reese's confidence in form echoes Frost's sense of poetry as "a momentary stay against confusion" and parallels his use of simple, everyday diction coupled with love and respect for nature. Like him, she "recreated once more the beauty of familiar things,"[33] while her reticence and ability to move the reader without shouting forecast many of his more effective lyrics. Making explicit Reese's connection with modern poetry, Kreymborg observed of "A Flower of Mullein" that "this is an Imagistic sonnet, thoroughly modern in its psychologic implications. It is never intellectual; the lexicon of psychoanalysis is absent."[34] Working out of a tradition of women's nature poetry that included writers such as Celia Thaxter, Helen Hunt Jackson, and Lucy Larcom, whose own "Flowers of the Fallow" celebrates the power and presence of common flowers like "sedge, hardhack, mullein, yarrow," Reese transforms the genre into something quintessentially modern—and associatively masculine.[35] As the next section explores, Frost had other affiliations with women's poetry, and by extension feminine voices, that would prove more problematic to the guardians of a manly high culture.

### "Rarely and barely very intellectual": Poetry and Popularity

In 1904 Jessie Rittenhouse complained, "Poetry grows more and more an intellectual pleasure for the cultured classes, less and less a possession of the people."[36] As Andreas Huyssen would observe nearly eighty years later, "Modernism constituted itself through a conscious strategy of exclusion, an anxiety of contamination by its other: an increasingly consuming and engulfing mass culture." He goes on to point out that "it is indeed striking . . . how the political, psychological, and aesthetic discourse around the turn of the century consistently and obsessively genders mass culture and the masses as feminine, while high culture, whether traditional or modern, clearly remains the privileged realm of male activities." Of course, the participation of modernism in an obsessive newness itself suggests the commodification of art and hence its own implication in mass culture, but, as Huyssen affirms, in spite of attempts to destabilize "the opposition between modernism and mass culture [this opposition] has remained amazingly resilient over the decades."[37]

These analyses are particularly important for a discussion of Frost, given his situation as what Leslie Fiedler calls a "middlebrow" poet. From one perspective Frost participated in the segregation of mass from elite culture via his many positions at prestigious U.S. colleges and universities, for, as Fiedler points out, Frost was the first writer in residence in the United States.[38] On the other hand, Frost's lifelong antipathy to academics made his role in the university a constant compromise or form of negotiation between high and low art, and his consistently high level of popularity suggested, however indirectly, his continuing affiliation with the sentimental poets and regionalist writers of the nineteenth century. Coupled with his putative accessibility, this affiliation continued to engender suspiciousness among elite professional critics who constructed the idea of literature as "difficult," needing interpretation, and who consciously or not resisted his removal of cultural power from the university.[39] Frost's resistance to elite culture was evident in a talk delivered at Amherst College in 1930: "Who are professors that they should attempt to deal with a thing as high and fine as poetry? Who are *they?*"[40] He was not the only one among his contemporaries to attempt this negotiation between high and low culture, for another New England poet, although separated from Frost by politics, age, and gender, would share in her distinctive manner his concerns with poverty, popularity, and canonicity: the young Edna St. Vincent Millay. A brief comparison of their lives as well as their work is instructive for a better understanding of the gendered nature of popularity and Frost's transformations of his voice; as one of Millay's critics has observed in terms equally apropos to Frost, "Millay allows the critic to observe the ways in which sentimentality and modernism, pop and high culture, and feminine and masculine writing intersected and diverged during this period."[41]

Born and raised in Maine, Millay's family, like Frost's, struggled with poverty in part due to an absent father; Millay's mother had divorced her father when the poet was eight years old, and "Vincent" grew up in a family headed by a strong-minded woman. Unlike Frost, Millay gained early recognition (perhaps notoriety is the better word) for her poem "Renascence," yet their first work appeared in the United States at about the same time (Millay's poem was published in 1912, her first book of poems in 1917). As her career gained momentum, she became the unofficial voice of a generation of women who sought freedom from gender roles, and she traveled the country giving immensely popular readings that coupled her irreverent social vision with the power of her personality in performances that were often called theatrical.[42] Describing her in terms reminiscent of Frost, one critic affirmed, "she remained an individualist until she died."[43] Millay's popularity reached its height in the 1920s, after she had lived a bohemian life in Greenwich Village and traveled in Europe. Like Frost, she was labeled a New England poet in strategies of critical confinement that, while ostensibly celebrating her strengths, also highlighted her "limitations." Kreymborg compared the two, affirming that "Miss Millay has the Yankee restlessness of Frost," while Van Wyck Brooks later waxed nostalgic about her work, noting that "her poems were full of the odours and flavours of New England, bayberry, hay, clover, seaweed and sorrel, and the salt smell of the ocean in them, of weedy mussels on rotting hulls, mingled with the rustle of eel-grass in the cove and the tinkling of cow-bells in stony pastures." In spite of the comparison with Thoreau that follows this assessment, Millay had already, by 1940, been effectively minimized, in particular by vicious attacks on her poetic maturity, her politics, and her gender (most famously by John Crowe Ransom, to whom I will return in a moment).[44] Nevertheless, she retained her appeal for popular audiences and was both "the first American woman poet to become a media personality" and the first to win a Pulitzer Prize for poetry.[45] Like Frost's, Millay's critical acclaim (though not her popularity) peaked in the 1920s, and, like him, she was the subject of harsh revaluation after her death in 1950.[46]

As her nineteenth-century precursors had done, Millay sometimes relied on a discourse of sentimentality to forward her politics, and her political work (such as *The Murder of Lidice* and *Make Bright the Arrows*) was not only immensely popular but also highly effective. Jo Ellen Green Kaiser observes: "Millay was discovering that the modernist representation of the crisis of modernity was not one she shared. Whereas the modernists had little faith in the political present . . . and in the general public's ability to recognize and reform its world, Millay increasingly turned to the public and to local politics to enact immediate change."[47] At the same time, she recognized the incommensurability of poetry and politics in her letters to friends, worrying to Charlotte Sills: "How many more books of propaganda poetry . . . [my] reputation can withstand without falling under the weight of it and without becoming irretrievably lost, I do not know—probably not more than one. But I have enlisted for the duration."[48] This concern is not terribly far removed from Frost's joking worry, in his later years, that "what begins in felicity and privacy, ends in publicity."[49]

Millay presented a problem for developing modernist criticism and poetic practice from at least three directions: her subjects, her subjectivity, and her relationship with her audience.[50] While we might argue, for example, that Millay's principal subject was not so much love but the difficulty or impossibility of love in the modern era given the cultural baggage of gender roles—and, hence, her participation in a modernist rather than sentimental tradition—her unabashed use of a very personal and intimate "I," which, as Huyssen has noted, signified "a lapse into [feminine] subjectivity or kitsch" for the masculinist modernist critic, doomed her at the very least to diminishment, if not to damnation and obscurity.[51] Furthermore, her intimate appeal to an audience, and in particular to a mass audience, feminized her as well. Reaching toward this mass audience was by definition to risk exclusion from a circle of elite artists: "In the literary world defined by modernism, the writer who wrote for women, whose audience included 'the ladies,' opened herself to the most terrible critical scorn."[52] Scorn is precisely what she received, for Ransom's infamous essay "The Poet as

Woman" highlights this very audience: "Miss Millay is the best of the poets who are 'popular,' and loved by Circles and Leagues of young ladies." The conclusions that he draws from this fact range from the ad feminam assertion, repeatedly echoed by masculinist critics, that "Miss Millay is rarely and barely very intellectual, and I think everybody knows it," to the remark that the poems of *Second April* reveal an "author [who] at twenty-nine is not consistently grown up."[53] Being not impersonal but personal, incorporating real life and politics into the aesthetic, enacting not the extinction of personality but the performance and presence of a personality, and appealing (in both senses) to a large, nonelite audience composed principally of women rendered Millay vulnerable to such sugarcoated acid attacks.

In spite of the poets' differences, many of the criticisms leveled at Millay were also aimed at Frost, though sometimes with different inflection or effect. For one thing, they shared a concern for women and gender; both were (as one reader observes of Millay) "ready to immerse [themselves] in the detailed sufferings and tribulations of human beings (not least of women) within modern social circumstances."[54] Like Millay's work, much of Frost's earlier published poetry focused on love or its loss, sometimes from an alarmingly personal perspective; much of it could be read as sentimental in its ostensibly nostalgic tone and setting; most poems were readily available to a nonelite audience via a (deceptively) transparent language and traditional formality in a period when "the modernist aesthetic separated literary language from ordinary language and, in particular, from the personal."[55] By emphasizing the everyday over the aesthetic, and (supposedly at least) the past over the present, as well as by appealing to a large audience, Frost was also assumed in some ways not to have "grown up."[56] This "immaturity" extended, ironically, to discussion of the disengaged quality of his work, its elision of contemporary hardships and modern life: its "apolitical" stance. When in response to some of these criticisms he began to write more explicitly political poetry, he was damned for his narrow and conservative stance—the same he had held all along, now made overt. If we consider the case of Millay's relation to politics and her critics' response to it, we can more easily understand Frost's position: the problem with his early work from the developing modernist critical stance was not the poet's disengagement from contemporary life but his feminine attitude toward it, based, many asserted, in sentimental nostalgia that proved equally problematic for leftist and conservative academic critics.[57] Allied with this attitude was a transparent everyday language, and intimate voice (as embodied in "The Pasture," for example), that enabled a mass audience also construed as

feminine to appreciate his work. As with Millay, popularity itself was sus-
pect, not simply because of its investment in this audience but also because
of its contamination by a successful history of American women's activism
energized by and manipulated via sentimental language.

In response to these criticisms, both Frost and his critical allies over a
period of time would go to work once again. The poet transformed this
intimate and nostalgic voice to a harder bardic or more elusive lyric one
while retaining the "simple" diction accessible to a mass audience that
continued to confirm his popularity. Frost avoided direct gender disputes
in public, though he enacts them via form and a bidirectional stance
toward audience. Finally, it is less Frost's use of irony, his partial disem-
bodiment of voice in the later lyrics, that suggests and indeed enables his
modernism than his divorce from his sentimental history (in many senses)
and from its characters. This divorce also enabled his reconstruction by
later critics—including contemporaries like Kearns—who would be able,
for example, to read his early dramatic poems as detached and objective,
in alliance with developing modernist principles of subjectivity, in spite of
his retention of an ostensibly "whole" and romantic "I." As I have repeat-
edly indicated, the personal and sympathetic nature of his work and the
feminine voice that often emerged could retrospectively be translated by
those who sought to recuperate Frost's work for modernism, possibly in
recognition that the new poetry and its elite followers needed him at least
as much as he needed them.

As we consider their commonalities, we might recall that in 1920 both
Frost and Millay contributed to a special "American" issue of a (high cul-
ture) British monthly (*Chapbook*) that featured most of the important figures
of modernism, and they figured prominently in Harriet Monroe's collec-
tion, *The New Poetry,* Frost with twelve poems occupying fifteen pages and
Millay with ten poems filling nine pages—yet both poets transgressed the
boundaries of "seriousness" necessary to establish and maintain an elite
modernism.[58] As Richard Poirier has observed, "Modernism can be
thought of as a period when, more than any other, readers were induced to
think of literary texts as necessarily and rewardingly complicated," repre-
senting "an attempt to perpetuate the power of literature as a privileged
form of discourse."[59] The popular realms in which both Frost and Millay
participated contaminated the purity and threatened the cultural privilege of
literature. Frost, for example, was "the first poet whose work was ever dis-
tributed to its mass readership by the Book-of-the-Month Club, the only
others having been Rod McKuen and Erica Jong."[60] This company alone—

a sentimental versifier and a "pornographic" novelist—would render him suspect for some present-day readers, as his inclusion on this list surely did for his critical contemporaries. In a similar vein Millay "made most of her money and certainly the better part of her fame by publishing in such popular culture magazines as *Ainslee's, Vanity Fair,* and *Literary Digest.*"[61] Millay's comments about "propaganda poetry" also point to the utilitarian function of poetry, in this instance against the Nazis, in which her dramatic work, followed by a collection of poetry on the same subject, became part of popular culture via a radio broadcast "that reached hundreds of thousands of listeners."[62] The personalities of Frost and Millay were featured widely in the media, the former in radio broadcasts and on his trips to England and Russia and the latter in a 1920 *Vanity Fair* article and later in a *Ladies Home Journal* article that focused on the poet's kitchen.[63]

Perhaps most notably, both poets did a considerable amount of work in another feminized realm that was entirely respectable for serious nineteenth-century American writers, male and female: children's literature. In 1929 Harper and Brothers published *Edna St. Vincent Millay's Poems Selected for Young People,* which included a wide range of works, from "Renascence" and her famous "First Fig" ("My candle burns at both ends") to the comic-serious "Grown-Up," which highlights the discrepancies between children's imagination of adulthood and its actualities.[64] Obviously meant for a wide age group, the collection focuses on themes of nature, death, and love in formal rhyme and meter and is inhabited by a range of persons, from the alluring nonconformist woman in "Portrait by a Neighbor," who suns by day and does housework by night, "weeds her lazy lettuce / By the light of the moon," to the charming little girl in "From a Very Little Sphinx" who has a tomboyish attachment to "weeds" and "thistles" rather than roses.[65] As it did for many nineteenth-century American women writers, "children's literature" offered Millay an opportunity to interrogate "adult" values and perspectives, as we see in section 6 of the latter poem:

All the grown-up people say,
"What, those ugly thistles?
Mustn't touch them! Keep away!
Prickly! Full of bristles!"

Yet they never make me bleed
Half so much as roses!
Must be purple is a weed,
And pink and white is posies.[66]

Signifying love to adult female readers still adept in the nineteenth-century language of flowers, Millay's image of the thorny rose recapitulates, in a mock-sentimental child-woman voice, the theme of painful love so evident elsewhere in her adult work, as it makes a sardonic indirect commentary on form and popularity that recalls Reese's "Flower of Mullein." That is, work that appears common, mundane, and rough like the thistle—or like children's literature itself—may be misjudged as less beautiful and less aesthetically significant. In any event Millay's children's book conducts a species of genre mixing that effectively interrogates the segregation of high from low, elite from popular art.

The broad appeal of this book is extended by its illustrations, which include innocent images that recall the "Dick and Jane" books of my own childhood (a little girl with bows in her hair and hearts on her dress), fairytale images like Jack (associated with "The Bean-Stalk"), and a gingerbread cottage, along with more subversive and menacing ones such as that which opens part 2. In this striking suggestion of male lust and female sexual desire, a woman and a satyr perch on a teeter-totter balanced in a tree. Outlined in leaves and flowers and seeming herself to be part of the natural scene, the woman is perched at the top left with her head held back in apparent ecstasy as the phallic log penetrates between her extended legs, while the satyr (ambiguously gendered—at the least, feminized) smiles slightly as he prepares for the next thrust. While this is an image that might appeal to children on one level, on another it encodes modernist concerns with ambiguous sexuality, as it echoes the earlier decadent images of Aubrey Beardsley. Highly susceptible to an elite interpretation as well as to a child's pleasure, it remains firmly planted in two worlds.[67]

Frost's children's writing is similarly amenable to dual interpretation. As I noted earlier, many of his poems, like "The Sound of the Trees," were frequently reprinted in collections of children's verse. His 1959 collection merely represented the culmination of a career's work that satisfied the needs of multiple audiences, and the poems that were included represent not only his earlier, more obviously sentimental work, such as "The Pasture" (which opens this collection as it does all of Frost's "adult" collections), "Going for Water," "Good-by and Keep Cold," and The Telephone," and dramatic poems such as "Mending Wall," "The Death of the Hired Man," and "Christmas Trees," but also a few of his "elite" lyrics, such as "Birches," "After Apple-Picking," "Acquainted with the Night," "Hyla Brook," and "The Oven Bird." The mixing of high and low realms is indicated plainly in the dedication to a person who had contributed powerfully to Frost's propensity to engage in such blending: "To Belle Moodie Frost, who knew as a teacher that no poetry was good for children that wasn't equally good for their elders."[68] In a striking inversion of the expected, Frost focuses on adults' participation in the nonelite, and he slyly underscores the morally healthy qualities of this amalgamation.

"A Young Birch" suggests the bidirectional audience for much of Frost's poetry:

> The birch begins to crack its outer sheath
> Of baby green and show the white beneath,
> And whosoever likes the young and slight
> May well have noticed.

Opening with an invocation to growth that would appeal to children concerned with leaving behind the "baby" and, at the same time, to adult nostalgia for precisely this state, the poem moves toward a (modernist) gesture toward the aesthetic:

> It will stand forth, entirely white in bark,
> And nothing but the top a leafy green—
> The only native tree that dares to lean,
> Relying on its beauty, to the air.[69]

The air of New Hampshire or the air of the poet's breath: both are conjured in these lines that lean toward the wise adult and ironic lyricist, who steps forward in the next parenthetical aside—"(Less brave perhaps than trusting are the fair)"—that simultaneously undercuts the aesthetic quality of the preceding image (by offering a potentially sentimental evocation of childhood innocence to the adult reader), while it situates the child listener or reader directly in the concrete realm of the beautiful and daring. The images to which Frost humorously compares the young tree include those that both children and adults can appreciate ("a cane," "a fishing pole"), as he locates it within everyday experience and language ("And zeal would not be thanked that cut it down / When you were reading books or out of town"). Yet, in spite of its sentimental overtones and simple language, the poem can easily be recuperated by an elite audience because of its undercurrent of irony and its central focus on the aesthetic, for the tree, like the poem itself, is "there to be admired": "It was a thing of beauty and was sent / To live its life out as an ornament." The bidirectionality of this lovely poem, resonant once again with the delicate masculinity explored in the preceding chapter, becomes even more apparent when we realize that it was first published as Frost's 1946 Christmas poem.[70] Frost's children's poetry emblematizes his brilliant ability to walk a tightrope between "popularity" and "sophistication," retaining respectability in some academic circles while he engendered affective and effective mainstream readings.

The versatility of Frost's voice and its interest to a wide range of popular as well as elite and academic audiences are apparent from a brief review of several poems' anthology history. Like "The Runaway" and "The Road Not Taken," "The Pasture" has appeared over many decades in children's collections (*Golden Journey: Poems for Young People* [1965]; *Talking to the Sun: An Illustrated Anthology of Poems for Young People* [1985]) and popular anthologies (*Favorite Poems Old and New* [1957]; *Best Loved Poems in Large Print* [1983]), in secondary and college texts (*Time for Poetry* [1959]; *How Does a Poem Mean?* [1975]; *Norton Anthology of American Literature* [1985]), and in ostensibly more "authoritative" canon-making collections (*Oxford Book of American Verse*, ed. F. O. Matthiessen [1950]; *Seven Centuries of Verse, English and American* [1967]; *Poetry in English: An Anthology* [1987]).[71] In spite of its acclaimed lyricism and modernist difficulty, "Birches" shows a remarkably similar pattern, having been published in such diverse collections as *Treasury of the Familiar* (1942), *Oxford Book of American Verse* (1950), *Poetry for Pleasure: The Hallmark Book of Poetry* (1960), *The Family Book of Verse* (1961), *Beginnings in Poetry* (1973), *Favorite Poems in Large Print* (1981), and three Norton anthologies, including the *Norton Anthology of Modern Poetry* (1988).[72] Although "Stopping by Woods on a Snowy Evening" predictably confirms Frost's nomination for "my best bid for fame," "The Tuft of Flowers" is also deemed a children's poem (*Home Book of Verse for Young Folks* [1929]), a college text (*College Book of Modern Verse* [1958]), and a "classic" (*Oxford Book of American Verse* [1950]).[73]

As this brief accounting and the discussion that precedes it suggest, to question the *type* of complexity and difficulty in a poem is not to question the *value* of such concepts as "complexity" and "difficulty" themselves. To engage in the latter interrogation is in some sense to risk deauthorizing the professional interpretive voice with respect to literary matters. Should we in fact value simplicity and accessibility (as ostensible parallels to complexity and difficulty), we are still faced with the problem of what these terms mean. And if a nursery rhyme—or a "children's" poem by Frost—is indeed simple and accessible, wherein lies its value? and for whom? In some concrete economic sense, in fact, it is more "valuable" than a poem like "Directive" or "The Love Song of J. Alfred Prufrock" because more people can

understand, appreciate, and buy it. But in terms of cultural capital and access
to institutional power the opposite is true. That Frost understood this para-
dox on a fundamental basis is clear from the shape and attitude of his poems
published after the 1922 appearance of "The Waste-Land," the concrete
embodiment of high modernism, and after the ascent of New Criticism.
That his work functions superbly at both "levels" is evident early on, and
Frost's contemporaries must surely have admired or envied his duplicity, his
ability to "go both ways." Yet, like the indiscriminate or indiscreet blend-
ing of poetry and narrative early in his career, Frost's dual position as popu-
lar and modern poet represents another kind of generic promiscuity: inas-
much as the former was identified with the feminine and the latter with the
masculine, this promiscuity was in effect like being bisexual. Hence the
need, ironically, to insist (as Frost often did) on both his difficulty-com-
plexity (emerging in humor and irony) and his penetrability (emerging in
the sentence sounds of ordinary speech).

Like Millay in so many respects, Frost also sought to "put Chaos into
fourteen lines / And keep him there."[74] But, unlike Millay, who is named
only once (in a list) in *The Continuity of American Poetry,* Frost features
significantly along with male high modernists like Eliot and Pound.[75] We
might reasonably conclude this discussion of the intersection of popular
with elite literature with the question: What happened to Millay; why
couldn't she be recuperated for modernism like Frost? As Suzanne Clark
points out, over the years "the assumption which has come to prevail [is]
that the revolution of poetic language has nothing to do with a revolution
in human society," in spite of the fact that a number of modernists, both
male and female, were politically active; in recent years a number of femi-
nist critics have begun to attempt this recuperation as part of a process of
redefining modernism itself.[76] Yet this affirmative perspective was not pos-
sible during Millay's lifetime, for a number of reasons. A principal disquali-
fying feature, of course, was not only that she was female—something that
writers like Bogan and Moore would overcome by adhering (at least osten-
sibly) to the doctrine of extinction of personality and to what Leslie Fiedler
calls "the avoidance of excessive feeling, the substitution of irony for senti-
mentality and pathos"[77]—but that she announced and highlighted the fact.
Furthermore, her career path moved toward *more* political-sentimental
poems, not less, as she deliberately sought to increase her influence over a
large public. As Kaiser points out, "given that sentimental discourse not
only pervaded American life, but actually had been used effectively to
advance women's political goals . . . it should not surprise us that Millay,

active in women's politics and an important voice of popular culture, should cease her experiments in modernism and return to sentimentality."[78] By ultimately refusing modernist aesthetic standards of complexity, irony, detachment, and darkness, Millay provided an illustration for Frost of the (divided) road that he needed to take.

## "I put it shining anywhere I please": The Designing Poet

> Never were poets so "hidden in the light of thought."
> —Edna St. Vincent Millay, *Conversation at Midnight*

In 1917 Harriet Monroe attempted a definition of the new poetry that was solidifying into an established aesthetic in the hands of Pound and Eliot. Beginning by asserting that it "strives for a concrete and immediate realization of life," she affirmed that "it is less vague, less verbose, less eloquent, than most poetry of the Victorian period and much work of earlier periods." It is "objective," presenting emotion via "exteriority" and concreteness.[79] That is, it strove to dissociate itself from feminine feelings. But voice was only one of the criteria by which this new poetry would be judged; form was another. In contrast to many of his contemporaries, Frost's early work in particular incorporated what Marjorie Perloff calls "narrative," or story. As Perloff has pointed out, "the dominant poetic form of early modernism remains the lyric . . . in which the isolated speaker (whether or not the poet himself), located in a specific landscape, meditates or ruminates on some aspect of his or her relationship to the external world, coming finally to some sort of epiphany, a moment of insight or vision with which the poem closes."[80] Furthermore, in contemporary criticism "the equation of poetry with the lyric is almost axiomatic."[81] As we saw in the introduction, this lyric is romantic, and it has a strong and assertive subjectivity that has been called masculine. Yet, as Perloff explains elsewhere, there are two versions of the romantic ideology for poetry, one "low-brow," which she identifies with Frost's favorite collection ("the most popular poetry anthology in the English-speaking world"), Palgrave's *Golden Treasury,* and another "high-brow," which she identifies with Pound and which possesses a high degree of "impersonality," or "objectivity."[82] The gendered nature of this distinction emerges quite plainly when we recall Pound's description of Palgrave as "that stinking sugar teat": the source of effeminate, sentimental poetry.[83] Significantly, several of Frost's poems were included in C. Day

Lewis's 1954 revision of Palgrave, while Pound and Williams were excluded; "[a] decade after World War II, then, poetry still means lyric."[84]

The point, of course, is that *lyric* is a historically situated term, signifying different things at different times.[85] In Frost's time, and through the early modern period, it continued to mean poetry in the Palgravian sense, and Frost's work suggests that he was acutely aware of this definition, both conjuring and reinventing the poem. From a strict Palgravian perspective, he "de-lyricizes" it with plain language, with rhetoric or didacticism or playfulness. While he often returns to the quintessential feature of the genre, namely, the singular speaker engaged in a solitary search for insight, his later published work allows the reader admission to that experience only indirectly and sometimes, I would say, inadvertently or even grudgingly, as the speaker and the poet become more detached, more distant, more ironic. Here I will attempt briefly to concretize this affirmation. Focusing first on "Design" as an exemplary instance, this section puts into play poems that perform this more masculine perspective; at the same time, it emphasizes the fundamentally mixed and circuitous nature of this performance, for the road that Frost takes is not wholly paved over with irony but also looks backward to his earlier, more sentimental subjectivity and delight in region.

At this point in his career Frost was taking the measure of poetic selfhood—however consciously or unconsciously—not only from its historical associations with femininity and effeminacy, and their affiliated genres, but, increasingly, from newly masculinized standards for *all* writing. Perhaps, at some level, the modernist novel (as Kearns and Lentricchia argue) *could* be viewed as masculine, though this perspective meant (and means) that once again the work of such women writers as Stein, Barnes, Larsen, Cather, and Fauset had to be repressed.[86] As Gilbert and Gubar remind us, the modernist novel was as contested as the poem on the terrain of gender, with each side strategizing for dominance; it was hardly unambiguously masculine. Perhaps what this conflict best illustrates is the nonessential connection between gender and genre, in which neither fiction nor poetry was inherently masculine or feminine but, rather, gendered and engendered by critics. If the traditional nineteenth-century novel incorporated a variety of characters, representing a diffusion of the author's self, and the nineteenth-century poem demanded a central and assertive selfhood, then twentieth-century versions of each transfigured these incarnations (at least this is one way to tell the story).[87]

What is important here to Frost's public self-representation is his stylistic and formal transformation from the mostly narrative and dramatic mode of *North of Boston* to more traditionally lyric poems: these poems, even with a (subversive, modernist, ostensibly masculine) veil of irony and stab of wit, echoed the short, self-contained, and self-reflexive pieces by writers like Reese and others that were setting the standard at the turn of the century and that by definition omitted virtually all of the characteristics of Frost's early work: the narrative, the personal, the dramatic, the regional, the vernacular.[88] In spite of what I have just observed about the nonessential connection between gender and genre, however, in Frost's own concrete and formal terms, genre intimates gender because the narrative poems tend to attempt a different task, elaborate a different gesture, and seek a different response than poems such as "Design" (from *A Further Range* [1936]) and "Directive" (from *Steeple Bush* [1947]).[89] While one group creates character, tells a story, and invites reader empathy, the other represents the writer's detached, ironic, metaphoric voice. Although this second approach was not poetry in the Palgravian sense, it was far closer to certain poems by Keats and Wordsworth (or, for that matter, to work by Dickinson, Sarah Piatt, and Frances Osgood, or Stevens, Eliot, and Pound) than to Whitman or Browning. In his narrative mode Frost speaks as the amateur, the conjuring village gossip, and in his lyric one as the crafty professional Poet.[90]

"Design" epitomizes Frost's lyric sleight-of-hand:

> I found a dimpled spider, fat and white,
> On a white heal-all, holding up a moth
> Like a white piece of rigid satin cloth—
> Assorted characters of death and blight
> Mixed ready to begin the morning right,
> Like the ingredients of a witches' broth—
> A snow-drop spider, a flower like a froth,
> And dead wings carried like a paper kite.
>
> What had that flower to do with being white,
> The wayside blue and innocent heal-all?
> What brought the kindred spider to that height,
> Then steered the white moth thither in the night?
> What but design of darkness to appall?—
> If design govern in a thing so small.

> (*CP* 275)

This designing poem has lured generations of readers to contemplate death, order, evil, and the nature of poetry. The three elements of nature, all sideshow freaks, combine in a whimsical and dreadful drama of murder that is fostered by the sensibility of the speaker-poet. As if stirring "a witches' broth," conjuring a spell that captivates not simply the protagonists but the reader–listener as well, he elicits the tragicomic scene whose ostensible inadvertence mirrors the whimsical relationship between himself and the reader. Taking back with one hand what he gives with the other, Frost offers a "dimpled spider," "a flower like a froth," and "dead wings carried like a paper kite." The mood is fostered by this bizarre conjunction of images, in which the spider is like a baby (a jab at sentimental "dead baby" poems? at his own "Home Burial"?), the flower is like food (or, more ominously, foam at the mouth of a madman), and the "dead wings" (reminiscent of Clara Robinson's poetry in "A Fountain") are a child's toy. All of these come together in a line that sounds like a jingle for breakfast cereal: "Mixed ready to begin the morning right."

The rhetorical gestures of the second stanza enforce our uncertainty and the narrator's power, for the questions suggest a knowledge of which we cannot partake, as he simultaneously claims membership in a secret society whose rituals confound the ordinary eye as he mocks that membership. We are provided a glimpse into the sacred chambers, however, with the second question: "What brought the kindred spider to that height, / Then steered the white moth hither in the night?" The controlling consciousness is, of course, the poet's own, as his apparently innocuous first words indicate: "I found." We might read right over this opening, and even later we might be tempted to emphasize the role of chance in the configuration of characters. But, as the poem progresses, retrospection insists that we assign ultimate weight to the "I," the mediating poetic consciousness that creates the utterly strange (and beautiful-ugly) meeting. By "finding" spider, moth, and flower, he becomes their creator, for his words bring them into daylight, onto the whiteness and blankness of the page. Hence, the last question and its "answer," "What but design of darkness to appall?— / If design govern in a thing so small," at once expresses doubt and satisfaction at his own magic in the recreation of the scene, just as the ambiguity of "appall" challenges the reader to interpret "correctly": Does it mean "to shock"? "To make white?" "To kill?" All of the preceding?

The sestet meditates on the issue of design, for the rhyme scheme is overdetermined, having little variation, while the stress system of the last line, and particularly the emphasis on "If," remains entirely ambiguous. Having pulled back the curtain on his Wizard of Oz ever so slightly, the speaker leaves us, like Dorothy, to contemplate our own method of escape from Oz itself. The poet is a performer, a confidence man, and if we are drawn into the world of the poem, we have been "had"—and I always am.

Professional readers as a whole, I think, find this verbal intercourse irre-
sistible. Nevertheless, even a perfunctory review of "Design" underlines its
radical difference from the narrative poems: human relationships and other
voices are erased in favor of intellectual challenge. The feminine voice that
concerns itself with labor and love and that enacts a generous relationship
with the reader metamorphoses into the ingenious and virtuoso Poet. As
Walton Beacham remarks, "'Playing' involves the whole spirit, while 'play-
fulness' can be the result of detached observation without real commitment
to the game."[91] Here Frost gives a performance that delights, amuses, and
confuses, but he also enforces his distance from his audience, as he empha-
sizes in his letter to Sidney Cox. Here he knows more, has access to artifice
that nonpoets, amateurs, lack. Ironically, it is precisely this knowledge and
authority that are appealing to modernist trained readers: the dazzling,
show-off quality of "Design," its swagger (here we're back to manly Whit-
man) and metaphoric ease, offer endless delight.

It is instructive to compare "Design" with "The Mariposa Lily" by Ina
Coolbrith, which was published in 1901 in E. C. Stedman's *American
Anthology, 1787–1900:*

> Insect or blossom? Fragile, fairy thing,
> Poised upon a slender tip, and quivering
> To flight! a flower of the fields of air;
> A jeweled moth; a butterfly, with rare
> And tender tints upon his downy wing,
> A moment resting in our happy sight;
> A flower held captive by a thread so slight
> Its petal-wings of broidered gossamer
> Are, light as the wind, with every wind astir,—
> Wafting sweet odor, faint and exquisite.
> O dainty nursling of the field and sky,
> What fairer thing looks up to heaven's blue
> And drinks the noontide sun, the dawning's dew?
> Thou wingèd bloom! thou blossom-butterfly![92]

Images of innocence and childlike newness, references to the poem's par-
ticipation in the sentimental tradition, structure Coolbrith's sonnet: the
"tender tints upon his downy wing" (suggestive of baby's skin) are occasions
for an almost maternal love that cherishes its "dainty nursling." In spite of
the sometimes precious language ("broidered gossamer," "wingèd bloom")
the vision of the poem, and some of its language, amply forecasts—if it does

not provide the model for—"Design." Most notable in this parallel are the deliberate confusion between the flower and insect that motivates the poem, the rhetorical questions that frame it, and, in contrast to the images of innocence, the distinctly modern "jeweled moth," juxtaposing hard and soft, constructed and natural.

The most striking difference, of course, between "The Mariposa Lily" and "Design" resides in the subjectivities of their speakers. Whereas Coolbrith's, to recall Annie Finch's framework for sentimental poetry, "is structured to allow the natural world an independent identity no less privileged than the poetic self," Frost's "effuse[s] from a 'poet' in the traditional sense of a seer or 'priest.'"[93] While "The Mariposa Lily" represents more an ode to beauty or to nature, Frost's celebrates, even revels in, the vision (design) of the artist, while, by adding the weird, babylike "dimpled spider," he also provides a bitter taste that serves as an antidote to the potentially cloying sweetness of his spider and heal-all flower. Nevertheless, Coolbrith's poem does not neglect the vision of the artist: "our happy sight." Could Frost have read "The Mariposa Lily" and (consciously or not) been responding to it? The correspondences seem dramatic. The poet was in his mid-twenties when Stedman's popular and widely available anthology appeared. Whether literal model or not, "The Mariposa Lily" demonstrates once again Frost's affiliations with sentimental and genteel poetry, and it points toward the borrowing by modernist poets of the late-nineteenth-century female-authored nature poem. In this context "Design" represents a reprise and reinvention of earlier lyric modes that retrospectively seem far safer than the intensely human and emotional dramas often enacted in the narrative poems. To recall Jarrell: "The younger Frost is surrounded by his characters, living beings he has known or created; the older Frost is alone."[94]

I've chosen to focus initially on "Design" in this section because it is one of Frost's most revered poems, but a study of *West-Running Brook,* published in 1928, reveals that, as might be expected, the movement toward masculine selfhood that I have described is not linear. In spite of their darker undertones, "Spring Pools" and the moody "On Going Unnoticed" gesture back to the sentimentally inflected poems of *A Boy's Will,* just as "Mowing" and "Birches" (the latter in *Mountain Interval*) anticipate the virtuoso poet of "Design" (though with a healthy dash of humility and quietness). If less flamboyant, "The Freedom of the Moon" (also in *West-Running Brook*) stage-directs like (and anticipates) "Design"; it is as lovely and precious as the diamond tiara that it conjures:

I've tried the new moon tilted in the air
Above a hazy tree-and-farmhouse cluster
As you might try a jewel in your hair.
I've tried it fine with little breadth of luster,
Alone, or in one ornament combining
With one first-water star almost as shining.

I put it shining anywhere I please.
By walking slowly on some evening later,
I've pulled it from a crate of crooked trees,
And brought it over glossy water, greater,
And dropped it in, and seen the image wallow,
The color run, all sorts of wonder follow.

                                                            (*CP* 224)

"I've put it shining anywhere I please"—even in poems like "The Death of the Hired Man" and "In the Home Stretch." From one perspective the moon's a piece of furniture, a prop to be moved at will to create the right effects, and the narrator's voice is the "voice of the poet talking to himself, or to nobody."[95] Yet the narrator's performance is less brazen, less accomplished, and more inviting and spacious than the voice of "Design," which is clearly talking to other people with the design to be impressive. The poem's (masculine) audacity is mitigated further when we acknowledge that it was included in the children's collection *You Come Too*.

Although a poem like "The Freedom of the Moon" highlights Frost's difference from the reader and exemplifies the shift in his attitude, other poems of the period recall his earlier feminine voices. "The Cocoon," also in *West-Running Brook*," gestures back to Frost's overt sympathy with women's lives, for, although the narrator is ostensibly detached, a seer of "one poor house alone, / With but one chimney to call its own," he diverts his sympathy and encouragement to the inhabitants:

The inmates may be lonely women-folk.
I want to tell them that with all this smoke
They prudently are spinning their cocoon
And anchoring it to an earth and moon
From which no winter gale can hope to blow it,—
Spinning their own cocoon did they but know it.

                                                            (*CP* 227)

Yes, there are overtones of death (the cocoon can double as a winding sheet) and the narrator is safely separated from these "inmates," who could as easily live in a poorhouse or an asylum, but the mood of the poem also resonates with what my students would call "warm fuzzies": the comfort and consolation also offered by mainstream nineteenth-century poetry.

With their closing references to God, "Once by the Pacific" and "Bereft" hearken back to the nineteenth century, the former to undercut surface certainties and the latter (as sentimental poets often did) to offer self-comfort. Like "Bereft" depicting the vulnerable self that appeared in *A Boy's Will,* "The Thatch" shows Frost engaged in the hard-hearted, ostensibly masculine task of clearing birds' nests from the thatch to prevent the rain from entering. In thrusting the birds from their homes, he acknowledges his "grief," a grief that must be assuaged, though he doesn't say so directly, by the knowledge that he is protecting his own family and family life, both of which are vulnerable to the elements:

> They tell me the cottage where we dwelt,
> Its wind-torn thatch goes now unmended;
> Its life of hundreds of years has ended
> By letting the rain I knew outdoors
> In on to the upper chamber floors.

> (CP 232)

Nothing of distancing irony or humor (with which to keep his "enemies" at bay) here; my response to this poem is a flush of nostalgia and sadness. Playful poems like "Canis Major," on the other hand, anticipate the more ponderous "fooling" of "Directive," as *West-Running Brook* inaugurates in force the smart-aleck countrified voice that becomes in later poems a self-caricature: "The Birthplace," "Dust in the Eyes," "The Door in the Dark," "What Fifty Said," and the strange "Egg and the Machine." Frost even writes a parody of himself: "Sitting by a Bush in Broad Sunlight" is surely a self-mocking (and reader-mocking) rendition of "Stopping by Woods on a Snowy Evening."

The voices of *West-Running Brook,* while they sometimes echo those that Frost gives us in earlier volumes, effectively leave behind the feminine voices most audible in those predecessors. Nevertheless, many of these poems and those in *A Further Range* ("Design" among them) invite our imaginative collusion or, at the very least, reflection: "Two Tramps in Mud Time"; "The White-Tailed Hornet" (a wonderful, self-conscious rumination that, unlike "Maple," does not engender hostility and detachment but makes me laugh, admire, and think); the scary-funny answer to modernist

alienation and despair, "Desert Places"; the brilliant "The Strong Are Say-
ing Nothing"; the bitter "Provide, Provide"; and "At Woodward's Gar-
dens," with its marvelous drop-dead surprise ending line. Of course, these
poems, like "Design" itself, have as much in common with female-authored
modernist poetry as they do with any precursors. A representative sample,
published only four years earlier than Frost's famous sonnet, on the same
subject and in the same form is Elinor Wylie's "Pretty Words."[96]

Once again, perhaps the most interesting comparison to make between
Frost and female modernist poets, given his complex attitude toward her, is
with Amy Lowell. Lowell's lesbian love poems, many written in the same
period as *West-Running Brook,* assume the aesthetic authority of both
"Design" and "Pretty Words." Though in a very different context Lowell
often handles the moon as decisively and self-consciously as Frost in "The
Freedom of the Moon" (or "The Death of the Hired Man," for that mat-
ter), as we see in the lovely "Interlude":

> When I have baked white cakes
> And grated green almonds to spread upon them;
> When I have picked the green crowns from the strawberries
> And piled them, cone-pointed, in a blue and yellow platter;
> When I have smoothed the seam of the linen I have been working;
> What then?
> To-morrow it will be the same:
> Cakes and strawberries,
> And needles in and out of cloth.
> If the sun is beautiful on bricks and pewter,
> How much more beautiful is the moon,
> Slanting down the gauffered branches of a plum-tree;
> The moon
> Wavering across a bed of tulips;
> The moon,
> Still,
> Upon your face.
> You shine, Beloved,
> You and the moon.
> But which is the reflection?
> The clock is striking eleven.
> I think, when we have shut and barred the door,
> The night will be dark
> Outside.[97]

Like "The Freedom of the Moon," "Interlude" celebrates poetic vision.
Insisting on the figurative status of the moon, Lowell places it alone on two

lines and reiterates it elsewhere twice; like Frost, she asserts her ability to "put it shining anywhere I please." She too "combines" it, here with "grated green almonds," "the green crowns of strawberries," and "the gauffered branches of a plum-tree." If the virtuosity of Lowell's poem is something it shares with Frost's, it has a different "design," for, beyond the self-celebration of her counterpart, Lowell imagines a different relationship with her reader that evokes the intimacy of "A Servant to Servants"—here the reader is "Beloved"—and she incorporates a female voice speaking to a female reader-beloved, affiliated with the virgin goddess Diana, who is eventually brought into the narrator's home (and, by extension, her body). The sensuality that floods the poem fosters the final linking of selves in the soft climax of the closing lines. The imaginative region invoked in "The Freedom of the Moon" parallels the liberating, interstitial space conjured in the title (and the performance) of "Interlude," but, while Frost's poem represents a kind of self-display, a connection with an implied masculine reader with whom he intends to share his power over a "beloved" (nature), Lowell's reaches toward the reader in a more intimate dispersal of her self at the moment of its (the poem's and the self's) consummation.

## Directives: Real Man and Real Poet

> A writer can live by writing to himself alone for days and years. Sooner or later to go on he must be read. . . . For long the public received him not. Then the public received him. When were the public right?
> —Robert Frost, "The Doctrine of Excursions"

After shifting definitively and finally from the dramatic and narrative mode to the reinvented lyric one of *West-Running Brook,* Frost had to confront new criticisms. Linda Wagner observes that "only the reviews of *West-Running* Brook (1928), Frost's fifth collection, show in retrospect that 1923 was the peak of Frost's critical reception" (*CR* xvi).[98] One reader charged, "Mr. Frost's work is weakest in ideas," and a second argues that "he lacks power" and "has not the cosmic imagination which creates its own world," while another affirmed, "Robert Frost is both as a thinker and an artist subtle and elusive" and "is the most passionate poet America has ever produced" (*CR* 95, 111, 110, 105). Among the most negative remarks, however, were those made by Louise Bogan and Muriel Rukeyser. In her influential column for the *New Yorker,* Bogan accused Frost of a lack of development, a stasis, and claimed that Frost's forays into political criticism were ill advised, criticizing

him, in a review of the 1939 *Collected Poems,* for his "later carping and con-
servatism." She observed: "one reads 'Collected Poems: 1939' waiting for a
crack of upheaval, with some unforeseen growth thereafter. The tone is
curiously static throughout. . . . In the later Frost, the mold, unbroken, has
stiffened a little" (*CR* 152). Working along the same lines, Muriel Rukeyser
complained in a review of the same volume that "the strain and violence
and sharp contrasts have been *controlled* out of his poems" (*CR* 161; emph.
added); she also identified Frost as "conservative," though perhaps less in
Bogan's political use of the word. But she echoed the criticism of the poet's
lack of development, substance, and passion: "He stokes, and banks, and
gauges the fires; there is little work of enduring intensity." The problem is
one of excess control: "Frost stays close, and guards" (*CP* 160, 161).[99]

A *Further Range* provoked a storm of controversy in part because of
Frost's generally conservative social position in the era of the Great Depres-
sion.[100] Untermeyer records the debate in a headnote to a 1937 Frost letter.
After the book had provoked "a barrage of criticism" from such reviewers
as Horace Gregory in the *New Republic,* Richard Blackmur in the *Nation,*
and Newton Arvin in the *Partisan Review*—all enormously influential pub-
lications—Robert Hillyer wrote a defense of the poet that was published in
the *Atlantic Monthly.* Granville Hicks wrote a parody in response to Hillyer's
piece that the *Saturday Review* initially refused and then later decided to
publish. Obviously sympathetic, Untermeyer describes the attack on Frost
by Hicks as "a typically unrestrained piece of savagery" (*LU* 452). Perhaps it
was little wonder, then, that the acutely sensitive Frost increasingly played a
role, attempting to become a smooth image, resistant to penetration in
every sense. Possibly no poem exemplifies this attitude more fully than
"Directive," on which I will focus in this section, after a brief accounting of
other poems that move me in ways that are very different than the earlier
dramatic poems.

If they strike out in new directions, the poems of *A Further Range* also
represent a further constriction (or "A Further Shrinking," as Rolfe
Humphries snidely titled his review for the *New Masses*) when viewed from
the perspective of human relationships, including the poet's more generous
connection with the reader in the poems of earlier volumes. *A Witness Tree,*
*Steeple Bush,* and *In the Clearing* all evince a mixture of the professional
Poet's voice with that of the shaggy countrified sage, even when individual
poems resonate with an earlier mode of intimacy and sympathy. This is not
to say that these volumes do not have many poems that I love and admire,
among them the quietly gorgeous "The Silken Tent," to which I will

return. Others: "The Most of It," "Never Again Would Birds' Song Be the Same," "The Subverted Flower," of course; but also self-mocking "Willful Homing," "The Quest of the Purple-Fringed," old-new-fashioned "The Discovery of the Madeiras," achingly vulnerable "To a Moth Seen in Winter" (far too sentimental and even, I suspect, self-pitying, for some), "The Fear of Man," "The Middleness of the Road," "The Draft Horse," "Ends," delicate and ecstatic "Questioning Faces," moments of the outrageous "How Hard It Is to Keep from Being King When It's in You and in the Situation."[101]

In spite of the tenor of these remarks, I have to confess that there are mere romps of poems that I also find appealing: "Away!" "A-Wishing Well" and Frost's answer to Keats, "Lines Written in Dejection on the Eve of Great Success" among them. Many of these poems are relatively remote, "guarded," requiring different attitudes toward reading than the narratives. Whether "serious," "ironic," "comic," or all three, some of Frost's later work is like popcorn—tasty and even addictive, though not nourishing as a steady diet. Take "Away!" in which the Yankee sage narrator plays whimsically with rhyme and with Frost's own earlier work, for the first stanza echoes in comic form the emptiness of "Desert Places":

> Now I out walking
> The world desert,
> And my shoe and my stocking
> Do me no hurt.

Reflecting further on his "well-wined friends" and on "the myth" of his own grudges ("There is no one I / Am put out with / Or put out by"), Frost also engages in a subtle power play, for being "put out" refers not only to being angry but to being replaced. The gentleman doth protest a bit too much here about his grudges, methinks, but still it's difficult not to have a soft spot for this trickster who's willing to assert his own immortality:

> And I may return
> If dissatisfied
> With what I learn
> From having died.

> (CP 426–27)

Ironically, given the consummate and seductive performance of "Away," many of the poems in the last three volumes (*Collected Poems* and *Masques* aside) represent a protest against poetry as commerce, while they themselves are fundamentally commercial products and well aware of that fact; this ambivalence is at once a cause and an effect of the guardedness that Rukeyser so astutely observes. Still, the distancing that we discover in Frost differs fundamentally from the difficulty, say, of Eliot and Pound, for in them we find an assumption of privilege or education, while Frost does not ostensibly require this privilege—in fact, he consciously attempts to deconstruct it, becoming "the ordinary man's modernist."[102]

Nowhere, perhaps, do we see his detachment more explicitly than in "Directive"; in contrast to Judith Oster's optimistic account of this poem as hospitable and welcoming, in certain moods I regard it as remote, stagy, and irritating in the extreme.[103] If "Design" performs the comic and engaging aspects of Frost's confidence man, "Directive" acts out his more manipulative and stilted mode. The opening lines invoke a sentimental nostalgia that is countered by an incipiently hostile—or at least standoffish—reference to "a house that is no more a house / Upon a farm that is no more a farm / And in a town that is no more a town" (*CP* 341–42). On one level (get at this one if you can, he seems to say) we are supposed to understand that, to the apparently numbed voice of the narrator, the dissolution of the familiar landscape represents a kind of death and loss of identity. The loss of "home" seems to precipitate his seeing it as merely a "house," and this loss engenders the dereliction of the entire community. Like the narrator in "Design," this narrator provides the guiding principle:

> The road there, if you'll let a guide direct you
> Who only has at heart your getting lost,
> May seem as if it should have been a quarry—
> Great monolithic knees the former town
> Long since gave up pretense of keeping covered.
>
> (*CP* 341)

Playfully, he admits his ambiguous motives toward his listeners; "getting lost" is part of the point of the journey. The sententious tone is at once aimed at those who would take him (too) seriously and at those who see his tongue planted firmly in cheek. But why should we care? Part of the joke is the feminization of the American landscape (Mother Nature), for here it seems at once bleak, obscene, and silly, like the scandalous revelation of female anatomy, with knees uncovered. Traveling the road to this town and this house suggests a passage back to the feminine territory, the home. Even more self-conscious and explicit than "Design," "Directive" points out, "there's a story in a book about it." What's the "it"? The getting lost? The landscape? The movement of the glacier? ("The ledges show lines ruled southeast northwest, / The chisel work of an enormous Glacier / That braced his feet against the Arctic Pole"). The overtones of violence that lurk behind the rocky knees in "Directive" are contained in this stagy description, which resonates with the voice of the professional writer. Indeed, the "enormous Glacier" is none other than the poet himself, "chiseling" (when did "chisel" acquire the secondary meaning of "cheat"?) out "lines," speaking with a kind of haunting "coolness" (*CP* 341). If the poet writes himself into the poem, he also locates the reader there as well. "The Arctic Pole," against which the Glacier must brace himself, is a critical, contending force that epitomizes remoteness, distance, cold: a masculine reader, on whom Frost understood he must ultimately rely for canonization.

Frost situates a reader firmly in the poem with the narrator's reiterated address to "you." As a representation of paranoia and claustrophobia, the next few lines are admittedly unexcelled; the narrator transforms the eyes looking at him into the spectacle of the reader: "Nor need you mind the serial ordeal / Of being watched from forty cellar holes / As if by eye pairs out of forty firkins." The nightmarish "forty eyes" are the poet's own, surveying and supervising this imaginative journey down to its utmost details. We're *supposed* to feel uneasy, jittery, like the boy whistling through the cemetery: "Make yourself up a cheering song of how / Someone's road home for work this once was / Who may be just ahead of you on foot" (*CP* 341). In this domain, where the poet-speaker is "just ahead" of us and punningly "on foot," home isn't "what you somehow haven't to deserve"; it's a place to go at the end of the workday, a place to store your grain, a place to protect you from prying eyes. This adventure, the poet acknowledges, isn't real; it's a head trip, an imaginative journey to find the home that never was (too sentimental, too feminine, too—in Frost's word—soft) and the self that never was either:

> And if you're lost enough to find yourself
> By now, pull in your ladder road behind you
> And put a sign up CLOSED to all but me.
> Then make yourself at home.

> (*CP* 341–42)

The "ladder road," the lines of the poem, are like the tape in "Mission Impossible" that self-destructs when the message is once conveyed. Nothing lasts, "things fall apart" (thank God—then the poetic self can't be traced), and all that's left is the world-building voice of the Poet, with whom the reader must find himself at home or have no home at all.

What's left is a diminished field (of vision?) "no bigger than a harness gall," "the children's house of make believe" (no children), and their "shattered dishes" and other "playthings in the playhouse." The place that was once a home becomes "no more a house, / But only a belilaced cellar hole, / Now slowly closing like a dent in dough." Mom's gone from the kitchen, like her fleshy dough, and she's also gone from the house and voice of poetry. Meant to be utterly disarming—in all senses, if we think back to Frost's letter to Cox about the use of humor—the closing lines are simply, depending on my mood, annoyingly pompous, stubbornly resistant, or simply silly, with their "hidden" "broken drinking goblet like the Grail, / Under a spell so the wrong ones can't find it," that is stolen "from the children's playhouse." The final invocation to "drink and be whole again beyond confusion" (*CP* 342) falls flat for me; I love a mystery, but I don't care how clever Frost is here or that he knows he's being clever and witty, (anti)poetic and (anti)modernist—this poem still grates like a door on bad hinges, even though it retains traces of a sentimental-nostalgic appeal to a country past.[104]

Frost's distancing in "Directive" and elsewhere may reflect his deliberate separation from "intercourse" with a critical masculine reader, his refusal to be "penetrated" to his full depth. In effect, then, he reconfirms his own real masculinity, which is, paradoxically, both separate from other men and defined by them. Manliness is defined not only in opposition (and hence relation) to women but also to other ("gay") versions of male selfhood. In modernist concepts of poetry both femininity and gayness acquire the status of the touchstone other, but for the proclaimedly heterosexual Frost the former subsumes and stands in for the latter as a way of erasing it more effectually.[105] Perhaps because he had proven his "prowess" with four Pulitzer Prizes to accompany his numerous other awards and honors, his competitiveness with other poets could be less preoccupying; to a certain degree he had to worry more about solidifying his image as he sought to insure his place in the still-developing literary canon.

In this connection the same critic who comments on Elinor's status as Muse until the time of her death adds, "As they wear onward, Frost's *Collected Poems* show an increasing self-complacence of poetic purpose: from the initial effort to write true things acceptable to his Muse to writing good things acceptable to himself" (*CR* 156). This metamorphosis parallels the continuing tension not just between feminine and masculine in Frost's work but between female and male in the critical world, emerging with virulence in a *New England Quarterly* review of the same volume seemingly aimed directly at Bogan and Rukeyser:

> This reviewer . . . proposes to tell how he feels about Frost simply because he is sick and tired of reading heavy-laden, academic comments on poetry, or the hoity-toity, heliotrope words of poetasters who write for little "arty" magazines. . . .
>
> Frost's poetry is both good and strong. Nothing anyone says about it can ever hurt it. Yearning spinsters who lay claim to poetic genius review Frost's work with an envy not easy to conceal. (*CR* 163–64)

More noteworthy for its misogyny than for its insight, this review brings into stark relief the polarization of gender in the literary community as well as within Frost's work, for the alliances in this community between women hating and homophobia lurk as a subtext in the reviewer's assertion that the poet's work is "strong." But these are not the only forces at work, for this review incorporates another thrust against the class structure of literary modernism. To this reader Frost's work represents a conservative approach to poetry, based in an accessible "plain language." Part of Frost's appeal for this reader, though he does not say so explicitly, is the poet's reliance upon traditional forms, such as ballad, sonnet, and blank verse.

We can see these forms, I have argued, as indicative but not predictive of gender identity; more important is what I have called the poems' gestures. What is at stake in contemporary reviews and in current readings of Frost is not only the status of the poet but also the status of the reader as Frost imagines it. The poet's continuing remarks about academic criticism highlight his defensive engagement with these actual readers. Writing to Lawrance Thompson in 1954 about an impending radio broadcast for which the pair were preparing, he complains, "I don't mind operators on poetry any more than I mind operators on the human body (divine) but I hate to have everybody that goes to college treated as if he was going to be an operator on either poetry or the human body (divine)." Conceived as surgeons who dissect the poem, critics also threaten to usurp the poet's proper authority: "Besides the danger of seeing figures or symbols where none are intended is the dangerous presumption on the part of the critics that they can go the poet one better by telling him what he is up to. He may think he knows what he means but it takes a modern critic to catch him at what he is up to" (*SL* 557). Thompson observes that Frost "was determined to use his time on the program as a means of attacking what he considered to be the misuses of poetry exemplified by the analytical procedures of the 'new critics' and college professors" (*SL* 556). To some degree this conception of criticism presupposes and/or creates an antagonistic relationship with the poem: the poet speaks an inscrutable tongue that must be translated. Frost's apparent transparency and popularity throughout his career controvert and, later, mock and mimic this assumption. Walton Beacham's remarks about Frost underscore the contemporaneity of this concern: "In dealing with Frost's play, or irony, the difficulty is that while all irony is personal and sub-jective, it is particularly troublesome with Frost because he intentionally eludes and deceives all but the cleverest readers."[106] These remarks point to an elite corps of readers skilled in interpreting an adversarial voice. Frost's defensiveness against academics did not relieve him of the necessity of play-ing their game, however much he might engage in one-upmanship. Whereas many of Frost's early published poems negotiate (however vari-ably) between sentimentality and detachment to engender an emotional response mediated and moderated (in both senses) by intellect, his later lyrics typically foreground the latter and seek intellectual attention as aes-thetic objects (like "Anecdote of the Jar") rather than as participatory dra-mas, leaving no space for the reader except as opponent, and a hard mascu-line one at that.

### "The slightest bondage": Toward a Conclusion

I want to suggest, finally, that in later books like *A Witness Tree* there exists a residue of the earlier poet whose delicate masculinity would foster a poet-ics of empathy before he turned more regularly to a self-consciously bardic stance. Frost has many poems that elaborate the conjunction between love, art, and nature in ways that do not necessarily exclude the female-feminine-feminist reader or entirely objectify the female other. An awareness of his readers emerges perhaps most invitingly and gracefully in "The Silken Tent," which studies the relationship between gender and genre:

> She is as in a field a silken tent
> At midday when a sunny summer breeze
> Has dried the dew and all its ropes relent,
> So that in guys it gently sways at ease,
> And its supporting central cedar pole,
> That is its pinnacle to heavenward
> And signifies the sureness of the soul,
> Seems to owe naught to any single cord,

But strictly held by none, is loosely bound
By countless silken ties of love and thought
To everything on earth the compass round,
And only by one's going slightly taut
In the capriciousness of summer air
Is of the slightest bondage made aware.

(*CP* 302)

This poem evinces a disposition for romantic lyric detachment, order, and timelessness; Frost follows Shakespearean form precisely. Establishing a mood of "ease" and gentleness, the poet invites us to imagine a graceful, fragile being who participates in traditionally feminine activities, such as needlework ("tent" stitch done in silk) and who partakes of the loveliness of nature (the "silken tent" constructed by various insects, which sways in the warmth of a "summer breeze").

At the same time that the poem refers to the beloved, it gestures gently toward the reader through its structure, style, and central metaphor. As we progress through the lines of this single, loosely but carefully constructed sentence, we lose sight of the initial association between the beloved and the silken tent. The speaker draws us along by frequent enjambment and by the loveliness of the sounds of his language; the poem's organizing principle seems to be less the sonnet form and more his own breath, his inspiration. As Poirier remarks, "The whole poem is a performance, a display for the beloved."[107] In some sense, though he does not say so, we can argue that the reader becomes this beloved as she—and the reader is feminized here—enacts the poem.

The last lines echo the experience that the poem itself performs: we find the last line "going slightly taut"—referring to bondage, to structure—and, hence, we acquire retrospectively a sense of our own gentle bondage within the confines of the poem. If we look back, we discover that the speaker has been playful, "capricious," all along. After he creates the mood in the opening two lines, he focuses less on the tent and more upon its supporting members—the ropes that "relent," paralleling the soft lines of the poem itself; the steadying "guys" (or "guise"), whose lightness engenders "ease" for the tent and for the reader; and the "supporting central cedar pole," perhaps a slanted reference to the sonnet form, perhaps to the central metaphor, and certainly a phallic image. At the same time, the "pinnacle to heavenward" evokes the idea of sexual delight, a delight echoed in the reader's experience of intercourse. Ironically, in view of the delicate ambiguity of the images and of the syntactic constructions in which they appear, the speaker defines in line 7 the "meaning" of the image of the pole: "the sureness of the soul." We discover in the next line, however, that the speaker's certainty is tentative, because unlocatable: it "seems" to come from nowhere. The shadow of this "seems" hovers over the rest of the poem, in part because Frost emphasizes it by placing it in the line-initial position. Like the tent itself, the poem seems not to depend on any single cord; "seamless," it is "strictly held by none," "loosely bound / By count-less silken ties of love and thought / To everything on earth the compass round." Frost's esteem for the relationship between poetry and life, partic-ularly sensual life, emerges in these lines. What holds the image, the poem, and the world together is in fact "love and thought"—the intercourse between the poet and his beloved, speaker and reader, and the way he con-structs that connection. If "any single cord" creates and sustains connection, it is the "vocal" "chords" of the speaker, his intimate, loving, and playful voice, as the silken tent becomes the silk intent.

I have to confess as a female reader that I am lured time and again by this poem that perhaps more than any other in Frost's oeuvre objectifies the woman whom it imagines. From one angle "The Silken Tent" reinscribes the normal configurations of speaker, reader, and object in romantic lyric as outlined by Rachel Blau DuPlessis: "There is often a [homoerotic] triangu-lated situation in the lyric: an overtly male 'I,' speaking as if overheard in front of an unseen but postulated, loosely male 'us' about a (Beloved) 'she.' "[108] Viewed in this light, Frost's poem appears as a paradigm of patri-archal appropriation, and it is easy to point to his "pole" in feminist wrath as a phallic image that embodies the centrality of a masculine consciousness to transcendence.

I want, however, to attempt to reclaim this poem as one that women can read with pleasure. "The Silken Tent" differs fundamentally from "Design" in its attitude toward and affinities with the reader, for, while the latter "stays close, and guards," the former engages and invites on more hos-pitable terms. Once again it is clear that the generic changes toward "Direc-tive" and "Design" mirror the transformation of Frost's voice from more feminine to more masculine, but such changes are not formally inherent; they are shaped by attitude played out in rhetorical and stylistic gesture. As Rita Felski points out in another context, "forms of textuality cannot be defined as either intrinsically liberatory or oppressive."[109] Frost does jostle the triangular situation of the traditional love lyric, however slightly, in 'The Silken Tent." It is, ironically, the possibility of evoking the reader not as male critic or collaborator but as the beloved ("loosely bound / By countless silken ties of love and thought") that mitigates this configuration. Yes, "The Silken Tent" is both romantic and sentimental; yes, the beloved is an object rather than a subject speaking her own language; yes, there is a gentle challenge to the reader. We are a long way from the voice of "A Servant to Servants." But this voice does not regard us—even women readers—as one of the enemies, to be kept at a distance. This is playing, not playfulness.[110]

At the same time that Frost leaves behind his narrative-dramatic forms, he retains a soft strand in his modern lyric voice. But that voice, he thought, would help ensure his reputation beyond sentiment and region. With echoes of Whitman, a section of his Oberlin College Commencement Address in 1937 ("What Became of New England?") makes these ambitions clear:

> New England now . . . What's become of it? It's not necessarily to be found in a literature to be restricted to New England. The little nation that was and was to be gave itself as Virginia gave herself, westward, into the great nation that she saw coming, and so gave help to America. And so any of us are not New Englanders particularly; any writers we were, any statesmen we were, were to be Americans, United States statesmen, United States writers. (*CP* 757)

That he had achieved this status is clear from the reviews of *A Witness Tree*, in which "The Silken Tent" first appeared, for they were full of "nearly uniform praise" (*CR* xviii), and the book won Frost his record fourth Pulitzer Prize. By this time the poet's transformation of both gender and genre was not only essentially completed (with some of the exceptions noted earlier) but also certified with the seal of public approval. The man who had written twenty-seven years earlier to Louis Untermeyer, "Do you know, I think that a book ought to sell. Nothing is quite honest that is not commercial" (the last sentence one he liked so well that he repeated it a month later)—and in 1931, in one of his characteristic "moods," confessed to the same correspondent, "Sometimes I almost cry I am afraid I am such a bad poet"—must have been gratified to have been recognized as a Real Poet, and by extension no sissy, but a Real Man indeed (*LU* 8–9, 10; *SL* 378).

# Coda: "An Impregnable Harbor for the Self"

Published in the World War II era, Frost's verse dramas *A Masque of Reason* (1945) and *A Masque of Mercy* (1947) seem to occasion little more than (and more than a little) embarrassment in Frost criticism; it's as if a distinguished and beloved older man suddenly took to exposing himself on street corners—everyone who knows him wants desperately not to see it. Wagner regards them as "both products of the 'Build Soil' impulse (Frost as institution, as voice of a people's conscience)" (*CR* xvii–xviii).[1] Early critics were less doubtful of *A Masque of Reason,* although Wagner points out that "Mark Van Doren finally took the responsibility—in the midst of a positive review—for assaying the weakness of the masque." Van Doren had observed: "there is also the danger that a man who *has* a voice will decline into a man who *is* one. . . . To be a Voice is not to be enviable, for it means taking whatever you say as valuable merely because you hear yourself saying it (*New York Herald Tribune,* March 25, 1945)" (xviii). A more critical reviewer called it "a volume of verse"; in the *New Republic* Conrad Aiken described "the pattern as 'unrewardingly blank . . . there are times when the cracker-barrel wisecrack grates a little, and when the texture and text alike become too thin'" (xviii). That these critics were either confused by Frost's new approach or "embarrassed by their own ambivalence toward the first masque," as Wagner notes, is suggested by their relative silence on *A Masque of Mercy.* Or perhaps, as I shall explore in a moment, they were abashed by some of its belated nastiness.

Roy Harvey Pearce's more recent discussion of the poems highlights Frost's hostility to the reader ("The sense of withdrawal in Frost . . . culminates in the wry [masques]. . . . Frost has come to taunt his reader, not to challenge him as he had done formerly"),[2] while the usually sympathetic Randall Jarrell is even more severe: "*A Masque of Reason* . . . is a frivolous, trivial, and bewilderingly corny affair, full of jokes inexplicable except as the contemptuous patter of an old magician certain that *he* can get away with anything in the world: *What fools these readers be!*"[3] Contemporary criticism of Frost seems to perpetuate the mode of quizzical or disconcerted silence that has often surrounded the poems. Lentricchia (in both *Modernist Quartet* and his earlier study) ignores the *Masques* entirely, while Oster mentions one in passing. Kearns cites *A Masque of Reason* as another example of the poet's repression of "his own prophetic femininity," replacing it with "the voice of the prophet, controlled, virile in its moderation, and relatively safe from attack."[4] In his usual sympathetic manner Poirier gives them more positive attention, mainly as examples of Frost's attitude toward Christianity; he observes that "even when he is most expressly Christian in his poetry, as in the *Masques,* little is affirmed that is not implicit in 'Design'" and that a "relationship between humans and God in Frost can, as in the *Masques,* be consciously and explicitly founded in complaints and in wonderings about mercy and justice." More pointedly, he suggests that "the knowledge that no one can at last depend on being taken care of by governments—or even God—is the necessary inducement to further creation in life, in poetry, in the imagination of the self." In a specific set of reflections on *A Masque of Reason* Poirier points out Frost's jab at the obscurity of much modern poetry and underlines his "positive attitude toward the elusiveness of meaning [that] applies at once to the difficulties of life and of poetry."[5] Overall, these remarks occupy a small proportion of Poirier's discussion, and his descriptive (rather than evaluative) tone indicates another approach that is taken to the *Masques.*[6] Finally, Jeffrey Meyers refers to the poems as "his most conspicuous failures . . . [they] add nothing to his poetic reputation."[7]

These are very funny poems, if wholly irregular in implied attitudes to their readers, which range from ploddingly didactic to playfully provoking to puzzlingly obscure. The *Masques* reveal more than Frost's perspectives on God and faith; they are also, as Kearns's argument suggests (though with a very different outcome), barometers of his attitude toward women and women's cultural roles. In *A Masque of Reason* and *A Masque of Mercy* we see the poet exhibiting a range of attitudes, from affirmation to ambivalence to ostensible sexism. *A Masque of Mercy* poses more difficulty—both personal and aesthetic—for many readers, and it was dismissed even more forcefully by contemporaries than *A Masque of Reason,* with Meyers's observation that the poem was only "a similar, much longer and even more lifeless work" extending Leslie Fiedler's earlier remark that it was "a bad book, shallow, corny, and unmercifully cute."[8]

*A Masque of Mercy* skewers verse collector Jessie Belle Rittenhouse, whose 1912 *Little Book of Verse* sold over 100,000 copies in its first edition. If imitation is indeed the sincerest form of flattery—or, in this case, the best way to make a buck—Untermeyer's 1919 anthology and its successor editions "managed to include poems that Rittenhouse would have admired and that, through no one's stretch of the imagination, would be included under anyone's definition of modernism." Certainly not of a *canonical* modernism that has until recently been defined solely by male standards. Rittenhouse's success as "a major literary journalist in America in the first two decades of this century," her power to "say who was in and who (usually by omission) was out" seems to irritate Frank Lentricchia as much as it did Frost, for the former notes (in what seems a rather gratuitously nasty tone, given her current obscurity) that "not one writer she took up has survived in recent accounts of American literary history (not even for a sentence)."[9] Using Frost as a cover, Lentricchia castigates "all those enemies [Rittenhouse among them] of a living, (that is, a 'contemporary,' a genuinely 'modern') literature who come at us from the feminized crypt of manliness, the book,"[10] and he points toward Frost's transformation of Jessie Belle into the "whorish" Jesse Bel (Jezebel) in *A Masque of Mercy*.

Ironically, given the early stage of his career when her volume was published, Rittenhouse's second collection had actually included a significant number of Frost poems, and one could hardly take issue with the choices: "The Road Not Taken," "Birches," "The Hill Wife," and "After Apple-Picking."[11] Furthermore, it should be pointed out that she had given Frost pride of place, for "The Road Not Taken" is the first poem in this new collection. Along with Frost we find many poets who are unknown today, to be sure, but we also discover a number who have regularly been studied, if not as high modernists (Sandburg and Robinson), along with several who have drawn increasing interest in recent years, including Amy Lowell, Millay, and H.D. Similarly, Rittenhouse's third collection controverts the idea that "not one writer she took up has survived in recent accounts of American literary history," including poems by Louise Bogan, Eliot, Crane, cummings, H.D., Jeffers, Amy Lowell, MacLeish, Millay, Moore, Pound, Ransom, Robinson, Sandburg, Tate, Edith Thomas, Williams, and Wylie—hardly an obscure group of writers—in addition to (presumably to vary the grouping from her previous book) Frost's "To Earthward," "Misgiving," "Stopping by Woods on a Snowy Evening," and "The Onset."[12]

Years after Rittenhouse's dominance in the world of poetry had subsided, Frost carries a grudge (in his terms, a "grievance"), and a nasty one, at that. Possibly for calling him a "dreamer" and implying that he is an aesthete, for representing him as un–American and, perhaps most unforgivably, comparing him indirectly to a masculine Amy Lowell and seeing in him "the boy" as much as the man,[13] he makes Jesse Bel dream that "someone took curved nail scissors and snipped off / My eyelids so I couldn't shut my eyes / To anything that happened any more" (*CP* 397). The woman who envisioned poetry "indiscriminately" is condemned to look at everything (and she's a drunk as well). But Rittenhouse (along with God and faith) isn't the only one to take it on the cheek here; there's another lusciously vicious attack on modern poetry that's compared with the deliciously punning "Babel":

> everyone developing
> A language of his own to write his book in,
> And one to cap the climax by combining
> All language in a one-man tongue-confusion.
>
> (*CP* 398)

I will grant that from one perspective not only is Frost is irritable here (and elsewhere in the poem), he's easily read as a little whiny and smug:

> When a great tide of argument sweeps in
> My small fresh water spring gets drowned of course.
> But when the brine goes back, as go it must
> I can count on my source to spring again,
> Not even brackish from its salt experience.
> No true source can be poisoned.
>
> (*CP* 410)

These lines actually belong to Keeper, who is in equal measure sententious (*CP* 411–12), but in spite of their potential humor and irony they suggest an uneasy alliance with the attitudes that Frost expresses elsewhere in his manifestation as bardic Poet.

Jesse Bel's voice and performance in *A Masque of Mercy* are far less important than Thyatira's in *A Masque of Reason;* in the former's role as a whore she comes in for it not only for her drunkenness and promiscuity but also for her (lack of) commercialism (ironically and unlike her real-life model, she tells the ostensible customer who knocks on the closed bookstore door that "we can't always be selling people things" [*CP* 389]). Perhaps most striking and most significant, however, is her castrating bitchiness: when Keeper accuses her of not offering to share her drinks, she counters, "We're poor—that's why. My man can't earn a living" (*CP* 392). Frost's grievances, long cherished, are embarrassingly exposed, and they are clearly related to perceived manliness. Although *A Masque of Mercy* has its wonderfully funny moments, when it comes to representing intellectual or powerful women, Frost's ambivalence (to put it gently) is only too evident. This modern-day whore will sell anything—even her man's pride and masculinity—for a buck. If I'm effeminate, you're a slut, he shouts. The aim is not song but to prove one's a man—at any cost. But even here, at one of his most difficult moments for feminist readers, Frost affirms (via Keeper) that "Bel gets some things right," namely, her affirmation of "courage": "Courage is of the heart by derivation, / And great it is" (*CP* 416).

One problem for contemporary readers of the earlier *A Masque of Reason* may have been what Louise Bogan implied was Frost's ostensibly flip attitude toward pain and suffering in an era that had had more of its share. Beyond this motive for criticism, however, lies another familiar one: Frost's affiliation with popular, negatively coded, critically constructed femininity. Of the ending Bogan affirms that it "will, indeed, bring down the house in a gathering of, say, the Ladies' Aid Society"; the rhetorical posturing of this affirmation, echoing Ransom's description of Millay's audience, amply testifies to its tone and attitude.[14] Yet I think that Frost gets far too little credit for the raunchy, affirmatively "feminine" voice of Job's Wife in *A Masque of Reason;* far from being merely decorative or entertaining, Thyatira is central to our understanding of Frost at this moment.[15] For example, though at times her voice is pushy (when she propels Job to face God: "Go over / And speak to Him before the others come. / Tell Him He may remember you: you're Job" [*CP* 373]), she performs some of the best lines in the poem. When the scene opens *she* is the one who recognizes God:

> It's God
> I'd know Him by Blake's picture anywhere.
> Now what's He doing?
>
> (*CP* 372)

If Job himself is a bit of a dope (and a dupe), and more than a little passive, Thyatira is not willing to let God off the hook: "—I have a protest I would lodge with You. / I want to ask You if it stands to reason / That women prophets should be burned as witches, / Whereas men prophets are received with honor" (*CP* 375). God looks a bit doltish as well; he can't find a record of having burned the Witch of Endor, whom Thyatira claims as a friend; his throne keeps collapsing; he doesn't have much of an answer to "why there is still injustice," only observing, "That's the way it is"; and he is utterly stereotypical in his conception of her and his defenses against her accusations. When (not surprisingly) Job pleads, "Oh, Lord, let's not go back to anything," God asks, "Because your wife's past won't bear looking into?——" (*CP* 376).

The sexual slur has frequently worked to silence women, but this one doesn't stop Thyatira. In her longest speech of the poem she highlights the violence and irrationality of God's world; for example, she reiterates some of the earlier Frost's visible compassion for the economically disadvantaged, although Frost assigns some irony to this passage that he does not allot earlier:

> No, let's not live things over. I don't care.
> I stood by Job. I may have turned on You.
> Job scratched his boils and tried to think what he
> Had done or not done to or for the poor.
> The test is always how we treat the poor.
> It's time the poor were treated by the state
> In some way not so penal as the poorhouse.
> That's one thing more to put on Your agenda.
> Job hadn't done a thing, poor innocent.
> I told him not to scratch: it made it worse.
> If I said once I said a thousand times,
> Don't scratch! And when, as rotten as his skin,
> His tents blew all to pieces, I picked up
> Enough to build him every night a pup tent
> Around him so it wouldn't touch and hurt him.
> I did my wifely duty. I should tremble!
> All You can seem to do is lose Your temper
> When reason-hungry mortals ask for reasons.
> Of course, in the abstract high singular
> There isn't any universal reason;
> And no one but a man would think there was.
> You don't catch women trying to be Plato.
>
>                                        (*CP* 377)

"You don't catch women trying to be Plato": in spite of the ostensibly carping tone, this is one of the best (and most outrageous) lines of the poem, and, while Frost pokes fun at her motherliness and excessive pragmatism, he has considerable sympathy with her, representing her (to my mind, anyway) as by far the most appealing character in *A Masque of Reason*.

Both Job and God patronize and stereotype her. To Thyatira's reiterated complaint that God doesn't allow women to be prophets (visionaries, poets?)—or if he does, "it's mostly women / Get burned for prophecy, men almost never"—Job says "God needs just as much as you or I / To get things done. Reformers fail to see that.—" And then he too indulges in a snide intellectual-sexual dig: "She'll go to sleep. Nothing keeps her awake / But physical activity, I find. / Try to read to her and she drops right off." She has no mind, just body, he implies, and God approves his stance by objectifying her further: "She's beautiful" (*CP* 377), and, a bit later, "I'm charmed with her." The latter statement is more than the polite middle-class male's false appreciation; it points back to the theme of witchcraft and women's exclusion from vision. It's difficult to read the level of Frost's self-consciousness here. Is he pointing back to his own witches and effectively "burning them at the stake"? When God asks Job, "What are her interests," Job makes the subject explicit:

> Witch-women's rights.
> Humor her there or she will be confirmed
> In her suspicion You're no feminist.
> You have it in for women, she believes.
>
> (*CP* 378)

Job and God are so egregiously condescending that it is impossible (at least if one loves Frost) to believe that the poet meant their perspectives to be taken seriously. He is, of course, cagey and ultimately silent on the subject of witchcraft and women as prophets; perhaps the matter is posed as a question more to himself than to anyone else. Certainly, there is a defensive tone—for, if Frost is Job and Thyatira, he is also God, of whom Thyatira has to suspect "You're no feminist." The alternations in voice and perspective suggest Frost's continued ambivalence about the role of visionary women in the world (God's and the Poet's); indeed, as Donald Sheehy has recently argued, "Revisionist as they may be in theological argument, the *Masques* are traditionally masculinist in discrediting a 'feminist' philosophical voice."[16]

The passage that Poirier cites as a jab at modern poetry represents another kind of self-defensive gesture on the part of the poet:

> The chances are when there's so much pretense
> Of metaphysical profundity
> The obscurity's a fraud to cover nothing.
> I've come to think no so-called hidden value's
> Worth going after. Get down into things
> It will be found there's no more given there
> Than on the surface.
>
> (*CP* 381)

In part a challenge, in part a stuck-out tongue, these lines defy the prying reader to find meaning as much as they accuse poets of having none. Torn between being popular, appreciated for what he appeared to be, and being valued for his depth, the poet hedges his bets once again. *A Masque of Reason* is at bottom as much a poem about interpretation as it is about God: What's meaningful? How? Why? What's the proper attitude of the interpreter, Job's or Thyatira's (or, for that matter, God's)? The gender of the "reader"—and the "writer"—does seem to matter but *how* remains unclear.

Still, it seems more than a little significant that Job's wife is finally the stage director, arranging God, the Devil, and Job for her Kodak photograph. Are women the ultimate managers? Merely consumers? Are they (thank God!) invisible (she won't show in the final photograph) but ultimately powerful? Job's Wife has the last words in the poem, spoken at first to Satan and then to the three males:

> I want you in my group beside the throne—
> Must have you. There, that's just the right arrangement.
> Now someone can light up the Burning Bush
> And turn the gold enameled artificial birds on.
> I recognize them. Greek artificers
> Devised them for Alexius Comnenus.
> They won't show in the picture. That's too bad.
> Neither will I show. That's too bad moreover.
> Now if you three have settled anything
> You'd as well smile as frown on the occasion.
>
> (*CP* 388)

In this closing portrait I see my grandmother taking photos as she did on every family gathering—arranging, fussing, telling everyone to smile, dipping as she pushed the button. And cutting off everyone's head.

On the day that I discovered the Robert Frost Interpretive Trail, it was doing a modest but steady business. One older couple got out of their green

van with Pennsylvania plates and headed down the boardwalk with a twen-
tyish young woman in a wheelchair sporting a Day-Glo orange flag, while
a boy and girl bounced away from their parents after heaving three white,
yellow, and red McDonald's bags in the trash barrel. As I knelt in the field
to gather blueberries, a pair of women in their fifties (possibly conferees at
nearby Bread Loaf, where Frost was to become "the presiding deity")[17]
approached and asked if it was all right to pick; as they crouched to gather,
their floral cotton dresses swept the ground. I caught up to the family a bit
later when they had paused for the father to read "A Young Birch" aloud in
a rhythmic and reverent fashion. As part of Frost's large contemporary audi-
ence, all of these readers were remapping the trail in their own ways.

At the beginning of this set of reflections I compared Frost very indi-
rectly to T. S. Eliot and—no doubt shockingly to some—implied that my
allegiances resided with the "popular modernist." My introduction to "The
Waste Land" in undergraduate school provoked nothing short of irritation
and disgust. In retrospect I see that my response could be attributed at least
as much to its detachment from me as a reader as to its difficulty—or per-
haps the two were allied. Frost was a different story—partly because I was a
New Englander and knew firsthand what he was talking about but partly, I
now believe, because he offered me more space, taking up less of his own.
Reiterating the feminine metaphor of "filament" with which this study
begins, his "Foreword to 'King Jasper'" indicates his desire for engagement
even at a time when he was consolidating himself into The Poet:

> We begin in infancy by establishing correspondence of eyes with eyes. We
> recognized that they were the same features and we could do the same things
> with them. We went on to the visible motion of the lips—smile answered
> smile. . . . From here on the wonder grows. It has been said that recognition
> in art is all. Better say correspondence is all. Mind must convince mind that it
> can uncurl and wave the same filaments of subtlety, soul convince soul that it
> can give off the same shimmers of eternity. At no point would anyone but a
> brute fool want to break off this correspondence. It is all there is to satisfaction;
> and it is salutary to live in fear of its being broken off. (LU 262)

The passion, intensity, and intimacy that Frost conjures here could not be
sustained; his shift from feminine to masculine voices indicates an increas-
ingly adversarial approach, a divorce between reader and speaker, and reader
and poet.

Not only did contemporary readers have the power to imagine and
shape the poet's voice, but current-day readers continue to "create" the

poet by interpreting him, and they do so often by suppressing or devaloriz-
ing his feminine voice. In my discussion of a variety of poems I have indi-
cated how even such fine readers as Poirier, Kearns, Oster, and Lentricchia
mute or silence Frost's femininity. Again representative, the latter makes a
distinction that, while it parallels my own attitude on Frost's eventual with-
drawal from the reader, illuminates even more clearly, if unwittingly, the
gender polarities within Frost and within Frost criticism:

> There is an affinity between the demented witch in "The Witch of Coös," the
> half-demented servant in "A Servant to Servants," the wife of "Home Burial,"
> and the selves created in "Design," "Desert Places" and other dramatic lyrics.
> . . . In both "Desert Places" and "Design" the poet's self-consciousness saves
> him; it allows the pressure of a difficult situation to be released. There is always
> an impregnable harbor for the self to retreat to, a room in the house of the
> mind that can never be penetrated, even if that room is sometimes only the
> self-directed ironic attitude.[18]

In strikingly pugilistic terms this distinction between these groups of poems
corresponds to the one I have made between Frost's feminine and mascu-
line voices. I noted earlier that Lentricchia comments that Frost's women
have no "drive to preserve self."[19] In what amounts to an elaboration of that
insight we see here the tension between earlier and later, more feminine and
more masculine—and, sometimes, narrative and lyric—dramatically
inscribed: the poet, conceived ironically as potentially feminine and vulner-
able, foils the appalling "design of darkness" by withdrawing into the
"impregnable [!] harbor" of the self. Most strikingly, the critic emphasizes
an "impenetrability" and self-containment that echo the masculine fear of
"merging" that we saw in Lawrence's criticism of Whitman and that defines
the autonomy (and anatomy?) of masculine selfhood and in particular,
canonical masculine lyric subjectivity as elaborated by both its poets and its
critics.[20]

   Hence, not only have poems like "Maple" and "In the Home Stretch,"
which embody complex substantive and formal concerns especially related
to gender, been largely ignored, but so also has the potential femininity of
many more familiar poems such as "Snow," "The Housekeeper," "The
Fear," "The Generations of Men," and "Paul's Wife." As Jarrell suggests,
the sheer length of some poems inhibits detailed admiration,[21] but the fact
that the poems that many contemporary readers foreground and admire—
and many tend to be later lyrics—conform more readily to a modernist
poetic and critical agenda in substance and, more significantly, in attitude

surely plays an important role in their relative prominence. This critical division, as well as the early assessment of Frost as a minor poet because of an ostensible absence of depth and modernist sophistication, is based in part on a predisposition to value poems that foreground a more distant, masculine intellectual thrust (and "sophistication" or "complexity") over those that evoke feminine participation and empathy and those that privilege the ironic, the ambiguous, and the "universal" over those that highlight the straightforward (on the surface, anyway), the vulnerable, and the "local": domesticated discourse. Whether we believe he consciously or only subconsciously inflected his work to meet the demands of the time and of posterity, we might reflect that Frost could be no slouch when it came to politics—whether it be cultivating Pound or Untermeyer or adopting a different voice—and if modern critics wanted complexity, ambiguity, alienation, and especially, ironic detachment, he could provide them, with a vengeance.[22]

Frost's inner battles, and his early feminine poems, were conducted and created against the backdrop of his marriage to Elinor, a connection that at once freed and bound him. Providing him with time and support to write, enabling him to see from a feminine perspective, his marriage to a working woman enabled a clarity of this vision that surely bewitched and terrified. By the same token Frost's early ability to "merge" with a feminine self, to express an empathy for the other both in his characters and in his gestures toward the reader, found its match in his own cultural role as husband and, ultimately, father, as well as in the patriarchal literary culture that fathered him by specifying the shape and voice of poetic utterance, requiring negotiations of popularity and masculinity on the road to canonicity. A public and self-promoting person like Whitman, Frost was bound by literary, sexual, and gender norms that shaped his work in a fundamental way. Stubbornly and vociferously heterosexual, Frost in many of his later poems enacts the potential hierarchy traditionally inscribed in that point of view, and the sense of loss in the replacement of feminine by more masculine poetic voices is poignant, if repressed. The price of this repression was an occasional, or even more than occasional, sinking into a self-parody, what Jarrell calls "the Only Genuine Robert Frost in Captivity."[23] What was at stake? Only everything: power, both cultural and literary, and finally identity itself.

In many of his best poems Frost evinces a complex understanding of feminine roles and voices and in guiding us to understanding expresses a sensibility that not only acknowledges his own feminine voices but celebrates them. Contemporary readers of any persuasion who elide these perspectives and the poet's gestures to the reader ultimately diminish Frost's complexity and appeal. On their faces many early poems may seem as politically "conservative" as Frost often represented himself: conserving a past peopled by those who found its deepest sustenance and satisfaction—as well as terror—in the earth. But, in spite of his resistance to a New Deal sensibility,[24] Frost was at times a closet "Democrat," that is, a radical propounder of strong, softer voices emerging from an ethic of relationship that also provided a "momentary stay against [the] confusion" proffered by the modernist vision of the wasteland. If some chose to view the New England hills and valleys as a microcosm of this wasteland, these viewers hadn't observed the ways in which the inhabitants found "waste" useful, whether creating friendship quilts, composing poetry out of feminine literary tradition, or feeding chickens and pigs.

# Notes

## Introduction

1. Sheldon W. Liebman, "Frost on Criticism," *New England Quarterly* 66.3 (1993): 399–415.

2. Lynn Keller and Cristanne Miller point out that "poetry—and particularly the relation of poetry to recent theoretical and feminist discourses—has received inadequate critical attention in the past few decades"; in addition, the kind of poetry that has received attention has been narrowly limited to "the personal lyric in the Romantic tradition." They remind us that "poetry, and particularly lyric poetry, enjoyed a critical heyday in the era of New Criticism. . . . As New Criticism has fallen from favor and been replaced by other methodologies and theories of literature, the lyric has yielded its position of critical prestige to narrative modes" ("Feminist Measures: Soundings in Poetry and Theory," in *Feminist Measures: Soundings in Poetry and Theory*, ed. Keller and Miller [Ann Arbor: University of Michigan Press, 1994], 1, 2).

Within discussions of poetry itself, feminist critics have frequently neglected male poets' use of feminine perspectives, other than as opportunities for castigation or as negative poles against which women writers have (assuredly and affirmatively) operated. We need to ask "why should one's empathetic engagement or curiosity go only to the gender or social identities the critic practices?"; "why might writing by men not be scrutinized by feminists in its social, economic, political situation, in the cultural work and life work it is accomplishing?" (Rachel Blau DuPlessis, "'Corpses of Poesy': Some Modern Poets and Some Gender Ideologies of Lyric," in Keller and Miller, *Feminist Measures,* 69–70).

3. Earl J. Wilcox, "Robert Frost and the 'Anxiety of Influence,'" in *His "Incalculable" Influence on Others: Essays on Robert Frost in Our Time* (Victoria, BC: English Literary Studies at the University of Victoria, 1994), 8. A brief survey of MLA Online—which is admittedly incomplete—indicates that since 1990 there have been only 4 full-length studies of the poet, compared to more than a dozen each for Eliot and Pound. When we consider total attention over the last sixteen years (the period that MLA Online encompasses), the consideration of Frost in relation to those contemporaries polarizes even more, with 1,746 entries for Eliot, 1,375

for Pound, and 482 for Frost. I was surprised to discover that the number of entries on Frost is actually much nearer to the figures for H. D. and Moore (351 and 259, respectively). All figures cited in this section include MLA Online data from 1 January 1981 to 28 February 1997. The four studies of Frost are: George F. Bagby, *Frost and the Book of Nature* (Knoxville: University of Tennessee Press, 1993); Judith Oster, *Toward Robert Frost, The Reader and the Poet* (Athens: University of Georgia Press, 1991); Katherine Kearns, *Robert Frost and a Poetics of Appetite* (Cambridge: Cambridge University Press, 1994); Edward Ingebretsen, S. J., *Robert Frost's Star in a Stone Boat: A Grammar of Belief* (Bethesda, MD: International Scholars, 1996). As this book was going to press, three additional volumes, whose accounts I have been able only to note occasionally, have been published: Robert Faggen, *Robert Frost and the Challenge of Darwin* (Ann Arbor: University of Michigan Press, 1997); Mark Richardson, *The Ordeal of Robert Frost: The Poet and His Poetics* (Urbana: University of Illinois Press, 1997); and Robert F. Fleissner, *Robert Frost's Road Taken* (New York: Peter Lang, 1997).

4. As will become apparent from my discussion, I see these terms as overlapping and extremely flexible; in formulating this list, I am purposely mixing the directionality (and hence potential hierarchy) of some of these categories.

5. Jay Parini, "Robert Frost and the Poetry of Survival," *The Columbia History of American Poetry,* ed. Jay Parini (New York: Columbia University Press, 1993), 279; Louise Bogan, "A Lifework," *A Poet's Alphabet: Reflections on the Literary Art and Vocation,* ed. Robert Phelps and Ruth Limmer (New York: McGraw-Hill, 1970), 173–74.

6. George Monteiro, *Robert Frost and the New England Renaissance* (Lexington: University Press of Kentucky, 1988), 6.

7. The preliminary recontextualization of Frost's work that this study represents has only become possible in the present cultural moment in which sentimental, regionalist, oral, gay, and popular literatures have gained cultural currency in the academy, and my account is deeply indebted not only to many specific works in these fields but also to the broader disposition toward inclusiveness everywhere evident in literary and cultural studies.

8. Rita Felski, *The Gender of Modernity* (Cambridge: Harvard University Press, 1995), 93. It is worth pointing out that queer theorists have conceptualized sexuality in analogously fluid terms; Diana Fuss, for example, argues that "sexual identity may be less a function of knowledge than performance, or . . . less a matter of final discovery than perpetual reinvention," while Judith Butler underlines that "sexuality always exceeds any given performance, presentation or narrative" (Fuss, "Inside/Out" [6–7]; and Butler, "Imitation and Gender Insubordination" [25], both in *inside/out, Lesbian Theories, Gay Theories,* ed. D. Fuss [New York: Routledge, 1991]).

9. Lisa Rado, "Lost and Found: Remembering Modernism, Rethinking Feminism," *Rereading Modernism: New Directions in Feminist Criticism,* ed. L. Rado (New York: Garland, 1994), 12, 7–9. In choosing to focus on Frost, I am consciously entering a number of important current debates in feminist criticism, including those described succinctly by Rado: the argument between "critics concentrating on the images of women in literary texts and those focusing on the lin-

guistic strategies of the texts themselves"; the matter of "whether we ought to devote our time to studying male or female authors"; "the relative merits of so-called 'psychological' versus 'cultural' criticism"; and "the preferential treatment afforded to the experimental as opposed to the realist text." I hope that the pages that follow demonstrate my attitude toward these debates, namely, that we need not and in fact should not pursue an either/or strategy (7–9, 11–13). Rado's discussion contains a useful bibliography of participants in these and other such debates. I will not enter the argument about what modernism is (or is not) but will look, instead, at Frost's stance toward the reader and his participation in the genre of "children's writing," among other matters. For a discussion of this debate, see Shari Benstock, "Expatriate Sapphic Modernism: Entering Literary History," in *Lesbian Texts and Contexts: Radical Revisions,* ed. Karla Jay and Joanne Glasgow (New York: New York University Press, 1990), 183–203 (reprinted in Rado, *Rereading Modernism,* 97–121); Marianne DeKoven, *Rich and Strange: Gender, History, Modernism* (Princeton: Princeton University Press, 1991), 4–16; and Astradur Eysteinsson, *The Concept of Modernism* (Ithaca: Cornell University Press, 1990). About the gender conflicts in modern literature, Cary Nelson observes, "Men did not always . . . write disparagingly about women, though they often did. Moreover, the range of sexist attitudes is so great that accounting for it may require distinct analytic categories rather than just a uniform category of misogyny or a description of a spectrum of deplorable stances" ("The Fate of Gender in Modern American Poetry," in *Marketing Modernisms: Self-Promotion, Canonization, Rereading,* ed. Kevin J. H. Dettmar and Stephen Watt [Ann Arbor: University of Michigan Press, 1996], 324; see 325).

10. As the account that follows indicates, I am aware of the dangers of using *we,* but I am hoping that my readers will perceive it as a gesture of invitation, bracketed by this awareness and by an understanding that disagreement is not only possible but likely.

11. Andreas Huyssen, *After the Great Divide: Modernism, Mass Culture, Postmodernism* (Bloomington: Indiana University Press, 1986), 44–62. See also Jane Tompkins, *Sensational Designs: The Cultural Work of American Fiction, 1790–1860* (New York: Oxford University Press, 1985), 3–39; Ann Douglas, *The Feminization of American Culture* (New York: Discus-Avon, 1977), 1–13, 95–99.

12. For the suggestion of Frost's declining popularity, see Hyatt H. Waggoner, *American Poets from the Puritans to the Present* (Boston: Houghton Mifflin, 1968), 293. On Frost's participation in popular culture, see Wilcox, *His "Incalculable" Influence,* 7.

13. Stanley Burnshaw, *Robert Frost Himself* (New York: George Braziller, 1986), 178; obituary cited in Jeffrey Meyers, *Robert Frost: A Biography* (Boston: Houghton Mifflin, 1996), 331.

14. Howard Willard Cox, *Our Poets of Today* (New York: Moffat, Yard and Co., 1918), 31.

15. Mark Van Doren, "The Permanence of Robert Frost," in *The Recognition of Robert Frost,* ed. Richard Thornton (New York: Henry Holt and Co., 1937), 5.

16. Lawrence Levine, *Highbrow/Lowbrow: The Emergence of Cultural Hierarchy in America* (Cambridge: Harvard University Press, 1988).

17. Jay Parini, "Robert Frost and the Poetry of Survival," 266.

18. Richard Poirier, "Frost, Winnicott, Burke," in *Transitional Objects and Potential Spaces: Literary Uses of D. W. Winnicott,* ed. Peter L. Rudnytsky (New York: Columbia University Press, 1993), 228. Nathaniel Hawthorne, *The Scarlet Letter,* ed. William Charvat et al., vol. 1 of *The Centenary Edition of the Works of Nathaniel Hawthorne* (Columbus: Ohio State University Press, 1962), 4.

Although we can plainly regard Frost's "duplicity" or "deceptiveness" as evidence of a postmodern sense of self, I am choosing to emphasize a historically embedded notion of a more "unified" self, in part because of Frost's increasingly single-minded representation of himself as "masculine."

19. We should observe the degree to which even the term *sex* is currently contested; see Judith Butler, *Bodies That Matter: On the Discursive Limits of "Sex"* (New York: Routledge, 1993). In spite of this developing theoretical perspective, I use the terms *sex* and *gender* as shorthand to refer roughly to *biology* and *culture.* Also, I should note here that, since race, class, and other identities traverse gender, this study will attempt to be alert to these crossings where they occur; nevertheless, it will focus on gender.

20. Alan Golding highlights two (often competing) views of canon formation and argues for a synthesis of the two in discussing twentieth-century American poetry: "the view that writers make canons (the aesthetic model) and the view that critics, teachers, and the academy do so (the institutional model)." Although the aesthetic model as Golding describes it accounts for the role of poets in creating canons, and in particular in canonizing other poets, it does not necessarily indicate their ability to shape their own reception. Golding provides an exemplary account of the difficulties inherent in each model of canon formation. As will be apparent from the discussion of Frost in the chapters that follow, I take a synthetic—or, perhaps more accurately, interactive—approach to canon formation, in which poet, critics, "ordinary" readers, and institutions all figure (Alan Golding, *From Outlaw to Classic: Canons in American Poetry* [Madison: University of Wisconsin Press, 1995], xv). On canon formation, see also G. Robert Stange, "1887 and the Making of the Victorian Canon," *Victorian Poetry* 25 (1987): 151–68; Robert von Hallberg, intro., in *Canons* (Chicago: University of Chicago Press, 1984), 1–4; Helen Vendler, *The Music of What Happens: Poems, Poets, Critics* (Cambridge: Harvard University Press, 1988); Hugh Kenner, "The Making of the Modernist Canon," in von Hallberg, *Canons,* 363–75; Harold Bloom, *Poetry and Repression: Revisionism from Blake to Stevens* (New Haven: Yale University Press, 1976); Bloom, "Criticism, Canon-Formation, and Prophecy: The Sorrows of Facticity," *Raritan* 3.3 (1984): 1–20.

In relation to Frost's construction of the reader, see Robert Frost, *SL* 299–300, 557; Robert Frost, *Robert Frost: A Living Voice,* ed. Reginald L. Cook (Amherst: University of Massachusetts Press, 1974), 77. In observing Frost's construction of the (negative) critic as masculine, we need to point out that his beloved and respected friend Edward Thomas managed to escape from this category; in part, I would suggest, this is due to the relative openness of Frost himself to intimacy and the "feminine" supportiveness of Thomas, as I discuss in chapter 4.

21. Felski, *Gender of Modernity,* 21. Michael Kimmel speaks of "masculini-

ties," not masculinity. Kimmel, *Manhood in America: A Cultural History* (New York: Free Press, 1996), 5–6.

22. For example, Oster takes this ahistorical approach to the poems; see *Toward Robert Frost*, xiv–xv.

23. It is possible to argue, for example, that Frost was virtually unaware of the gender dynamics of his self-transformation and to offer as support for this view three observations: (1) early in his career Frost did not change his work to accord with the ideas of an influential Ezra Pound, instead choosing to pursue his own path; (2) Frost seemed shaken by Trilling's famous birthday remarks about his participation in a "dark" modernist elite; and (3) Frost continued throughout his career, even at the end as his poems had changed radically, to read his poems publicly with deep emotion. To these observations we might counter that first, in the early years of his career, Frost was not subject to the weight of an already formulated modernist critical tradition; second, that he was performing a role; and, third, that he realized the power and popularity of his earlier poems and continued to read them as he thought audiences would want to hear them. I am grateful to Lisa Seale for these observations in a letter of September 1997. Given complexities such as these, my account will attempt to be suggestive rather than prescriptive about Frost's level of consciousness.

24. Roy Harvey Pearce, *The Continuity of American Poetry* (Princeton: Princeton University Press, 1961), 4, 5, 140, 166. I focus on Pearce here as an exemplary case that indicates how even the most thorough and thoughtful criticism of American poetry is gendered. For example, what he would do with Bradstreet's maternal notion of creativity he does not say; for Pearce, as for many of his critical descendants, a defining feature of the American poet is his (and it is his) Emersonian self-centeredness. The privilege of the unitary self in conceptions of poetic identity emerges perhaps most vividly in the trope of apostrophe, which Jonathan Culler has identified as the characteristic trope of lyric. See Culler, "Apostrophe," *The Pursuit of Signs: Semiotics, Literature, Deconstruction* (Ithaca: Cornell University Press, 1981), 137. See also T. S. Eliot, *The Three Voices of Poetry* (New York: Cambridge University Press, 1954); Sharon Cameron, *Lyric Time: Dickinson and the Limits of Genre* (Baltimore: Johns Hopkins University Press, 1979).

From a feminist psychological perspective, the Romantic "I," self-assertive and self-directed, that engages in and formulates a poetics of presence is gendered masculine; see Nancy Chodorow, *The Reproduction of Mothering* (Berkeley: University of California Press, 1978), 169. Chodorow chooses as her context the postindustrial, capitalist economic structure and the bourgeois nuclear family. Frost's situation in relation to this theory is complex. That he was raised by his mother, both before and after his father's premature death, suggests the possibility that it was even more urgent for him to define himself in contradistinction to her. On the other hand, his closeness with her may have enabled his great sympathy for women. Finally, Frost was white but not securely middle-class. Overall, however, Chodorow's account seems to accord with his self-presentation as both individuated and masculine. See also Jean Baker Miller, *Toward a New Psychology of Women* (Boston: Beacon Press, 1976); Carol Gilligan, *In a Different Voice* (Cambridge: Harvard University Press, 1982).

25. Pearce's account of the relationship between nineteenth-century readers and writers echoes the lament of Nathaniel Hawthorne in "The Custom House," as well as the latter's famous complaint about the "damned mob of scribbling women." Even discussions of Dickinson's mythical aversion to publication—an attitude recently controverted by Dickinson scholars—often omit the fact that her poems were from the beginning, and still are, enormously popular with "ordinary" readers.

26. Sandra M. Gilbert and Susan Gubar, *The Madwoman in the Attic: The Woman Writer and the Nineteenth-Century Literary Imagination* (New Haven: Yale University Press, 1979), 548; see 539–650; 16–19, 48, 64ff., 72–73. Margaret Homans seems to accept this concept of the self in *Women Writers and Poetic Identity: Dorothy Wordsworth, Emily Brontë, and Emily Dickinson* (Princeton: Princeton University Press, 1980), 32.

27. Janet Todd, *Feminist Literary History: A Defense* (Cambridge: Polity Press, 1988). Similarly, Mark Jeffreys points out that for most contemporary critics the idea of "lyric" means late-Romantic lyric, which is connected with "the imperial assertion of self, the programmatic exclusion of otherness or difference, and the logocentric quest for presence" ("Ideologies of Lyric: A Problem of Genre in Contemporary Anglophone Poetics," *PMLA* 110 [1995]: 196–205). This quest for presence has emerged in what Timothy Morris has called "the poetics of presence," which emphasizes the intensity and individuality of the poet's voice and which values "originality, organicism, and monologism" (*Becoming Canonical in American Poetry* [Urbana: University of Illinois Press, 1995], 1, 2). From a slightly different angle Lynn Keller and Cristanne Miller note that one possible reason for the recent theoretical turn to narrative and away from poetry is the perception that (a monologically defined) lyric incorporates a "naive . . . notion of a unified speaking subject" ("Feminist Measures," 3).

28. Marjorie Perloff, *The Dance of the Intellect: Studies in the Poetry of the Pound Tradition* (Cambridge: Cambridge University Press, 1985), 181.

29. The term *not poetry* comes from Sandra Gilbert's study of Dickinson and Whitman ("The American Sexual Politics of Walt Whitman and Emily Dickinson," in *Reconstructing American Literary History,* ed. Sacvan Bercovitch [Cambridge: Harvard University Press, 1986], 128; see also Annie Finch, "The Sentimental Poetess in the World: Metaphor and Subjectivity in Lydia Sigourney's Nature Poetry," *Legacy* 5.2 [1988]: 4, 3–15). As I shall explore in chapter 1, this diffused, absent, or composite subjectivity appears quite often in the culturally feminine poems that have been labeled "sentimental."

30. Homans, *Women Writers,* 4.

31. Nancy Chodorow, *Reproduction,* 169.

32. Adrienne Rich, "Three Conversations," in *Adrienne Rich's Poetry,* ed. Barbara Charlesworth Gelpi and Albert Gelpi (New York: Norton, 1975), 114–15.

33. Paula Gunn Allen, *Spider Woman's Granddaughters: Traditional Tales and Contemporary Writings by Native American Women,* ed. P. G. Allen (Boston: Beacon Press, 1989), 5.

34. Allen, *Spider Woman's Granddaughters,* 2; see also Paula Gunn Allen, *The*

*Sacred Hoop: Recovering the Feminine in American Indian Traditions* (Boston: Beacon Press, 1986), 1–7.

35. Allen's work also suggests to me that the genre mixing that many consider partially definitive of postmodernism may be less an effect of style or historical moment than of contemporary critics' increased willingness to regard that blending as affirmative—or even to perceive it in the first place.

36. Another risk, obviously, is ethnocentrism, even though there may be an analogical relationship between "feminine" and "Indian" voices.

37. As Cary Nelson so astutely observes, "totalizing, ahistorical myths of gender—whether men figure positively or negatively, whether women are valorized or degraded—are always self-undermining and reversible. Perhaps we are better off with no master narratives of the fate of gender that claim to transcend history. It is not only poets but also literary critics who have been enamored of such overarching stories about the essential nature of men and women" ("Fate of Gender in Modern Poetry," 356).

38. For a discussion of the gendering of reader-speaker relations, see Karen Oakes, " 'I stop somewhere waiting for you': Whitman's Femininity and the Reader of *Leaves of Grass*," in *Out of Bounds: Male Writers and Gender(ed) Criticism,* ed. Laura Claridge and Elizabeth Langland (Amherst: University of Massachusetts Press, 1990), 169–85; Oakes, "Welcome and Beware: The Reader and Emily Dickinson's Figurative Language," *ESQ: A Journal of the American Renaissance* 34 (1988): 181–206. The so-called masculine tradition represented by the work in one of Frost's avowedly favorite volumes, Palgrave's *Golden Treasury,* can itself be envisioned as "feminine"; I take up this discussion more fully in the next chapter.

39. Golding, *From Outlaw to Classic,* 92.

40. Ann Douglas [Wood], "The Literature of Impoverishment: The Woman Local Colorists in America, 1865–1914," *Women's Studies* 1.1 (1972): 3–45; Judith Fetterley, *Provisions: A Reader from Nineteenth-Century American Literature* (Bloomington: Indiana University Press, 1985), 23; Caroline Gephard, "The Spinster in the House of American Criticism," *Tulsa Studies in Women's Literature* 10.1 (1991): 79–91.

41. Malcolm Cowley, "Frost: A Dissenting Opinion," in *Critical Essays on Robert Frost,* ed. Philip L. Gerber (Boston: G. K. Hall, 1982), 103 (reprinted from *New Republic,* September 11, 1944, 312–13, and September 18, 1944, 345–47). Waggoner makes explicit his sympathy with this view in the pages that follow; see Waggoner, *American Poets,* 294; Pearce, *Continuity,* 271, 274, 283. Many of Frost's critics, from Carl Van Doren to the present, emphasize the strong selfhood highlighted by Pearce, alternatively conceptualized as "individualism." See, for example, Van Doren, "Soil of the Puritans," in Gerber, *Critical Essays,* 70; Harriet Monroe, *Poets and Their Art* (New York: Macmillan, 1926), 57; Burnshaw, *Robert Frost Himself,* 258.

42. Pearce, *Continuity,* 197. To be fair, Pearce argues at the end of his discussion of popular forms that "we must reach back to popular art and reconstruct its ambience so as to take the art as seriously as it deserves, only then to appreciate and judge it" (252). According to Timothy Morris, the problem with Sigourney for today's readers is her apparent lack of (masculine) individuation, and he suggests,

"The idea of degrees of individuation implies that at some level there is a common mass of poetic diction that most rank-and-file poets do not rise above; often, that common mass . . . is a rhetorical assumption rather than a demonstrable fact" (*Becoming Canonical*, 37–38).

43. As one measure of the contradictions (and complexities) inherent in New Criticism, Golding points to Frost's continuous and generous inclusion in the influential textbook *Understanding Poetry*, noting, "It is hard to assess the extent to which *Understanding Poetry* created or simply reflected Frost's influence; certainly few New Critics, with the exception of Warren, wrote major favorable essays on Frost" (*From Outlaw to Classic*, 106).

44. Kearns argues that Frost tried to create poems "able to appeal simultaneously to that maternal impulse to suspend (punitive) critical action and to the paternal impulse toward a decisive mediation that at once establishes both the truth and the merit of the poetic enterprise" (*Robert Frost and a Poetics of Appetite*, 47).

45. Morris, *Becoming Canonical*, 5, xi.

46. Joanna Russ, *How to Suppress Women's Writing* (Austin: University of Texas Press, 1983), 52–53; Henry James, "Mr. and Mrs. James T. Fields," reprinted in *Henry James: Literary Criticism—Essays on Literature, American Writers, English Writers* (New York: Library of America, 1984), 174; Amy Lowell, *Tendencies in Modern American Poetry* (New York: Macmillan, 1917), 81. Like James and many others, Warner Berthoff would highlight Jewett's "miniature competence" in her *Atlantic* stories, though he admires her achievement in *The Country of the Pointed Firs*. See Warner Berthoff, *The Ferment of Realism: American Literature, 1884–1914* (New York: Free Press, 1965), 96.

47. My description of Frost's movement toward a more masculine self-representation is intended to be just that, without judgmental tones suggesting that his more feminine poems are "better"; nevertheless, the more feminine poems are often more powerful and effective for me, and they engender a fuller emotional (as well as intellectual) experience than some, though by no means all, of the later lyrics.

48. Robert Frost, Bread Loaf School, 10 May 1950; cited in John Evangelist Walsh, *Into My Own: The English Years of Robert Frost, 1912–1915* (New York: Grove Weidenfeld, 1988), 13.

49. Keller and Miller, "Feminist Measures," 9. Similarly, Tey Diana Rebolledo observes of Chicano/a writers: "We have internalized the dominant ideology so that only by talking theory (construed as a superior form of logic) can our literature and our cultural practices be intellectually viable"; Gloria Anzaldúa describes the response of a woman of color graduate student to mainstream academic language practice: "she felt oppressed and violated by the rhetoric of dominant ideology, a rhetoric disguised as good 'scholarship' by teachers who are unaware of its race, class and gender 'blank spots.' It is a rhetoric that presents its conjectures as universal truths while concealing its patriarchal privilege and posture." In "The Race for Theory" Barbara Christian notes that "theory has become a commodity which helps determine whether we are hired or promoted in academic institutions"; because of this movement toward the hegemony of theory, she argues, "some of our most daring and potentially radical critics (and by *our* I mean

black, women, third world) have been influenced, even co-opted, into speaking a language and defining their discussion in terms alien to and opposed to our needs and orientation" (Rebolledo, "The Politics of Poetics: Or, What Am I, a Critic, Doing in This Text Anyhow?" in Gloria Anzaldúa, *Making Face, Making Soul / Haciendo Caras* (San Francisco: Aunt Lute, 1990), 348; and "Haciendo caras, una entrada" (xxiii); Barbara Christian, "The Race for Theory," 335–36, both in Anzaldúa, *Making Face*. In an observation with which Frost would probably have had considerable sympathy, Christian urges a reconnection between language and experience; she affirms, "what I write and how I write is done in order to save my own life. . . . [literature] is an affirmation that sensuality is intelligence, that sensual language is language that makes sense" (343).

As I will investigate in relation to the responses by contemporary critics to Frost himself, the immasculated ("rational," "objective") perspective that continues to shape his reception would also interpret the anecdote that opened this chapter as (merely) a folksy attempt to establish an emotional link with the reader, rather than as (also) an affirmation of another kind of interpretive authority. The term *immasculation* is Judith Fetterley's. As Fetterley notes of American women: "As readers and teachers and scholars, women are taught to think as men, to identify with a male point of view, and to accept as normal and legitimate a male system of values, one of whose central principles is misogyny" (*The Resisting Reader: A Feminist Approach to American Fiction* [Bloomington: Indiana University Press, 1978], xx; see also Elaine Showalter, "Women and the Literary Curriculum," *College English* 32 [1971]: 855; Patrocinio P. Schweickart, "Reading Ourselves: Toward a Feminist Theory of Reading," in *Gender and Reading: Essays on Readers, Texts, and Contexts*, ed. Elizabeth A. Flynn and Patrocinio P. Schweickart [Baltimore: Johns Hopkins University Press, 1986], 44–45).

50. Olivia Frey, "Beyond Literary Darwinism: Women's Voices and Critical Discourse," in *The Intimate Critique, Autobiographical Literary Criticism*, ed. Diane P. Freedman, Olivia Frey, and Frances Murphy Zauhar (Durham: Duke University Press, 1993), 43–44.

51. Frey, "Beyond Literary Darwinism," 48. The debate that we might call the "men in feminism" issue—which asks such questions as "can men be feminists? feminist critics?"—is obviously one that Frey's work conjures. For some voices in the discussion, see Laura Claridge and Elizabeth Langland, eds., *Out of Bounds: Male Writers and Gender(ed) Criticism* (Amherst: University of Massachusetts Press, 1990); Alice Jardine, *Men in Feminism* (New York: Methuen, 1987); David Porter, ed., *Between Men and Feminism* (New York: Routledge, 1992). As my account suggests, I believe a nonessentialist view would answer yes. See such exemplary texts as David Leverenz, *Manhood and the American Renaissance* (Ithaca: Cornell University Press, 1989); and Leland S. Person, *Aesthetic Headaches: Women and a Masculine Poetics in Poe, Melville, and Hawthorne* (Athens: University of Georgia Press, 1988).

52. Jane Tompkins, "Me and My Shadow," in Freedman et al., *Intimate Critique*, 26.

53. Another factor in selecting the use of a personal voice, which both Tompkins and Frey acknowledge, is the very concrete and pressing one of position

in the academy; both of these writers can afford to take the positions they have because of their relative power and status.

54. Frost came of age and began his career as a poet at a time of extreme upheaval in the United States. Among the many social and political events that provided the context for this period of his life were the massacre of Native Americans at Wounded Knee, the Spanish American War, the massive immigration movement, the women's suffrage movement, unprecedented technological improvements, the opening of Oklahoma for settlement, numerous labor strikes, Teddy Roosevelt's presidency, the San Francisco earthquake and fire, the opening of the Panama Canal, and the entrance of large numbers of women into the labor force.

55. As I attempt to demonstrate elsewhere, analytical tools and methods are not inherently coded "strong" or "weak," appropriative or innocent; instead, we should look to the uses to which such tools and methods are put. See Karen Oakes, "Reading Trickster; or, Theoretical Reservations and a Seneca Tale," in *Tricksterism in Turn-of-the-Century American Literature: A Multicultural Perspective,* ed. Elizabeth Ammons and A. White-Parks (Hanover: University Press of New England, 1994), 137–57.

56. Patricia Meyer Spacks, *Gossip* (New York: Knopf, 1985), 5, 31–32, 38–42, 130–31, 150–53.

57. Sheldon W. Liebman, "Frost on Criticism," 399, 400; Peter J. Stanlis, "Acceptable in Heaven's Sight: Robert Frost at Bread Loaf 1939–1941," in *Frost: Centennial Essays III,* ed. Jac Tharpe (Jackson: University Press of Mississippi, 1978), 197–98.

58. Amy Lowell, *Tendencies in Modern Poetry* (New York: Macmillan, 1917), 117–18; Jessie Rittenhouse, "Portraits of Women," in Thornton, *Recognition of Robert Frost,* 247, 248.

59. Richard Poirier, *Robert Frost: The Work of Knowing* (Oxford: Oxford University Press, 1977), 113, 43; Patricia Wallace, "The 'Estranged Point of View': The Thematics of Imagination in Frost's Poetry," in *Frost: Centennial Essays II,* ed. Jac Tharpe (Jackson: University Press of Mississippi, 1976), 179; Frank Lentricchia, *Robert Frost: Modern Poetics and the Landscapes of Self* (Durham: Duke University Press, 1975), 64, 62ff.; Robert H. Swennes, "Man and Wife: The Dialogue of Contraries in Robert Frost's Poetry," *American Literature* 42 (1970): 372; Robert Faggen, *Robert Frost and the Challenge of Darwin* (Ann Arbor: University of Michigan Press, 1997), 188; William H. Pritchard, *Frost: A Literary Life Reconsidered* (New York: Oxford University Press, 1984), 99, 93. See also Mordecai Marcus, "The Whole Pattern of Robert Frost's 'Two Witches': Contrasting Psycho-Sexual Modes," *Literature and Psychology* 26 (1976): 69–78.

60. Katherine Kearns, "'The Place Is the Asylum': Women and Nature in Robert Frost's Poetry," *American Literature* 59 (1987): 191; Kearns, *Robert Frost and a Poetics of Appetite,* 23, 28, 29. In both of these works Kearns apparently equates *feminine* with *female.* Community represents another threat to identity: "Community, with its necessary imposition of public values, threatens to subvert personal autonomy" (26). On Frost's "insubordination," see Frank Lentricchia, *Modernist Quartet* (Cambridge: Cambridge University Press, 1995), 85–86.

61. Kearns, *Robert Frost and a Poetics of Appetite,* 43, 69. I believe that Kearns

overstates her case about the poet's hostility because of her synchronistic view of his work.

62. Oster, *Toward Robert Frost,* 2, 3.

63. Ibid., 78. Robert Langbaum argues that participation, and then judgment, is characteristic of the dramatic monologue (*The Poetry of Experience* [New York: Random House, 1957], 94, 104ff., 204ff.). On Frost's subjectivity, see also Lentricchia, *Robert Frost,* 61 (in which Lentricchia responds directly to Pearce); and Mark Richardson, *The Ordeal of Robert Frost: The Poet and His Poetics* (Urbana: University of Illinois Press, 1997), 167, 175, 220, 225.

64. Randall Jarrell, *Poetry and the Age* (New York: Ecco, 1980), 32, 33.

65. Cited by Stanley Burnshaw, *Robert Frost Himself,* 172. This concept of the reader-speaker relation from 1961 is ironic in view of the detachment that I will argue overwhelmingly characterizes Frost's work in the latter part of his career.

66. Walt Whitman, "A Backward Glance O'er Travel'd Roads," in *Leaves of Grass,* ed. Sculley Bradley and Harold W. Blodgett (New York: Norton, 1973), 570; Liebman, "Frost on Criticism," 407. Judith Oster observes: "he leaves openings for us to enter, where we also enter *into* the creative process—the process of making meaning" (*Toward Robert Frost,* x).

67. Feminist criticism has damaged Frost's reputation as much or more by its sins of omission than by those of commission; for example, where Gilbert and Gubar roundly chastise Whitman for his egocentric and self-aggrandizing project, they seem to consider Frost as too obviously in the other camp for sustained study (*Madwoman,* 556–57; *The War of the Words* [New Haven: Yale University Press, 1988], vol. 1 of *No Man's Land: The Place of the Woman Writer in the Twentieth Century,* 3 vols. [1988–94]).

68. On the history and development of the self-made man in America, see Kimmel, *Manhood in America,* 13–42.

**Chapter 1**

1. As the following account indicates, there is ostensibly a difference between *sentimentality,* the *sentimental,* and *sentimentalism.* While the first two terms relate more frequently to popular culture and everyday life, the third commonly signifies an aesthetic genre. Yet some confusing overlap remains, because readers might refer to the scene of little Eva's death as "sentimental," or even cite its appeal to "sentimentality." Even within the so-called genre of sentimentalism, considerable variability exists, as much critical debate (and this chapter) suggests. For an excellent description of this debate and a substantial accounting of the debaters, see Joanne Dobson, "The American Renaissance Reenvisioned," in *The (Other) American Traditions: Nineteenth-Century Women Writers,* ed. Joyce Warren (New Brunswick: Rutgers University Press, 1993), 168–72, 177–78 n. 11. Dobson also argues that "it is more useful to see [sentimentalism] as a specific type of imaginative energy rather than as a literary form or as a body of conventions" (172). In a similar vein I have suggested that we might properly think of sentimentalism as a style rather than a genre; see intro., *Nineteenth-Century American Women Writers: An Anthology* (Cambridge, MA, and Oxford, UK: Blackwell Publishers, 1997),

xliii–xlv. It is not my aim to resolve this terminological tangle, only to suggest some of its strands in relation to Frost.

2. As I argue elsewhere, Twain not only critiques the nineteenth-century discourse of sentimentality, he also participates in it; see Karen L. Kilcup, "'Quite Unclassifiable': Crossing Genres, Crossing Genders in Twain and Greene," in *New Directions in American Humor Studies*, ed. David E. E. Sloane (Birmingham: University of Alabama Press, 1998). See also Gregg Camfield, *Sentimental Twain: Samuel Clemens in the Maze of Moral Philosophy* (Philadelphia: University of Pennsylvania Press, 1994); and Laura Skandera-Trombley, *Mark Twain in the Company of Women* (Philadelphia: University of Pennsylvania Press, 1994).

3. Mark Richardson emphasizes Frost's belief that "the artist should work to *establish* fellowship with the larger patterns of culture rather than work (Emerson-like) to escape the consequences of that fellowship." Yet this desire was counterbalanced, Richardson suggests, by Frost's feeling of himself as culturally oppositional, a position exacerbated by the feminization of the poetic enterprise (*The Ordeal of Robert Frost: The Poet and His Poetics* [Urbana: University of Illinois Press, 1997], 4, 11).

4. On critical uneasiness with emotions more generally, see Susan K. Harris, *Nineteenth-Century American Women's Novels: Interpretive Strategies* (New York: Cambridge University Press, 1990), 2–8.

5. Jane Tompkins, *Sensational Designs: The Cultural Work of American Fiction, 1790–1860* (New York: Oxford University Press, 1985), 123; see 17, 32. Tompkins is of course writing about novels, but the responses that she cites apply equally to poetry (160).

6. Fred Kaplan, *Sacred Tears, Sentimentality in Victorian Literature* (Princeton: Princeton University Press, 1987), 17.

7. Writers such as Ann Douglas and Karen Halttunen have emphasized the investment of the sentimental in consumerism and argued that it is imbued with class affiliations, for it marks off a space in which middle-class culture defines itself. More positively, Elaine Sargent Apthorp highlights the affiliation between sentimental fiction and movements of social reform. See Ann Douglas, *The Feminization of American Culture* (New York: Discus-Avon, 1977); Karen Halttunen, *Confidence Men and Painted Women, A Study of Middle-Class Culture in American, 1830–1870* (New Haven: Yale University Press, 1982), xiv, xvi; Elaine Sargent Apthorp, "Sentiment, Naturalism, and the Female Regionalist," *Legacy: A Journal of Nineteenth-Century American Women Writers* 7.1 (1990): 3–21. These commentators represent only a small number of the voices engaged in this energetic discussion. See, for example, Nina Baym, *Woman's Fiction: A Guide to Novels by and about Women in America, 1820–1870* (Ithaca: Cornell University Press, 1978); Mary Kelley, *Private Woman, Public Stage: Literary Domesticity in Nineteenth-Century America* (New York: Oxford University Press, 1984); Nancy Cott, *The Bonds of Womanhood: "Woman's Sphere" in New England, 1780–1835* (New Haven: Yale University Press, 1977); Barbara Epstein, *The Politics of Domesticity: Women, Evangelism, and Temperance in Nineteenth-Century America* (Wesleyan University Press, 1981); Herbert Ross Brown, *The Sentimental Novel in America, 1789–1860* (Durham: Duke University Press, 1940); Mary Kelley, "The Sentimentalists: Promise and Betrayal in the Home," *Signs* 4.3

(1979): 434–46. See also Richard Brodhead, "Sparing the Rod: Discipline and Fiction in Antebellum America," *Representations* 21 (1988): 67–96; Philip Fisher, *Hard Facts: Setting and Form in the American Novel* (New York: Oxford University Press, 1992); Rosemarie Garland Thomson, "Crippled Girls and Lame Old Women: Sentimental Spectacles of Sympathy in Nineteenth-Century American Women's Writing," in *Nineteenth-Century American Women Writers: A Critical Reader,* ed. Karen L. Kilcup (Malden, MA, and Oxford, UK: Blackwell Publishers, 1998), 128–45.

8. Joanne Dobson, "American Renaissance Reenvisioned" 168, 171, 175.

9. Some of the most recent discussions of sentimentalism have been even more damning than Douglas's important early study. Laura Wexler suggests that the conflict between Douglas (as a critic of sentimentalism) and Tompkins (as a supporter) is limited to tidy, middle-class debate: "It is in both cases as if the issue of the moral stimulation of sentimentalism raises questions for a literary consciousness alone, more or less observant, more or less well educated, more or less discriminating." Raising the troubling issue of the location of marginalized groups within sentimental fictions and their position as readers of those fictions, Wexler argues that "it may be useful to speak . . . of sentimental fiction not only as a literary genre, but as a generic cultural category on its own—that is, as *the* sentimental fiction. It would designate the alliance of the double-edged, double-jeopardy nature of sentimental perception with the social control of marginal domestic populations" ("Tender Violence: Literary Eavesdropping, Domestic Fiction, and Educational Reform" in *The Culture of Sentiment: Race, Gender, and Sentimentality in Nineteenth-Century America,* ed. Shirley Samuels [New York: Oxford University Press, 1992], 15, 18).

10. Even feminist readers like Joanne Dobson, Cheryl Walker, and Paula Bennett, who seek to recuperate the body of sentimental poetry for contemporary study and upon whose work I draw in the discussion of Frost that follows, sometimes reiterate the marginalization of emotion and in some cases the valorization of both individualism and modernist coolness. For example, Dobson appears to value the potential for "uniqueness or individuality" in sentimental poetry; the interpretive assumptions that underlie this affirmation suggest that for poetry to be good it must be unique rather than representative, or express an individual voice rather than a communal one. Similarly, though Walker's task is to renovate our perceptions of nineteenth-century women's poetry, she has until recently been somewhat apologetic, seeking to focus our attention on atypical responses to representative topics; she ambivalently reassigns to modernism the privilege that her account attempts in part to dismantle. In their studies of the prototypical sentimentalist, Nina Baym explores Sigourney's historical poetry, while Annie Finch focuses on her nature poetry. In a related interpretive gesture Paula Bennett outlines superbly the transition of women's nature poetry from sentimental to modernist, implicitly providing an ancestry for Frost as well. Citing a protomodernist poem from the *Atlantic,* Bennett observes, "'Bloodroot' is an unequivocal foretaste of things to come: a movement in this [early women's] poetry toward greater concrete detail, more ambiguous and flexible stylistic expression, and toward a much wider—and more disturbing—range of themes and voices than high sentimentalism, with its commitment to religiously-based domestic and cultural values, allowed." Contemporary critics' continued elevation of such modernist norms as "wider," "more disturbing,"

and "more ambiguous and flexible" render it difficult for us not only to appreciate but even to hear strains of a complex sentimental poetic tradition as a tone of modernist verse. This difficulty is compounded by critics' continued engendering of sentimental poetry as essentially feminine and the quarantine to which we subject our emotional responses to poetry. For the Bennett quotation, see "Late Nineteenth-Century American Women's Nature Poetry and the Evolution of the Imagist Poem," *Legacy* 9.2 (1992): 92. On the subjectivity and subjects of the sentimental poet, see Annie Finch; on her subjectivity, see Paula Bennett and Joanne Dobson; on her connection with the reader, see Joanne Dobson; on her content and form, see Cheryl Walker. (See also Finch, "The Sentimental Poetess in the World: Metaphor and Subjectivity in Lydia Sigourney's Nature Poetry," *Legacy* 5.2 [1988]: 5; Paula Bennett, "Late Nineteenth-Century American Women's Nature Poetry," 91; Joanne Dobson, "Reclaiming Sentimental Literature," *American Literature* 69 [1997]: 263–88; Cheryl Walker, intro., *American Women Poets of the Nineteenth Century, An Anthology* [New Brunswick: Rutgers University Press, 1992], xxiv–xxvi.) Centering on prose fiction, Dobson mentions the investment of male writers in the sentimental ("American Renaissance Reenvisioned," 172, 178 n. 15), as does Douglas (*Feminization of American Culture,* 284–89).

11. I am using these terms as a form of distinction between poets like Lydia Sigourney, Helen Hunt Jackson, and Longfellow, on the one hand, and the elite, academic tradition represented by Whitman and Dickinson, on the other.

12. Helen Gray Cone, "Woman in American Literature," *Century Magazine* 40.6 (1890): 922.

13. Amy Lowell, "Two Generations in American Poetry," in *Critical Essays on American Modernism,* ed. Michael J. Hoffman and Patrick D. Murphy (New York: G. K. Hall, 1992), 45.

14. Criticism of sentimentalism in the United States began well before Cone, as the poems of Frances Osgood, Sarah Piatt, Emily Dickinson, and others make apparent.

15. Louise Bogan, letter to John Hall Wheelock, 1 July 1935, *What the Woman Lived: Selected Letters of Louise Bogan, 1920–1970,* ed. Ruth Limmer (New York: Harcourt Brace Jovanovich, 1973), 86; Roy Harvey Pearce, *The Continuity of American Poetry* (Princeton: Princeton University Press, 1961), 269; Rita Felski, *The Gender of Modernity* (Cambridge: Harvard University Press, 1995), 28.

16. Cornelius Weygandt, "New Hampshire," in *The Recognition of Robert Frost,* ed. Richard Thornton (New York: Henry Holt and Co., 1937), 70; George Monteiro, *Robert Frost and the New England Renaissance* (Lexington: University of Kentucky Press, 1988), 97; see 20–21, 40–43; John Evangelist Walsh, *Into My Own: The English Years of Robert Frost, 1912–1915* (New York: Grove Weidenfeld, 1988), 70–71; Jay Parini, *The Columbia History of American Poetry* (New York: Columbia University Press, 1993), 266; Randall Jarrell, "To the Laodiceans," *Poetry and the Age* (New York: Ecco Press, 1980), 37. These accounts indicate current as well as historical attitudes toward the relationship between men and sentimentalism. See Samuel Coale, "The Emblematic Encounter of Robert Frost," *Frost: Centennial Essays* (Jackson: University Press of Mississippi, 1974), 93; Robert Fleissner, *Frost's Road Taken* (New York: Peter Lang, 1997), 81–97, 115–19. A project that needs

urgent attention is the role of male sentimental poets (Longfellow and company) in engendering modernist poetry.

17. Bennett separates the "high sentimentalism" of earlier (before the late 1850s) women poets like Lydia Sigourney, Elizabeth Oakes Smith, and Frances Sargent Osgood from the work of later writers: "High sentimentalism (c. 1825–50) is an epistemologically based discourse. It claimed that the intimations of the heart could serve as reliable guides to moral and spiritual truths. Low sentimentalism is the kind of sentimentalism still with us today. It is loose, subjective, personal, and makes no claims to knowledge, only to feeling." See Paula Bennett, " 'The Descent of the Angel': Interrogating Domestic Ideology in American Women's Poetry, 1858–1890," *American Literary History* 7.4 (1995): 606 n. 2; 592, 594. Bennett's argument is based on her groundbreaking recovery work, part of which is collected in *Nineteenth-Century American Women Poets: An Anthology* (Cambridge, MA, and Oxford, UK: Blackwell Publishers, 1998). This important account poses some potential difficulties. For one thing, the distinction between "high" and "low" sentimentalism is not always easy for contemporary readers to assess. Where, and how, can we draw the line? Second, earlier poets like Osgood were themselves often critical of domestic ideology, as the poems touched upon later will reveal; there could be significant overlap, not only between high and low sentimentalism but also between what I call "transparent" and "ironic" sentimentalism (the latter, though she does not explicitly name it such, the subject of Bennett's article). Finally, the language of high and low itself may be problematic to some, inasmuch as it encodes a hierarchy that often separates "elite" from "popular," "highbrow" from "lowbrow," art, and it assumes that "knowledge" and "feeling" are incommensurate. On Osgood's perspective, see Joanne Dobson, "Sex, Wit, and Sentiment: Frances Osgood and the Poetry of Love," *American Literature* 65.4 (1993): 631–50.

18. As Philip Fisher notes in another context, many American writers, including Frost, "preserved the core of sentimental technique even in the process of adapting it to later conditions or obscuring it beneath a veneer of toughness, elegance, or self-irony" (*Hard Facts,* 93–94).

19. A number of writers have discussed the continuity between the romantic and the modern. See Robert Langbaum, *The Poetry of Experience: The Dramatic Monologue in Modern Literary Tradition* (New York: Random House, 1957), 9–37; Marjorie Perloff, *The Dance of the Intellect: Studies in the Poetry of the Pound Tradition* (Cambridge: Cambridge University Press, 1985), 1–32. Except indirectly, I will not enter the debate on Frost as modernist. For one extended discussion of the subject, see Robert Kern, "Frost and Modernism," *American Literature* 60.1 (1988): 1–16.

20. Lawrance Thompson, *Robert Frost: The Early Years, 1874–1915* (New York: Holt, Rinehart and Winston, 1966), 92.

21. Harrison H. Harkesheimer, "One Day in June," *Youth's Companion,* 4 June 1891, 326; other references to this issue are: Molly Elliott Seawell, "Through Thick and Thin" (chap. 5), 317–18; Laura J. Rittenhouse, "Mrs. Darrow's Poorhouse," 318–19; Gen. John Gibbon, "Reading Indian 'Sign,' " 321–22; Annie R. Ramsey, "Directions for a Trip to Europe," 322–23; Celia Thaxter, "The Path of Peace," 326; advertisements (inside back cover); "Contagiousness of Diseases" 332. There were a number of different telescope offers made by the serial during 1888 to

1890, with the smaller ones requiring recruitment of one subscription plus a small premium of 85¢, and the larger ones requiring five new subscriptions and a premium of $3.45, postage included. For an example, see 26 October 1899, 543.

22. On the role of the *Youth's Companion* in the Frost household, see Lesley Lee Francis, *The Frost Family's Adventure in Poetry: Sheer Morning Gladness at the Brim* (Columbia: University of Missouri Press, 1994), 27, 124.

23. Walker, *The Nightingale's Burden: Women Poets and American Culture before 1900* (Bloomington: Indiana University Press, 1982), 88–91. Sentimental poems that were published in the same issue of the *New England Magazine* include: "Consummation," by Gertrude Brooke Hamilton, "Colonial Dames," by William Addison Houghton, and "To a Brown Thrush," by Anna Perlsius Chandler (*New England Magazine* 40.3 [May 1909]: 297, 289, 281). Frost's poem appeared on 338. It is interesting to consider the popular context in which "Into Mine Own" appeared: the same issue included a wide variety of materials, including photos of "Beautiful New England," nonfiction prose including "The Woman's Congressional Club," "Great Fights in Early New England History" (a story about King Philip's War), and "Our Birds"; as well as short fiction like the orientalist "Miss Yin Yang, of Shanghai" and the comic children's dialect piece "The Wax Works at Warsaw"; columns on drama, music, art, and literature; and reader-authored opinions like "A 'Plain Farmer's' View of the Forestry Question," signed by "A Plain Old Farmer."

24. "Although *The Companion* is now a family paper, it was established three generations ago for the express purpose of furnishing what did not then exist; namely, reading-matter for the young, that should entertain, educate, and inspire them" (*Youth's Companion,* 7 November 1912, 610).

25. Robert Frost, "Ghost House," *Youth's Companion,* 15 March 1906, 132. There were also a number of items for parents, with anecdotes, current events, essays on such matters as "Railroad Rates," and the like (see 130, 134).

26. Mark Richardson highlights the importance of what we might call the literary atmosphere in poets' coming-of-age. See *Ordeal of Robert Frost,* 120.

27. Robert Frost, "The Prerequisites," in *Selected Prose of Robert Frost,* ed. Hyde Cox and Edward Connery Lathem (New York: Collier Books, 1968), 97.

28. Francis Turner Palgrave, ed., *The Golden Treasury of the Best Songs and Lyrical Poems in the English Language* (London: Macmillan, 1892). On Frost and the male poetic tradition, see, for example, Samuel Coale, "The Emblematic Encounter of Robert Frost," in Tharpe, *Frost: Centennial Essays,* 90; Charles Carmichael, "Robert Frost as a Romantic," in ibid., 147–65; R. F. Fleissner, "Like 'Pythagoras' Comparison of the Universe with Number': A Frost-Tennyson Correlation," in ibid., 207–20; Poirier, *Robert Frost: The Work of Knowing* (New York: Oxford University Press, 1977), 162–65, 220–22; George F. Bagby, *Frost and the Book of Nature* (Knoxville: University of Tennessee Press, 1993).

29. Jeffrey Meyers, *Robert Frost: A Biography* (Boston: Houghton Mifflin, 1996), 71, 73; see also Pritchard, *Frost: A Literary Life Reconsidered* (New York: Oxford University Press, 1984), 42–43; Richardson, *Ordeal of Robert Frost,* 105ff.; Fleissner, *Frost's Road Taken,* 1–77.

30. For an account of Frost's mother reading poetry to him, see Thompson, *Robert Frost: The Early Years,* 90.

31. On Frost's reading, see Meyers, *Robert Frost,* 55–59. See also "To 'Books We Like'" (*CP* 738) and "Books That Have Meant the Most" (*CP* 852).

32. Suzanne Clark, *Sentimental Modernism, Women Writers and the Revolution of the Word* (Bloomington: Indiana University Press, 1991), 1–16. Robert Langbaum makes the distinction between romantic and sentimental poetry (*Poetry of Experience,* 9–37). Langbaum's definition of romanticism remains one of the most useful; he distinguishes between romanticism as a transtemporal impulse exploring the relation between emotion and intellect and Romanticism as a specific literary moment occurring as a result of the Enlightenment (21–22).

33. In addition to Bennett's and Walker's collections of nineteenth-century American women poets, see Janet Gray, ed., *She Wields a Pen: American Women Poets of the Nineteenth Century* (Iowa City: University of Iowa Press, 1997). See also Angela Leighton and Margaret Reynolds, *Victorian Women Poets* (Cambridge, MA, and Oxford, UK: Blackwell Publishers, 1995).

34. For the "Romantic" poems cited, see Palgrave, *Golden Treasury,* 265, 268–69, 291, and 339; for the women poet's selections, see Cheryl Walker, *American Women Poets,* 72, 19, 281.

35. Howells is cited by Shirley Samuels, intro., *Culture of Sentiment,* 5. Ezra Pound, *Letters to Ibbotson, 1935–62,* ed. Vittorio I. Mondolfi and Margaret Hurley (Orono: National Poetry Foundation and the University of Maine, 1979), 24.

36. Rufus Wilmot Griswold, ed., *The Poets and Poetry of America* (Philadelphia: Carey and Hart, 1848), 538.

37. In 1849 Griswold split the bursting anthology into a separate volume for women, *The Female Poets of America,* which itself went through numerous editions and printings between 1849 and 1892. After 1849 "The Poets and Poetry of America" actually meant the *male* poets and poetry of America.

38. See Joanne Dobson, "Reclaiming Sentimental Literature," *American Literature* 69 (1997): 263–88; Walker, intro., *American Women Poets,* xxviii.

39. Frank Lentricchia, "The Resentments of Robert Frost," *American Literature* 62.2 (1990): 176–86.

40. Griswold, *Poets and Poetry of America,* 538.

41. Bennett, "Late Nineteenth-Century American Women's Nature Poetry," 91.

42. Finch, "Sentimental Poetess," 5. Finch argues that sentimental poetry also sparks fears in American readers wary of unprovoked intimacy (4, 5). Her account complements Jonathan Culler's description of the (romantic) poet, who asks "inanimate objects to bend themselves to your desire" and for whom the "sentient," responsive world exists "to constitute an image of self. He makes himself poet, visionary" (Culler, "Apostrophe," *The Pursuit of Signs: Semiotics, Literature, Deconstruction* [Ithaca: Cornell University Press, 1981], 139, 142). Finch's description of sentimental poets' lyric voice evokes almost a "poetics of absence" or, in my earlier phrase, a poetics of empathy.

43. Robert Frost, *LU* 64, 111–12; see 144. See Sandra L. Katz, *Robert Frost: A Poet's Wife* (Westfield: Institute for Massachusetts Studies, 1988), 7–8, for two of Elinor's own poems. Frank Lentricchia notes Frost's affiliations with the (male-

authored) tradition of genteel poetry (*Modernist Quartet* [Cambridge: Cambridge University Press, 1994], 49–50, 72–74, 114).

44. Andrew W. Angyal, "Robert Frost's Poetry before 1913, A Checklist," *Proof 5, The Yearbook of American Bibliographical and Textual Studies* (Columbia, SC: J. Faust, 1977), 98; Jeffrey S. Cramer, *Robert Frost among His Poems: A Literary Companion to the Poet's Own Biographical Contexts and Associations* (Jefferson, NC: McFarland, 1996), 10.

45. Meyers, *Robert Frost*, 161.

46. Richard Reed remarks that the poems in *A Boy's Will* "are marred by several shortcomings," one of which is "excessive sentimentality"; he claims that "the sentimentality evident in so many of these early poems is often evoked through the presence or absence of animals" ("The Animal World in Frost's Poetry," in *Frost: Centennial Essays II*, ed. Jac Tharpe [Jackson: University Press of Mississippi, 1976], 159, 160).

47. Bennett, "Late Nineteenth-Century American Women's Nature Poetry," 91; Finch, "Sentimental Poetess," 5. Frost identifies five tones in the poem ("Lecture to the Browne and Nichols School, 1915," in *Robert Frost on Writing*, ed. Elaine Barry [New Brunswick: Rutgers University Press, 1973], 143–44).

48. William H. Pritchard, *Lives of the Modern Poets* (New York: Oxford University Press, 1980), 119–20.

49. Poirier, *Robert Frost: The Work of Knowing*, 59, 60.

50. Frost does use natural objects as metaphors for his own purposes; this is a gesture that Finch associates with traditional romantic lyric ("Sentimental Poetess," 6–14). Poirier's description of the strong lyric speaker also parallels Rachel Blau DuPlessis's outline of the traditional "lyric triangle": "an overtly male 'I,' speaking as if overheard in front of an unseen but postulated, loosely male 'us' about a (Beloved) 'she'" ("'Corpses of Poesy': Some Modern Poets and Some Gender Ideologies of Lyric," in *Feminist Measures, Soundings in Poetry and Theory*, ed. Lynn Keller and Cristanne Miller [Ann Arbor: University of Michigan Press, 1994], 71).

51. Poirier, *Robert Frost: The Work of Knowing*, 31; Meyers, *Robert Frost*, 99.

52. Walker, *Nightingale's Burden*, 88–91; see Walker, intro., *American Women Poets*, xxiv–xxv.

53. It is also a familiar figure in such regionalist fiction as Mary E. Wilkins Freeman's story "A New England Nun" and Susan Glaspell's story "A Jury of Her Peers."

54. Rose Terry (Cooke), *Poems* (Boston: Ticknor and Fields, 1861), 176–77.

55. Frances Sargent Osgood, "The Daisy's Mistake," *Poems* (Philadelphia: Carey and Hart, 1849), 328–31; reprinted in Walker, *American Women Poets*, 127–29.

56. Osgood, *Poems* (Philadelphia: Carey and Hart, 1850), 435–36. This poem is also titled "The Lily's Delusion" in Frances S. Osgood, *Poems* (New York: Clark and Austin, 1846), 67–68.

57. Walker, intro., *American Women Poets*, xxviii.

58. From another perspective poems like Cooke's and Osgood's point to women poets' ironic critique of sentimental domestic ideology, an ideology that Frost would also appropriate and transform in poems like "The Pasture," while they also anticipate Frost's own critique of that ideology in poems like "Home Burial."

59. On the relationship between Ward and the Frosts, see Francis, *Frost Family's Adventure*, 8; and Francis, "Robert Frost and Susan Hayes Ward," *Massachusetts Review* 26 (1985): 341–50.

60. Clement Wood, *Poets of America* (New York: E. P. Dutton, 1925), 159.

61. Samuels, intro., *Culture of Sentiment*, 4–5.

62. Celia Thaxter, *The Poems of Celia Thaxter* [ed. Sarah Orne Jewett], Appledore edition (Boston: Houghton Mifflin, 1896), 153–54 (reprinted in Karen L. Kilcup, ed., *Nineteenth-Century American Women Writers: An Anthology* [Cambridge, MA, and Oxford, UK: Blackwell Publishers, 1997], 283).

63. Jane E. Vallier compares Thaxter to Margaret Fuller and highlights her "shunning of the sentimental" (*Poet on Demand: The Life, Letters, and Works of Celia Thaxter* [1982; reprint, Portsmouth, NH: Peter E. Randall, 1994], 16).

64. There are elements of uncertainty even within this regularity. While Thaxter's ballad is essentially regular iambic tetrameter throughout, Frost manipulates the meter to convey the doubt that lurks in the narrator's mind: lines one and three have seven stresses, each with a "feminine" ending, while the second quatrain of "Flower-Gathering" becomes more irregular, with eight, eight, nine, and six syllables, respectively. Unpredictably arranged, the stresses emphasize the lover's uncertainty and questioning of the beloved, and they unsettle the reader's sense of certainty as well, especially in the solitary extended nine-syllable line ("Are you dumb because you know me not[?]"). As the poem concludes, the line lengths and metrical scheme restore a measure of predictability, but the feminine endings remain ("question," "beside you," "measure," and "treasure"). The words on which the feminine line endings occur (especially *question, measure,* and *treasure*) confirm Frost's sense of the redemptive power of form to conserve not only meaning but also relationships. In its reliance on structural irregularities "Flower-Gathering" invokes a modernist sensibility, but the attitudes of the poem, and its language, retain their powerful sentimental force.

65. Poirier, *Robert Frost: The Work of Knowing*, 200, 206; see 210–12. Robert Faggen situates "A Prayer in Spring" "within a tradition of religious lyrics" (*Robert Frost and the Challenge of Darwin* [Ann Arbor: University of Michigan Press, 1997], 249). On "Rose Pogonias," see Frank Lentricchia, *Robert Frost: Modern Poetics and the Landscapes of Self* (Durham: Duke University Press, 1975), 32–34.

66. Poirier, *Robert Frost: The Work of Knowing*, 217, 218.

67. As it was in seventeenth-century verse (Poirier, *Robert Frost: The Work of Knowing*, 289); see Finch, "Sentimental Poetess," 10–11. Others have explored Frost's relation to religious faith and God; for example, see Dorothy Judd Hall, *Robert Frost: Contours of Belief* (Athens: Ohio University Press, 1984); and Fleissner, *Frost's Road Taken*, 163–73. Here I am more interested in the rhetorical gesture than in the poet's attitudes toward belief.

68. Poirier, *Robert Frost: The Work of Knowing*, 211.

69. Angyal dates Frost's poem ("Robert Frost's Poetry before 1913, A Checklist," 98). On the difference between modernist and nineteenth-century poetry, see Walker, intro., *American Women Poets*, xxvii, xxviii; on the realism in some nineteenth-century women poets, see Walker, "Nineteenth-Century Women

Poets and Realism," in *American Realism and the Canon,* ed. Tom Quirk and Gary Scharnhorst (Newark: University of Delaware Press, 1994), 37.

70. Emily Dickinson, *The Poems of Emily Dickinson* (Cambridge: Harvard University Press, 1955), 3:1015–16, P1466.

71. Bennett, "Late Nineteenth-Century American Women's Nature Poetry," 91.

72. Elizabeth Oakes Smith, "Strength from the Hills," *The Female Poets of America,* 2d ed. (Philadelphia: Parry and McMillan, 1854), 194; reprinted in Walker, *American Women Poets,* 76–77.

73. See Emily Stipes Watts, *The Poetry of American Women from 1632 to 1945* (Austin: University of Texas Press, 1977), 97–105; Bennett, "Descent of the Angel," 592–93.

74. Lucy Larcom, "Swinging on a Birch-Tree," *Our Young Folks* 3 (June 1867): 355–56. I could also emphasize the similarities between the two poems, the most notable of which are the New England setting and the boy's perspective. George Monteiro connects "Birches" with a passage from Thoreau's *Journals.* Monteiro notes of Frost's poem that "in some ways it is unfortunate that Frost stopped calling the poem by this title ['Swinging Birches']. I say unfortunate because the activity at the heart of the poem—the activity that generates whatever cohesion the poem has—is the boy's swinging of birches and the poet's ruminations on the possibility that the birches he sees have been bent by boys at play" (104–5). I cite this passage because it seems so relevant to Larcom's admittedly very different poem. See Monteiro, *Robert Frost and the New England Renaissance* (Lexington: University of Kentucky Press, 1988), 99–111.

Frost could not easily have avoided Larcom's work. Although she did not occupy a prominent position in the anthologies by either Rufus Griswold or E. C. Stedman, Larcom was a popular New England poet whose work appeared widely in mid- to late-nineteenth-century periodicals and whose collected poems went through many editions. A feminist, abolitionist, intellectual, and naturalist, and a friend of Whittier, she became a worker in the Lowell textile mills at the age of eleven after the premature death of her father, and she contributed regularly to the *Lowell Offering.* She also became an editor of the children's magazine *Our Young Folks* from 1865 to 1870. Finally, and perhaps most significantly, Larcom was the teacher of Frost's lifelong supporter (and publisher of his first poem) Susan Hayes Ward. For a discussion of the relationship between Ward and Larcom, see Shirley Marchalonis, *The Worlds of Lucy Larcom, 1824–1893* (Athens: University of Georgia Press, 1989), 246–47, 262–63; Daniel Dulany Addison, *Lucy Larcom: Life, Letters, and Diary* (Boston: Houghton Mifflin, 1895), 53, 223–24, 238. Addison's book contains letters from Larcom to Ward, and he cites Ward's assistance for preparing the volume (vii–viii). For the relationship between Frost and Ward, see Lesley Lee Francis, "Robert Frost and Susan Hayes Ward," *Massachusetts Review* 26 (1985): 341–50.

75. Clark, *Sentimental Modernism,* 1.

76. Timothy Morris, *Becoming Canonical in American Poetry* (Urbana: University of Illinois Press, 1995), 21.

77. Jane Tompkins, "Me and My Shadow," in *The Intimate Critique, Autobi-*

*ographical Literary Criticism,* ed. Diane P. Freedman, Olivia Frey, and Frances Murphy Zauhar (Durham: Duke University Press, 1993), 25–26.

78. Marjorie Barrows, ed., *One Hundred Best Poems for Boys and Girls* (Racine, WI: Whitman Publishing Co., 1930), 108, 48, 96, 79–80.

79. Pritchard, *Lives of the Modern Poets,* 113; Oster, *Toward Robert Frost,* 158, 11, 148–56; Poirier, *Robert Frost: The Work of Knowing,* 235, 179. See also Donald J. Greiner, "The Indispensible Robert Frost," in *Critical Essays on Robert Frost,* ed. Philip L. Gerber (Boston: G. K. Hall, 1982), 232.

80. Walker, intro., *American Women Poets,* xxv.

81. Rufus Wilmot Griswold, *The Female Poets of America* (New York: James Miller, 1877), 459.

82. One might sensibly question whether or not all elegies are to a greater or lesser degree sentimental.

83. Walsh, *Into My Own,* 130, 251.

84. Jarrell, *Poetry and the Age,* 28–29.

85. Exemplary texts on this subject are Poirier, "The Difficulties of Modernism and the Modernism of Difficulty," in *Critical Essays on American Modernism,* ed. Michael J. Hoffman and Patrick D. Murphy (New York: G. K. Hall, 1992), 104–14; and Leslie Fiedler, "Literature as an Institution" and "What Happened to Poetry," *What Was Literature? Class Culture and Mass Society* (New York: Simon and Schuster, 1982), 57–63, 83–95.

86. Katz, *Robert Frost: A Poet's Wife,* 57–58; Meyers, *Robert Frost,* 60. For a very different view, see Walsh, *Into My Own,* 64–69. Had I read Walsh before I had given my presentation, its shape would undoubtedly have been much more tentative, for it now seems likely that this incident never happened.

87. Lionel Trilling, "A Speech on Robert Frost: A Cultural Episode," in *Robert Frost: A Collection of Critical Essays,* ed. James M. Cox (Englewood Cliffs, NJ: Prentice-Hall, 1962), 156 (reprinted from *Partisan Review* 26 [Summer 1959]: 445–52); mentioned by Frost in a letter to Trilling (*SL* 582–83). See also Linda W. Wagner, *CR* xix; and John Ciardi, "Robert Frost: American Bard," in *CR* 241–45.

88. Paul Lauter et al., eds., *The Heath Anthology of American Literature,* 1st ed. (Lexington, MA: D. C. Heath, 1990), 2:xi–xii. The second edition of the *Heath* retains the choices of the first, while the *Norton* fourth edition includes many of the same choices, and, in addition, such "characteristic" poems as "Mowing," "After Apple-Picking," and "Neither Far Out nor in Deep," as well as three long dramatic poems, 'The Death of the Hired Man," "Home Burial," and "A Servant to Servants" (it excludes "The Fear") (Nina Baym et al., eds., *The Norton Anthology of American Literature,* 4th ed. [New York: Norton, 1994], 2:xi–xii).

89. In contrast to this representation of Frost is the earlier view, which Jarrell suggests is heavily imbued with popularism, of Louis Untermeyer's best-selling anthologies. My 1942 edition reveals at least partial confirmation of this view, including among its thirty-six poems "The Pasture," "The Tuft of Flowers," "Reluctance," "The Runaway," "Bereft," "Stopping by Woods on a Snowy Evening," "Nothing Gold Can Stay," and "The Road Not Taken" (Untermeyer, ed., *Modern American Poetry: A Critical Anthology* [New York: Harcourt, Brace, 1942], xvi–xvii).

90. Lentricchia, *Modernist Quartet,* 76.

91. Richardson, *Ordeal of Robert Frost,* 21.

92. Edward Connery Lathem, *The Poetry of Robert Frost* (New York: Holt, Rinehart and Winston, 1975), 610.

93. Frost, *SL* 86; see Walsh, *Into My Own* (117), on Frost's worries about reviews and his future reputation.

94. Many other women poets, from Margaret Fuller to Lucy Hooper, addressed similar supposedly "public" and ostensibly "indecorous" subjects for women; one famous example is Lucy Larcom's powerful abolitionist poem "Weaving" (*The Poetical Works of Lucy Larcom* [Boston: Houghton Mifflin, 1884], 93–95; reprinted in Kilcup, ed., *Nineteenth-Century American Women Writers,* 175–77).

95. Nina Baym, "Reinventing Lydia Sigourney," in *The (Other) American Traditions, Nineteenth-Century Women Writers,* ed. Joyce W. Warren (New Brunswick: Rutgers University Press, 1993), 55–59. Walker argues that the poet belongs as much to a category of early national poetry as sentimental poetry ("Nineteenth-Century American Women Poets Revisited," in *Nineteenth-Century American Women Writers: A Critical Reader,* ed. Karen L. Kilcup [Malden, MA, and Oxford, UK: Blackwell Publishers, 1998], 231–44).

96. Baym, "Reinventing Lydia Sigourney," 59, 64.

97. Rufus Wilmot Griswold, *The Female Poets of America* (Philadelphia: Parry and McMillan, 1854), 99. The Griswold version of "Indian Names," one of several by Sigourney, is reprinted in Kilcup, *Nineteenth-Century American Women Writers: An Anthology,* 46–47. Sigourney included the poem in earlier collections of her own poetry, such as *Poems* (1834), where it contains additional stanzas. This 1834 version is reprinted in Paula Bernat Bennett, *Nineteenth-Century American Women Poets: An Anthology,* 12–13.

98. Fisher, *Hard Facts,* 19.

99. Baym, "Reinventing Lydia Sigourney," 63.

100. "Indian Names" appears to be vulnerable to Wexler's critique of nineteenth-century sentimental fiction ("Tender Violence: Literary Eavesdropping, Domestic Fiction, and Educational Reform," in Samuels, *Culture of Sentiment,* 8–38). For one thing, the poem addresses a white middle-class reader, employing the image of the Indian as a mean of eliciting (at the least) guilt; the location of an Indian reader ("they") remains outside the poem's margins. But, in spite of the poem's inability to give Indians subjectivity, it would be difficult to say how the poem's sentimental stance—if we want to call it that—serves as a means of "the social control of marginal domestic populations" (18). Furthermore, it is possible to argue that Sigourney's rhetorical stance and depiction of Indians' approaching absence are merely rhetorical devices aimed at strengthening her message. As *A Sketch of Connecticut, Forty Years Hence* reveals, she was well aware of the living (if threatened) presence of Native Americans even in the northeastern United States. Finally, if this poem were a single effort on the poet's part, we might be able to attack her for participation in a troubling sentimentalism that erases Indians from middle-class culture—but Sigourney wrote literally thousands of lines in both poetry and prose to ensure their continuing presence. Coming—like Frost, we might note—from family circumstances of economic hardship may have enabled her to have the sympathy for Native Americans that resonates in "Indian Names."

101. Culler, "Apostrophe," 143.

102. Much nineteenth-century fiction and nonfiction by women represented Native Americans in an affirmative (if sometimes stereotypical) light, including Lydia Maria Child's *Hobomuk* (1824), Catherine Maria Sedgwick's *Hope Leslie* (1827), Helen Hunt Jackson's *A Century of Dishonor* (1881) and *Ramona* (1884), and Mary Wilkins Freeman's *Madelon* (1896). In the context of this discussion it is noteworthy that all of these writers were from New England and that Frost would have been likely to know at least some of their work.

103. Bogan provides a tactful overview of the response to Frost's political poetry in an essay published shortly before the poet's death; see "A Lifework," in *A Poet's Alphabet: Reflections on the Literary Art and Vocation,* ed. Robert Phelps and Ruth Limmer (New York: McGraw-Hill, 1970), 180–81. Poirier is characteristically sympathetic to "Kitty Hawk" (*Robert Frost: The Work of Knowing,* 301–3; see 236–37).

104. Robert Frost, "Introduction to Sarah Cleghorn's 'Threescore,'" *CP* 751, 750.

105. Meyers points out that Frost's attitude changed over time; "as he became increasingly influential, he wanted a 'division of spoils; between poetry and power'" (*Robert Frost,* 323).

106. Frost was seven years old when the massacre at Wounded Knee occurred, an event that was widely publicized across the country.

107. Frost's sympathy for Native Americans is particularly noteworthy given the racism (as well as antifeminism and nativism) endemic in turn-of-the-century U.S. culture; this racism was one means of consolidating masculinity to white middle-class males (Michael Kimmel, *Manhood in America: A Cultural History* [New York: Free Press, 1996], 90).

108. Roy Harvey Pearce, *Savagism and Civilization: A Study of the Indian and the American Mind* (Berkeley: University of California Press, 1988), 189.

109. My account contrasts with that of Faggen, who argues that "the narrator coldly refrains from judging the miller's actions" (*Robert Frost and the Ordeal of Darwin,* 121; see also Fleissner, *Frost's Road Taken,* 203).

110. The sentimental background for this poem also obviously includes Longfellow's *Hiawatha.* Pearce notes of Longfellow that "in *Hiawatha* (1855) he was able, by matching legend with a sentimental view of a past far away enough in time to be safe and near enough in space to be appealing, fully to image the Indian as the noble savage" (*Savagism and Civilization,* 192; see 191–94). Fisher also provides us with a subtle link between Frost and Native Americans; in the context of a discussion of Cooper, Fisher connects "Spring Pools" to "the history of beginnings damaged by violence" (*Hard Facts,* 30).

## Chapter 2

1. Mary E. Wilkins [Freeman], "A Poetess," *A New England Nun and Other Stories* (London: James R. Osgood, 1892), 154–55.

2. Ibid., 153. Josephine Donovan points to the external, "translocal discipline," imposed on Betsey as the source of her "silence and erasure" ("Breaking the

Sentence: Local-Color Literature and Subjugated Knowledges," in *The [Other]
American Traditions: Nineteenth-Century Women Writers,* ed. Joyce W. Warren [New
Brunswick: Rutgers University Press, 1993], 239). Like Barbara H. Solomon and
Mary R. Reichardt, Perry D. Westbrook accepts at face value Freeman's intimation
about Betsey's poetry, calling it "mawkish," while Ann Romines and Linda Grasso
highlight Freeman's hints that we should regard this poetry in more complex and
affirmative ways. See Solomon, ed., intro., *Short Fiction of Sarah Orne Jewett and Mary
Wilkins Freeman* (New York: New American Library, 1979), 25; Reichardt, *A Web
of Relationship: Women in the Short Stories of Mary Wilkins Freeman* (Jackson: Univer-
sity Press of Mississippi, 1992), 144–45; Westbrook, *Mary Wilkins Freeman,* rev. ed.
(Boston: Twayne, 1988), 48; Romines, *The Home Plot: Women, Writing and Domes-
tic Ritual* (Amherst: University of Massachusetts Press, 1992), 112–15; Grasso,
"'Thwarted Life, Mighty Hunger, Unfinished Work': The Legacy of Nineteenth-
Century Women Writing in America," *American Transcendental Quarterly* 8.2 (1994):
99–101.

    3. Freeman, "A Poetess," 147, 146, 153.

    4. Grasso, "'Thwarted Life, Mighty Hunger, Unfinished Work,'" 101.

    5. William H. Pritchard, *Frost: A Literary Life Reconsidered* (New York:
Oxford University Press, 1984), 147.

    6. As I note elsewhere, Randall Jarrell praises early Frost's sympathy for
people with diminished lives; a 1919 letter from the poet to Untermeyer also sug-
gests his personal understanding of economic hardship. Commenting on another
writer's work, he moves toward a broader meditation on the relationship between
economics and art:

> Form is with the rich, material with the poor, though to the poor it sometimes
> may seem that material is just what they lack to eat and cover their backs with.
> The rich are too vague from their remoteness from things ever to make real-
> izing artists. Things belong to the poor by their having to come to grips with
> things daily. And that's a good one on the poor. They are the only realists.
> Things are theirs and no one else's, though of course it is forbidden the poor
> to wear or eat the things.

Realism is inevitable to the poor, Frost claims; material life is inescapable. Privi-
lege, which buffers the rich from this realism, also prevents them from being
"realizing artists." The voices of *North of Boston,* published three years earlier, put
these ideas into practice. As the letter continues, Frost appears to disavow the
sympathy he has just expressed; perhaps he didn't want to appear too soft, but, at
any rate, his ambivalence is clear (Louis Untermeyer, ed., *LU* 80). John C. Kemp
suggests that the change in form paralleled the poet's construction of a mythic past
for himself as farmer-poet of New England (*Robert Frost and New England: The
Poet as Regionalist* [Princeton: Princeton University Press, 1979], 41). Frost
bridged his movement from sentimental lyric to narrative and dramatic work by
transforming the social activism of much of the former tradition into the region-
alism of the latter.

    7. In addition to Lowell, Howells, Westbrook, and Kemp, see Lawrence

Lipking, *The Life of the Poet: Beginning and Ending Poetic Careers* (Chicago: University of Chicago Press, 1981), 10; George W. Nitchie, *Human Values in the Poems of Robert Frost: A Study of a Poet's Convictions* (Durham: Duke University Press, 1960), 117–18.

8. Kemp, *Robert Frost and New England,* 13, 162; emphasis added. Kemp does not distinguish between regional and local color writing, though he seems more critical of the latter. While I am somewhat sympathetic to Kemp's assessment of Frost's development toward self-caricature as Yankee poet, he offers little appreciation of the sympathy, and even empathy, that the poet has for women. One measure of this omission is Kemp's suggestion that the narrators in Frost's best poems regard their characters from the outside, yet his sensitivity to the range of the poet's characters, and the tension that he creates between insider and outsider, forms a useful starting point (195). Kemp also provides a helpful bibliography of responses to Frost's regionalism (237–61).

9. Perry D. Westbrook, "Robert Frost's New England," in *Frost: Centennial Essays,* ed. Jac Tharpe (Jackson: University of Mississippi Press, 1974), 246; emphasis added. In fact, a letter by Frost suggests that he almost certainly knew the work of at least one regionalist, Alice Brown, for he writes to his close friend Edward Thomas about "my friend Alice Brown the novelist" (*SL* 166).

10. Richard Poirier points to Frost's grounding in home and its love relationships as a precondition for "extravagances" and the discoveries that such extravagances enable (*Robert Frost: The Work of Knowing* [Oxford: Oxford University Press, 1977], 89).

11. Judith Fetterley and Marjorie Pryse, intro., *American Women Regionalists, 1850–1910* (New York: Norton, 1992), xi–xx; David Jordan, ed., *Regionalism Reconsidered: New Approaches to the Field* (New York: Garland, 1994); Robert L. Dorman, *Revolt of the Provinces: The Regionalist Movement in America, 1920–1945* (Chapel Hill: University of North Carolina Press, 1993), 1–25. As the remarks that follow suggest, the distinction between local color and regionalism seems at present to be more a matter of critical revaluation than of any conscious practice on the part of the writers involved.

12. David Jordan, for example, attempts to distinguish between "nostalgic 'local color'" and "regionalism," with its "dynamic interplay of political, cultural, and psychological forces," while Warren Johnson highlights how regionalism is "sometimes reduced to 'local color'" (Jordan, intro., *Regionalism Reconsidered,* ix; Johnson, "Regionalism and Value Structure in Erckmann-Chatrian," in Jordan, *Regionalism Reconsidered,* 105.

13. Jim Wayne Miller, "Anytime the Ground Is Uneven: The Outlook for Regional Studies and What to Look Out For," *Geography and Literature: A Meeting of the Disciplines* (Syracuse: Syracuse University Press, 1987), 2; see also Kemp, *Robert Frost and New England,* 225, Johnson, "Regionalism and Value Structure in Erckmann-Chatrian," 105–6. As Eudora Welty observes, "'Regional' is an outsider's term; it has no meaning for the insider who is doing the writing, because as far as he knows he is simply writing about life" ("Place in Fiction," *The Eye of the Story: Selected Essays and Reviews* [New York: Random House, 1978], 132).

14. Michael Kowaleski, "Writing in Place: The New American Regionalism," *American Literary History* 6.1 (1994): 175.

15. Francesco Loriggio, "Regionalism and Theory," in Jordan, *Regionalism Reconsidered,* 3.

16. As Jim Wayne Miller observes, "regionalism has been considered, correctly and incorrectly, as reactionary; as a simplistic approach to a complex reality; as a denial of the wholeness of American culture and the great Western tradition" ("Anytime the Ground Is Uneven," 5).

17. Caroline Gebhard, "The Spinster in the House of American Criticism," *Tulsa Studies in Women's Literature* 10.1 (1991): 83; see Joanna Russ, *How to Suppress Women's Writing* (Austin: University of Texas Press, 1983), 52–53.

18. Lentricchia seems to presume that Frost rejects the "local-color" writers because of their inherent sentimentality (*Modernist Quartet* [Cambridge: Cambridge University Press 1994], 59–60, 115).

19. Jill Franks, "The Regionalist Community: Indigenous versus Outsider Consciousness in Deledda's *La madre* and Lawrence's *Sea and Sardinia,*" in Jordan, *Regionalism Reconsidered,* 90. Regionalism can come out the loser in the native-exotic dyad, inasmuch as the former may appear essentially "conservative" and "nostalgic," whereas "exoticism appeals to the transgressive imagination" and the unfamiliar. See Johnson, "Regionalism and Value Structure," 105.

20. This precedence of character is, not surprisingly, an important characteristic of the dramatic monologue (Robert Langbaum, *The Poetry of Experience: The Dramatic Monologue in Modern Literary Tradition* [York: Random House, 1957], 182).

21. Fetterley and Pryse, *American Women Regionalists,* xv, xvi, xviii, xvii.

22. Ibid., xvii; emphasis added.

23. Dobson, "The American Renaissance Reenvisioned," in *The (Other) American Traditions: Nineteenth-Century Women Writers,* ed. Joyce Warren (New Brunswick: Rutgers University Press, 1993), 167.

24. Lentricchia, *Modernist Quartet,* 109.

25. Lentricchia points out that "neither Frost's mother nor his wife could qualify in the technical sense as working-class, but both were tied to toiling joylessly and without hope of respite in jobs of no glamour and to lifetime grooves of family obligation that permitted no life in high cultural activity for themselves." Such connections prohibited a facile writing out of "the privileged-class woman upon whom ideals of cultural feminization in America are typically based"; rather, as Lentricchia notes significantly though parenthetically, "Frost's experiments in fact often featured at their very center economically disadvantaged female voices" ("The Resentments of Robert Frost," *American Literature* 62.2 [1990]: 192, 186). Another potential source of his sympathy for the "outsider" lies in his mother's status as an immigrant; Frost's remarks on this subject in an interview are intriguing, to say the least (Rose C. Feld, "Robert Frost Relieves His Mind," in *Critical Essays on Robert Frost,* ed. Philip L. Gerber [Boston: G. K. Hall, 1982], 54, 55).

26. Robert Faggen, *Robert Frost and the Challenge of Darwin* (Ann Arbor: University of Michigan Press, 1997), 187.

27. Frost inscribed what Robert Langbaum has called a "poetry of experience" that gives "the facts from within" and that establishes a sympathy between

writer and character, and hence, reader and character (*Poetry of Experience*, 52, 78). Langbaum, however, emphasizes the poet's ultimate detachment (25, 27, 85).

28. Robert Frost, "Poverty and Poetry," *CP* 759. Writing about the tension in postmodernist theory between narrative and lyric, Susan Stanford Friedman argues for the recuperation of a radical narrative practice in poetry and, in particular, in contemporary female-authored long poems. Friedman's insights are useful for a discussion of narrative in poetry more generally and for Frost's work more specifically. For one thing, she points out the slippage between genres, our inability to specify accurate and solid distinctions between poetry and narrative. More significantly for this discussion, she underscores "the radical potential of narrative for writers of any group that has been absent in or trivialized by hegemonic historical discourses" as well as "the function of tales to 'bear witness.'" She asserts, "it is . . . premature, I believe, to dismiss narrative for those denied the authoritative voice and position of the storyteller by the dominant symbolic order" (Friedman, "Craving Stories: Narrative and Lyric in Contemporary Theory and Women's Long Poems," in *Feminist Measures: Soundings in Poetry and Theory*, ed. Lynn Keller and Cristanne Miller [Ann Arbor: University of Michigan Press, 1994], 21, 16).

29. Richard Brodhead argues that regionalism enabled groups who usually didn't have access to literature to write, though sometimes at the cost of self-estrangement ("Regionalism and the Upper Class," in *Rethinking Class: Literary Studies and Social Formations*, ed. Wai Chee Dimock and Michael T. Gilmore [New York: Columbia University Press, 1994], 150–74).

30. Richard Poirier, *Robert Frost: The Work of Knowing*, 125, 134, 135. Roger Ekins argues that "home is a house of refuge and a source of protection" ("'At Home' with Robert Frost," *Frost: Centennial Essays*, 192). See also Vivian C. Hopkins, "The Houses of Robert Frost," *Frost: Centennial Essays*, 182–90. Katherine Kearns points out the space for interpretation that Frost creates for the reader of "Home Burial" (*Robert Frost and a Poetics of Appetite* [Cambridge: Cambridge University Press, 1994], 71).

31. Lawrance Thompson and R. H. Winnick, *Robert Frost: A Biography*, ed. Edward Connery Latham (New York: Holt, Rinehart and Winston, 1981), 114. See also William H. Pritchard, *Frost: A Literary Life Reconsidered*, 54. I agree with Pritchard's argument for a more generous view of Frost's life than the one elaborated by Thompson.

32. As I will do in the discussion of "A Servant to Servants" that follows, I have purposely emphasized the value and legitimacy of the woman speaker's perspective and experience, for it is through these doors that Frost enters into the feminine literary traditions of both mainstream poetry and woman-authored New England regionalist fiction; the other side of this story has already been told.

33. Richard Poirier, *Robert Frost: The Work of Knowing*, 128. See also Faggen, *Robert Frost and the Challenge of Darwin*, 218–25; Faggen sees Amy as more manipulative than I do.

34. Amy Lowell, *Tendencies in Modern Poetry* (New York: Macmillan, 1917), 117–18; Jessie Rittenhouse, "Portraits of Women," in *The Recognition of Robert Frost*, ed. Richard Thornton (New York: Henry Holt and Co., 1937), 247, 248.

35. Fetterley and Pryse, *American Women Regionalists*, xvii.

36. Judith Oster, *Toward Robert Frost: The Reader and the Poet* (Athens: University of Georgia Press, 1991), 192–99. The poem's violent subtext again recalls the famous "loaded gun" incident. Whether Lesley dreamed it or not, it indicates a charged atmosphere in the Frost household (Katz, *Robert Frost: A Poet's Wife*, 57–58; see also Jeffrey Meyers, *Robert Frost: A Biography* [Boston: Houghton Mifflin, 1996], 60; but see Walsh, *Into My Own: The English Years of Robert Frost, 1912–1915* [New York: Grove Weidenfeld, 1988], 64–69).

37. For a more concentrated discussion of this issue, see Karen L. Kilcup, "'"Men work together," I told him from the heart': Frost's (In)Delicate Masculinity," *ELH* 65.3 (1998): 731–56. For important discussions of the construction of masculinity in the nineteenth and early twentieth centuries, see E. Anthony Rotundo, *American Manhood: Transformations in Masculinity from the Revolution to the Modern Era* (New York: Basic Books, 1993); Michael Kimmel, *Manhood in America: A Cultural History* (New York: Free Press, 1996).

38. Poirier, *Robert Frost: The Work of Knowing*, 126, 128. In sharp contrast to my view, Lentricchia blames the wife for the disruption of home, observing that she "needs to see her husband as unfeeling and unresponsive because she needs, in her masochism, to destroy their marriage as a context of mutuality." Katherine Kearns sees the husband as less powerful and threatening than I do (Lentricchia, *Robert Frost: Modern Poetics and the Landscapes of Self* [Durham: Duke University Press, 1975], 64; Kearns, "'The Place Is the Asylum': Women and Nature in Robert Frost's Poetry," *American Literature* 59.2 [1987]: 192–93).

39. Kearns, *Robert Frost and a Poetics of Appetite*, 77; see Oster, *Toward Robert Frost*, 215.

40. Joseph Brodsky, "On Grief and Reading," *New Yorker* 70.30 (26 September 1994): 78, 74–78. In a similar vein Kearns emphasizes that "the narrators in poems like 'The Death of the Hired Man' and 'Home Burial' are by definition objectively reportorial, and as such they keep the reader back from the immediacies of emotion as well" (*Robert Frost and Poetics of Appetite*, 148). Similarly, Barton Levi St. Armand argues for Frost's outsider status, in contrast to the "insider" status of regionalists like Jewett and Freeman ("The Power of Sympathy in the Poetry of Robinson and Frost: The 'Inside' vs. the 'Outside' Narrative," *American Quarterly* 19 [1967]: 564: 74).

41. Fetterley and Pryse, *American Women Regionalists*, xvii.

42. Elizabeth Ammons discusses the freedom from marriage and child rearing as the basis of much of late-nineteenth-century American women's writing; Elinor's choice to marry Robert virtually destined her to a nonartistic life (Ammons, *Conflicting Stories: American Women Writers at the Turn into the Twentieth Century* [New York: Oxford University Press, 1991], 8–11).

43. *CP* 58. In the original edition of the poem the wife's plea reads, "You can't because you don't know how"; Frost's addition of *to speak* in all subsequent editions underlines the couple's specifically linguistic difficulty. See Edward Connery Lathem, ed., *The Poetry of Robert Frost* (New York: Holt, Rinehart and Winston, 1969), 536.

44. For another example, see the darkly comic account of infant death in Rose Terry Cooke's "Freedom Wheeler's Controversy with Providence." In Fet-

terley and Pryse, *American Women Regionalists,* 94–122. Another much less familiar text that is more directly analogous is Dinny Gleeson's death in Sarah Pratt McLean Greene's novel *Flood-Tide* (New York: Harper, 1901).

45. Freeman, "A Poetess," 143.

46. Ibid., 159. Grasso, "'Thwarted Life, Mighty Hunger, Unfinished Work,'" 105.

47. Lydia H. Sigourney, "Death of an Infant," in *Female Poets and Poetry of America,* ed. Rufus Wilmot Griswold (Philadelphia: Parry and McMillan, 1854), 96.

48. Elizabeth A. Petrino takes a critical view of Sigourney's child elegies as she locates Emily Dickinson in the tradition of the child elegy ("'Feet so precious charged': Dickinson, Sigourney, and the Child Elegy," *Tulsa Studies in Women's Literature* 13 [1994]: 317–38). In a recent paper Wendy Dasler Johnson takes a more affirmative and recuperative view of Sigourney ("Reading Lydia Huntley Sigourney: Problems of Sentimental Convention and Class," paper presented at "Woman to Woman: 19th-Century American Women Writers in the 21st Century," Hartford, CT, May 1996).

49. Wendy Dasler Johnson (on Sigourney), 11.

50. Paula Bennett, "God's Will, Not Mine: Mourning and Rage in Sarah Piatt's Poetry on Child Death," Northeast Modern Language Association Convention, 19 April 1996. For a different view of Frost's relationship to the sentimental, see Faggen, *Robert Frost and the Challenge of Darwin,* 216–17.

51. Jeffrey Meyers, *Robert Frost,* 58, 73.

52. Francis Turner Palgrave, *Golden Treasury of the Best Songs and Lyrical Poems in the English Language* (London: Macmillan, 1892), 268–69.

53. Pritchard, *Frost: A Literary Life Reconsidered,* 78.

54. Freeman, "A Poetess," 147.

55. In a discussion that is particularly resonant for the account of "In the Home Stretch" that follows, Kemp argues that Frost was never really a farmer but at heart and by upbringing an urbanite and that he composed a myth for the purposes of self-publicity. Frost certainly composed many stories about himself, varying them for different audiences at different times. While there is surely some truth to Kemp's assertions, especially in relation to Frost's relation to a popular readership, he worried relentlessly about elite readers' inability to perceive his complexity and sophistication. Many of the latter, including Humphries, Winters, and Pearce, bought the rural story and attacked Frost for his smallness and limitation as a consequence (Kemp, *Robert Frost and New England,* 64–68; see Donald J. Grenier, *The Poet and His Critics* [New York: American Library Association, 1974], 116–17, 124–25, 126–27, 182ff.).

56. Wallace also observes, "critics have tended to see Frost's women as classic cases of hysteria or depression" ("The 'Estranged Point of View': The Thematics of Imagination in Frost's Poetry," in *Frost: Centennial Essays II,* ed. Jac Tharpe [Jackson: University of Mississippi Press, 1976], 178); in this vein, see Kemp, *Robert Frost and New England,* 124, 125, 198.

57. Kearns, *Robert Frost and a Poetics of Appetite,* 88; Lentricchia, *Robert Frost: Modern Poetics and the Landscapes of Self,* 66. Langbaum discusses the use of "reprehensible" speakers in the dramatic monologue, and he comments more specifically

on Frost's use of the form "to expose aberrations of mind and soul in New England" (85, 93); O'Donnell discusses his "abnormal people" in *North of Boston* ("Robert Frost and New England: A Revaluation," *Yale Review* 37 [1948]: 704). See also Mark Richardson, *The Ordeal of Robert Frost: The Poet and His Poetics* (Urbana: University of Illinois Press, 1997), 239.

58. Kearns, *Robert Frost and a Poetics of Appetite*, 89.

59. Thompson, *Robert Frost: The Years of Triumph, 1915–1938* (New York: Holt, Rinehart and Winston, 1970), 494. This feeling was probably exacerbated by the conflicting advice American men were receiving about sexuality and masculinity (Peter G. Filene, *Him/Her/Self: Sex Roles in Modern America* [Baltimore: Johns Hopkins University Press, 1986], 83).

60. Adrienne Rich, *Of Woman Born: Motherhood as Experience and Institution* (New York: Bantam, 1977), 61; see Thomas J. Schlereth, *Victorian America: Transformations in Everyday Life, 1876–1915* (New York: HarperPerennial, 1991), 272–74.

61. Filene, *Him/Her/Self*, 91–92.

62. See Meyers, *Robert Frost*, 35, 100, 161, 231, for Elinor's role as Muse; *CR* 156.

63. Poirier, *Robert Frost: The Work of Knowing*, 115.

64. As I will explore more fully in the next chapter, Frost commented on such "gossip" in an illuminating manner. See Thompson, *SL* 159. For an interesting discussion of the construction of the narrator as "sinner" or sufferer of an illness, see Faggen, *Robert Frost and the Challenge of Darwin*, 225–32.

65. On the relationship between female readers and texts, see Schweickart, "Reading Ourselves," 44ff.; Judith Kegan Gardiner, "On Female Identity and Writing by Women," in *Writing and Sexual Difference*, ed. Elizabeth Abel (Chicago: University of Chicago Press, 1982), 185.

66. Marcia McClintock Folsom, "'Tact Is a Kind of Mind-Reading': Empathic Style in Sarah Orne Jewett's *The Country of the Pointed Firs*," in *Critical Essays on Sarah Orne Jewett*, ed. Gwen Nagel (Boston: G. K. Hall, 1984), 77.

67. Rose Terry Cooke, "Mrs. Flint's Married Experience," in *How Celia Changed Her Mind and Selected Stories*, ed. Elizabeth Ammons (New Brunswick: Rutgers University Press, 1986), 97, 101.

68. Ibid., 112, 125.

69. Emily Dickinson, *The Poems of Emily Dickinson*, ed. Thomas H. Johnson (Cambridge: Belknap-Harvard University Press, 1955), 337, P435.

70. Another excruciating example of the violence done to women by degraded men occurs in Harriet Prescott Spofford's story "In the Maguerriwock," in which an isolated farm woman is driven crazy by her husband and brother-in-law who kill a travelling peddler for his money and beat her into enforced silence while she is pregnant. The mother loses her mind, and the daughter who is born later is "a fool." See Harriet Prescott Spofford, "In the Maguerriwock," in *The Amber Gods and Other Stories*, ed. Alfred Bendixen (New Brunswick: Rutgers University Press, 1989), 269–80. The story was originally published in 1868. Even Mary Wilkins Freeman's story "A New England Nun," which portrays its male protagonist with affection and humor, indicates an element of brutality in his mere physical presence (*A New England Nun and Other Stories*, 1–17).

71. Fetterley and Pryse, *American Women Regionalists,* xvii; Friedman, "Craving Stories," 16. Cooke's story includes a large dose of irony in the portrait of the foolish Mrs. Flint's choice to marry, but this irony is sympathetic rather than detached and judgmental.

72. Judith Fetterley, "'Not in the Least American': Nineteenth-Century Literary Regionalism," *College English* 56.8 (1994): 887.

73. Cited in Elaine Barry, *Robert Frost on Writing* (New Brunswick: Rutgers University Press, 1973), 45.

74. My reading of the poem differs from Richardson's, which emphasizes Frost's inclination to "*codify* gender rather than scrutinize it" (*Ordeal of Robert Frost,* 49–50).

75. Sarah Orne Jewett, "The Town Poor," first published in the *Atlantic Monthly* in 1890; reprinted in *Nineteenth-Century American Women Writers: An Anthology,* ed. Karen L. Kilcup (Cambridge, MA, and Oxford, UK: Blackwell Publishers, 1997), 384–90. Rosemarie Garland Thomson offers a provocative reading of the uses of sentimentality in this story; see "Crippled Girls and Lame Old Women: Sentimental Spectacles of Sympathy in Nineteenth-Century American Women's Writing," *Nineteenth-Century American Women Writers: A Critical Reader* (Malden, MA, and Oxford, UK: Blackwell Publishers, 1998), 128–45.

76. Kearns, *Robert Frost and a Poetics of Appetite,* 19.

77. For the affiliation in traditional, male-authored American literature between women and nature, see Annette Kolodny, *The Lay of the Land: Metaphor as Experience and History in American Life and Letters* (Chapel Hill: University of North Carolina Press, 1975).

78. Following Frost's own thoughts about life, Reuben A. Brower conceptualizes the poem's tension as one between mercy and justice (*The Poetry of Robert Frost: Constellations of Intention* [New York: Oxford University Press, 1963]), 162; see Robert Frost, "Poverty and Poetry," *CP* 762). We should also notice Frost's remark about Warren in "Poverty and Poetry"; after reading the poem, he tells his Haverford College audience: "The thing about that, the danger, is that you shall make the man too hard. That spoils it" (*CP* 763). It is Mary's role, I am suggesting, that enables us to see Warren's "feminine" softness.

79. Poirier, *Robert Frost: The Work of Knowing,* 106, 108.

80. Fetterley and Pryse, *American Women Regionalists,* xvii.

81. Suzanne Clark, *Sentimental Modernism, Women Writers and the Revolution of the Word* (Bloomington: Indiana University Press, 1991), 1–16.

82. Citing "the sharp actuality" of "The Housekeeper" as "worthy of Sarah Orne Jewett," Edward Garnett announces of "Home Burial" that "for tragic poignancy this piece stands by itself in American poetry" ("A New American Poet," *Atlantic Monthly* 116.2 [August 1915]: 220, 218). The anonymous reviewer for the *Independent* also highlights his participation in a regionalist tradition: "The New England that *North of Boston* introduces is the same bleak land that Mary Wilkins Freeman and Alice Brown have made so thoroughly their own in fiction: the bare hill-tops, and cold, harsh winds, where human beings, like the plants, must grapple close with roots deep in the flinty soil, to withstand the struggle for existence. It is a conflict that strips life of non-essentials, that under its barrenness locks up molten

drama, which is the more portentous for its suppression" (*CR* 27; *Independent,* 31 May 1915, 368).

83. William Dean Howells, "Editor's Easy Chair," *Harper's* 131.784 (1915): 635.

84. It is poignant indeed that only a few weeks after Jeanie sent her letter to Wilbur Rowell that we find Frost writing to Harriet Monroe about a check with an affectedly casual air: "I have carelessly let this cheque lie only to discover, now when I could use it, that it is unsigned. So I shall have to trouble you with it" (*SL* 120).

85. Jeffrey S. Cramer, *Robert Frost among His Poems: A Literary Companion to the Poet's Own Biographical Contexts and Associations* (Jefferson, NC: McFarland, 1996), 48.

86. Here the poem echoes the lengthy dialogue, in the first section of Lucy Larcom's regionalist-sentimental poem *An Idyl of Work,* on the definition of *lady;* one of Larcom's protagonists muses, "'Lady.' Who defines / That word correctly?" We discover that "There's something more in it than feeding folks / With bread or with ideas." Although Larcom's definition is inflected by religious overtones, like Frost's it has to do with notions of service, labor, and class: while her three factory girls embody the essence of being a "lady," the material signs of that status are more important to the world at large; we learn that the "town-dame" laments "that now even factory-girls / Shine with gold watches, and you cannot tell, / Therefore, who are the ladies" (Lucy Larcom, *An Idyl of Work* [1875; reprint, Westport, CT: Greenwood Press, 1970], 14, 19, 20).

87. As many writers on Frost have indicated, Elinor hated housework. But there is no reason to believe that, given their rural locations and the size of the family, she did not have to work hard nevertheless. On the effect of Elinor's poor health on her housekeeping, see Lesley Lee Francis, *The Frost Family's Adventure in Poetry: Sheer Morning Gladness at the Brim* (Columbia: University of Missouri Press, 1994), 16. On the response of many college-educated women to housework, see Filene, *Him/Her/Self,* 124, 125.

88. *CP* 108. For one view of the poem, see Warren French, "Frost Country," *Frost: Centennial Essays II,* 18–19.

89. Lesley Lee Francis connects this poem with Edward Thomas and the war (*The Frost Family's Adventure in Poetry: Sheer Morning Gladness at the Brim* [Columbia: University of Missouri Press, 1994], 172).

90. Oster highlights Frost's bawdy (*Toward Robert Frost,* 302–3 n. 35).

91. Faggen sees the poem as a set of reflections on change and progress; he also discusses "The Death of the Hired Man" in relation to the concept of progress (*Robert Frost and the Challenge of Darwin,* 192, 115).

92. For an interesting study of the positive force of rootedness in American literature, see Ozzie J. Mayers, "The Power of the Pin: Sewing as an Act of Rootedness in American Literature," *College English* 50 (1988): 664–80.

93. Sandra L. Katz, *Robert Frost: A Poet's Wife* (Westfield: Institute for Massachusetts Studies, 1988), 92, 93, 94ff.

94. My term *intellectual classism* represents an extrapolation of Brodhead's argument in "Regionalism and the Upper Class."

95. Sandra A. Zagarell, "Narrative of Community: The Identification of a

Genre," *Signs: Journal of Woman in Culture and Society* 13.3 (1988): 499. Zagarell's discussion represents the genre over time and cross-culturally.

96. Ibid., 499.

97. Paralleling my own argument, Elizabeth Ammons offers another necessary voice to the tendency to idealize female-centered rural communities; she points out the exclusive and ethnocentric basis of Jewett's Dunnet Landing (Karen Oakes, "'Colossal in Sheet-Lead': The Native American and Piscataqua-Region Writers," in *A Noble and Dignified Stream: The Piscataqua Region in the Colonial Revival, 1860–1930,* ed. Sarah M. Giffen and Kevin M. Murphy [York, ME: Old York Historical Society, 1992], 165–76; Ammons, "Material Culture, Empire, and Jewett's *The Country of the Pointed Firs,*" in *New Essays on* The Country of the Pointed Firs, ed. June Howard [Cambridge: Cambridge University Press, 1994], 81–99. See Fetterley, "'Not in the Least American,'" 892–93).

98. Fetterley, "'Not in the Least American,'" 891, 889.

99. Zagarell, "Narrative of Community," 517.

100. Barry, *Robert Frost on Writing,* 45.

101. Rose Terry Cooke, "The West Shetucket Railway," *Independent,* 12 September 1872, 2. Frost published his first poem, "My Butterfly," in the *Independent* in 1894.

102. "Local Color and After," editorial, *Nation,* 27 September 1919, 426–27.

## Chapter 3

1. One of the "old virtues" was lyricism; in 1936 Untermeyer noted that, "as late as 1928, most of the critics were surprised that the writer identified with the long monologs in *North of Boston* should turn to lyrics, forgetting that Frost's first volume (written in the 1890s and published twenty years later) was wholly and insistently lyrical" (*The Recognition of Robert Frost,* ed. Richard Thornton [New York: Henry Holt and Co., 1937], 179).

2. It is interesting that Frost planned to include both "Snow" and "The Witch of Coös" (along with "Paul's Wife," "West-Running Brook," and others) in an expanded edition of *North of Boston.* See Jeffrey S. Cramer, *Robert Frost among His Poems: A Literary Companion to the Poet's Own Biographical Contexts and Associations* (Jefferson, NC: McFarland, 1996), 60, 69, 70, 95; and Lawrance Thompson and R. H. Winnick, *Robert Frost: The Later Years, 1938–1963* (New York: Holt, Rinehart and Winston, 1976), 178.

3. Published in a San Francisco newspaper, Belle Moodie Frost's poem "The Artist's Motive" speaks explicitly of obtaining money for art in order to pay for food, shelter, and clothing. It opens: "'Tis nearly done! And when it is—my picture, here, / I'll cast it forth as naught into the hand that gives / To me what most I need—gold, gold!" See Lawrance Thompson, *Robert Frost: The Early Years, 1874–1915* (New York: Holt, Rinehart and Winston, 1966), 488–91; William H. Pritchard, *Frost: A Literary Life Reconsidered* (New York: Oxford University Press, 1984), 31–32.

4. Emily Dickinson, *The Poems of Emily Dickinson,* ed. Thomas H. Johnson (Cambridge: Harvard University Press, 1963), 544, P709.

5. Frank Lentricchia, *Modernist Quartet* (Cambridge: Cambridge University Press, 1994), 51.

6. Sandra M. Gilbert, "The American Sexual Politics of Walt Whitman and Emily Dickinson," in *Reconstructing American Literary History,* ed. Sacvan Bercovitch (Cambridge: Harvard University Press, 1986), 130.

7. *Selected Prose of Robert Frost,* ed. Hyde Cox and Edward Connery Lathem (New York: Collier Books, 1968), 141; emphasis added.

8. Walter J. Ong discusses the use of an educated "father speech" (*patrius sermo*) that has traditionally been used to exclude women from access to power; in contrast is the everyday speech of the "mother tongue" (*materna lingua*). See *Fighting for Life* (Ithaca: Cornell University Press, 1981), 36–37; also Ong, *The Presence of the Word: Some Prolegomena for Cultural and Religious History* (New Haven: Yale University Press, 1967), 249–50. For one application of Ong's ideas, see Sandra M. Gilbert and Susan Gubar, *No Man's Land,* Vol. 1, *The War of the Words* (New Haven: Yale University Press, 1988), 243, 253ff. For a direct comparison of Frost with Thoreau, see George Monteiro, *Robert Frost and the New England Literary Renaissance* (Lexington: University of Kentucky Press, 1988), 3–4, 57–111.

9. Henry David Thoreau, "Reading," *Walden and Selected Essays* (1854; reprint, New York: Hendricks, 1973), 95.

10. A variety of critics have observed that, since gay "identity" emerged only in the latter part of the nineteenth-century, the term *gay* (or *lesbian*) is anachronistic as applied to earlier writers. I use the term here, aware of its limitations, because of its legibility; I complicate the notion of sexuality in Frost in the next chapter. On terminology, see Lee Edelman, *Homographesis: Essays in Gay Literary and Cultural Theory* (New York: Routledge, 1994), 3–23; Ed Cohen, "Are We (Not) What We Are Becoming? 'Gay' 'Identity,' 'Gay Studies,' and the Disciplining of Knowledge," in *Engendering Men: The Question of Male Feminist Criticism,* ed. Joseph A. Boone and Michael Cadden (New York: Routledge, 1990), 161–75; Eve Kosofsky Sedgwick, *The Epistemology of the Closet* (Berkeley: University of California Press, 1990), 16–18; Bonnie Zimmerman, "What Has Never Been: An Overview of Lesbian Feminist Criticism," in *The New Feminist Criticism, Essays on Women, Literature, and Theory,* ed. Elaine Showalter (New York: Pantheon, 1985), 200–224; Louie Crew and Rictor Norton, "The Homophobic Imagination: An Editorial," *College English* 36 (1974): 285; Catharine R. Stimpson, "Zero-Degree Deviancy: The Lesbian Novel in English," *Where the Meanings Are: Feminism and Cultural Spaces* (New York: Methuen, 1988), 97; Adrienne Rich, "Compulsory Heterosexuality and Lesbian Existence," *Blood, Bread, and Poetry* (New York: Norton, 1986), 23–75; Catharine R. Stimpson, "Afterword: Lesbian Studies in the 1990s," in *Lesbian Texts and Contexts: Radical Revisions,* ed. Karla Jay and Joanne Glasgow (New York: New York University Press, 1990), 377–82; Marilyn R. Farwell, "Heterosexual Plots and Lesbian Subtexts: Toward a Theory of Lesbian Narrative Space," in Jay and Glasgow, *Lesbian Texts and Contexts,* 91–103; Penelope J. Engelbrecht, "'Lifting Belly Is a Language': The Postmodern Lesbian Subject," *Feminist Studies* 16.1 (1990): 85–114; Diana Fuss, "Inside/Out," in *inside/out, Lesbian Theories, Gay Theories,* ed. Diana Fuss (New York: Routledge, 1991), 2.

11. Karen Oakes, "'I stop somewhere waiting for you': Whitman's Femi-

ninity and the Reader of *Leaves of Grass*," in *Out of Bounds: Male Writers and Gender(ed) Criticism*, ed. Laura Claridge and Elizabeth Langland (Amherst: University of Massachusetts Press, 1990), 169–85.

12. Walter J. Ong, *Orality and Literacy: The Technology of the Word* (New York: Methuen, 1982), 160, 162.

13. Robert Frost, "The Unmade Word, Or Fetching and Far-Fetching," in *Robert Frost on Writing*, ed. Elaine Barry (New Brunswick: Rutgers University Press, 1973), 145. See George Monteiro, *Robert Frost and the New England Renaissance* (Lexington: University Press of Kentucky, 1988), 3–4.

14. Sarah Orne Jewett, "The Passing of Sister Barsett," *A Native of Winby* (Boston: Houghton Mifflin, 1893), 152–53.

15. Ibid., 158.

16. C. Day Lewis, Introduction, *Selected Poems of Robert Frost*, as cited in Louise Bogan, "Robert Frost," in *A Poet's Alphabet* (New York: McGraw-Hill, 1970), 176; Pritchard, *Frost: A Literary Life Reconsidered*, 93. Pritchard also highlights the powerful "digressiveness" of the minister's speech in "The Black Cottage" as a means to enhance the "actuality" and "intimacy" of Frost's art in *North of Boston* as a whole in relation to the lives of women (93). Walter Jost comments upon the poet's "ideal of relaxed everyday talk and gossip" and discusses "The Death of the Hired Man" as "a paradigm of gossip in the familiar sense, two people talking about an absent third person" ("Lessons in the Conversation that We Are: Robert Frost's 'Death of the Hired Man,'" *College English* 58.4 [1996]: 399, 401; see also Bogan, "Robert Frost," 176; Yvor Winters, "Robert Frost: or, the Spiritual Drifter as Poet," *The Function of Criticism: Problems and Exercises* [Denver: Swallow Press, 1957], 160).

17. Patricia Meyer Spacks, *Gossip* (New York: Alfred A. Knopf, 1985), 6, 8–9, 12.

18. Ibid., 17. Spacks constructs an analogy between gossip and fiction; here I am extending her account to include poetry as well.

19. Ibid., 5.

20. Ibid., 11.

21. Ibid., 40.

22. Alice Brown, "The Mortuary Chest," *Tiverton Tales* (Boston: Houghton Mifflin, 1898), 52. Oral traditions have been, and continue to be, important for women and other marginalized groups. See Carolyn G. Heilbrun, *Writing a Woman's Life* (New York: Ballantine, 1988), 44, 46; Adrienne Rich, *Blood, Bread, and Poetry: Selected Prose, 1979–1985* (New York: Norton, 1986), 137–38; Susan Stanford Friedman, "Craving Stories: Narrative and Lyric in Contemporary Theory and Women's Long Poems," in *Feminist Measures: Soundings in Poetry and Theory*, ed. Lynn Keller and Cristanne Miller (Ann Arbor: University of Michigan Press, 1994), 16; Lennard Davis, *Resisting Novels* (New York: Methuen, 1987), 143; Walter Benjamin, "The Storyteller," in *Illuminations*, ed. Hannah Arendt (New York: Schocken, 1968), 83–85. The role of storytelling as a survival mechanism also appears in much contemporary fiction by women, from Sandra Cisneros's *The House on Mango Street* to Toni Morrison's *Beloved*. While many of these contemporary accounts based in oral traditions are written down and while they sometimes

possess individual speakers, they often retain the traditions' emphasis on community-centered values.

23. Spacks, *Gossip,* 65.

24. Bogan, *Poet's Alphabet,* 172. In terms similar to Frost, Jewett was often located by critics in an intermediate state between "fiction" and "sketch"; for an indication of the shape of the debate, see Ann Romines, *The Home Plot: Women, Writing and Domestic Ritual* (Amherst: University of Massachusetts Press, 1992), 8; Elizabeth Ammons, "Going in Circles: The Female Geography of Jewett's *The Country of the Pointed Firs," Studies in the Literary Imagination* 16 (1983): 83–92.

25. Ann Douglas Wood, "The Literature of Impoverishment: The Women Local Colorists in America, 1865–1914," *Women's Studies* 1 (1972): 3–45; Josephine Donovan, *New England Local Color Literature: A Woman's Tradition* (New York: Frederick Ungar, 1983), 1–10. More recently, Linda Grasso traces elements of sympathy between the two generations of writers by focusing on "the muted boundaries, the overlaps, the ambiguities" that are especially visible in a text like Freeman's "A Poetess" ("'Thwarted Life, Mighty Hunger, Unfinished Work': The Legacy of Nineteenth-Century Women Writing in America," *American Transcendental Quarterly* 8.2 [1994]: 102).

26. E. C. Stedman, *An American Anthology, 1787–1900* (1901; reprint, New York: Glenwood Press, 1968), n.p.

27. Howells, "Editor's Easy Chair," *Harper's Monthly Magazine* 131.784 (September 1915): 635; Donald Sheehy, "'Not Quite All, My Dear': Gender and Voice in Frost," *Texas Studies in Literature and Language* 36.4 (Winter 1994): 416.

28. Susan Gillman, "Regionalism and Nationalism in Jewett's *Country of the Pointed Firs,*" in *New Essays on* The Country of the Pointed Firs, ed. June Howard (New York: Cambridge University Press, 1994), 101–17; Stephanie Foote, "'I Feared to Find Myself a Foreigner': Revisiting Regionalism in Sarah Orne Jewett's *The Country of the Pointed Firs," Arizona Quarterly* 52.2 (1996): 39, 42.

29. Foote, "'I Feared to Find Myself a Foreigner,'" 57–58.

30. Clement Wood, *Poets of America* (New York: E. P. Dutton, 1925), 156. Bogan, *Poet's Alphabet* 177; Jeffrey Meyers, *Robert Frost: A Biography* (Boston: Houghton Mifflin, 1996), 178; Robert Faggen, *Robert Frost and the Challenge of Darwin* (Ann Arbor: University of Michigan Press, 1997), 211; Katherine Kearns, *Robert Frost and a Poetics of Appetite* (Cambridge: Cambridge University Press, 1994), 135.

31. As Sandra M. Gilbert and Susan Gubar note of the early twentieth century, "male thinkers were daunted by women's new-found libidinous energy, and literary men tended to reenvision the battle of the sexes as an erotically charged sexual struggle" (*War of the Words,* 35).

32. Patricia Wallace, "The 'Estranged Point of View': The Thematics of Imagination in Frost's Poetry," in *Frost: Centennial Essays II,* ed. Jac Tharpe (Jackson: University of Mississippi Press, 1976), 184, 185, 182; emphasis added.

33. Gilbert and Gubar, *War of the Words,* 135.

34. Another, and perhaps much more frightening prospect for the poet who increasingly sought a unified, autonomous, and closely controlled sense of self is that the witch's voice is his own; "Frost here displaces his feminine and maternal identities so that they emerge in mediational constructs: the 'witch' becomes a speaker

whose 'otherness' allows her both behaviors and insights that the man of moderation must repudiate in himself" (Kearns, *Robert Frost and a Poetics of Appetite*, 137).

35. See Lawrance Thompson, *Robert Frost: The Early Years, 1874–1915*, 21, 35, 37, 38. On responses to the "effeminization" of public realms in America at this time, see Michael Kimmel, *Manhood in America: A Cultural History* (New York: Free Press, 1996), 121.

36. On Toffile's name, see Marcus, "Whole Pattern," 99. We should also notice that the first edition of *New Hampshire* has Lajway's name as Barre, which certainly implies his function as restrainer. See Edward Connery Lathem, *The Poetry of Robert Frost* (New York: Holt, Rinehart and Winston, 1975), 548.

37. Wallace, "'Estranged Point of View,'" 184.

38. Cited in Cook, *Living Voice of Robert Frost*, 77.

39. This recording is cited by Wallace, "'Estranged Point of View,'" 184; see also Robert Frost, *Robert Frost Reads His Poetry*, performed by Robert Frost, Caedmon CP1060, audiocassette (1956). One of the difficulties in sorting out reader-speaker-author relations here resides in the poet's conflation of fact and fiction, of actual local gossip and his own embroidery upon it. Frost once observed (though we must take this with as much salt as many of his pronouncements) that this witch is "a veritable witch in a county in upper New Hampshire. . . . Do not approach this witch with condescension" (cited in Reginald L. Cook, in "Robert Frost's Asides on His Poetry," in *On Frost: The Best From American Literature*, ed. Edwin H. Cady and Louis J. Budd [Durham: Duke University Press, 1991], 37).

40. Mrs. Moody P. Gore and Mrs. Guy E. Speare, eds., *New Hampshire Folk Tales* (n.p.: New Hampshire Federation of Women's Clubs, 1932), 150, 153, 158.

41. Randall Jarrell, *Poetry and the Age* (New York: Ecco Press, 1980), 62.

42. William Little, *The History of Warren, A Mountain Hamlet, Located among the White Hills of New Hampshire* (Manchester, NH: William E. Moore, 1870), 434, 440. Both *The History of Warren* and *New Hampshire Folk Tales* inscribe oral traditions, and, in writing "The Witch of Coös" and "The Pauper Witch of Grafton," Frost is consciously entering into such traditions while he "introduce[s] new elements into old stories" (Ong, *Orality and Literacy*, 42).

43. Sarah Orne Jewett, "A Farmer's Sorrow," *Manhattan* 3.3 (1884): 212–13. I have cited only the opening lines. I am grateful to Paula Bennett for pointing me toward this poem.

44. For a discussion of Thaxter's work in the context of regionalism, see Perry Westbrook, *Acres of Flint: Writers of Rural New England, 1870–1900* (Washington, DC: Scarecrow Press, 1951), 139–41; see also Jane Vallier, *Poet on Demand* (1982; reprint, Portsmouth, NH: Peter E. Randall, 1994), 1–136.

45. Howard, "Introduction: Sarah Orne Jewett and the Traffic in Words," 4.

46. On Jewett's use of nostalgia, see Foote, "'I Feared to Find Myself a Foreigner,'" 41. Writers have long been in disagreement about Jewett's relation to sentimentalism and nostalgia, their view often depending upon their agenda. See, for example, Fred Lewis Pattee, who observes: "With her there was no preliminary dallying with mid-century sentiment and sensationalism" (*A History of American Literature since 1870* [New York: Century, 1915], 231).

47. Pattee, *History of American Literature,* 234 (emphasis added), 221.

48. Granville Hicks, *The Great Tradition: An Interpretation of American Literature since the Civil War,* rev. ed. (n.p.: Biblio and Tannen, 1967), 103, 105, 245. Amy Lowell, *Tendencies in Modern American Poetry* (New York: Macmillan, 1917), 135.

49. Donald Davidson, "Regionalism and Nationalism in American Literature," *Still Rebels, Still Yankees and Other Essays* (n.p.: Louisiana State University Press, 1972), 270–71. More recently, Susan Gillman has suggested that "there is a significant link between regionalism and nationalism, one that includes but goes beyond simple rejection" ("Regionalism and Nationalism in Jewett's *Country of the Pointed Firs,*" 102).

50. Van Wyck Brooks, *New England: Indian Summer, 1865–1915* (n.p.: E. P. Dutton, 1940), 524, 543, 542, 509 n. 2.

51. In 1927 Elizabeth Shepley Sargent argued that "those who mistake his verse for a product local or provincial have been too literal. They have failed to catch the poet in his game of hide-and-seek. . . . his subject-matter, for all its clear geographical limits, is universal" (*Recognition of Robert Frost,* 147). And, as Robert P. Tristram Coffin would put it in 1938, "Frost's particulars everywhere run out to great universals," and "what begins as sectional and New England poetry . . . end[s] by being poetry wide enough to cover the world" (*New Poetry of New England: Frost and Robinson* [1938; reprint, New York: Russell and Russell, 1964], 60, 125). By 1948 W. G. O'Donnell would again argue, "In so far as Frost is a voice of New England, he is a minor figure in contemporary literature; to the extent that he makes New England universal in meaning and implication, he is a significant writer" ("Robert Frost and New England: A Revaluation," *Yale Review* 37.4 [1948]: 710). This "paradox" is one that contemporary readers are equally eager to foster; a recent television broadcast about the poet closed with the affirmation that Frost "wrote poems that were both local and universal" ("Robert Frost: Versed in Country Things," New Hampshire Public Television, 1989; re-aired September 1996).

52. Stedman, *American Anthology,* n.p.

53. Jac Tharpe, *Frost: Centennial Essays* (Jackson: University Press of Mississippi, 1974), 13.

54. Davidson, *Still Rebels,* 268.

55. Amy Kaplan, "Nation, Region, and Empire," in *Columbia Literary History of the American Novel,* ed. Emory Elliott (New York: Columbia University Press, 1991), 240–66; Eric J. Sundquist, "Realism and Regionalism," in *Columbia Literary History of the United States,* ed. Emory Elliott (New York: Columbia University Press, 1988), 501–24; James M. Cox, "Regionalism: A Diminished Thing," *Columbia Literary History of the United States,* 761–84; Howard, "Introduction: Sarah Orne Jewett and the Traffic in Words," 1–37.

56. Bogan, *Poet's Alphabet,* 178–79.

57. Foote, "'I Feared to Find Myself a Foreigner,'" 59n. Foote makes this observation in the context of a discussion of regionalism generally and Jewett in particular.

58. Even Alice Brown would succumb to the critical mood concerning regionalist writing, moving in the early part of the twentieth century from the

intense and accurate sketches of New England in *Meadow Grass* and *Tiverton Tales* to more popular romantic forms.

59. Stanley T. Williams and Nelson F. Adkins, *Courses of Reading in American Literature with Bibliographies* (New York: Harcourt, Brace, 1930), 100, 102, 114–16, 122, 127–31, 141–42.

60. Westbrook, *Acres of Flint,* 183 (emphasis added), 82, 139, 184–85.

61. Lionel Trilling, "A Speech on Robert Frost: A Cultural Episode," in *Robert Frost: A Collection of Critical Essays,* ed. James M. Cox (Englewood Cliffs, NJ: Prentice-Hall, 1962), 154, 157.

62. Henry W. Wells, *The American Way of Poetry* (New York: Columbia University Press, 1943), 107–8.

63. Sarah Orne Jewett, "The Foreigner," in *The Country of the Pointed Firs and Other Stories,* ed. Sarah Way Sherman (Hanover: University Press of New England, 1997), 236–37.

64. Ibid., 241.

65. See John Kemp, *Robert Frost and New England: The Poet as Regionalist* (Princeton: Princeton University Press, 1979), 177–84; Pritchard, *Frost: A Literary Life Reconsidered,* 155–63. Calling *New Hampshire* the poet's "most underrated book," Meyers praises it for revealing "his supremacy in shorter poems" (*Robert Frost,* 181). For Frank Lentricchia, *New Hampshire* represents a turning point in Frost's career (*Modernist Quartet,* 116, 118).

66. Robert Faggen is one of the few readers to offer a sustained and serious discussion of "Maple"; he sees it as a representation of the "possibilities of growth" (*Robert Frost and the Challenge of Darwin,* 203–8).

67. Whether in oral or in written form, the storyteller embodies and speaks to a community and attempts to let listeners draw their own conclusions; in the work of the master storyteller Benjamin writes about, "the psychological connection of the events is not forced upon the reader. It is left up to him to interpret things the way he understands them, and thus the narrative [the story] achieves an amplitude that information lacks" ("Storyteller," 89).

68. Judith Oster regards "Maple" as a poem about reading: "The question of how to read, or how much to read into, a text does not simply arise from the reading of a Frost poem. It is a question about which he wrote poems, such as . . . 'Maple'" (*Toward Robert Frost: The Reader and the Poet* [Athens: University of Georgia Press, 1991], 44).

69. Elaine Showalter, "Women and the Literary Curriculum," *College English* 32 (1971): 856–57.

70. Oster makes this comment about other lines in the poem (*Toward Robert Frost,* 46).

71. Peter Filene, *Him/Her/Self* (Baltimore: Johns Hopkins University Press, 1986), 121.

72. Thompson, *Robert Frost: The Early Years, 1874–1915,* 125.

73. Elinor's achievement was extremely rare for women of her day (Filene, *Him/Her/Self,* 26). Interestingly, Jeanie, like Elinor, was especially gifted; as Lawrance Thompson documents, Mrs. Frost confided to friends that "perhaps the good Lord had given the child more brains than she needed. Too bright for her age,

she was inclined to make a world of her own out of her imaginings and her reading." As she grew older, "Jeanie's desperate retreat into books . . . failed her. As long as she had asserted superiority over her brother, scholastically, she seemed to derive adequate sustenance from pride alone. When he surpassed her, during their first year in high school as freshmen, all her defenses began to collapse" (*Robert Frost,* 113).

74. Kearns reviews the poem in terms of the drama enacted between father, mother, and daughter, arguing that women "who fail to recognize their mothers may remain for a time domesticated and safe, temporary antitheses to the witch" (*Robert Frost and a Poetics of Appetite,* 100, 20).

75. Fetterley, *The Resisting Reader,* 89.

76. See Lesley Lee Francis, "'A Decade of Stirring Times': Robert Frost and Amy Lowell," *New England Quarterly* 59 (1986): 508–22; Pritchard, *Frost: A Literary Life Reconsidered,* 175–76; Nathaniel Hawthorne, *The Letters of Nathaniel Hawthorne to William Ticknor 1851–1879,* ed. C. E. Frazer Clark, Jr. (1910; reprint, Newark, NJ: Carteret Book Club, 1972), 78.

77. I am indebted to Paula Bennett for this observation.

78. Gilbert and Gubar, *War of the Words,* 143; Leslie Fiedler, "Literature and Lucre," *What Was Literature?* (New York: Simon and Schuster, 1982), 23–33; Ann Douglas, *The Feminization of American Culture* (New York: Knopf, 1977), 114, 282–85; Nina Baym, "Melodramas of Beset Manhood: How Theories of American Fiction Exclude Women Writers," *American Quarterly* 33 (1981): 123–39.

79. Robert Frost, notebook, c. 1919–21, #001723, Dartmouth College Library, Hanover, NH.

80. Sandra Zagarell, "Narrative of Community: The Identification of a Genre," *Signs: Journal of Woman in Culture and Society* 13.3 (1988): 502.

## Chapter 4

1. Walt Whitman, "A Woman Waits for Me," in *Leaves of Grass: A Textual Variorum of the Printed Poems,* ed. Sculley Bradley et al., 3 vols. (New York: New York University Press, 1980), 1:239–40, ll. 28–30.

2. Frost also evokes what Lentricchia calls, in another context, "a feat, a kind of performance, a display of prowess, the virtuosity, the poetry of work" (*Modernist Quartet* [Cambridge: Cambridge University Press, 1994], 102). On the development of the homosexual as an identity, see E. Anthony Rotundo, *American Manhood: Transformations in Masculinity from the Revolution to the Modern Era* (New York: Basic Books, 1993), 274–79. Marjorie Garber discusses the "back-formation" of "heterosexuality" from "homosexuality"; "before people began to speak of 'homosexuals' as a kind of person, a social species, there was no need for a term like 'heterosexual'" (*Vice Versa, Bisexuality and the Eroticism of Everyday Life* [New York: Simon and Schuster, 1995], 40).

3. Sandra M. Gilbert and Susan Gubar, *No Man's Land,* vol. 2, *Sexchanges* (New Haven: Yale University Press, 1989), 301, 302.

4. Elaine Showalter, *Sexual Anarchy: Gender and Culture at the Fin de Siècle* (New York: Viking, 1990), 8; see Michael Kimmel, *Manhood in America: A Cultural History* (New York: Free Press, 1996), 78; Peter G. Filene, *Him/Her/Self: Sex Roles*

*in Modern America*, 2d. ed. (Baltimore: Johns Hopkins University Press, 1986), 78–79.

5. As James Gifford aptly observes, "For too long critics have tended to view homosexual writing very narrowly, concentrating primarily on sexual attraction; but every 'homosexual' tale need not outline in overt form a romantic entanglement between men or between women" (*Dayneford's Library, American Homosexual Writing, 1900–1913* [Amherst: University of Massachusetts Press, 1995], 30).

6. Robert K. Martin's work on Whitman articulates vividly the academic suppression of the homoerotic. He affirms, "The history of Whitman criticism in this connection is shameful. I know of no parallel example of the willful distortion of meaning and the willful misreading of a poet in order to suit critics' own social or moral prejudices." Martin also acknowledges the poet's attempts, "late in his own lifetime, to conceal his homosexuality from outsiders" (*The Homosexual Tradition in American Poetry* [Austin: University of Texas Press, 1979], xvii, 6, xvi). Frost's increasing emphasis on his hypermasculinity, I am suggesting here, indicates a similar if less acute trajectory. For other accounts of Whitman's homosexuality, see Michael Moon, *Disseminating Whitman: Revision and Corporeality in* Leaves of Grass (Cambridge: Harvard University Press, 1991); Byrne R. S. Fone, *Masculine Landscapes: Walt Whitman and the Homoerotic Text* (Carbondale: Southern Illinois University Press. 1992); M. Jimmie Killingsworth, *Whitman's Poetry of the Body: Sexuality, Politics, and the Text* (Chapel Hill: University of North Carolina Press, 1989).

Acknowledging the complexity and the historical embeddedness of terms like *lesbian* and *gay*, some clarification of terminology is required at this point. For Eve Kosofsky Sedgwick *homosocial* encompasses "men-promoting-the-interests-of-men" to "men-loving-men," while for James R. Dawes (who borrows from Sedgwick), it signifies "the spectrum of male interaction ranging from the most superficial to the most intimate. It includes, but is not limited to homosexuality." These definitions parallel those of Adrienne Rich's "lesbian continuum" in "Compulsory Heterosexuality and Lesbian Existence." The problem with this kind of inclusiveness, as many gay and lesbian critics have observed, is the dispersal of uniquely "gay" or "lesbian" identities based on sexuality (Eve Kosofsky Sedgwick, *Between Men: English Literature and Male Homosocial Desire* [New York: Columbia University Press, 1985], 3; James R. Dawes, "Masculinity and Transgression in Robert Frost," *American Literature* 65.2 [1993]: 311–12n.; Adrienne Rich, "Compulsory Heterosexuality and Lesbian Existence" in *Blood, Bread, and Poetry, Collected Essays, 1979–1985* [New York: Norton, 1986], 23–75).

I will use *homosocial* in a somewhat more restricted fashion, to signify "same-sex," nonsexual social relations among men (a business lunch, a shared workout at the gym); *homoerotic* will indicate erotic feelings or desires that are not internally or explicitly defined and not consciously acted upon. *Homosexual* will represent self-aware, self-defined sexual behavior between members of the same sex. I acknowledge that there are difficulties with these distinctions as well, one such difficulty being that the boundaries between these terms are essentially arbitrary and highly permeable. We should bear in mind the notion of performativity of the sexualized self elaborated by Diana Fuss and Judith Butler (Fuss, "Inside/Out," in *inside/out, Lesbian Theories, Gay Theories,* ed. Diana Fuss [New York: Routledge, 1991], 6–7;

Butler, "Imitation and Gender Insubordination," in Fuss, *inside/out,* 25). What I hope to recuperate with these formulations is the relative absence of charge at one end of the continuum (homosocial) compared to the highly electric and intense connotations of homosexual. How this charge is coded depends, of course, on the social context in which the terms are applied, as the discussion that follows attempts to indicate.

7. As Thomas E. Yingling points out, it is particularly crucial to be attentive to "the politics and practices of reading" in relation to homosexual literature (*Hart Crane and the Homosexual Text: New Thresholds, New Anatomies* [Chicago: University of Chicago Press, 1990], 3). In another important remark for the present context Judith Butler points out: "It seems crucial to resist the model of power that would set up racism and homophobia and misogyny as parallel or analogical relations. The assertion of their abstract or structural equivalence not only misses the specific histories of their construction and elaboration, but also delays the important work of thinking through the ways in which these vectors of power require and deploy each other for the purpose of their own articulation" (*Bodies That Matter: On the Discursive Limits of "Sex"* [New York: Routledge, 1993], 18).

8. Gilbert and Gubar, *Sexchanges,* 216.

9. E. Anthony Rotundo, *American Manhood,* 275; Gifford, *Dayneford's Library,* 3–7.

10. Gilbert and Gubar, *Sexchanges,* 222.

11. D. H. Lawrence, "Ego-Bound Women," in *The Complete Poems of D. H. Lawrence,* ed. Vivian de Sola Pinto and F. Warren Roberts (New York: Penguin, 1977), 475. It is worth noting that the poem goes on to criticize the "ego-bound condition of mankind."

12. Rotundo, *American Manhood,* 227, 231. In the context of a cultural mandate for muscular masculinity Frost may have had some difficulties in another sense: he was frequently ill in his youth and younger adulthood. Affiliated with weakness, illness has traditionally been associated with femininity in the United States. See Diane Price Herndl, *Invalid Women: Figuring Feminine Illness in American Fiction and Culture, 1840–1940* (Chapel Hill: University of North Carolina Press, 1993); Kimmel, *Manhood in America,* 181.

13. In poem after poem we see masculinity also problematically related to economic concerns. If men's focus is merely financial or work related, as it is initially for Warren in "The Death of the Hired Man," ostensibly for Amy's husband in "Home Burial," and uniformly for Len in "A Servant to Servants," they are alienated from their female partners.

14. Rotundo, *American Manhood,* 44, 270.

15. Katherine Kearns, *Robert Frost and a Poetics of Appetite* (Cambridge: Cambridge University Press: 1994), 28.

16. Ibid., 24.

17. Nancy Chodorow, *The Reproduction of Mothering: Psychoanalysis and the Sociology of Gender* (Berkeley: University of California Press, 1978), 169; Jean Baker Miller, *Toward a New Psychology of Women* (Boston: Beacon Press, 1977), 83; Carol Gilligan, *In a Different Voice: Psychological Theory and Women's Development* (Cambridge: Harvard University Press, 1982), 70–71.

18. D. H. Lawrence, "Whitman," in *Whitman: A Collection of Critical Essays,* ed. Roy Harvey Pearce (Englewood Cliffs: Prentice-Hall, 1962), 13, 16, 15.

19. F. O. Matthiessen, *American Renaissance: Art and Expression in the Age of Emerson and Whitman* (London: Oxford University Press, 1941), 535; emphasis added.

20. To a certain degree Matthiessen's remarks reveal a great deal about his own poignant persona as guardian of heterosexual masculinity, and they underscore Kearns's assertion that Frost regarded critics as punitive and paternal (*Robert Frost and a Poetics of Appetite,* 47). For a valuable discussion of Matthiessen's life, see Susan Howe, *The Birth-mark: Unsettling the Wilderness in American Literary History* (Hanover: University Press of New England, 1993), 10–11, 13–18, 159–62. Matthiessen's connection between sexuality and gender once again highlights the intertwining of misogyny and homophobia in high literary culture. See Alan Golding, *From Outlaw to Classic: Canons in American Poetry* (Madison: University of Wisconsin Press, 1995), 101–2.

21. Kearns, *Robert Frost and a Poetics of Appetite,* 131; emphasis added.

22. Cited in Lentricchia, *Modernist Quartet,* 78, 90; cited in Gilbert and Gubar, *No Man's Land,* vol. 1, *The War of the Words* (New Haven: Yale University Press, 1988), 156.

23. Rotundo, *American Manhood,* 278, 273; Gifford, *Dayneford's Library,* 19; Kimmel, *Manhood in America,* 100, 122.

24. Lee Edelman, *Homographesis: Essays in Gay Literary and Cultural Theory* (New York: Routledge, 1994), 247n. This observation occurs specifically in relation to Lentricchia's blind spot in this regard. See also Dawes, "Masculinity and Transgression in Robert Frost," 303; Gifford, *Dayneford's Library,* 118–34. Edelman points out the way in which the image of the gay ("self-centered," phallocentric) man has been appropriated by patriarchal voices as representing a kind of false manhood, incorporating misogyny and hence absolving heterosexual male dominance and privilege. Nevertheless, I would argue that some gay men do use phallic centeredness as a means of cultural empowerment. That is, while there is no necessary connection between gayness and patriarchal privilege, there is a possible one.

25. Edelman, *Homographesis,* 28–29.

26. Frank Lentricchia, "The Resentments of Robert Frost," *American Literature* 62.2 (1990): 184; *Modernist Quartet,* 86.

27. Lentricchia, "Resentments," 184–85. Dawes explores the sexualized component of Frost's voice more generally, acknowledging that "criticism on Frost has . . . consistently traced the edges of the problem of homosocial relationships, building up a discourse that surrounds but never penetrates and creating, ultimately, a lacuna" ("Masculinity and Transgression," 298).

28. Dawes, "Masculinity and Transgression," 308.

29. Paula Bennett, "The Pea that Duty Locks: Lesbian and Feminist-Heterosexual Readings of Emily Dickinson's Poetry," in *Lesbian Texts and Contexts,* ed. Karla Jay and Joanne Glasgow (New York: New York University Press, 1990), 113, 114.

30. Paula Bennett, "Critical Clitoridectomy: Female Sexual Imagery and Feminist Psychoanalytic Theory," *Signs* 18.2 (1993): 237.

31. Ibid., 242.

32. Karl Keller, *The Only Kangaroo Among the Beauty, Emily Dickinson and America* (Baltimore: Johns Hopkins University Press, 1979), 309–10.

33. Robert Faggen, *Robert Frost and the Challenge of Darwin* (Ann Arbor: University of Michigan Press, 1997), 211; see also 211–15.

34. Edelman, *Homographesis,* 39. See Eve Kosofky Sedgwick, *The Epistemology of the Closet* (Berkeley: University of California Press, 1990), 31–32. Dawes elaborates on the homoerotic bonding between the men; citing Freud, he observes that in the poem "male heterosexuality can be defined as 'traffic in women,' in which the female is used as a 'conduit of a relationship in which the true *partner* is a man'" ("Masculinity and Transgression," 308; see also 308–10).

35. Kearns, *Robert Frost and a Poetics of Appetite,* 112. For a provocative discussion of Frost's poem "The Last Mowing" in the context of gender identity, see Mark Richardson, *The Ordeal of Robert Frost: The Poet and His Poetics* (Urbana: University of Illinois Press, 1997), 61–62.

36. See Josephine Donovan, "Breaking the Sentence: Local-Color Literature and Subjugated Knowledges," in *The (Other) American Traditions: Nineteenth-Century Women Writers,* ed. Joyce Warren (New Brunswick: Rutgers University Press, 1993), 229. One intriguing example of the witch in regionalist fiction occurs in Alice Brown's "At Sudleigh Fair," *Meadow-Grass: Tales of New England Life* (Boston: Copeland and Day, 1896), 191–228.

37. Robert P. Tristram Coffin, *New Poetry of New England: Frost and Robinson* (1938; reprint, New York: Russell and Russell, 1964), 28.

38. Harriet Monroe, "Comment: Edna St. Vincent Millay," in *Critical Essays on Edna St. Vincent Millay,* ed. William Thesing (Boston: G. K. Hall, 1993), 133. This essay is reprinted from *Poetry* (August 1924): 260–64.

39. Coffin, *New Poetry of New England,* 28.

40. The second edition of *The Oxford English Dictionary* lists a citation for *horny*—meaning "lecherous"—as early as 1889 (*OED,* prepared by J. A. Simpson and E. S. C. Weiner [Oxford: Clarendon Press, 1989], 7:394).

41. Kimmel, *Manhood in America,* 7.

42. Clara Robinson of "A Fountain" may be based on Frost's imaginative reconstruction of the life and work of a real woman, Clara Weaver Robinson (1854–1905), who taught at St. Lawrence University from the late 1870s to 1882. Although she was not on the faculty when Elinor attended (1892–95), she may have been well-known to the students, given her dedication to the institution and her involvement in its life. Her surviving poetry is metrically regular and substantively conventional, dealing mostly with faith, nature, and love—largely the kind of sentimental poetry that Frost's narrator (and by proxy, the poet himself) figuratively destroys and simultaneously appropriates in "A Fountain" (Clara Weaver Robinson, *Poems by Clara Weaver Robinson, Sonnets and Other Verses by Ethel Robinson Murphy,* ed. Ernest L. Robinson [Schenectady, NY: Riedinger and Riedinger, 1970]; for biographical information, see "Editor's Foreword," xi–xiii; and Marjory Robinson, "Clara Weaver Robinson," 1–3, in the same volume). In spite of my generalizations about Robinson's poems, there are a number that surprise and please, such as "The Country" (51).

43. Peter Filene comments on the menace of the new woman as well as on the general attitude of hostility between men and women in the opening decades of the twentieth century (*Him/Her/Self*, 42, 52).

44. Frost's reminiscence of Lowell's poetry, "The Poetry of Amy Lowell," which was published in *The Christian Science Monitor* for 16 May 1925, also subtly (and diminishingly) aligns her with an earlier and more floral tradition of poetry, in spite of his ostensibly generous assertion that "How often I have heard it in the voice and seen it in the eyes of this generation that Amy Lowell had lodged poetry with them to stay" (*CP* 712). Several writers argue that the relationship between the two poets was at least partially positive, including Jean Gould, Camille Roman, and Lesley Lee Francis. Gould remarks that their first meeting marked "the beginning of a kind of sparring friendship, a mixture of admiration, rivalry, and wit." Although Frost's posthumous tribute to the poet reflects his oversimplification of her work, he clearly felt some admiration for her. For her part Lowell remarked upon her "ever increasing admiration of his work, and a profound attachment to the man" (Gould, *Amy: The World of Amy Lowell and the Imagist Movement* [New York: Dodd, Mead, 1975], 169; see also 214, 335, 339–40; Roman, "Robert Frost and Three Female Modern Poets: Amy Lowell, Louise Bogan, and Edna Millay," *Robert Frost Review* [Fall 1995]: 62–69; Francis, "A Decade of 'Stirring Times': Robert Frost and Amy Lowell," *New England Quarterly* 59 [1986]: 508–22).

45. Amy Lowell, "Two Generations of American Poetry," *Poetry and Poets* (Boston: Houghton Mifflin, 1930), 116. Lowell also acknowledged the increasing power of women poets in the new poetry (121). For an important account of Lowell's life and work, see Cheryl Walker, "Amy Lowell and the Androgynous Persona," *Masks Outrageous and Austere: Culture, Psyche, and Persona in Modern Women Poets* (Bloomington: Indiana University Press, 1991), 16–43.

46. Jean Gould points out that Lowell's review in the *Atlantic* was a large part of what made *North of Boston* a best-seller (*Amy*, 159).

47. Cited in E. Claire Healey and Laura Ingram, "Amy Lowell," in *Dictionary of Literary Biography*, 3d ser., vol. 54, ed. Peter Quatermain (Detroit: Gale Research Press, 1987), 252. Louis Untermeyer, *The New Era in American Poetry* (New York: Henry Holt, 1919), 139.

48. Cited in Gould, *Amy*, 169; Lesley Lee Francis, "A Decade of 'Stirring Times,'" 511. Ironically, one element of Lowell's own attitude toward a popular audience is reflected in her comment to D. H. Lawrence about the potential reception of his Tortoise poems: "The public is a mole, a blind, blundering bat" (Elaine Healey and Keith Cushman, eds., *The Letters of D. H. Lawrence and Amy Lowell, 1914–1925* [Santa Barbara: Black Sparrow Press, 1985], 102). This quotation is part of Letter 65 (101–3).

49. John Kemp's suggestion that Lowell's critical frame for Frost would come to restrict future responses to the poet continues to hold true. See Jeffrey Meyers, *Robert Frost: A Biography* (Boston: Houghton Mifflin, 1996), 131, 152–53.

50. Cited in Francis, "A Decade of 'Stirring Times,'" 523.

51. Amy Lowell, "The Day that was That Day," in *Selected Poems of Amy Lowell*, ed. John Livingston Lowes (Boston: Houghton Mifflin, 1928), 150. For a

discussion of Lowell's dramatic poems, see Richard Benvenuto, *Amy Lowell* (Boston: Twayne, 1985), 85–94.

52. Gould, *Amy*, 348. In a letter to Albert Feuilleurat of early 1925, Lowell acknowledged, "Our attitudes [hers and Frost's] towards the natives of the New England countryside are rather different: he is much more sympathetic to them than I am and makes excuses for their idiosyncrasies (cited in S. Foster Damon, *Amy Lowell, A Chronicle* [Boston: Houghton Mifflin, 1935], 710). Damon informs us that one of Lowell's regionalist poems, "The Gravestone," "was an actual incident told her by Robert Frost" (712). The complex interactive component and mutual influences of this important relationship need to be explored more fully.

53. Amy Lowell, "A Critical Fable," *A Critical Fable* (Boston: Houghton Mifflin, 1922), 21. The poem was published anonymously; Lowell's identity as author was revealed in 1924. Lowell goes on to discuss Frost's role as a poet-in-residence and the creative compromises that such a role entailed (23–25). Perhaps it was difficult for the wealthy Lowell to understand fully Frost's financial and emotional predicament.

54. Like his contemporaries, Meyers depicts Lowell and her work—unfairly, I think—in severe and judgmental terms (*Robert Frost*, 130–31).

55. Lowell, *Selected Poems of Amy Lowell*, 154.

56. Gould, *Amy*, 356; see also 258, 275–78. On Frost's puritanical attitudes toward sexuality, see Meyers, *Robert Frost: A Biography*, 127. Many of Lowell's poems could be read as spoken by men, but as Gilbert and Gubar point out, "In the twentieth century . . . a number of lesbian writers have in various ways employed the strategy of male impersonation to usurp male authority and to reclaim the mother-muse for themselves" (*War of the Words*, 185, 217). On the masculine voice in Lowell's work as well as the connection between Frost and Lowell, see Emily Stipes Watts, *The Poetry of American Women from 1632 to 1945* (Austin: University of Texas Press, 1977), 159. As the twentieth century unfolded—in the years that Frost was beginning to be recognized—lesbian stories were common in such periodicals as the *Atlantic, Harper's,* and *Century,* though, as the second decade came to an end, such relationships were increasingly likely to be regarded with suspicion and censure (Lillian Faderman, *Surpassing the Love of Men: Romantic Friendship and Love between Women from the Renaissance to the Present* [New York: William Morrow, 1981], 302–8, 314–25).

57. Gould, *Amy*, 274.

58. Faderman, *Surpassing the Love of Men*, 332.

59. Mencken's comments continue in this vein for a rather lengthy paragraph ("The New Poetry Movement," in *Critical Essays on American Modernism,* ed. Michael J. Hoffman and Patrick D. Murphy [New York: G. K. Hall, 1992], 38).

60. Pound is quoted in C. David Heymann, *American Aristocracy: The Lives and Times of James Russell, Amy, and Robert Lowell* (New York: Dodd, Mead, 1980), 198.

61. Lowell is cited in Damon, *Amy Lowell: A Chronicle*, 604; and Gould, *Amy*, 318–19.

62. Louis Untermeyer, *From Another World: The Autobiography of Louis Untermeyer* (New York: Harcourt Brace, 1939), 102.

63. Clement Wood, *Amy Lowell* (New York: Harold Vinal, 1926), 173, 174; emphasis added to all of the Wood quotations. Cheryl Walker observes of Wood's biography that "this study of Lowell reflects the response to the poet's lesbianism by some of her contemporaries and is full of homophobia" ("Amy Lowell and the Androgynous Persona," 206 n. 29). In contrast to Wood's biography, Damon's is sympathetic and personal. It is interesting to note that, only two years before he published his Lowell biography, Wood had authored an advice book that "tried to reassure anxious young men that homosexuality was a stage of development out of which they would soon, thankfully, pass" (Kimmel, *Manhood in America,* 203; Wood, *Manhood: The Facts of Life Presented to Men* [Girard, KS: Haldeman-Julien, 1924]).

64. Cary Nelson, "The Fate of Gender in Modern American Poetry," in *Marketing Modernisms: Self-Promotion, Canonization, Rereading,* ed. Kevin J. H. Dettmar and Stephen Watt (Ann Arbor: University of Michigan Press, 1996), 336.

65. Van Wyck Brooks, *New England: Indian Summer, 1865–1915* (New York: E. P. Dutton, 1940), 532, 533–34.

66. Gould, *Amy,* 356; see Pritchard, *Frost: A Literary Life Reconsidered* (New York: Oxford University Press, 1984), 175–76.

67. Brown had a long-term intimate friendship with poet and critic Louise Imogen Guiney, as did Jewett with her publisher's widow, Annie Adams Fields. This labeling of Jewett and Brown occurs, of course, anachronistically and after the fact. As Marjorie Garber points out, many of the individuals subsequently identified as "lesbian" or "gay" could more accurately be described as "bisexual," and we need to be careful about this kind of narrow labeling (*Vice Versa,* 27–28).

68. W. Sutton, ed., *Newdick's Season of Frost: An Interrupted Biography of Robert Frost* (New York: New York University Press, 1976), 220–21.

69. Frost, c. 1913–17, notebook #001725, Dartmouth College Library, Hanover, NH. In a letter to Walter Pritchard Eaton of 1915, Frost affirmed his gratitude to Howells and Garnett for appreciating his blank verse, and he differentiated himself strongly from free verse poets (see *CP* 690). The notebook entry continues:

I am very much my own teacher
Now that we have settled that for the delight[?] of society
A word about my rhythm
I knew history whould [*sic*] want to know
I make it go this way
For the same reason that soldiers fall out of step in crossing a bridge
So the structure of the universe won't get to vibrating too much and break
        down
William Sharp had written such
Vers libre I am told
Never read him—or her

William Sharp (1855?–1905) was a Scottish poet and critic who wrote under the pen name of Fiona Macleod.

70. Rotundo, *American Manhood,* 251–52; Gifford, *Dayneford's Library,*

17–18, 188–21. See also Jackson Lears, *No Place of Grace: Antimodernism and the Transformation of American Culture, 1880–1920* (New York: Pantheon, 1981), 223; Lears points to the fluid, even "feminine," identifications available to men at the turn of the century.

71. Rotundo, *American Manhood*, 253.

72. Ibid., 277–78. On the development of a "visible gay subculture," see Kimmel, *Manhood in America*, 98–100.

73. Gifford, *Dayneford's Library*, 11.

74. As Gifford observes, however, the image of the aesthete was ubiquitous in American culture in the form of the ambiguous Arrow Collar Man (ibid., 17–18, 121–24). For another discussion of homosexuality and aestheticism, see Yingling, *Hart Crane and the Homosexual Text*, 31–32.

75. Brian Pronger, *The Arena of Masculinity: Sports, Homosexuality, and the Meaning of Sex* (New York: St. Martin's Press, 1990), 128; Gifford, *Dayneford's Library*, 98–117.

76. For an extended discussion of this story, see Gifford, *Dayneford's Library*, 124–26.

77. Meyers, *Robert Frost: A Biography*, 173.

78. This matrix of attitudes expressed toward Lowell and Cather suggests the very complicated nature of Frost's attitude toward homosexuality. Robert Frost, c. 1924, notebook #001734, Dartmouth College Library, Hanover, NH.

79. Dawes, "Masculinity and Transgression in Robert Frost," 300–301. Echoing Edelman, Dawes observes, "explicit homosexuality is a threat to the animus because of its traditional association with femininity, and thus with submission" (303); he also suggests that "The Axe-Helve" is the only affirmative representation of homosocial relations in Frost. See Norman Holland, *The Brain of Robert Frost: A Cognitive Approach to Literature* (New York: Routledge, 1988), 29–30.

80. Edelman, *Homographesis*, 19.

81. Walt Whitman, "Full of Life Now," *Leaves of Grass*, 2:407–8, ll. 1–8.

82. Karen Oakes, "'I stop somewhere waiting for you': Whitman's Femininity and the Reader of *Leaves of Grass*," in *Out of Bounds: Male Writers and Gender(ed) Criticism*, ed. Laura Claridge and Elizabeth Langland (Amherst: University of Massachusetts Press, 1990), 169–85.

83. Meyers, *Robert Frost: A Biography*, 63–64.

84. Willa Cather, *Introduction to The Best Stories of Sarah Orne Jewett* (Boston: Houghton Mifflin, 1924), xix.

85. Whitman, *Leaves of Grass*, 1:1, ll. 4–5. Lentricchia parallels this poem with Bryant's "To a Waterfowl"; see *Robert Frost: Modern Poetics and the Landscapes of Self* (Durham: Duke University Press, 1975), 36–38.

86. Ibid., 3:585, l. 2.

87. John Kemp, *Robert Frost and New England: The Poet as Regionalist* (Princeton: Princeton University Press, 1979), 69; William Pritchard seems ambivalent about the sentimental inflection of the poem (Pritchard, *Frost: A Literary Life Reconsidered*, 25, 27).

88. Faggen, *Robert Frost and the Challenge of Darwin*, 113; Dawes, "Masculinity and Transgression," 297–98.

89. Sarah Orne Jewett, "York Garrison, 1640," *Wide Awake* 23.1 (1886): 18–22.

90. Whitman, *Leaves of Grass*, 2:364–65, ll. 1–7.

91. Robert K. Martin, *The Homosexual Tradition in American Poetry*, 55. For a supporting voice for this reading, see Burton R. S. Fone, "This Other Eden: Arcadia and the Homosexual Imagination," in *Essays on Gay Literature*, ed. Stuart Kellogg (New York: Harrington Press, 1983), 13–34. Fone outlines a provocative set of criteria for the way in which "the Arcadian ideal has been used in the homosexual literary tradition," one of which is "to imply the presence of gay love and sensibility in a text that otherwise makes no explicit statement about homosexuality" (13).

92. Martin, *The Homosexual Tradition in American Poetry*, 56.

93. He would not necessarily have been aware of the fact that in homosexual poetry as a whole "one of the most frequent guises of the male genitals is as a plant or flower" (Gregory Woods, *Articulate Flesh: Male Homo-eroticism and Modern Poetry* [New Haven: Yale University Press, 1987], 33).

94. Frost may be inserting a secretive pun in his use of *scythe* here, for in many parts of New England—including the northeastern Massachusetts and southern New Hampshire areas in which he spent much of his earlier life—the word is often pronounced very close to *sigh*.

95. Faggen's discussion of the orchid in the context of Darwin is fascinating (*Robert Frost and the Challenge of Darwin*, 46–48).

96. Dawes, "Masculinity and Transgression," 299; Kearns, *Robert Frost and a Poetics of Appetite*, 112.

97. Kearns, *Robert Frost and a Poetics of Appetite*, 58.

98. Ibid., 44.

99. John D'Emilio and Estelle B. Freedman, *Intimate Matters: A History of Sexuality in America* (New York: Harper and Row, 1988), 171–235. For one of the best recent discussions of lesbian identity in the twentieth century, see Lillian Faderman, *Odd Girls and Twilight Lovers: A History of Lesbian Life in Twentieth-Century America* (New York: Penguin, 1991).

100. Edelman, *Homographesis*, 6.

101. Gifford, *Dayneford's Library*, 103.

102. Frost clearly regarded the poem as comic, as letters to F. S. Flint and Untermeyer indicate. See Elaine Barry, ed., *Robert Frost on Writing* (New Brunswick: Rutgers University Press, 1975), 82–83; *LU* 40. See also Faggen, *Robert Frost and the Challenge of Darwin*, 145–48.

103. Gifford, *Dayneford's Library*, 99.

104. Kimmel, *Manhood in America*, 105.

105. Whitman, *Leaves of Grass*, 1:240, ll. 26–28.

106. Gifford, *Dayneford's Library*, 99.

107. At the same time that Garber describes this process of finalization, she also draws convincingly on the historical record to indicate the historical basis of sexual categories and their cultural valences. Her seductive account of the 1920s, for example, depicts a wide range of behavior that might fall into the unstable category of "bisexuality," and the individuals whom she discusses range from Edna St. Vincent Millay to Langston Hughes. She argues that, "whether as experiment, desire,

or lifestyle, bisexuality was an intrinsic part of the culture of the twenties" (*Vice Versa*, 122).

108. Ibid., 324.

109. Ibid., 297–316.

110. Ibid., 66. See also David Gadd, *The Loving Friends: A Portrait of Bloomsbury* (New York: Harcourt Brace Jovanovich, 1974); Fred Klein, *The Bisexual Option: A Concept of One Hundred Percent Intimacy* (New York: Arbor House, 1978). It is worthwhile noting that Havelock Ellis observed, "the basis of the sexual life is the bisexual" (*Studies in the Psychology of Sex*, vol. 2: *Sexual Inversion* [1910; reprint, New York: Random House, 1936], 86–87, 88).

111. In spite of this rather bland reading of *gay*, I have to wonder if for Frost the term is not also inflected with a secondary meaning of "licentious." The word *gay* came to be affiliated with homosexuality beginning in about 1935 (*Oxford English Dictionary*, 6:409).

112. Meyers, *Robert Frost: A Biography*, 118, 120; see Lesley Lee Francis, *The Frost Family's Adventure in Poetry: Sheer Morning Gladness at the Brim* (Columbia: University of Missouri Press, 1994), 105. Francis cites several studies of the Frost-Thomas relationship.

113. Edward Thomas, review of *North of Boston, New Weekly*, 8 August 1914, 249. Other poems associated, sometimes more indirectly, with Thomas include: "The Exposed Nest" and "Range Finding" (which Frost showed to his friend while in England); "Not to Keep," which was inspired by Thomas's letters to Frost; and "On Talk of Peace at This Time," which he sent a copy of to Thomas. See Cramer, *Robert Frost among His Poems*, 44–46, 47, 54, 75–76, 82, 119, 128, 233–34. Another poem that Frost composed in connection with Thomas was "A Soldier"; unlike the other three poems I will discuss, this poem seems more detached, more "poetic," to me.

114. Edward Thomas, "The Sun Used to Shine," in *The Recognition of Robert Frost*, ed. Richard Thornton (New York: Henry Holt and Co., 1937), 59–60; Pritchard, *Frost: A Literary Life Reconsidered*, 88.

115. Kearns comments (in obvious contrast to my view) that "The Road Not Taken" is atypical in its willingness to loosen the boundaries of selfhood: "A rare instance in Frost's poetry in which there is a loved and reciprocal figure, the poem is divested of the need to keep the intended reader at bay." She attributes this divestment to a source that she does not explore: "Here Frost is not writing about that contentiously erotic love which is predicated on the sexual battles between a man and a woman, but about a higher love, by the terms of the good Greek, between two men" (*Robert Frost and a Poetics of Appetite*, 73).

116. Thompson gives the context for this poem (*Robert Frost: The Early Years, 1874–1915* [New York: Holt, Rinehart and Winston, 1966], 455–56); see Meyers, *Robert Frost: A Biography*, 126; Francis, *Frost Family's Adventure in Poetry*, 176–78.

117. Lowell, *Selected Poems*, 25. Gifford points out a "desire to locate the Other, the Homosexual, in exotic surroundings. . . . Clearly it was easier to 'read' sexual inversion outside of one's repressive culture rather than within it" (*Dayneford's Library*, 111).

118. In some sense it was "safe" to publish "Iris by Night" in *A Further Range* because by this time Frost's public masculinity was well established.

119. D'Emilio and Freedman, *Intimate Matters*, 226, 228.

120. Rotundo, *American Manhood*, 278.

121. Cited in D'Emilio and Freedman, *Intimate Matters*, 228.

122. For the use of the word *come* meaning "to climax," see *Oxford English Dictionary* 3:528.

123. Edelman, *Homographesis*, xiv, xv.

124. Showalter, *Sexual Anarchy*, 173.

125. Sedgwick, *Between Men: English Literature and Male Homosocial Desire* (New York: Columbia University Press, 1985), 207.

126. Gifford, *Dayneford's Library*, 13, 98–117. See also Woods, *Articulate Flesh*, 53; Lears, *No Place of Grace*, 102; Georges-Michel Sarotte, *Like a Brother, Like a Lover: Male Homosexuality in the American Novel and Theater from Herman Melville to James Baldwin*, trans. Richard Miller (New York: Anchor-Doubleday, 1978), 70–91.

127. Sedgwick, *Between Men*, 89. On the relationship between Helen Thomas and the Frosts, see Francis, *Frost Family's Adventure in Poetry*, 116, 188.

128. Cited in Gilbert and Gubar, *Sexchanges*, 301.

129. Walt Whitman, "Reconciliation," in *Leaves of Grass: A Textual Variorum of the Printed Poems*, 2:555–56.

130. Edelman, *Homographesis*, 12.

131. Edelman, *Homographesis*, xvi.

132. Yingling, *Hart Crane and the Homosexual Text*, 6. Yingling makes explicit this connection (or lack of connection) between the homosexual and the national, pointing to a necessary marriage between homophobia and nationalism (11–12).

**Chapter 5**

1. Jessie B. Rittenhouse, *My House of Life: An Autobiography* (Boston: Houghton Mifflin, 1934), 288.

2. Cassandra Laity, "H. D., Modernism, and the Transgressive Sexualities of Decadent-Romantic Platonism," in *Gendered Modernisms: American Women Poets and Their Readers,* ed. Margaret Dickie and Thomas Travisano (Philadelphia: University of Pennsylvania Press, 1996), 46; see also Cassandra Laity, "H. D. and A. C. Swinburne: Decadence and Modernist Women's Writing," *Feminist Studies* 15.3 (1989): 465–70.

3. Robert L. Dorman, *Revolt of the Provinces: The Regionalist Movement in America, 1920–1945* (Chapel Hill: University of North Carolina Press, 1993), 35.

4. Emily Dickinson, *The Selected Letters of Emily Dickinson,* ed. Thomas H. Johnson (Cambridge: Belknap-Harvard University Press, 1958), 411–12, L268. In an observation resonant for Frost, Robert Langbaum notes that, after critical disparagement about his self-revelation in early poems, Robert Browning issued a disclaimer to his 1842 *Dramatic Lyrics:* "so many utterances of so many imaginary persons, not mine" (cited in Robert Langbaum, *The Poetry of Experience: The Dramatic Monologue in Modern Literary Tradition* [New York: Random House, 1957], 79). Browning's dramatic monologues often represent individuals who are morally

problematic, while Frost's more frequently speak in the voices of those who are troubled; this different stance suggests the latter's relatively greater sympathy for and investment in his characters.

5. H. L. Mencken, "The New Poetry Movement," in *Critical Essays on American Modernism,* ed. Michael J. Hoffman and Patrick D. Murphy (New York: G. K. Hall, 1992), 39. Cleanth Brooks, "Frost, MacLeish, and Auden," *Modern Poetry and the Tradition* (1939; reprint, London: Poetry London, 1945), 113, 114.

6. Dorman, *Revolt of the Provinces,* 50, 29–53. Dorman identifies groups of writers and artists in different locations, such as Mary Austin and Willa Cather in the west and the Agrarians in the south, but he insists that "with its credo of decentralization, the movement itself had no center, no directing or dominating group. It was a *movement* less from its formal or organizational cohesiveness than from its simultaneity across the country" (34).

7. As Harvey Green points out, "between 1920 and 1937, 30 million people moved from farms to towns, villages, and cities, and 21 million from towns to farms." More significantly, perhaps, "By 1930 the 40 million first- or second-generation immigrants constituted one-third of the population of the United States" (*The Uncertainty of Everyday Life, 1915–1945* [New York: HarperPerennial, 1992], 5).

8. Mary Austin, *The American Rhythm,* enlarged ed. (New York: Cooper Square, 1970), 54.

9. Frost seems obliquely to confirm this shift; for example, *North of Boston's* dedication reads: "To E. M. F. THIS BOOK OF PEOPLE" (Edward Connery Lathem, ed., *The Poetry of Robert Frost: The Collected Poems, Complete and Unabridged* [New York: Holt, Rinehart and Winston, 1975], 534). We should also take note that Jarrell is not entirely disapproving of the shift (*Poetry and the Age* [New York: Ecco Press, 1980], 33–34).

Oster points out the move in Frost toward increasing self-consciousness: "While in earlier poems such as 'Birches,' 'Mowing,' or even 'The Death of the Hired Man' perfect artistic fusions seem just to 'happen,' such issues as metaphor and figuring, the creating word or vision, artistic process and transformation surface more overtly and self-consciously as subjects in the poems published in 1923 and 1928 ('Maple,' 'Paul's Wife,' 'A Boundless Moment,' 'A Hillside Thaw,' 'Gathering Leaves,' 'The Aim was Song,' 'For Once Then Something' in 1923; 'The Rose Family,' 'The Freedom of the Moon,' 'Fireflies in the Garden,' in 1928. 'Time Out,' with its focus not on nature but on how we read it, was published later still, in 1942)" (*Toward Robert Frost: The Reader and the Poet* [Athens: University of Georgia Press, 1991], 270–71 n. 42).

10. Bogan, *Achievement in American Poetry, 1900–1950* (Chicago: Henry Regnery, 1951), 50–51.

11. Roy Harvey Pearce, *The Continuity of American Poetry* (Princeton: Princeton University Press, 1961), 283.

12. Sandra M. Gilbert and Susan Gubar, *No Man's Land,* 3 vols. (New Haven: Yale University Press, 1988, 1989, 1994). Because she seems to construct the narrative voice as more masculine in the terms of this discussion, Katherine Kearns, like her modernist precursors, affiliates traditional lyric with femininity or, perhaps more tellingly, with "effeminacy." In describing narrative and poetic genres in this

way, Kearns tells one story of cultural affiliations; it is, of course, as easy to tell an opposing story, of the novel affiliated with femininity and the everyday and the poem with masculinity and transcendence, as Gilbert and Gubar do (*Robert Frost and Poetics of Appetite* [Cambridge: Cambridge University Press, 1994], 169, 33). Frank Lentricchia elaborates a more historically grounded narrative of Frost's relation to lyric. By the standards of contemporary literary tastemakers, as Lentricchia tells the story, a pure, "unadulterated" lyric would exclude features that constituted the hallmarks of much of Frost's earliest published work, such as narrative, evocation of region, dramatic event, and blank verse (*Modernist Quartet* [Cambridge: Cambridge University Press, 1994], 55–61). In Lentricchia's version the (masculine) novel becomes a key to understanding the poet's aesthetic: "the new lyric poet's key technical liaison with the already powerfully emerged realist novel . . . might win for him, an American male lyricist, social acceptance in an American capitalist context which typically encoded economic and cultural roles in engendered opposition" ("The Resentments of Robert Frost," *American Literature* 62.2 [1990]: 185).

13. Lentricchia, *Modernist Quartet*, 95, 113.

14. Sharon Cameron, *Lyric Time: Dickinson and the Limits of Genre* (Baltimore: Johns Hopkins University Press, 1979), 22–23.

15. Or, as Suzanne Clark points out, to the sentimental novel (*Sentimental Modernism: Women Writers and the Revolution of the Word* [Bloomington: Indiana University Press, 1991], 19–31).

16. Jo Ellen Green Kaiser, "Displaced Modernism: Millay and the Triumph of Sentimentality," in *Millay at 100: A Critical Reappraisal,* ed. Diane P. Freedman (Carbondale: Southern Illinois University Press, 1995), 37.

17. Paul Lauter, "Race and Gender in the Shaping of the American Literary Canon: A Case Study from the Twenties," *Feminist Studies* 9 (1983): 447, 449. Lauter observes, "the map of American literature which most of us have used was drawn fifty years ago" (435).

18. Lentricchia, "Resentments of Robert Frost," 185; emphasis added. Lentricchia echoes the homoerotic image that he foregrounded earlier in his essay; as interestingly, he also purges this *second* reference to homoeroticism from *Modernist Quartet.*

19. Michael Kimmel, *Manhood in America: A Cultural History* (New York: Free Press, 1996), 7.

20. Bogan, *Achievement in American Poetry*, 23, 24, 23. Emily Stipes Watts, *The Poetry of American Women from 1632 to 1943* (Austin: University of Texas Press, 1977), 147.

21. Paula Bennett, "Late Nineteenth-Century American Women's Nature Poetry and the Evolution of the Imagist Poem," *Legacy: A Journal of American Women Writers* 9.2 (1992): 92, 94, 97.

22. Ibid., 91.

23. I can give only a brief indication of these connections, and the account of Lizette Woodworth Reese that follows is meant to be merely suggestive. A number of Guiney poems, such as "Hylas," "The Japanese Anemone," "The Still of the Year," "Emily Brontë," "Sanctuary," "When on the Marge of Evening," "Fog," and "Sunday Chimes in the City," while they often sound notes of nineteenth-cen-

tury romanticism, also possess moments of modernist subjectivity that anticipate Frost in poems such as "For Once, Then, Something" and "The Need of Being Versed in Country Things" (Louise Imogen Guiney, *Happy Ending: The Collected Lyrics of Louise Imogen Guiney* [Boston: Houghton Mifflin, 1927]).

Pearce includes both Guiney and Lizette Woodworth Reese among the writers on his "depressing list" of decidedly second-rate poets who are noted, he asserts, for "exercises in rhetoric, too-delicate evocations of the trivial or too-robust summonings up of the 'sublime'" (Pearce, *The Continuity of American Poetry,* 255, 56). For a more balanced view of Guiney, see Van Wyck Brooks, *New England: Indian Summer, 1865–1915* (New York: E. P. Dutton, 1940), 434, 451; for a more positive view, see Sheila A. Tully, "Heroic Failures and the Literary Career of Louise Imogen Guiney," *American Transcendental Quarterly* 47–48 (1982): 171–86; Bogan, *Achievement in American Poetry,* 24–25; Alfred Kreymborg, *A History of American Poetry: Our Singing Strength* (New York: Tudor, 1934), 255, 256; Horace Gregory and Marya Zaturenska, *A History of American Poetry, 1900–1940* (New York: Harcourt, Brace, 1946), 83–91; Watts, *Poetry of American Women,* 139–40; Jessie B. Rittenhouse, *The Younger American Poets* (Boston: Little, Brown, 1918), 75–93. For a relatively uncritical view, see Alice Brown, *Louise Imogen Guiney* (New York: Macmillan, 1921).

24. Lawrance Thompson, *Robert Frost: The Years of Triumph, 1915–1938* (New York: Holt, Rinehart and Winston, 1964), 305.

25. Ibid., 305–6.

26. H. L. Mencken, "The New Poetry Movement," *Critical Essays on American Modernism,* 41–42. For a discussion of Mencken's hostility to mainstream culture, see Mark Richardson, *The Ordeal of Robert Frost: The Poet and His Poetics* (Urbana: University of Illinois Press, 1997), 4, 29.

27. David M. Robinson, "Address: Lizette Woodworth Reese, The Poet," in *Lizette Woodworth Reese, 1856–1935* (Baltimore: Enoch Pratt Free Library, 1944), 12; Bogan, *Achievement in American Poetry,* 25.

28. Kreymborg, *A History of American Poetry: Our Singing Strength* (New York: Tudor, 1934), 261; Untermeyer, ed., *Modern American Poetry: A Critical Anthology* (New York: Harcourt, Brace, 1936), 113. In an appreciation of Reese at the dedication of a statue to her memory, Robinson notes the connection between Reese's poetry and the later work of Sara Teasdale and Edna St. Vincent Millay, observing, "In a period of sugared sentiment and lace valentine lyrics, Miss Reese's crisp lines were a generation ahead of the times" ("Address: Lizette Woodworth Reese, The Poet," 12–13; Untermeyer, cited in Robinson, "Address," 12; see also Rittenhouse, *Younger American Poets,* 27–45; Gregory and Zaturenska, *History of American Poetry,* 79–83; Watts, *Poetry of American Women,* 145–46).

29. Alicia Ostriker, *Stealing the Language: The Emergence of Women's Poetry in America* (Boston: Beacon Press, 1986), 44. For a discussion of both Guiney and Reese, see Cheryl Walker, *The Nightingale's Burden: Women Poets and American Culture before 1900* (Bloomington: Indiana University Press, 1982), 120–37. On Reese, see Edmund Wilson, "The All-Star Literary Vaudeville," in *Critical Essays on Edna St. Vincent Millay,* ed. William B. Thesing (Boston: G. K. Hall, 1993), 140 (excerpted from the *New Republic* 47 [30 June 1926]: 161–62).

30. Lizette Woodworth Reese, *A Branch of May* (Baltimore: Cushings and Bailey, 1887), 38.

31. We might recall here that in nineteenth-century American women's poetry the spider is an important emblem for female creativity. Dickinson's poems on the subject are well-known, but Rose Terry Cooke's "Arachne," which is beginning to reappear in contemporary anthologies, is another example. See Rose Terry Cooke, *Poems* (New York: William S. Gottsberger, 1888), 101–2.

32. Lizette Woodworth Reese, *The Selected Poems of Lizette Woodworth Reese* (New York: George H. Doran, 1926), 185.

33. Robinson, "Address," 16.

34. Kreymborg, *History of American Poetry,* 261.

35. See Lucy Larcom, *The Poetical Works of Lucy Larcom,* Household Edition (Boston: Houghton Mifflin, 1884), 296–97. Larcom's flowers can be interpreted as a commentary on the life of older, "barren" women, and it is entirely possible that Reese could have been familiar with "Flowers of the Fallow," which was first published in the *Atlantic* in October 1881. For a discussion of this poem from a different perspective, see Shirley Marchalonis, *The Worlds of Lucy Larcom, 1824–1893* (Athens: University of Georgia Press, 1989), 222–23; 292–93 n. 10.

36. Rittenhouse, *Younger American Poets,* 34.

37. Andreas Huyssen, *After the Great Divide: Modernism, Mass Culture, Postmodernism* (Bloomington: Indiana University Press, 1986), vii, 47. Huyssen argues persuasively against postmodern theory that genders modernist writing as feminine (49). On the participation of modernism and modernist artists in consumerism, see Stanley Aronowitz, *The Crisis in Historical Materialism* (South Hadley, MA: J. F. Bergin, 1981); Fredric Jameson, "Reification and Utopia in Mass Culture," *Social Text* 1 (1979): 130–48; and Ian Willison et al., eds., *Modernist Writers and the Marketplace* (Houndmills, Basingstoke: Macmillan, 1996). On the uses of mass culture as critique of mainstream society, see Tania Modleski, *Loving with a Vengeance: Mass Produced Fantasies for Women* (New York: Methuen, 1982). Marcus Klein points out that modernist poetry was reacting to a commercialization of American culture that was actually worse in an earlier period, the late nineteenth century, and that immigration served as a crucial impetus for the separation between mass and elite culture ("Tradition and History," *Critical Essays on American Modernism,* 117; excerpted from *Foreigners: The Making of American Literature: 1900–1940* [Chicago: University of Chicago Press, 1981], 7–16). A number of recent writers have argued that the modern university was instrumental in securing and reinforcing this separation; see, for example, Thomas Strychacz's discussion of how the commodification of competence in the face of a symbiotically difficult literature ensured the self-perpetuating cultural power of academics (*Modernism, Mass Culture, and Professionalism* [Cambridge: Cambridge University Press, 1993], 1–44; see also Gail McDonald, *Learning to Be Modern: Pound, Eliot, and the American University* [Oxford: Clarendon Press, 1993]; Leslie Fiedler, *What Was Literature? Class Culture and Mass Society* [New York: Simon and Schuster, 1982]; and John Guillory, *Cultural Capital: The Problem of Literary Canon Formation* [Chicago: University of Chicago Press, 1993], 139–41). As these writers suggest, the juxtaposition of popular against high culture is both specious and historically implicated.

38. Leslie Fiedler, "What Happened to Poetry" and "Literature as an Institution," *What Was Literature?* 83, 58.

39. As Thomas Strychacz has pointed out, even popular audiences are extremely diverse and often highly specialized (*Modernism, Mass Culture, and Professionalism,* 21).

40. Frost, "Education by Poetry: A Meditative Monologue," *CP* 717.

41. Jo Ellen Green Kaiser, "Displaced Modernism," 29. A number of writers remark upon Millay's sentimentality, whether to confirm or to refute it. One of the most influential instances occurs in a 1945 essay by Marshall McLuhan: "Edna Millay, for example, has never been anything but a purveyor of cliché sentiment" ("The New York Wits," in *Critical Essays on Edna St. Vincent Millay,* 155); see the essays by Tate and Fletcher in this volume for other examples, as well as Suzanne Clark, "Uncanny Millay," *Millay at 100,* 13; and Colin Falck, "Introduction: The Modern Lyricism of Edna Millay," in *Edna St. Vincent Millay: Selected Poems,* ed. Colin Falck (New York: HarperPerennial, 1992), xv. For an interesting discussion of the relationship between popularity and canonicity in the case of Marianne Moore, see Timothy Morris, *Becoming Canonical in American Poetry* (Urbana: University of Illinois Press, 1995), 81–103.

The personal relationship between Frost and Millay deserves more attention. As he did with many other poets, Frost seemed to regard Millay as a competitor; see Thompson, *Robert Frost: The Years of Triumph, 1915–1938,* 651 n. 29.

42. Sandra M. Gilbert, "Female Female Impersonator: Millay and the Theatre of Personality," in *Critical Essays on Edna St. Vincent Millay,* 293–312.

43. Patricia A. Klemans, "'Being Born a Woman': A New Look at Edna St. Vincent Millay," in *Critical Essays on Edna St. Vincent Millay,* 200

44. Kreymborg, *History of American Poetry,* 442; Brooks, *New England: Indian Summer,* 540.

45. Cheryl Walker, "The Female Body as Icon: Edna Millay Wears a Plaid Dress," *Millay at 100,* 89. As Sandra M. Gilbert points out, "*A Few Figs From Thistles* made her the 'It-girl' of American poetry in 1922." "'Directions for Using the Empress': Millay's Supreme Fiction(s)," *Millay at 100,* 170.

46. William B. Thesing, intro., *Critical Essays on Edna St. Vincent Millay,* 1, 13. Cary Nelson points to two very different Millays: "the articulately antiromantic Millay that the culture has largely chosen to forget" and "the rhapsodically romantic Millay who has been both remembered and belittled" ("The Fate of Gender in Modern American Poetry," in *Marketing Modernisms: Self-Promotion, Canonization, Rereading,* ed. Kevin J. H. Dettmar and Stephen Watt [Ann Arbor: University of Michigan Press, 1996], 348).

47. Kaiser "Displaced Modernism," 39

48. Allen Ross Macdougall, ed., *Letters of Edna St. Vincent Millay* (New York: Harper and Brothers, 1952), 311–12.

49. Cited in Pritchard, *Frost: A Literary Life Reconsidered* (New York: Oxford University Press, 1984), 242.

50. Clark, *Sentimental Modernism,* 69, 71.

51. Huyssen, *After the Great Divide,* 46; Clark, "Uncanny Millay," 9, 15.

52. Clark, *Sentimental Modernism,* 10, 34.

53. John Crowe Ransom, "The Poet as Woman," *The World's Body* (1938; reprint, Baton Rouge: Louisiana State University Press, 1968), 76, 78, 104. Clark cites Delmore Schwartz's remarks in a similar vein (*Sentimental Modernism,* 78). Many of Millay's critics over the years have responded to this criticism; see Klemans, "'Being Born a Woman,'" 211; and Genevieve Taggard's brilliant essay (anticipating Ransom) "Edna St. Vincent Millay," in *Critical Essays on Edna St. Vincent Millay,* 137–40, 139.

54. Falck, intro., *Edna St. Vincent Millay,* xvii. In this connection Millay's sequence, "Sonnets from an Ungrafted Tree," is a must-read, especially in relation to Frost. See Sandra M. Gilbert and Susan Gubar, *Letters from the Front,* vol. 3 of *No Man's Land* (New Haven: Yale University Press, 1994), 83. Gilbert and Gubar's reading of these poems compares them to Frost's narratives but once again elides the feminine subjectivity in the latter.

55. Clark, "Uncanny Millay," 4.

56. Bogan, *CR* 152; see my later discussion.

57. Poirier observes that "from the late twenties until his death in 1963, Frost regarded himself as the necessary enemy of two forces in American cultural life which had formed an unexpected and perplexing alliance: the political left and the modernist literary élite" (*Robert Frost: The Work of Knowing* [New York: Oxford University Press, 1977], 226).

58. Harriet Monroe and Alice Corbin Henderson, eds., *The New Poetry: An Anthology of Twentieth-Century Verse in English* (New York: Macmillan, 1924). Amy Lowell occupies more space in Monroe than either Frost or Millay, with thirteen poems and nineteen pages.

Shari Benstock discusses the seriousness of high modernism as embodied in Eliot and Pound, which suggests another reason for Frost's controversial place in the canon of modernist poetry: he was too engaged in practices of playfulness and humor ("Expatriate Sapphic Modernism: Entering Literary History," in *Rereading Modernism: New Directions in Feminist Criticism,* ed. Lisa Rado [New York: Garland, 1994], 100).

59. Richard Poirier, "The Difficulties of Modernism and the Modernism of Difficulty," *Critical Essays on American Modernism,* 106, 105.

60. Fiedler, *What Was Literature?* 83.

61. Kaiser, "Displaced Modernism," 29.

62. Ibid., 40; Walker, "Female Body as Icon," 90.

63. Walker, "Female Body as Icon," 89.

64. See Edna St. Vincent Millay, *Edna St. Vincent Millay's Poems Selected for Young People* (New York: Harper and Brothers, 1929), 42.

65. Ibid., 73, 3–6.

66. Ibid., 5.

67. This image conjures Frost's "The Subverted Flower" for me, though the poem retains a far more negative view of male sexuality and ambivalent view of female desire.

68. Robert Frost, *You Come Too: Favorite Poems for Young Readers* (New York: Henry Holt and Co., 1959), 5. Lesley Lee Francis describes effectively the creative environment that Frost and Elinor helped create for their children, as well

as the collaboration between children and adults in various writing projects. This collaborative approach and attitude toward children were shared by Edward Thomas, indicating another bond between the two poets. See Francis, *The Frost Family's Adventure in Poetry: Sheer Morning Gladness at the Brim* (Columbia: University of Missouri Press, 1994), 12, 29, 119. Frost's stories for his children also indicate his delight in crossing the boundaries between "children's'" and "adult" literature; see *Stories for Lesley,* ed. Roger D. Sell (Charlottesville: University Press of Virginia, 1984).

69. Robert Frost, "The Young Birch," *You Come Too,* 32.

70. Jeffrey S. Cramer, *Robert Frost among His Poems: A Literary Companion to the Poet's Own Biographical Contexts and Associations* (Jefferson, NC: McFarland, 1996), 144. As the Beatles would do in another media, Frost frequently issued "Christmas poems." His and Millay's (continuing) popular appeal is borne out in the many occasions on which their verse has been set to music.

71. Clearly, the categories of "college text" and "authoritative canon-making text" are sometimes virtually identical. This discussion of Frost's history in anthologies and that which follows are based on *Grainger's World of Poetry on CD ROM* (New York: Columbia University Press, 1992).

72. On the reception history of "Birches," see George Monteiro, *Robert Frost and the New England Renaissance* (Lexington: University Press of Kentucky, 1988), 100.

73. These distinctions are themselves merely categorical conveniences, for "teachers of literature [were] becoming more responsible for overseeing the canon in the two decades after 1900." As Alan Golding points out, beginning with Stedman, anthologists "responded [to public indifference to the higher forms of poetry] by emphatically separating popular and cultivated taste" (*From Outlaw to Classic,* 21). Golding's discussion of Frost's (puzzling) dominance over other American poets in the New Critical *Understanding Poetry* provides a useful understanding of the interconnection between pedagogy and critical practice (105–7).

74. Millay, "I will put Chaos into fourteen lines," *Edna St. Vincent Millay: Selected Poems,* 153.

75. Pearce, *Continuity of American Poetry,* 284.

76. Clark, *Sentimental Modernism,* 6, 32.

77. Fiedler, *What Was Literature?* 92.

78. Kaiser, "Displaced Modernism," 40.

79. Harriet Monroe and Alice Corbin Henderson, "Introduction to the First Edition," *The New Poetry: An Anthology of Twentieth-Century Verse in English,* new ed. (New York: Macmillan, 1924), xxxv–xxxvi.

80. Marjorie Perloff, *The Dance of the Intellect: Studies in the Poetry of the Pound Tradition* (Cambridge: Cambridge University Press, 1985), 156–57. Perloff cites "Desert Places" from *A Further Range* (1936) as one example.

81. Ibid., 159. Perloff observes, "the poetry of modernism was wedded to a sharp distinction between *poetry,* the lyric expression of personal emotions, and *prose,* the language of fiction, of the novel" (*Dance of the Intellect,* 158). Alan Golding, *From Outlaw to Classic: Canons in American Poetry,* 26–27, 88.

82. On the divisions within modernism, see Gilbert Allen, "Millay and Modernism," *Critical Essays on Edna St. Vincent Millay,* 266–72. See also David

Perkins, *A History of Modern Poetry: From the 1890s to the High Modernist Mode* (Cambridge: Belknap-Harvard, 1976).

83. Ezra Pound, *Letters to Ibbotson, 1935–62*, ed. Vittorio I. Mondolfi and Margaret Hurley (Orono, ME: National Poetry Foundation, 1979), 24; see Perloff, *Dance of the Intellect*, 178–79.

84. Perloff, *Dance of the Intellect*, 178. Connecting the two modes of modern poetry, Perloff goes on to discuss postmodernist poetry's elimination of the distinctions between "poetry" ("lyric") and "prose": "Postmodernism in poetry . . . begins in the urge to return the material so rigidly excluded . . . to the domain of poetry, which is to say that the Romantic lyric . . . gives way to a poetry that can, once again, accommodate narrative and didacticism, the serious and the comic, verse *and* prose" (180–81). Frost was, of course, including all of these materials in his work. The Frost poems in Lewis's edition were: "To Earthward," "The Road Not Taken," "The Runaway," and "Reluctance." All of these poems have strong resonances with mainstream nineteenth-century poetry, and all but "The Runaway" reflect the taste for lyric to which Perloff points. See Francis Turner Palgrave and C. Day Lewis, eds., *Palgrave's Golden Treasury* (London: Collins, 1954), 472–75. Lowell and Millay are both excluded from this edition, although T. S. Eliot is represented, with "The Journey of the Magi," "Marina," and "The Hollow Men" (represented by an "extract"), as is Ezra Pound, with "[What thou lovest well remains]." Lewis's choices continue Palgrave's tradition.

85. See Chaviva Hošek and Patricia Parker, *Lyric Poetry: Beyond New Criticism* (Ithaca: Cornell University Press, 1985), esp. Jonathan Arac, "Afterword: Lyric Poetry and the Bounds of New Criticism," 345–55.

86. On the dismissal of Willa Cather, see Sharon O'Brien, "Becoming Noncanonical: The Case of Willa Cather," in *Reading in America, Literature and Social History*, ed. Cathy N. Davidson (Baltimore: Johns Hopkins University Press, 1989), 240–58.

87. Sandra M. Gilbert and Susan Gubar, *The Madwoman in the Attic* (New Haven: Yale University Press, 1979), 548.

88. Lentricchia, "Resentments of Robert Frost," 177.

89. George Monteiro observes how Frost's revisions of the earlier "In White" "turn the poem to narrative and away from unadorned lyric, thereby enhancing the mystery that surrounds the incident he wishes to describe" (*Robert Frost and the New England Renaissance* [Lexington: University Press of Kentucky, 1988], 36; see also Poirier, *Robert Frost: The Work of Knowing*, 245–52). "Design" is nevertheless far closer to traditional lyric than poems like "Home Burial" and "A Servant to Servants."

90. On the connection between Frost and Dickinson, see Monteiro, *Robert Frost and the New England Renaissance*, 9–33.

91. Walton Beacham, "Technique and the Sense of Play in the Poetry of Robert Frost," in *Frost: Centennial Essays II*, ed. Jac Tharpe (Jackson: University of Mississippi Press, 1976), 246.

92. Ina Coolbrith, "The Mariposa Lily," in *An American Anthology, 1787–1900*, ed. Edmund Clarence Stedman (1901; reprint, New York: Greenwood Press, 1968), 495.

93. Annie Finch, "The Sentimental Poetess in the World: Metaphor and Subjectivity in Lydia Sigourney's Nature Poetry," *Legacy: A Journal of American Women Writers* 9.2 (1992): 5.

94. Jarrell, *Poetry and the Age,* 34.

95. T. S. Eliot, *The Three Voices of Poetry* (New York: Cambridge University Press, 1954), 6.

96. Wylie's concrete images refer more overtly to a domestic world, at least in the first stanza of her poem, but both she and Frost highlight artificially created scenes and objects—for her the "gold-enamelled fish" and for him, the "dimpled spider." Both voices sport the assurance and confidence of the autonomous lyric self, and both are clearly modernist in their vision, their self-reflexive cool, their emphasis on the aesthetic. We could cite many examples of female-authored modernist poetry that take this masculine stance, from Bogan's "Medusa," "The Crows," "Cassandra," and "Women" to many of H. D.'s classical lyrics. As with Frost, modernist women did not *always* assume such positions, as Bogan's "Betrothed" and "Evening in the Sanatarium" suggest (Louise Bogan, *The Blue Estuaries: Poems, 1923–1968* [New York: Octagon Books, 1975], 4, 17, 33, 19, 7, 111).

97. Amy Lowell, "Interlude," *The Complete Poetical Works of Amy Lowell* (Boston: Houghton Mifflin, 1955), 212. Obviously, this poem, like many others by Lowell, also retains its modernist attitudes; my goal here has been to distinguish between the different stances possible within feminine and masculine modernist practice.

98. This was the same year in which Millay received the Pulitzer Prize for poetry.

99. Warner Berthoff has also commented on Frost's guardedness, observing that the "wide popularity [of Frost's poems] is a further source of interest, having grown up around the skillfully idealized projection of an ethos of American individualism in its guarded, sly, New England aspect" (*The Ferment of Realism: American Literature, 1884–1919* [New York: Free Press, 1965], 281; see also 280).

100. The critique of Frost as unengaged with "real life" seems a surprisingly conservative one coming from the 1930s Left and incredibly problematic in view of his consistent empathy for working-class people (usually agrarian) as well as his own and his family's experience with hard labor. It is also problematic in view of the notable conservatism and fascism of Eliot, Pound, and others, reenacted, in some sense, by the elusive eliteness and opacity of their poems, however self-mocking or ironic those qualities might be. In his early poems Frost was a democratic poet in the tradition of Sigourney and Whitman. From this perspective, in making this criticism of Frost, the leftists were ironically consolidating their positions as possessors of cultural and intellectual power. See Strychacz, *Modernism, Mass Culture, and Professionalism,* 34, 35.

101. Later poems like "The Fear of Man" and the bitter "Ends" also show much of the understanding of women's perspectives or imply sympathy for a reader who may find him- or herself in similarly severe circumstances. Nevertheless, these poems evince different forms of subjectivity, and hence different attitudes toward the reader, than earlier parallels.

102. Frank Lentricchia, "Lyric in the Culture of Capitalism," *American Literary History* 1.1 (Spring 1989): 66.

103. Oster, *Robert Frost: The Reader and the Poet*, 255–58. In spite of its ubiquity in anthologies and its status in the canon, contemporary opinion on and contexts for the poem are diverse and often divided; most, however, address the poem with high seriousness. For a range of different views, see George W. Nitchie, *Human Values in the Poetry of Robert Frost: A Study of a Poet's Convictions* (Durham: Duke University Press, 1960), 145–46; Frank Lentricchia, *Robert Frost: Modern Poetics and the Landscapes of Self* (Durham: Duke University Press, 1975), 112–19; Harold Bloom, intro., in *Modern Critical Views: Robert Frost*, ed. Harold Bloom (New York: Chelsea House, 1986), 4–5; John F. Lynen, "Du Coté de Chez Frost," in *Frost: Centennial Essays*, ed. Jac Tharpe (Jackson: University of Mississippi Press, 1974), 562–94; Perry Westbrook, "Abandonment and Desertion in the Poetry of Robert Frost," *Frost: Centennial Essays II*, 295–96; George Monteiro, *Robert Frost and the New England Renaissance*, 1–2; Donald J. Greiner, "The Indispensable Robert Frost," in *Critical Essays on Robert Frost*, ed. Philip L. Gerber (Boston: G. K. Hall, 1982), 237–38; Poirier, *Robert Frost: The Work of Knowing*, 99; Mark Richardson, *Ordeal of Robert Frost*, 238ff.; Robert Faggen, *Robert Frost and the Challenge of Darwin* (Ann Arbor: University of Michigan Press, 1997), 273–76.

104. To a certain degree "Directive" possesses the kind of self-consciousness that we see in a poem like Marianne Moore's "Poetry"; both are self-reflexive, and both have a strong central speaker. But Moore's opens toward the reader in a way that is to me much more (affirmatively) disarming. We might also observe that Moore is only apparently collaborating in a male modernist project of remasculinizing the lyric, for, as Rachel Blau DuPlessis points out, both she and Mina Loy were working "in opposition to the romantic lyric" ("'Corpses of Poesy': Some Modern Poets and Some Gender Ideologies of Lyric," in *Feminist Measures, Soundings in Poetry and Theory*, ed. Lynn Keller and Cristanne Miller [Ann Arbor: University of Michigan Press, 1994], 77).

Lentricchia's view of this poem is decidedly different from my current one and representative of a characteristic attitude toward "Directive" in particular and the Poetic Pronouncements of later Frost:

The awesome "Directive" (*Steeple Bush*, 1947) . . . gathers up elements in the poetic landscape he had been fashioning since *A Boy's Will*, as if to rewrite, in a single sweeping and triumphant gesture, both *The Waste Land* and *The Four Quartets*: as if he were saying he could do it better than Eliot had—more economically, more accessibly—and with a lightness of touch beyond Eliot's ken. "Drink and be whole again beyond confusion," directs the bard in the wicked last line. . . . With that gesture, Frost plays a joke on his mythic projection as the speaker of maxims, and on anyone not used to reading him with close slowness of attention, any reader who takes Frost in once only, for the bardic impression, as if Frost were speaking to him from the platform like a media phenom. (*Modernist Quartet*, 116–17)

The problem is, I don't buy it; the emperor has no clothes; there's nothing beyond the presence of the bard. I get the joke, and I'm still not amused. This kind of poet's exercise is like masturbation—feeling sometimes a bit naughty, often a lot of fun, but in large doses pretty lonely. Lentricchia's comment suggests Frost's mood of schoolboy competition with Eliot that this poem conveys to me: mine's *bigger,* it says—so much bigger and better that I don't have to wave it in anyone's face. I'm the Real Thing: a Real Man, and a Real Poet.

105. We might consider the possibility that for Frost, World War I—like the Civil War for Whitman—sparked part of his growing cynicism.

106. Beacham, "Technique and the Sense of Play," 246.

107. Poirier, *Robert Frost: The Work of Knowing,* xiv. The account of the poem that follows is inflected by Poirier's insights.

108. DuPlessis, "'Corpses of Poesy,'" 71, 72.

109. Felski, "Modernism and Modernity: Engendering Literary History," *Rereading Modernism,* 202.

110. Beacham, "Technique and the Sense of Play," 246.

## Coda

1. W. W. Robson makes a similar connection, though he is more critical: "In things like 'A Masque of Reason' he is plainly out of his depth. The manner of that 'masque,' contriving as it does to be both smart and naïve, would be an affront if we were to bring it seriously into comparison with the tragic poetry of the Book of Job. . . . Although a generalized geniality and a weak whimsicality are unfortunately common in Frost's work, they do not represent its strength." See Robson, "The Achievement of Robert Frost," in *Critical Essays on Robert Frost,* ed. Philip L. Gerber (Boston: G. K. Hall, 1982), 215; for other extended comments on the *Masques,* see Arthur M. Sampley, "The Myth and the Quest: The Stature of Robert Frost," *Critical Essays on Robert Frost,* 192; W. R. Irwin, "The Unity of Frost's Masques" *American Literature* 32.3 (1960): 302–12.

2. Roy Harvey Pearce, *The Continuity of American Poetry* (Baltimore: Johns Hopkins University Press, 1961), 282. Hyatt H. Waggoner discusses *A Masque of Mercy* as an illustration for his discussion of Frost's relinquishment of his "masks" late in life, suggesting a very different view from my own. See Waggoner, *American Poets from the Puritans to the Present* (Boston: Houghton Mifflin, 1968), 316–18.

3. Randall Jarrell, "The Other Frost," *Poetry and the Age* (New York: Ecco Press, 1980), 34; see also Yvor Winters, "Robert Frost: or, the Spiritual Drifter as Poet," in *Robert Frost: A Collection of Critical Essays,* ed. James M. Cox (Englewood Cliffs: Prentice-Hall, 1962), 69–74. In a 1945 review Louise Bogan had also been critical of the poem, comparing Frost unfavorably to Rilke, Eliot, and Auden (Bogan, *A Poet's Alphabet: Reflections on the Literary Art and Vocation,* ed. Robert Phelps and Ruth Limmer [New York: McGraw-Hill, 1970], 162–63).

4. Once again, Kearns's story of this poem diverges from mine; in line with her argument that women are primarily threatening to Frost, she observes about Thyatira's question about why women get burned for prophecy: "The answer lies, of course, in what Frost believes that femality knows, for by traditional masculinist

terms its knowledge is of anarchic truths whose powers to subvert rationality must be silenced, burned into nothing" (Katherine Kearns, *Robert Frost and a Poetics of Appetite* [Cambridge: Cambridge University Press, 1994], 136).

5. Richard Poirier, *Robert Frost: The Work of Knowing* (New York: Oxford University Press, 1977), 252, 290, 263, 254. Other readers focus very briefly on the *Masques* as an opportunity to discuss Frost's theology (see Marice C. Brown, "Introduction: The Quest for 'all creatures great and small,'" in *Frost: Centennial Essays,* ed. Jac Tharpe [Jackson: University of Mississippi Press, 1974], 5–6; Robert Fleissner, *Frost's Road Taken* [New York: Peter Lang, 1997], 136–37; or, on his connection with Emersonian precursors, George Monteiro, *Robert Frost and the New England Renaissance* [Lexington: University of Kentucky Press, 1988], 150–51). See also Robert Faggen, *Robert Frost and the Ordeal of Darwin* (Ann Arbor: University of Michigan Press, 1997), 3, 260.

6. Frost himself has very little to say about these volumes in his letters, either to Untermeyer or to anyone else, other than promising to send copies of each to Earle J. Bernheimer, the collector of the poet's work (*SL* 520–22).

7. Jeffrey Meyers, *Robert Frost: A Biography* (Boston: Houghton Mifflin, 1996), 278.

8. Ibid., 281; Leslie Fiedler, "Poetry Chronicle," *Partisan Review* 3 (1948): 381.

9. Frank Lentricchia, *Modernist Quartet* (Cambridge: Cambridge University Press, 1994), 59, 78.

10. Ibid., 86.

11. Jessie B. Rittenhouse, ed., *The Second Book of Modern Verse* (Boston: Houghton Mifflin, 1919), 3, 91–93, 116–19, 185–86. The first collection, which was published in 1913, would not have included Frost; it does, however, incorporate significant selections of Louise Imogen Guiney and Lizette Woodworth Reese, in addition to reprinting Millay's "Renascence."

12. Jessie B. Rittenhouse, *The Third Book of Modern Verse: A Selection from the Work of Contemporaneous American Poets* (Boston: Houghton Mifflin, 1927), 4, 272, 275–76. "To Earthward" also occupies a prominent position on the second page of the volume.

13. Jessie B. Rittenhouse, *My House of Life: An Autobiography* (Boston: Houghton Mifflin, 1934), 288–89.

14. Bogan, *Poet's Alphabet,* 162.

15. In one of the few essays that takes the *Masques* with the seriousness they deserve, Peter J. Stanlis relegates Thyatira to secondary status, arguing that "Job's wife supplies the comic subplot for the serious theme." Stanlis offers a detailed and useful analysis of the poems in the historical context of "the masque as conscious literary and dramatic form in English literature," the theological context of the Bible, and the literary context of Emerson's philosophy. See Peter J. Stanlis, "Robert Frost's Masques and the Classic American Tradition," in Tharpe, *Frost: Centennial Essays,* 450, 443, 440–68. Similarly, W. R. Irwin regards "her disturbance" as "really no more than whimsical" ("The Unity of Frost's Masques," 306). Meyers takes Thyatira to be a transformed Kay Morrison (*Robert Frost,* 264–65).

16. Donald G. Sheehy, "'Not Quite All, My Dear': Gender and Voice in Frost," *Texas Studies in Literature and Language* 36.4 (1994): 422.

17. Meyers, *Robert Frost,* 236.

18. Lentricchia, *Robert Frost: Modern Poetics and the Landscapes of Self* (Durham: Duke University Press, 1975), 98–99.

19. Ibid., 64.

20. An element in the formalization (and masculinization) of Frost's language has occurred in the editing process. Lathem's edition "normalizes" much of the "countrified" or domesticated discourse in Frost by erasing the hyphens the poet often used to separate words; a random glance at any page of his notes reveals what are for me unsettling changes. For example, if we look at page 541 of the Notes, Lathem substitutes "sleigh bells" for "sleigh-bells" and "jewelweed" for "jewel-weed" in "Hyla Brook"; in "Birches," he changes "ice-storms" to "ice storms," "matter-of-fact" to "matter of fact," and "snow-crust" to "snow crust." The effect of these emendations is actual revision of the poet, eliding his deliberately "untutored" linguistic gestures. This kind of editing represents a Frostian version of what contemporary critics of Dickinson argue is problematic about Thomas Johnson's editing; see Susan Howe, *The Birth-mark: Unsettling the Wilderness in American Literary History* (Hanover: University Press of New England, 1993), 130–53; and Martha Nell Smith, *Rowing in Eden: Rereading Emily Dickinson* (Austin: University of Texas Press, 1992). Richard Poirier's and Mark Richardson's new edition of the poems corrects these editorially introduced errors.

21. Jarrell, *Poetry and the Age,* 62.

22. See William H. Pritchard, *Frost: A Literary Life Reconsidered* (New York: Oxford University Press, 1984). Pritchard discusses Frost's self-conscious shaping of his own career (esp. 70ff., 112ff., 241). With Pritchard, Poirier describes what we might call Frost's "engagements" with literary modernism and its proponents (*Robert Frost: The Work of Knowing,* 226–31).

23. Jarrell, *Poetry and the Age,* 33. On Whitman's similar move toward self-parody, see Justin Kaplan, *Walt Whitman: A Life* (New York: Simon and Schuster, 1980), 303ff.

24. Poirier, *Robert Frost: The Work of Knowing,* 24, 231–32.

# Index

Addison, Daniel Delaney, 264 n. 74
Adkins, Nelson F., 127–28
Aiken, Conrad, 233
*Ainslee's,* 207
Alcott, Louisa May, 128
Allen, Gilbert, 302–3 n. 82
Allen, Paula Gunn, 7–8, 251 n. 35
Ammons, Elizabeth, 272 n. 42, 277 n.
    97, 278 n. 24
*An American Anthology,* 216
Angyal, Andrew W., 262 n. 44, 263 n. 69
Anzaldúa, Gloria, 252–3 n. 49
Apthorp, Elaine Sargent, 256 n. 7
Aronowitz, Stanley, 299 n. 37
Arvin, Newton, 222
*Atlantic Monthly,* 19, 106, 222, 290 n.
    56, 299 n. 35
Auden, W. H., 47, 306 n. 3
Austin, Mary, 194, 296 n. 6

Bagby, George, 246 n. 2
Barnes, Djuna, 213
Barry, Elaine, 262 n. 47
Bartlett, John, 30, 88, 106
Baym, Nina, 51–52, 53, 256 n. 7,
    257–58 n. 10
Beacham, Walton, 228
Benjamin, Walter, 279 n. 22, 283 n. 67
Bennett, Paula, 28, 80; high and low
    sentimentalism, 259 n. 17; on the
    language of gems and flowers,
    155; on the modernist element in
    nineteenth-century women's

poetry, 257–58 n. 10; on the
    movement of women's poetry
    from sentimental to modern, 197
Benstock, Shari, 301 n. 58
Benvenuto, Richard, 289–90 n. 51
Berthoff, Warner, 242 n. 46, 304 n. 99
Bloom, Harold, 248 n. 20
Bogan, Louise, 2, 44, 114, 227, 235,
    237, 304 n. 96; on Frost as bard,
    194–95; on Frost and industrial-
    ism, 127; on Frost's political
    poetry, 267 n. 103; on Frost's sta-
    sis, 220–21; on *A Masque of Rea-
    son,* 306 n. 3; on Reese, 199, 211;
    on the sentimentalization of
    American poetry, 19, 197–98
Bradstreet, Anne, 73
Braithwaite, William, 110
Brodhead, Richard, 256–57 n. 7, 271
    n. 29, 276 n. 94
Brodsky, Joseph, 70
Brooks, Cleanth, 193
Brooks, Van Wyck, 126, 167; on Mil-
    lay as New England poet, 203
Brower, Reuben A., 275 n. 78
Brown, Alice, 63, 110, 111, 113, 167,
    168, 282–83 n. 58; Frost compared
    to, 88, 275–76 n. 82; Frost's
    "good friend," 198, 269 n. 9; and
    Guiney, 291 n. 67, 298 n. 23;
    "The Mortuary Chest," 279 n. 22;
    "At Sudleigh Fair," 288 n. 36; in
    Yale textbook with Frost, 128

Brown, Herbert Ross, 256 n. 7
Browning, Robert, 214, 295–96 n. 4
Bryant, William Cullen, 188
Burnshaw, Stanley, 247 n. 13
Butler, Judith, 246 n. 8, 248 n. 19, 285
    n. 6, 286 n. 7

Cameron, Sharon, 195–96
canon, and canonicity, 2, 4, 5–6, 7, 10,
    11, 28, 91, 93, 105–6, 107, 111,
    112, 143, 144, 171, 172, 193, 203,
    210, 225, 226, 235, 242, 300 n. 41,
    302 n. 71
Carmichael, Charles, 260 n. 28
Cary, Alice, 6, 125
Cary, Phoebe, 6
Cather, Willa, 128, 168, 174, 213, 292
    n. 78, 296 n. 6, 303 n. 86
*Century Magazine,* 19, 290 n. 56
*Chapbook,* 206
Child, Lydia Maria, 267 n. 102
children's literature, 5, 10, 175, 218,
    301–2 n. 68; Frost's, 45, 208–10
Chodorow, Nancy, 7, 249 n. 24
Christian, Barbara, 252–53 n. 49
Cisneros, Sandra, 279 n. 22
Claridge, Laura, 253 n. 51
Clark, Suzanne, 43–44, 211, 301 n. 53
Cleghorn, Sarah, 54
Coale, Samuel, 260 n. 28
Coffin, Robert P. Tristram, 147, 151,
    160, 161, 282 n. 51
Cone, Helen Gray, 19
Cooke, Reginald L., 281 n. 39
Cooke, Rose Terry, 63, 128, 262 n. 58;
    "Arachne," 299 n. 31; "Captive,"
    33–35, 42, 162; "Freedom
    Wheeler's Controversy with
    Providence," 272–73 n. 44; "Mrs.
    Flint's Married Experience,"
    81–82, 100, 275 n. 71; "The West
    Shetucket Railway", 101; in Yale
    textbook with Frost, 128
Coolbrith, Ina, "The Mariposa Lily,"
    216–17

Cornos, John, 89
Cott, Nancy, 256 n. 7
*Courses of Reading in American Literature,*
    128
Cowley, Malcolm, 9–10
Cox, Howard Willard, 247 n. 14
Cox, James M., 282 n. 55
Cox, Sidney, 90, 106, 107, 186, 192,
    197; Frost separated from "the
    ladylike and the hyperaesthetic,"
    168
Cramer, Jeffrey S., 262 n. 44
Crane, Hart, 235
Culler, Jonathan, 249 n. 24, 261 n. 42
cummings, e. e., 235

Damon, S. Foster, 290 n. 52, 291 n. 63
Davidson, Donald, 126, 127
Dawes, James R., 285 n. 6, 287 nn. 24,
    27, 288 n. 34, 292 n. 79
Deland, Margaret, 112
delicate masculinity/tender male,
    151–52, 158, 170, 173, 174, 177,
    178–79, 181, 182, 184–85, 187,
    189, 209, 228
D'Emilio, John, 182
*Dial,* 194
Dickinson, Emily, 27, 41, 45, 82, 105,
    106, 155, 174, 214, 250 n. 25,
    258 nn. 11, 14, 299 n. 31,
    308 n. 20
Dobson, Joanne, 18, 66, 257–58 n. 10,
    259 n. 17
Donovan, Josephine, 112, 267–68 n. 2,
    288 n. 36
DuPlessis, Rachel Blau, 230, 262 n. 50,
    305 n. 104
Dwyer (Russell), Ada, 165–66

Edelman, Lee, 153–54, 170, 176, 188,
    278 n. 110, 287 n. 24
Ekins, Roger, 271 n. 30
Eliot, T. S., 1, 17, 47, 144, 153, 191,
    195, 196, 210, 211, 214, 235, 241,
    245–46 n. 2, 249 n. 24, 301 n. 58,

303 n. 84, 304 n. 100, 305 n. 104,
  306 n. 3
Ellis, Havelock, 294 n. 110
Emerson, Ralph Waldo, 54, 188, 196
Engelbrecht, Penelope, 278 n. 10
Epstein, Barbara, 256 n. 7

Faderman, Lillian, 290 n. 56, 293 n. 99
Faggen, Robert, 14, 67, 114, 156, 174,
  267 n. 109, 273 n. 50, 274 n. 64,
  276 n. 91, 283 n. 66, 293 n. 95
Falck, Colin, 300 n. 41
Farrar, John, 103, 106
Farwell, Marilyn R., 278 n. 10
Fauset, Jessie Redmon, 213
Felski, Rita, 20, 230
feminine literary tradition, 2, 3, 67, 72,
  196; outlined, 6–11
feminine voice, 6–11, 21, 22, 23, 29,
  30, 35, 39, 42, 50, 58, 62, 80, 91,
  104, 105, 113, 114, 118, 123, 130,
  137, 138, 140, 142, 148–49, 159,
  160, 163, 192, 193, 202, 206, 216,
  218, 219, 237, 242, 244. *See also*
  delicate masculinity
Fetterley, Judith, 66, 80, 82, 100, 138,
  253 n. 49
Fiedler, Leslie, 211, 234, 265 n. 85;
  Frost as "middlebrow" poet, 202
Fields, Annie Adams, 291 n. 67
Filene, Peter, 274 n. 59, 276 n. 87, 289
  n. 43
Finch, Annie, 7, 217, 250 n. 29, 257–58
  n. 10, 261 n. 42, 262 n. 50
Fireside Poets, 6, 195
Fisher, Philip, 53, 257 n. 7, 259 n. 18,
  267 n. 110
Fleissner, Robert, 246 n. 2, 263 n. 67
Flint, F. S., 293 n. 102
Folsom, Marcia McClintock, 81
Fone, Byron R. S., 285 n. 6, 293 n. 91
Foote, Stephanie, 127, 281 n. 46, 282
  n. 57
Francis, Lesley Lee, 260 n. 22, 263 n.
  59, 264 n. 74, 276 n. 87, 276 n.

89; on Edward Thomas, 294 n.
  112, 301–2 n. 68
Franks, Jill, 270 n. 19
Freedman, Estelle, 182
Freeman, Mary Wilkins, 112, 113;
  Frost compared to by critics, 63,
  88, 275–76 n. 82; *Madelon,* 267 n.
  102; "A Mistaken Charity," 84;
  "A New England Nun," 262 n.
  53, 274 n. 70; "A Poetess," 61–62,
  72, 73, 75, 99, 160; on regionalism
  and gossip, 110, 111; "The Revolt
  of 'Mother,'" 100; in Yale text-
  book with Frost, 128
French, Warren, 276 n. 88
Frey, Olivia, 11–12, 253–54 n. 53
Friedman, Susan Stanford, 271 n. 28
Frost, Belle Moodie, 25, 118; "The
  Artist's Motive," 277 n. 3, 283–84
  n. 73; *You Come Too* dedicated to,
  209
Frost, Carol, 153, 154
Frost, Elinor, 32, 37, 67, 68, 72,
  75–76, 78, 79, 91, 92–93, 136,
  226, 243, 276 n. 87, 283 n. 73,
  288 n. 42, 301 n. 68; as poet, 71,
  272 n. 42
Frost, Jeanie, 25, 67, 276 n. 84, 283–84
  n. 73
Frost, Lesley, 48, 272 n. 36; and Reese,
  198–99
Frost, Robert
  ambivalence about strong women,
    163–67, 234, 239
  in anthologies, 45, 210; in the *Heath
    Anthology of American Literature,*
    48–49, 265 n. 88; in the *Norton
    Anthology of American Literature,* 49,
    265 n. 88; in Palgrave, 212–13; in
    Rittenhouse, 235
  attitudes toward emotion and senti-
    mentality, 29–30
  empathy, poetics of, 3, 8, 21, 62, 64,
    69, 70, 75, 80–81, 85, 87, 101,
    105, 123, 228, 243

Frost, Robert (*continued*)

genre, Frost's shift in, 5, 8, 122–23, 128–29, 138, 139–40, 143–45, 194–96, 221, 230, 231, 268 n. 6, 277 n. 1

as immature, 205; as both sentimental and modern, 22, 37–38, 206

popularity, 3, 5, 11, 41, 49–50, 107, 202, 203

reputation and contemporary critics, 1–2, 4–5, 13–14, 20, 44, 48–49, 50–51, 88–90, 105–6, 122–23, 138–40, 193–95, 220–21, 227–28, 231, 233–34

and social class, 50, 66–67, 75–76, 92–93, 134, 151, 154, 178, 195, 227, 235, 268 n. 6, 304 n. 100

works, books: *A Boy's Will*, 5, 17–59, 62, 90; *In the Clearing*, 222; *Collected Poems* (1939), 194, 222, 223, 226; *A Further Range*, 189, 214, 219, 220, 221, 222; *A Masque of Mercy*, 104, 143, 223, 233, 234, 235–37, 307 n. 5; *A Masque of Reason*, 104, 143, 223, 233, 234, 237–40, 307 n. 5; *Mountain Interval*, 63, 64, 91, 103, 105, 122, 130, 148, 149, 164, 191; *New Hampshire*, 5, 103–45, 148, 149, 159, 189, 191, 192, 283 n. 65; *North of Boston*, 39, 51, 61–101, 103, 112, 122, 139, 148, 149, 214, 268 n. 6; *Steeple Bush*, 214, 222; *West–Running Brook*, 217, 219, 220; *A Witness Tree*, 222, 228, 231; *You Come Too*, 218

works, essays and talks: "The Doctrine of Excursions," 221; "Education by Poetry," 203; "The Figure a Poem Makes," 29; "Foreword to 'King Jasper,'" 241 "Introduction to Sarah Cleghorn's 'Threescore,'" 54; "The Poetry of Amy Lowell, 29, 163, 289 n. 44; "Poverty and Poetry, 67, 271 n.

28, 275 n. 78; "A Romantic Chasm," 179; "The Unmade Word, or Fetching and Far-Fetching," 108; "What's Become of New England," 231

works, poems: "Acquainted with the Night," 208; "After Apple Picking," 91, 208, 235; "The Aim Was Song," 104; "At Woodward's Gardens," 220; "Away!" 223; "A-Wishing Well," 223; "The Axe-Helve," 49, 170; "Bereft," 219; "Birches," 43, 45, 91, 208, 210, 217, 235; "Brown's Descent," 63; "Build Soil," 140, 233; "Canis Major," 219; "Christmas Trees," 103, 208; "The Cocoon," 218–19; "The Code," 193; "The Death of the Hired Man," 64, 83–87, 90–91, 94, 96, 98, 120, 125, 134, 137, 144, 148, 151, 170, 173, 191, 192, 196, 208, 217, 220, 286 n. 13; "Desert Places, 48, 220, 223; "Design," 48, 213, 214–16, 217, 218, 219, 220; "Directive," 48, 159, 193, 210, 214, 219, 222, 224–26, 225, 226, 230, 305 n. 104; "The Discovery of the Madeiras," 223; "The Draft Horse," 223; "Ends," 223, 304 n. 101; "Evening in a Sugar Orchard," 47; "The Exposed Nest," 90; "The Falls," 51, 55; "The Fear," 49, 75, 90, 110, 113, 121, 242; "The Fear of Man," 223, 304 n. 101; "Fire and Ice," 104, 200; "Flower-Gathering," 36–38, 39, 98, 156, 263 n. 64; "For Once, Then, Something," 104; "A Fountain, a Bottle, a Donkey's Ears, and Some Books," 159–63, 170, 177, 187–88, 215, 288 n. 42; "Fragmentary Blue," 123; "The Freedom of the Moon," 217–18, 220; "Genealogical," 55; "The

Generations of Men," 242; "Ghost House, 20, 23, 24–25; "Going for Water," 36, 68, 208; "Good-by and Keep Cold," 40, 141, 208; "The Gum-Gatherer," 63; "The Hill Wife," 13, 235; "A Hillside Thaw," 142–43; "Home Burial," 3, 13, 48, 64, 67, 68–75, 77, 78, 80, 82, 85, 87, 90, 95, 97, 99, 106, 137, 148, 151, 173, 177, 215, 275 n. 82, 286 n. 13; "The Housekeeper," 75, 110, 114, 121, 138, 242; "How Hard It Is to Keep from Being King When It's in You and in the Situation," 223; "A Hundred Collars," 177–79, 187; "Hyla Brook," 208; "In the Home Stretch," 64, 91–98, 99, 120, 137, 148, 151–52, 164, 170, 187, 218; "Into Mine Own," 23; "In a Vale," 158; "The Invest-ment," 49; "Iris by Night," 185, 187, 191; "Kitty Hawk," 54; "A Line-Storm Song," 98; "Lines Written in Dejection on the Eve of Great Success," 223; "A Lone Striker," 127; "Love and a Ques-tion," 36, 68; "Maple," 99, 104, 105, 113, 129, 130–37, 140, 145, 148, 152, 159, 219, 283 n. 66; "Meeting and Passing," 91, 136, 184; "Mending Wall," 45, 48, 91, 170, 208; "The Middleness of the Road," 223; "Misgiving," 235; "Moon Compasses," 200; "The Most of It," 223; "Mowing," 158, 176, 177, 217; "My Butterfly," 35, 158, 277 n. 101; "My Giving," 54; "My November Guest," 45; "The Need of Being Versed in Country Things," 142; "Neither Out Far Nor In Deep," 193; "Never Again Would Birds' Song Be the Same," 223; "New Hampshire," 105; "Nothing Gold Can Stay," 1, 142;

"October," 23, 36; "An Old Man's Winter Night," 49, 66; "On Being Chosen Poet of Ver-mont," 112; "Once by the Pacific," 48, 219; "On Going Unnoticed," 217; "The Onset," 47, 140, 235; "Our Hold on the Planet," 200; "Our Singing Strength," 140; "Out, Out—" 48, 127; "The Oven Bird," 1, 48, 200, 208; "The Pasture," 30–31, 35, 39, 41, 45, 46, 142, 170, 185, 187, 205, 210; "The Pasture," first in You Come Too, 208; "Paul's Wife," 130, 242, 277 n. 2; "The Pauper Witch of Grafton," 105, 114, 130, 143, 158–59, 281 n. 42; "A Prayer in Spring," 39, 40–43, 98; "Provide, Provide," 48, 220; "Putting in the Seed," 40; "Ques-tioning Faces," 223; "The Quest of the Purple-Fringed," 222; "Range-Finding," 200; "Reluc-tance," 23, 36, 303 n. 84; "The Road Not Taken," 48, 49, 91, 210, 235, 294 n. 115, 303 n. 84; "Rose Pogonias," 39, 156; "The Runaway," 142, 210, 303 n. 84; "The Sachem of the Clouds (A Thanksgiving Legend)," 55, 57; "The Self-Seeker," 66, 127; "A Servant to Servants," 3, 64, 75, 76–83, 87, 90, 91, 95, 99, 110, 113, 118, 119, 120, 121, 124, 130, 134, 148, 151, 160, 164, 177, 185, 187, 220, 231, 271 n. 32, 286 n. 13; "The Silken Tent," 148, 184, 222, 228–30; "Snow," 104, 113, 188, 242, 277 n. 2; "The Sound of the Trees," 1, 208; "Spring Pools," 217; "Stopping by Woods on a Snowy Evening," 45, 47, 48, 49, 106, 140, 210, 235; "The Strong Are Saying Nothing," 189, 220; "The Subverted Flower,"

Frost, Robert (*continued*)
136, 174, 223, 301 n. 67; "The
Telephone," 90, 208; "The
Thatch," 219; "To a Moth Seen
in Winter," 223; "To E. T.," 148,
184–87, 189; "To Earthward,"
235, 303 n. 84, 307 n. 12; "The
Tuft of Flowers," 148, 171–74,
177, 187, 191, 210; "Two Tramps
in Mud Time," 219; "Unhar-
vested," 200; "The Vanishing
Red," 54, 55–59, 127; "Waiting,"
36, 98; "West-Running Brook,"
130, 277 n. 2; "The White-Tailed
Hornet," 219; "Wild Grapes,"
104, 138; "Wind and Window
Flower," 31–36, 41, 156; "The
Witch of Coös," 79, 99, 104, 111,
113, 114–21, 123, 124, 130, 135,
143, 145, 152, 154–55, 158, 159,
161, 277 n. 2, 281 n. 42; "A
Young Birch," 1, 209–10
   writer: as amateur, 104, 115, 196,
214, 216; as professional, 104, 108,
111, 112, 113, 130, 131, 137, 196,
214, 222
Fuller, Margaret, 266 n. 94
Fuss, Diana, 246 n. 8, 278 n. 10, 285 n.
6

Gadd, David, 294 n. 110
Garber, Marjorie, 179–80, 284 n. 2,
291 n. 67, 293–94 n. 107
Gardiner, Judith Kegan, 274 n. 65
Garnett, Edward, 186, 275 n. 82, 291 n.
69
genre, 5, 6, 195, 244, 277 n. 1, 303 n.
89; feminine voice and dramatic
poems, 242; Frost as detached lyric
poet, 192, 195, 214–16, 217;
Frost's movement toward lyric,
143–44, 189; Frost's shift in,
122–23, 195–96, 221, 230, 231,
268 n. 6, 277 n. 1; gender and
genre, 9–11, 18, 64, 65, 88–89,

104–12, 136, 141–45, 169–70, 186,
193, 196–97, 201–2, 212–14, 228;
mixing, 7–8, 9, 12, 62, 64, 111,
139–45, 208, 251 n. 35, 271 n. 28;
privilege of lyric, 6–7
Gephard, Caroline, 251 n. 40
Gifford, James, 168–69, 177, 285 n. 5,
292 nn. 74, 76, 294 n. 116
Gilbert, Sandra, 106, 150, 213, 250 n.
29, 255 n. 67, 278 n. 8, 280 n. 31,
290 n. 56, 300 n. 45, 301 n. 54
Gilligan, Carol, 249 n. 24
Gillman, Susan, 280 n. 28, 281 n. 49
Glaspell, Susan, 262 n. 53
Golding, Alan, 248 n. 20, 252 n. 43,
287 n. 20, 302 n. 73
Gore, Mrs. Moody P., 121, 281 n. 40
gossip, 61, 80, 104, 109–11, 124, 128,
148, 214; and the erotic, 111, 115;
and feminine voice, 116, 117;
folktales as, 121, 123; and homo-
erotic, 118, 160, 162; and inti-
macy, 110, 114, 137; negative, and
power, 110–11, 113–18, 160; not
neutral, 13; and regionalism, 109,
129, 130, 137, 143
Gould, Jean, 289 n. 44, 289 n. 46
Grasso, Linda, 62, 268 n. 2
Graves, Robert, 186
Gray, Janet, 261 n. 33
Gray, Thomas, 40
Green, Harvey, 296 n. 7
Greene, Sarah Pratt McLean, 273 n. 44
Gregory, Horace, 222
Grenier, Donald J., 305 n. 103
Griswold, Rufus, 27, 261 n. 37, 264 n. 74
Gubar, Susan, 150, 213, 255 n. 67, 278
n. 8, 280 n. 31, 290 n. 56, 301 n.
54
Guillory, John, 299 n. 37
Guiney, Louise Imogen, 144, 198,
297–98 n. 23, 307 n. 11

H. D. (Hilda Doolittle), 235, 246 n. 2,
304 n. 96

Hale, Sarah Josepha, 26–29, 32
Hall, Dorothy Judd, 263 n. 67
Halttunen, Karen, 256 n. 7
Harkesheimer, Harrison H., 21, 75
Harper, Frances E. W., 51
*Harper's*, 290 n. 56
Harris, Susan K., 256 n. 4
Hawthorne, Nathaniel, 4, 139, 250 n.
     25
Healey, E. Claire, 289 n. 47
Heilbrun, Carolyn, 279 n. 22
Herndl, Diane Price, 286 n. 12
Hicks, Granville, 126, 127, 222
highbrow/lowbrow art, 4, 41, 111,
     144, 202; and cultural power, 44;
     Frost as "middlebrow" poet," 202;
     Frost mixing, 208
Hillyer, Robert, 222
*A History of Warren, A Mountain Ham-
     let, Located among the White Hills of
     New Hampshire*, 123
Holland, Norman, 292 n. 79
Homans, Margaret, 250 n. 26
homoerotic writing, 5–6, 117, 118, 230,
     285–86 n. 6; and the aesthete/the
     aesthetic, 168–69, 177–79, 185;
     and the athlete, 169–70, 177–79;
     bisexuality, 179–80; delicate mas-
     culinity of, 170, 171–75, 181–82,
     184–85; female sexual power in,
     155–63; and gender, 148–49,
     153–54, 176, 187–88; and homo-
     phobia, 150, 156, 170, 174, 183,
     227; and lesbian sexuality, 165–68,
     182, 183–84, 188; loss of individu-
     ated self in, 152–53; and masculin-
     ity, 150–52, 153–54, 170–71,
     181–82, 185
Hood, Thomas, 26
Hooper, Lucy, 54, 266 n. 94
Howard, June, 125
Howe, Susan, 308 n. 20
Howells, William Dean, 112, 291 n.
     69; on Frost's masculinity, 88–89,
     167; on sentimentalism, 26

Hughes, Langston, 293 n. 107
Humphries, Rolfe, 222, 273 n. 55
Huyssen, Andreas, 3, 299 n. 37; mod-
     ernism vs. mass culture, 202

*Independent*, 277
Ingebretsen, Edward, 246 n. 3
Ingram, Laura, 289 n. 47
Irwin, W. R., 306 n. 1, 307 n. 15

Jackson, Helen Hunt, 196, 258 n. 11; *A
     Century of Dishonor* and *Ramona*,
     267 n. 102; "Down to Sleep,"
     46–47; nature poet, 201; "Poppies
     on the Wheat," 26, 125; in Yale
     textbook with Frost, 128
James, Henry, 10
Jameson, Fredric, 299 n. 37
Jardine, Alice, 253 n. 51
Jarrell, Randall, 20, 21, 242, 265 n. 89,
     268 n. 6; on Frost "the greatest
     actor," 195; on Frost's change
     from "radical" to "conservative,"
     192; on Frost's shift from dramatic
     to lyric, 194; on *A Masque of Rea-
     son*, 233–34; on older Frost alone,
     217; "the Only Genuine Robert
     Frost in Captivity," 243; "ordi-
     nary" vs. "intellectual" readers of
     Frost, 47; on sexuality in Frost,
     123
Jeffers, Robinson, 235
Jeffreys, Mark, 250 n. 27
Jewett, Sarah Orne, 81, 112, 113, 168,
     281 n. 46; *The Country of the
     Pointed Firs*, 11, 129; "A Farmer's
     Sorrow," 124–25; "The For-
     eigner," 131; Frost compared to
     by critics, 63, 88; lesbian writer,
     126, 167, 291 n. 67; "The Passing
     of Sister Barsett," 109, 110, 111;
     "The Town Poor," 83–84; in
     Yale textbook with Frost, 128;
     "York Garrison, 1640," 174–75
Johnson, Thomas H., 308 n. 20

Johnson, Warren, 269 n. 12
Johnson, Wendy Dasler, 273 n. 48
Jong, Erica, 206–7
Jordan, David, 269 n. 12
Jost, Walter, 279 n. 16
Joyce, James, 153

Kaiser, Jo Ellen Green, 211–12, 300 n. 41
Kaplan, Amy, 282 n. 55
Kaplan, Fred, 18
Kaplan, Justin, 308 n. 23
Katz, Sandra, 98, 261 n. 43
Kearns, Katherine, 14, 76, 78, 85, 114, 152, 153, 154, 158, 176, 195, 206, 213, 234, 242, 252 n. 44, 254 n. 60, 254–55 n. 61, 271 n. 30, 272 nn. 38, 40, 280–81 n. 34, 283 n. 74, 287 n. 20, 294 n. 115, 296–97 n. 12, 306–7 n. 4
Keats, John, 25, 214
Keller, Lynn, 245 n. 1, 250 n. 27
Kelley, Mary, 256–57 n. 7
Kemp, John, 62, 63, 65, 268 n. 6, 269 n. 8, 273 n. 55
Kennedy, John F., 49
Kern, Robert, 259 n. 19
Kilcup, Karen, 256 n. 2; 272 n. 37. *See also* Karen Oakes
Killingsworth, M. Jimmie, 285 n. 6
Kilmer, Joyce, 45
Kimmel, Michael, 248–49 n. 21, 255 n. 68, 267 n. 107, 281 n. 35, 291 n. 63
Klein, Fred, 294 n. 110
Klein, Marcus, 299 n. 37
Klemans, Patricia, 300 n. 43
Kolodny, Annette, 275 n. 77
Kowaleski, Michael, 270 n. 14
Kreymborg, Alfred: on Millay and Frost, 203; on Reese and Frost, 199; on Reese as modernist, 201

*Ladies' Home Journal,* 207
Laity, Cassandra, 191

Lamb, Charles, 26, 73–74
Langbaum, Robert, 255 n. 63, 259 n. 19, 270–71 n. 27, 273–74 n. 57, 295–96 n. 4; Romanticism vs. romanticism, 261 n. 32
Langland, Elizabeth, 253 n. 51
language of gems and flowers, 155–63
Larcom, Lucy, 128; "Flowers of the Fallow," 201–2, 299 n. 35; *An Idyl of Work,* 276 n. 86; New England/ regional writer, 25, 125; popular poet, 6; "Swinging on a Birch Tree," 43, 264 n. 74, 266 n. 94
Larsen, Nella, 213
Lathem, Edward Connery, 272 n. 43, 281 n. 36, 308 n. 20
Lauter, Paul, 196, 265 n. 88, 297 n. 17
Lawrence, D. H., 150, 152, 171, 242, 286 n. 11, 289 n. 48
Lazarus, Emma, 128
Lear, Edward, 45
Lears, Jackson, 292 n. 70
Leighton, Angela, 261 n. 33
Lentriccia, Frank, 13, 49, 66, 154, 195, 196, 213, 234, 235, 242, 254 n. 60, 261–62 n. 43, 270 n. 18, 270 n. 25, 272 n. 38, 283 n. 65, 284 n. 2, 287 n. 24, 292 n. 85, 297 nn. 12, 18, 305 n. 104
Leverenz, David, 253 n. 51
Levine, Lawrence, 247 n. 16
Lewis, C. Day, 212–13, 303 n. 84
Liebman, Sheldon W., 13
Lindsay, Vachel, 166
Lipking, Lawrence, 268–69 n. 7
Littel, Robert, 122, 123
*A Little Book of Verse,* 235
Little, William, 281 n. 42
Longfellow, Henry Wadsworth, 10, 45, 107, 188, 258 n. 11, 259–60 n. 16, 267 n. 110
Loriggio, Francesco, 270 n. 15
Lowell, Amy, 44, 181, 188, 191, 290 n. 54, 292 n. 78, 301 n. 58, 304 n. 97; attitude toward popular audi-

ence, 289 n. 48; as challenge to
Frost, 163; "A Critical Fable,"
164–65, 290 n. 53; critics on,
166–67; "The Day That Was That
Day," 164, 165; desire for best-
seller, 163–64; "In Excelsis," 165;
Frost on, 29, 167, 289 nn. 44, 45;
on Frost, 11, 13, 45, 88, 126; Frost
as source for "The Gravestone,"
290 n. 53; "The Garden by
Moonlight," 165, 182; "Inter-
lude," 220–21; "July Midnight,"
165; as lesbian/lesbian poet, 165;
"Madonna of the Evening Flow-
ers," 165; male speaking voices in
poems, 290 n. 56; "Number
Three on the Docket," 164; pow-
erful critic, 164, 167; as publicity
agent for poetry, 163, as regional-
ist poet, 164; Rittenhouse, 235,
236; "The Rosebud Wall-Paper,
164; vs. sentimental poetry, 19;
sexual independence, 170; and
Untermeyer, 138–39; "Venus
Transiens," 165
Loy, Mina, 305 n. 104
Lynen, John, 304 n. 103

MacLeish, Archibald, 54, 235
Marchalonis, Shirley, 264 n. 74, 299 n.
35
Marcus, Mordecai, 281 n. 36
Martin, Robert K., 175, 285 n. 6
Marvell, Andrew, 39
mass audience, 202, 204–6; and mass
culture, 10, 20, 29, 44, 196
Masters, Edgar Lee, 194
Matthiessen, F. O., 152, 153, 183, 196,
210, 287 n. 20
Mayers, Ozzie J., 276 n. 92
McCuen, Rod, 206–7
McDonald, Gail, 299 n. 37
McLuhan, Marshall, 300 n. 41
Melville, Herman, 27
Mencken, H. L., 166, 193, 298 n. 26;

disparages Lowell, 290 n. 59;
praises Reese, 199
Meyers, Jeffrey, 25, 114, 234, 267 n.
105, 283 n. 65, 290 n. 54
Millay, Edna St. Vincent, 203–12, 237,
293 n. 107, 301 n. 58, 302 n. 70,
304 n. 98; "The Bean-Stalk," 208;
children's author, 207–8; com-
pared to Reese, 298 n. 28; Conver-
sation at Midnight, 212; elite and
popular, 208; "First Fig," 207; first
woman to win Pulitzer, 204;
"From a Very Little Sphinx,"
207–8; "Grown-Up," 207; imma-
ture, 205; life compared to Frost's,
203–4; Make Bright the Arrows,
204; media personality, 204; The
Murder of Lidice, 204; political
poet, 204, 205; "Portrait by a
Neighbor," 207; "Renascence,"
203, 307 n. 11; in Rittenhouse,
235; Second April, 205; sentimental
and modern, 203; sentimental
writer, 300 n. 41, 300 n. 46; "Son-
nets from an Ungrafted Tree, 301
n. 54
Miller, Cristanne, 245 n. 1, 250 n. 27
Miller, Jean Baker, 249 n. 24
Miller, Jim Wayne, 269 n. 13, 270 n.
16
modernism and modern literature, 247
n. 9, 308 n. 22; critics construct
Frost as, 18, 32, 37, 100, 206; and
critics' discomfort with sentimen-
talism, 41, 44, 99; and cultural
power, 5, 195; Frost's modern
sentimentality, 18, 21, 22, 30–48,
59, 74; and genre, 242, 243; and
Guiney, 297–98 n. 24; and mascu-
line voice, 18, 141, 243; and mas-
culinity, 226, 242, 243; premod-
ernists, 144, 217
Modleski, Tania, 299 n. 37
Monroe, Harriet, 44, 106, 206, 212,
276 n. 84, 301 n. 58

Monteiro, George, 2, 20, 264 n. 74, 278 n. 8, 302 n. 72, 303 nn. 89, 90, 307 n. 5

Moon, Michael, 285 n. 6

Moore, Marianne, 195, 211, 235, 246 n. 2, 300 n. 41, 305 n. 104

Morris, Timothy, 44, 250 n. 27, 251–52 n. 42, 300 n. 41

Morrison, Toni, 277 n. 22

Mosher, Thomas B., 50, 89

*Nation,* 194

Native Americans, 51–59, 266 n. 100, 267 nn. 102, 106, 107

Nelson, Cary, 247 n. 9, 251 n. 37, 300 n. 46

New Critics, 9, 43, 108

*New England Magazine,* 23

*New England Quarterly,* 227

*New Hampshire Folk Tales,* 121–22

*New Masses,* 222

"new poetry," 36, 163, 193, 199, 201, 206, 212

*New Poetry, The,* 206

*New Republic,* 19, 139, 222, 233

Nitchie, George W., 269 n. 7, 305 n. 103

Oakes, Karen, 251 n. 38, 254 n. 55, 277 n. 97, 278–79 n. 11. *See also* Karen Kilcup

Oakes Smith, Elizabeth, 6, 25, 26, 41–43, 107

O'Brien, Sharon, 303 n. 86

O'Donnell, W. G., 274 n. 57, 282 n. 51

Ong, Walter J., 108, 278 n. 8, 281 n. 42

oral tradition and oral literature: gender of, 107–9, 113, 114, 121, 137; and cultural power, 127; and listener's power, 283 n. 67; survival mechanism, 279–80 n. 22

Osgood, Frances Sargent, 214; "A Cold, Calm Star," 33, 34–35; crit-ical of sentimentalism, 258 n. 14, 259 n. 17, 262 n. 58; "The Daisy's Mistake," 33–34, 196

Oster, Judith, 14, 114, 234, 242, 249 n. 22, 255 n. 66, 276 n. 90, 283 nn. 68, 70, 296 n. 9

Ostriker, Alicia, 199

Palgrave, Francis Turner: and *Palgrave's Golden Treasury,* 25–26, 49, 212, 213, 214, 251 n. 38, 303 n. 84

Parini, Jay, 2, 4, 20

*Partisan Review,* 222

Pattee, Fred Lewis, 126, 281 n. 46

Pearce, Roy Harvey, 6, 10, 19, 22, 28, 58, 194, 196, 199, 211, 233, 249 n. 24, 250 n. 25, 251 nn. 41, 42, 267 n. 110, 273 n. 55, 298 n. 23

Perkins, David, 302–3 n. 82

Perloff, Marjorie, 6, 212, 302 n. 81, 303 n. 84

Person, Leland, 253 n. 51

Petrino, Elizabeth, 273 n. 48

Phelps, Elizabeth Stuart, 125

Piatt, Sarah, 6, 214, 258 n. 14

Poe, Edgar Allan, 114, 188

*Poetry,* 106

*Poetry and Poets,* 163

*Poets and Poetry of America,* 27

Poirier, Richard, 4, 13, 32, 79, 87, 206, 229, 234, 239, 242, 262 n. 50, 265 n. 85, 269 n. 10, 301 n. 57, 308 nn. 20, 22

politics and poetry, 51–59, 203–5, 211–13, 243

Pope, Alexander, 39

Porter, David, 253 n. 51

Pound, Ezra, 26, 51, 88, 144, 166, 191, 212, 213, 214, 235, 243, 245–46 n. 2, 249 n. 23, 301 n. 58, 303 n. 84, 304 n. 100

Pritchard, William, 14, 45, 62, 75, 110, 271 n. 31, 279 n. 16, 292 n. 87, 306 n. 22

Pryse, Marjorie, 66, 80

Rado, Lisa, 246–47 n. 9

Ransom, John Crowe, 235; on Millay, 204–5, 237

readers, amateur/popular/"ordinary," 1, 22, 30, 45, 47–49, 87, 105–6, 113, 142, 143, 191–92, 204–5, 210

readers, professional/elite/academic, 1, 4, 6, 10–11, 13, 17–18, 28, 41, 43–44, 47–49, 54, 63, 87, 105–6, 113, 128, 143, 144, 191, 196, 202–4, 205, 206–7, 208, 209, 210, 216, 227–28

Rebolledo, Tey Diana, 252–53 n. 49

Reed, Richard, 262 n. 46

Reese, Lizette Woodworth, 144, 195; "August," 199, 200; "Emily," 200; "A Flower of Mullein," 200–201, 207; and later women modernists, 298 n. 28; "Mid-March," 199; "Nina," 200; Pearce critical of, 298 n. 23; poems anticipate Frost's, 198–202; positive reputation, 199; in Rittenhouse, 307 n. 11

regionalism and regionalist writing, 5, 9–10; and connection with reader, 61–62, 66, 69, 79–81, 85–87, 124; as critical not nostalgic, 67, 99–101; critics see as limited, 126–27; detachment from the reader in, 132–38, 139–40; female and male regionalists, 127–28; feminine tradition, 9–10, 63, 83, 194, 271 n. 32; and folktales, 121–24; Frost as regional and modern, 74; Frost's "transcendence" of, 62–63, 65, 128; Frost's unease with, 104, 115–20; menace of men in, 68–70, 72, 78, 113, 131; and nationalism, 101, 105, 124–29, 143–44; "new regionalism" (of early twentieth century) 191, 194; positive male-female relationships in, 91–98; regional poetry, 125; and sentimentalism,

62, 66, 72–75, 84, 87, 125, 139–44, 194, 202

Reichardt, Mary, 268 n. 2

Reynolds, Margaret, 261 n. 33

Rich, Adrienne, 7, 79, 278 n. 10, 285 n. 6

Richardson, Mark, 49, 256 n. 3, 260 n. 26, 275 n. 74, 288 n. 35, 298 n. 26, 308 n. 20

Rittenhouse, Jessie, 13, 49; on *A Masque of Mercy*, 235–37; on poetry as elitist, 202; selections of Frost for anthologies, 235

Robert Frost Interpretive Trail, 1, 15, 240–41

Robinson, Clara Weaver, 288 n. 42

Robinson, David M., 298 nn. 27, 28

Robinson, Edwin Arlington, 11, 17, 20–21, 125, 128, 235, 241

Robson, W. W., 306 n. 1

Roman, Camille, 289 n. 44

romanticism and romantic poetry, 144, 182, 191; critics value, 18; Frost associated with, 45; and lyric/individual subjectivity, 6–7, 21, 53, 58, 150; and sentimentalism, 25–26

Romines, Ann, 268 n. 2, 278 n. 24

Roosevelt, Teddy, 168

Rotundo, E. Anthony, 150, 151, 168

Rukeyser, Muriel, 222, 227

Russ, Joanna, 242 n. 46

St. Armand, Barton Levi, 272 n. 40

*St. Nicholas,* 25

Sampley, Arthur M., 304 n. 1

Samuels, Shirley, 266 n. 100

Sanborn, Kate, 75

Sandburg, Carl, 166, 194, 235

Sargent, Elizabeth Shepley, 282 n. 51

Sarotte, Georges-Michel, 295 n. 126

*Saturday Review,* 222

Schneider, Isdor, 194

Schweickart, Patrocinio, 253 n. 49

Scott, Sir Walter, 25

Sedgwick, Catharine Maria: *Hope Leslie*, 267 n. 102
Sedgwick, Eve Kosofsky, 278 n. 10, 285 n. 6
sentimentalism and sentimental poetry, 5, 17–59, 194; aesthetic predictability, 27–29; allied with romanticism, 25–26, 42–43, 73–74; animals and sentimentality, 262 n. 46; balance between emotion and restraint in, 19, 21, 29, 30–31, 32, 33, 37–39, 40; and Coolbrith, 216–17; critical dismissals of, 19–20; definitions, 255 n. 1; dispersed subjectivity of, 17, 21, 35, 53–54; elision of in anthologies, 48–49; female vulnerability in, 31–35; Frost to Cox ("too soft to look . . . for the sentiments"), 192, 197; Frost identifies self as sentimental, 36; Frost separated from, 20–21, 63; Frost's use of, 21–59; and the homoerotic, 182, 186; oversimplified, 18–19; and the political, 17–59, 204, 211; and popular journals, 22–25, 27–28, 36; power of, 17, 18; Reese's rejection of, 199; and religion, 18, 40–43; retrospectively feminized, 9–11; sentimental modernism of Frost, 18, 21, 22, 30–48, 59, 74; visibility of nineteenth-century sentimental poets, 25
Shakespeare, William, 25, 166
Sheehey, Donald, 239
Shelley, Percy Bysshe, 25, 26, 54
Showalter, Elaine, 131
Sigourney, Lydia, 25, 196, 251–52 n. 42, 257 n. 10, 304 n. 100; "Death of an Infant," 26, 73–74; "Indian Names," 52–59, 266 nn. 97, 100; "Niagara," 51; popular poet, 6, 10, 112; *Traits of the Aborigines of America*, 52, 58; writing for money, 50

"sissy poem," 153, 154, 170, 187, 191, 231
Smith, Martha Nell, 308 n. 20
Smith, Seba, 27–29, 75
Solomon, Barbara, 268 n. 2
Spacks, Patricia Meyer, 110–11
Speare, Mrs. Guy E., 121, 281 n. 40
Spenser, Edmund, 39
Spofford, Harriet Prescott, 274 n. 70
Stange, G. Robert, 248 n. 20
Stanlis, Peter J., 307 n. 15
Stedman, Edmund Clarence, 112, 127, 216, 264 n. 74, 302 n. 73
Stein, Gertrude, 213
Stevens, Wallace, 153, 154, 214, 228
Stimpson, Catherine R., 278 n. 10
Stowe, Harriet Beecher, 17, 54
Strychasz, Thomas, 299 n. 37, 300 n. 39, 304 n. 100
subjectivity and poetic selfhood: dispersed/feminine selfhood, 6–8, 17, 21–22, 35, 39, 53, 58, 64, 75, 80–81, 152, 204, 243; Frost as autonomous, 70–71; intimacy of poetic speaker and reader, 221, 243; masculine, 119, 130–32, 134, 137, 192, 193, 195, 196, 197, 198, 200, 201, 214; refusal of intimacy/detachment from, 192, 224, 225–26, 228, 242, 243; strong lyric "I," 6, 14, 21–22, 35, 53, 58, 80, 101
Sundquist, Eric, 282 n. 55
Sutton, W., 291 n. 68

Taggard, Genevieve, 301 n. 53
Tate, Allen, 235
Teasdale, Sarah, 29, 298 n. 28
*Tendencies in American Poetry*, 165
Tennyson, Lord Alfred, 26, 31
Tharpe, Jac, 127
Thaxter, Celia: "Alone," 38–40, 45, 263 n. 64; compared to Margaret Fuller, 263 n. 63; nature poet, 201; "The Path of Peace," 23;

popular poet, 6; regionalist poet, 281 n. 44; "The Sandpiper," 125; in Yale textbook with Frost, 128
theory, literary, 2, 11–13, 254 n. 55
Thomas, Edith, 235
Thomas, Edward, 179–87, 248 n. 20, 269 n. 9, 276 n. 89, 294 nn. 112, 113, 301 n. 68; and children's writing, 301–2 n. 68; Frost's claim of Thomas's manliness, 186; Frost's letters to Thomas's widow about, 185–86; Frost's most intimate friend, 181; homoerotic relationship with Frost, 185; "Iris by Night," 181–82; "The Sun Used to Shine" (poem on Frost), 181
Thompson, Lawrance, 78–79, 91, 117, 185, 227, 271 n. 31, 283–84 n. 73, 294 n. 116, 300 n. 41; Frost's mother reading to him, 260 n. 30; on Reese, 198
Thomson, Rosemarie Garland, 256 n. 7, 275 n. 75
Thoreau, Henry David, 107–8, 109, 113, 264 n. 74; Millay compared to, 203
Todd, Janet, 250 n. 27
Tompkins, Jane, 12, 18, 253–54 n. 53
Trilling, Lionel, 48, 128, 143, 249 n. 23
Twain, Mark, 17, 43, 61

Untermeyer, Louis, 3, 49, 50, 51, 106, 231, 268 n. 6, 293 n. 102, 307 n. 6; and Amy Lowell, 138–39, 163; on Amy Lowell as "pretty," 166; anthologizing Frost, 265 n. 89; Frost advises on anthology, 188–89; Frost cultivates, 243; on Frost and politics, 54; Frost's defender and promoter, 89, 103, 222; on Frost's genre shifts, 277 n. 1; Frost's intimacy with, 180–81; Frost writes to about lesbian readers, 183; loans Frost a thousand

dollars, 122; on Reese, 199; true emotion in poetry, 29

Vallier, Jane, 263 n. 63
Van Doren, Carol, 251 n. 41
Van Doren, Mark, 4, 233
Vanity Fair, 207
Vendler, Helen, 248 n. 20
von Hallberg, 248 n. 20

Waggoner, Hyatt, 247 n. 12, 251 n. 41, 306 n. 2
Wagner, Linda, 103, 193, 220, 233
Walker, Cheryl: on Amy Lowell, 289 n. 45, 291 n. 63; on the difference between modernist and nineteenth-century poetry, 263 n. 69; on Guiney and Reese, 298 n. 29; "poem of secret sorrow," 23, 33, 257–58 n. 10; on realism in nineteenth-century American women's poetry, 263–64 n. 69; on Reese, 199
Wallace, Patricia, 13, 76, 114, 273 n. 56
Walsh, John Evangelist, 20, 265 n. 86
Ward, Susan Hayes, 263 n. 59; editor and publisher of Frost's first poem, 35; Frost calls self a "sentimental sweet singer" to, 36, 163; Frost sends Christmas poems to, 35–36; Larcom's student, 264 n. 74
Watts, Emily Stipes, 290 n. 56
Wells, Henry W., 129
Welty, Eudora, 269 n. 13
Westbrook, Perry, 63, 65, 268 n. 2, 281 n. 44
Wexler, Laura, 266–67 n. 100
Weygandt, Cornelius, 20
Wharton, Edith, 128
Whitman, Walt, 130, 166, 214, 231, 243, 255 n. 67, 258 n. 11, 292 n. 85, 304 n. 100, 306 n. 105, 308 n. 23; Edward Thomas compares Frost to, 181; Frost compared to by critics, 2; "gay"/homoerotic,

Whitman, Walt (*continued*)
108, 149, 170–79, 183, 242; genre
mixing, 9, 106; loss of (masculine)
self, 152–53; masculine, 147, 168;
and military, 184–85, 187; orality
in 107–9; "Osceola," 54; reader's
role in poetry, 15
Whittier, John Greenleaf, 264 n. 74
Wilcox, Earl J., 245–46 n. 2, 247 n. 12
Wilde, Oscar, 110, 150, 168
Williams, Stanley T., 127–28
Williams, William Carlos, 213, 235
Winters, Yvor, 273 n. 55
witches, 85, 104–5, 111, 113–24, 280–81
n. 34, 281 n. 39; and female eroti-
cism, 114–19, 155–56; Frost's sym-
pathy for, 124; and powerful femi-
nine voice, 113–24, 152

Wood, Ann Douglas, 112, 256 n. 7
Wood, Clement, 36, 114, 166–67, 188,
291 n. 63
Woods, Gregory, 293 n. 93
Wordsworth, William, 2, 25, 26, 54,
149, 181, 214
Wylie, Elinor, 220, 235,
304 n. 96

Yeats, W. B., 191, 195
Yingling, Thomas E., 286 n. 7, 292 n.
74, 295 n. 132
*Youth's Companion,* 22–25, 35, 36,
260 nn. 22, 24

Zagarell, Sandra, 99, 100, 144, 276–77
n. 95
Zimmerman, Bonnie, 278 n. 10